"DO IT MY WAY
OR YOU'RE FIRED!"

The Wiley Management Series on Problem Solving, Decision Making, and Strategic Thinking

The Hidden Agenda: Recognizing What Really Matters at Work
  Priscilla Elfrey

"Do It My Way or You're Fired!": Employee Rights and the Changing Role of Management Prerogatives
  David W. Ewing

"DO IT MY WAY OR YOU'RE FIRED!"

Employee Rights and the
Changing Role of Management
Prerogatives

David W. Ewing

JOHN WILEY & SONS, INC.

New York   Chichester   Brisbane   Toronto   Singapore

Copyright © 1983 by David W. Ewing.
Published by John Wiley & Sons, Inc.

All rights reserved. Published simultaneously in Canada.

Reproduction or translation of any part of this work
beyond that permitted by Section 107 or 108 of the
1976 United States Copyright Act without the permission
of the copyright owner is unlawful. Requests for
permission or further information should be addressed to
the Permissions Department, John Wiley & Sons, Inc.

This publication is designed to provide accurate and
authoritative information in regard to the subject
matter covered. It is sold with the understanding that
the publisher is not engaged in rendering legal, accounting,
or other professional service. If legal advice or other
expert assistance is required, the services of a competent
professional person should be sought. *From a Declaration
of Principles jointly adopted by a Committee of the
American Bar Association and a Committee of Publishers.*

Library of Congress Cataloging in Publication Data:

Ewing, David W.
   "Do it my way or you're fired!"

   (Wiley series on problem solving, decision making, and strategic thinking)
   Includes index.
   1. Employee rights—United States.   I. Title.
II. Series.

HD6971.8.E95   1982   658.3   82-13414
ISBN 0-471-86843-4

Printed in the United States of America

10 9 8 7 6 5 4 3 2 1

To H.E.E. and W.B.E.

PREFACE

"Do it my way or you're fired!" In words like these generations of American managers have maintained discipline and compliance when subordinates threatened to get out of line. They have exercised a prerogative that managers all over the world for centuries took for granted. In recent years, however, the prerogative has been weakened, and signs point to continued weakening throughout this decade. (In most other countries, the prerogative to fire at will has been not only weakened but destroyed.)

The purpose of this book is twofold. For managers in corporations, government agencies, and other organizations it's meant to help them understand (1) how and why their prerogatives are being redefined, and (2) how to respond constructively to the new trend, both as individuals and as policy makers. I believe that the only thing that stands between effective management and effective employee civil liberties is, to borrow Marvin Bower's famous phrase, the "will to manage." The book is also intended as a guide for the employee and general interest reader on the rights one has or doesn't have when entering the company door. Such an understanding can help an employee act appropriately when transgressions take place.

I began this book by compiling the trials and tribulations of twenty-odd employee objectors and whistleblowers. For these write-ups I drew on interviews, court records, newspaper and magazine articles by careful journalists, and other factual sources. For every write-up completed and used I dropped several others that, however dramatic and unusual, could not be sufficiently attested to.

Next I reviewed the programs and policies of a half dozen organizations that responded to the movement for broader employee rights and civil liberties. The majority of these accounts are based on interviews originally conducted for the *Harvard Business Review*.

The next stage was an analysis of a series of court cases decided since the mid-1970s. In a surprisingly short period, the courts have produced significant changes in the law. In this stage, I took advantage of my own legal training as well as conversations with a number of fine lawyers.

Finally, in an attempt to conceptualize what has been going on and to point out the practical implications for managers, I wrote the expositions that join the accounts of employee objectors, organizational programs, and court decisions. In general, these interpretive sections take up where my previous book *Freedom Inside the Organization* (Dutton, 1977) left off.

I am grateful to two former secretaries at the *Harvard Business Review*, Linda B. Lord and Cynthia K. Shaw, for typing endless early drafts of the manuscript and handling voluminous correspondence. For most of the typing of the long final draft that went to the editors and publisher I am indebted to Catherine Michaud of Arlington, Massachusetts. In addition I wish to thank my literary agent Julian Bach for keeping my hopes alive in the early stages of the writing, and my editor at Wiley, John B. Mahaney, who made a series of very helpful suggestions for attacking the final draft. For a long, careful job of indexing I am indebted to Rebecca L. Ewing. Last, but certainly not least, I take my hat off to those hardy individualists in corporations, government agencies, and the legal system whose actions and aspirations have opened a new era in the history of American human rights.

DAVID W. EWING

Winchester, Massachusetts
October 1982

CONTENTS

ACCOUNTS AND CASES

xii   ACCOUNTS AND CASES

xii   ACCOUNTS AND CASES

1

THE ENDLESS WAVE

Never in American history has there been so much confusion over the prerogatives of managers to manage and the rights of their subordinates to be managed within limits. On this point, if nothing else, there is complete agreement among executives, lawyers, consultants and academics. Some of the confusion arises from laws about collective bargaining, civil rights, sexism, and safety. But these encroachments on traditional management prerogatives are only part of the problem. The most important changes have to do with a whole new way of regarding the manager–subordinate relationship. These changes have altered the organizational climate gradually and ubiquitously; they are more like what sailors call a "sea change" than a thunderhead or line squall. What they have produced is a new way of thinking about human dignity in the workplace—among managers as well as among nonmanagers. For the time being, the new way coexists with the old; this is what causes so much confusion. To illustrate, here are two brief samples from the sea of current experience.

A woman in a mid-western company adopted a child and got into an argument with her superior about the amount of leave she was entitled to. The superior thought she was entitled to the equivalent of sick leave, whereas she insisted she was entitled to maternity leave, which was considerably longer. When, unable to accept the superior's answer, she complained to managers higher up in the company, she was dismissed. She had become, I was told by a company executive, "a pain in the neck." The outcome of an almost identical case in a West Coast company was very different. When the superior tried to penalize the complaining employee, she appealed to a special group established for hearing such cases and was granted leave without prejudice to her position in the organization. Her superior was the one who was reprimanded and instructed to change his ways.

An officer of a bank in West Virginia learned of some illegal overcharges that were being made on customers' accounts. When he brought the matter tactfully to the attention of his superiors, he was told to forget it; "we know what we're doing," they said. Dissatisfied with this answer, he went to a top executive in the organization. When his boss learned about this, the boss fired him. Yet in an organization in New England, where a similar story was unfolding, the complainant went up the line when the angry boss tried to fire him. Not only was the situation corrected but he was thanked for his effort and enjoyed the satisfaction of seeing the perpetrators discharged.

Such contrasting pairs of stories are not unusual. They are taking place all over the country and in ever-increasing abundance. They illustrate a significant shift in the balance between management prerogatives and employee rights in corporate, government, educational, and other types of organizations. (Strictly speaking, managers are employees, too, but the term *employee rights* has become so firmly associated with the rights of subordinates and nonmanagers that the usage will be continued in this book.) Whether this shift is good or bad, whether it is due to excessive permissiveness or to the democratic spirit, whether it will lead to more capitalism or more socialism—these are questions that need not concern us for the time being. The fact is that the shift is going on, it proceeds independently of political fortunes in Washington, D.C., it is changing the life of every manager and subordinate, and it is affecting the fortunes of almost every corporate and public organization, large or small. The questions that should concern us first are these: What is going on? Why is it happening?

From many thousands of careful studies of the U.S. work force, several significant and durable features emerge. It is larger than ever, more volatile than ever, and more knowledgeable. So much attention has been given to these features individually, and to their economic significance in terms of productivity and quality of goods and services, that an important cumulative effect of the features has received little attention. This effect is *dissidence*. If there has been any lingering doubt about the importance of professional management, that doubt should now be erased forever. Employee dissidence makes the task of the manager not only more difficult and challenging than ever before, but also more indispensable.

According to business historian Alfred D. Chandler, modern management was born in the second half of the nineteenth century when technology and organization size made it essential to safe and efficient business operations.[1] The phenomenon of dissidence escalates the need for modern management, and to a new level of sophistication. Administrators now find themselves in roles comparable to the atomic "glue" that holds the forces of the nucleus together. Without good administration, the "nuclei" of the corporation and government agency—individuals, groups, departments—fly apart. The effect on the economy, when this happens, is disastrous.

More than a century ago, according to Chandler, railroads led the way to modern management, developing organization and control systems to take the place of arbitrary leadership by executive pooh-bahs. In the Western Railroad (western Massachusetts and eastern New York), a series of accidents, including a head-on collision, made the owners realize that business was getting too complicated for the traditional boss system. Today, new concepts for the management of dissidence have been pioneered by a great variety of companies—banks, airlines, chemical producers, automotive parts manufacturers, insurance firms, and many others. This fact reflects the universality of the pressures for change. They come from the chemistry of the work force everywhere, whether in a plywood company in Seattle or a camera-manufacturing firm in Boston.

As for the changing nature of the American work force, five features stand out. First is its enormousness—106 million employees altogether, including 11 million in government and 95 million in private industry, education, and public agencies. About 70 million of the latter work in about 80,000 businesses employing 100 or more people (the largest is AT&T, employing more than 1 million people). Second is the rise of technically trained "knowledge workers" and professionals. The late Nelson A. Rockefeller once noted that both of his famous grandfathers who founded Standard Oil Company, John D. Rockefeller and Winthrop Aldrich, were high-school dropouts. But today in Exxon, the corporate descendant of Standard Oil, highly educated employees hold the top 45,000 posts in the company—about 30% of the jobs. Thousands of other organizations also depend heavily on highly trained people.

Third is the astonishing variety of employees. The majority are white but substantial minorities are composed of blacks, Mexican Americans, and Orientals. The majority are Protestants but many millions are Catholics, Jews, Mormons, agnostics, and atheists. Close to 80% are nonunionized but three trade unions alone (Teamsters, United Auto Workers, and United Steelworkers) boast a membership of 4.5 million working at critical points in the economy. The majority are on the payrolls of corporations but im-

[1] Alfred D. Chandler, The Visible Hand (Cambridge: Harvard University Press, 1977), pp. 81–121.

pressive minorities are paid by universities, health management organizations, consulting firms, churches, the military, and civic organizations, as well as federal, state, and municipal governments.

A fourth feature is the mobility of American employees. The woman who was a secretary five years ago is on a corporate legal staff today. The man who worked in a university lab in San Diego last year now works in a scientific company in Georgia. There is great mobility between levels of jobs, types of responsibility, areas of work, and even between the work force and the at-home population, for growing numbers of people are trading back and forth between jobs and leisure.

Fifth, and in some ways most import₄nt of all, is the influence on employees of the variegated American culture. Some employees are materialistic, others are aesthetic; some are conservatives, others are heretics; some worship authority, others only tolerate it; some revel in teamwork and group membership, others prefer to go it alone in field selling or research; some "think like farmers" whereas others "think like Madison Avenue."

These features combine to produce the phenomenon of dissidence, which so many thousands of American organizations are experiencing. Dissidence could not happen in many other countries where there is more uniformity and less variety, nor could it have happened in the United States a few generations ago when there were fewer knowledge workers, less employee mobility, and a weaker union tradition. Sometimes critics blame dissidence on structures that various organizations have developed to accommodate it—employee assistance departments, civil-service-type regulations governing dismissal, labor–management problemsolving committees, and so on. This interpretation misses the point. Dissidence is in the wind, and as W. MacNeile Dixon once observed, "It is not the lofty sails but the unseen wind that moves the ship."

Why do the five characteristics mentioned produce dissidence? They do that because they produce interaction and interchange. They are like ingredients in a recipe that combine to produce a new flavor or dish, or chemicals interacting in a test tube to produce a new material. The enormousness of the American work force increases the mathematical possibilities for change and conflict; the rise of technically trained people gives more employees a basis for challenging the judgments of superiors; the mix of employee types brings people with divergent backgrounds into contact with one another; mobility exposes employees to a broader range of possible conflicts; and our heterogeneous culture multiplies the variety of values, norms, customs, and expectations that meet, not always harmoniously, in plants and office buildings.

How does dissidence manifest itself? In its most obvious form, it shows up in employee actions, not only strikes and slowdowns, the most dramatic

form, but also arguments with superiors, letters to the organization president, suggestions to management, demands for a voice in job planning and
work control systems, protests against a company decision to sell to, let us
say, the Arabs or the Pentagon, outspoken criticism in the media of company policies, blasts at management in stockholder meetings, and other
ways. Anthony Athos, an astute observer of the business scene, once predicted that employees some day would surround the chief executive's office
and hold him hostage, in order to gain compliance with a demand.[2] That
event has not yet happened, but almost every possible action short of such
a mutiny has taken place.

Dissidence also manifests itself in attitude surveys and other studies of
employee thinking. Daniel Yankelovich reports a marked shift in attitude
surveys toward what he calls a "psychology of entitlement" among employees. Instead of saying that they would *prefer* to have more influence on how
things are run, the growing tendency now is to insist that they have a *right*
to take part in decisions affecting their jobs. And whereas management,
only a few generations ago, could get away with water pollution or poor
working conditions by threatening layoffs, today a substantial minority tell
Yankelovich surveyors that they are prepared to risk their economic security, if necessary, in order to improve and preserve the quality of life.[3]
Opinion Research Corporation, the Conference Board, and other such organizations also have reported pronounced shifts in employee attitudes—more
discontent, more willingness to challenge management, more questioning
of superiors' decisions.

Ask almost any veteran supervisor about changes in attitude observed
and he or she will support what the pollsters report. When they began their
careers, they were taught to fear authority ("respect for authority" was the
accepted phrase). What the boss said was right because he was the boss,
and whatever club he used to enforce compliance was his prerogative.
These once-automatic, knee-jerk beliefs still exist, still are strong here and
there, but no longer prevail. Nor does loyalty to the company prevail. Over
the *Chicago Tribune* there used to fly a banner reading, "My country right or
wrong—but my country." Corporate managements often succeeded in in-
culcating a similar loyalty to the company—whatever it decided to do, it
deserved all-out employee support. Not any more. Most managements
think very hard about how a proposed action or policy may affect employment, work conditions, or employee relations, often altering or eliminating
the proposal rather than taking the chance of alienating many employees.

[2] Anthony Athos, "Is the Corporation the Next to Fall?," *Harvard Business Review*, January–
February 1970, p. 49.
[3] Daniel Yankelovich, "We Need New Motivational Tools," *Industry Week*, August 6, 1979,
p. 60.

Several years ago a company in the Southwest conducted a formal vote of employees concerning a proposed move to another location. And the head of Monsanto, John Hanley, told me that much as he wanted to prohibit cigarette smoking during working hours, he had decided not to do so after listening to the counsel of his public relations advisers.

Increasingly, employees think of "self" in terms quite different from management's usual definition. Employees insist that they want to reserve something of themselves from the clutch of the institutions that employ them, to keep a distance between themselves and their superiors, psychologically as well as cognitively. Like the radicals of the 1960s who had something to do with the chain reaction leading to the contemporary state of mind, they are keenly sensitive to the importance of form and procedure. They understand how a corporation's or agency's rules of order, propriety, civility, and appropriateness can demean the spirit, policing it as effectively as armed guards could. They resist the brittleness of corporate oligarchy, they protest the presumption that policies and directives should flow down and reports flow up. "In this grand tree, from root to crown," an anonymous employee wrote under a copy of the organization chart posted on one company's bulletin board, "ideas flow up and vetoes down."

A well-known New York public relations firm started its periodic report to employees and clients with these paragraphs:

> Remember those good old pre-whistle-blowing days when company loyalty was considered a virtue? The ideal employee was one who spent 50 years with the same employer without once uttering a word of complaint. At least not loud enough to be heard. For such durability, he received a gold watch upon retirement to mark time till the end of his days.

> The trouble with that image is not that it never existed, but that it runs counter to the nature of our society, which is based upon the right to air grievances, express opinions and voice disapproval—in short: to be heard. Our government rules by consent of the governed. Those in authority may not quell the voice that cries out in protest—no matter how discomfiting.

> In the past many corporations believed they were exempt from this political ideal. They abided, so they thought, in another realm. But gradually, enlightened companies have come to realize that they are social organisms, too, and they cannot function in a manner that goes against the grain of the broader society. To be sure, their adaptation has been slow, and the reasons are not hard to find. By definition, a

corporation is not a pure or even a representative democracy; its employees are not empowered to elect their management or decide who their bosses will be. We do not say this has been bad for the country or its economy. We merely say that corporations have never pretended to be paragons of political democracy. That was not their aim.

Nevertheless, progressive companies have systematically built bridges between the managers and the managed so that employees could speak out without fear of reprisal. Unfortunately, many companies failed to open such channels of communication, and they found themselves beset by increasing numbers of disgruntled employees, especially as they grew. The more layers of management one inserts between an employee and his chief executive, the more disenfranchised that employee is likely to feel.[4]

Feelings of dissidence are aggravated, not reduced, by many employers' willingness to retaliate against employees who talk back. Although this fact perplexes and bemuses old-guard managers, it does not surprise younger generations of employees, who perversely may accept management's power and their own powerlessness as a kind of challenge, a throwing down of the gauntlet.

Let us consider the ultimate form of retaliation by a supervisor, which is dismissal. Estimates of the number of victims of unfair discharge vary enormously because no records need to be kept—after all, such acts usually are perfectly legal. However, one careful and knowledgeable estimate comes from Jack Stieber, director of Michigan State University's School of Labor and Industrial Relations. Beginning with the annual number of unjust discharges as ruled in arbitration cases, and applying this ratio, with various adjustments, to the rest of the work force, Stieber estimates conservatively that about half a million employees are fired unjustly every year. I believe this to be a reasonable figure. Taking some confidential estimates of attempted discharges in a few companies that maintain due process procedures for their employees, and projecting these estimates to the rest of the work force, I arrive at a figure at least as large as Stieber's. Note that both Stieber's estimate and my own are concerned with what we call unjust discharge; that is, a dismissal not because of incompetence or uncooperativeness but because of a supervisor's arbitrary whim or capricious judgment—for instance, dislike of a subordinate who "doesn't part his hair in the right way," anger against an assistant who objects to an unreasonable suggestion, frustration with an employee who criticizes working conditions.

[4] *Burson–Marsteller Report*, Summer 1981, p. 1.

So long as most employees want to be individualistic, unjust discharges add to latent employee anger and exacerbate discontent with management.

GATHERING MOMENTUM

Will employee dissidence continue during the 1980s? Will it continue to challenge the balance between management prerogatives and employee rights? Some observers feel that it has reached a peak preliminary to tapering off, as happened with the campus rebellions of the late 1960s. Most of the signs, however, indicate that dissidence will keep on growing, that it is not a rogue wave that breaks at one time and place on the shore but, to borrow the surfboarders' phrase, an endless wave that goes on and on. Some of the most important indicators are the following.

Societal Encouragement. Despite the rise of a new conservatism in American politics—or perhaps because of it—our schools, churches, community associations, clubs, youth groups, and other social organizations continue to emphasize democratic ideals. Although it is difficult to measure such forces objectively, it appears to many observers that at the grass roots American society is irreversibly committed to standards of fair play and individual dignity. Society's "basic training" emphasizes participation, speaking out, open dialogue, egalitarianism. Long before the time we take our first jobs, most of us are infused with notions of authority-sharing and a fairly democratic style of decision-making. I remember visiting the sixth-grade schoolroom that two of my daughters attended. Walking into the room, I first heard the ubiquitous buzz of conversation, then saw all the students in small groups at round tables, collaborating on group projects. A teacher and a couple of assistants went back and forth among the tables to answer questions and give guidance. All the children were free to talk and question. Groups were the thing. What a contrast, I thought, with the grade-school classrooms I had been raised in, where we sat in straight rows of desks all facing the front of the room where the teachers stood, like sea gulls standing facing an oncoming storm.

"The secret of the matter is," says a man in Charles Dickens's *Going into Society*, "that it ain't so much that a person goes into Society, as that Society goes into a person." Because notions of American society "go into a person" at a more impressionable age than the more authoritarian values of industry, they stay in most employees' thinking indefinitely.

New Notions of Job Rights. By emphasizing the value of employer property and stockholders' interests, capitalism—albeit unwittingly and unintentionally—has promoted the idea that an employee has a kind of property right in his or her job. This idea fuels dissidence because it leads to the conviction that a job is too precious to be destroyed by a capricious supervisor or oppressive department head. Ironically, although many conservative managers consider the notion of job property rights un-American, the conservative capitalist ethic, by popularizing the ideal of property, pulls the rug out from under them.

Martin J. Morand points out that the notion of property rights in jobs has historical roots in the West.[5] As late as the seventeenth century, Morand says, the notion of property was broad. It included a person's capacities, rights, and liberties, not just chattels and lands. Indeed, the intangible rights came to be viewed as the source and justification of ownership of material things. Because of a historical flip-flop, however, material ownership came to be viewed as the source and justification of intangible rights, and when modern market societies developed, the rights became dependent on ownership. To oversimplify what happened, the individual who once had been considered justified in pursuing material wealth because of inalienable properties possessed by all humans now had to "earn" many rights by ownership. Later, when certain individuals succeeded in acquiring (or inheriting) more material possessions than others, and thus became able to exercise and dictate their desires more freely than other people, the concept of property narrowed to include land, buildings, and bank accounts, exclusive of rights. In recent decades, however, the concept of property has been expanding. Morand argues:

> Our legal system is designed to protect property rights and, therefore, contracts. Jobs have become recognized as property, at least, to some extent. Certainly, they are seen and felt as property by workers. Unions function to strengthen the degree of "property" in a job.

> The worker whose job is threatened reacts. When it is the "invisible hand" of the market that he has been socialized to accept as inevitable or unavoidable, he still responds. However, when his job is threatened because of what appears to him to be "social engineering" manipulation . . . he sees human capital being stripped from him and he feels this as not only inequitable but inequitous. The result is not just worker response, but worker backlash.[6]

[5] Martin J. Morand and Donald S. McPherson, "Encouraging Alternatives to Seniority-Based Layoffs through Modifications of Unemployment Insurance," working paper circulated in February 1979 (Indiana: Center for the Study of Labor Relations, Indiana University of Pennsylvania).

[6] Ibid., pp. 5–6.

Dissidents Holding Levers of Power.   In generations past, dissidence generally came from employees near the bottom of the economic barrel, especially blue-collar workers in manufacturing plants. What we are seeing today, however, is a growing inclination to dissidence among well-paid employees who often work close to top management and participate in vital forms of decision-making. Among the militant groups of employees we now hear about, for instance, are movie and television writers, airport traffic controllers, communications specialists, hospital medics, and baseball players. The high status and visibility of these militants make dissidence contagious in the work force. What is more, high-status dissidents are increasingly sensitive to shortcomings in management. They want not only equitable pay, flexible working hours, good lighting, clean rest rooms, safe working conditions, and so on, but such psychological benefits as recognition in policymaking and freedom from unnecessary stress. Stress, says Stanley Aronowitz, a labor writer and activist, "is the black lung of the technical classes." During the air traffic controllers' strike in 1981, Robert Schrank of the Ford Foundation called the stoppage a striking example of the airy expectations of employees in strategic operating positions. "Here you have guys making $30,000 a year or more and their basic complaint is the insensitivity of management."

In generations past, employees in textile mills, automotive factories, steel mills, and railroads sold their time and stamina. They were more or less interchangeable, like worker ants. But today's high-status dissidents sell neither their bodies nor their time; they sell their unique capacities, knowledge, and power. Moreover, often there are few of them engaged in any one specialty—yet that specialty is essential to the operation of the agency or company. This combination of facts means that the specialists have unique powers over the organization. They can cripple it, if they want to. They can hijack it. They can paralyze it. Simply by withdrawing, they can devastate it.

Now, the dependence is mutual, for the same abilities that give the specialist power over the organization also give the organization power over the specialist, who may have to look far and wide to find another organization that has a need for his or her special talents. Nevertheless, the specialist has a bargaining power that hired hands never possessed in the past. Result: The boss who wants to fire a critic or conscientious objector in the word-processing department or metallurgy division must think twice. That person may be irritating, but will getting rid of him or her be like cutting off the departmental nose to spite the face? Management audiences laugh at the old saw about the employee who says, "My boss and I are engaged in a power struggle. He's got the power and I've got the struggle." But in reality it may be the other way around, or partly the other way. In the United

States and other countries there is growing agreement with Pehr Gyllen-hammer, the veteran head of Volvo, that management can no longer be based on power. In most shows of power today, observes Gyllenhammer, the workers will "win" and management will "lose," though the inevitable result sooner or later is that everyone loses.

Belief in Self-Responsibility. For several generations corporations and government agencies have sought, in indoctrination and training, to develop a sense of individual responsibility among employees so that they will report problems early and take the initiative in correcting errors, rather than pass the buck. This effort, which is spreading in many ways and forms, makes some kinds of dissidence seem loyal rather than (as in the past) disloyal. If the company or agency wants and trains you to sound the alarm right away when you discover an error in the computer program or a malfunction in a quality-control program, doesn't it make sense that you should also protest an immoral directive from your boss or blow the whistle on a cover-up in a product testing program?

In past generations leaders were presumed to have special knowledge, abilities, capacities, and powers. Ordinary people lived vicariously with the few heroes who challenged authority—the Galileos, Michael Servetuses, Oliver Cromwells, Nikolai Lenins, George Washingtons, Simon Bolivars, and others. Today there is less willingness to let someone else be the hero. More and more of us picture *ourselves* as Davids willing to take on Goliath. We want to feel, sense, touch, understand, and discover personally, ver-idically rather than vicariously. We are more willing to stand up to the boss ourselves, blow the whistle ourselves, rather than always leaving it to a Jane Fonda, Ralph Nader, or Senator William Proxmire. As Duncan E. Littlefair puts it, the growing popular conviction is that "not one hundred or two hundred gifted leaders but *millions* of people have the right and freedom to become heroes." [7]

What is significant is that employer organizations themselves are encouraging such individual initiative. In its corporate code for employees, Bank of America urges anyone anywhere on its payroll to report suspected acts of fraud, embezzlement, or deception. Atlantic Richfield tells employees to report violations of pollution laws to management and/or the appropriate government agency. Increasingly, companies and agencies are telling train-ees how much depends on *their* prompt action when they discover some-thing that is illegal or suspicious.

Moreover, when organization leaders and personnel officials talk about things like fulfillment at work, fun on the job, and rewarding task chal-

---

[7] Duncan E. Littlefair, *The Glory within You* (Philadelphia: Westminster Press, 1973), p. 24.

lenges, as they do so often, they tend to legitimize the employee who objects to a psychotic or unfair supervisor, or to surreptitious monitoring of employee phone calls, or to unreasonable interferences in after-hours activities. "What's all this talk about quality of work life," people ask, "if we have to submit to lie detector tests?"

Consider an example. Late in the 1960s, Eaton Corporation began changing the conventionally dull, stuffy, autocratic atmosphere of thirteen manufacturing plants where about 5,000 employees worked. It couldn't do this overnight, of course, and the process is still going on, but it began eliminating what employees considered a stupid, denigrating, time-clock-punching, rules-obsessed philosophy of management in favor of weekly departmental meetings where everyone is expected to chip in with thoughts and criticisms, round-table discussions of problems, and what the company calls an "open floor" concept, meaning that everyone who works is entitled to a voice in discussions about the way work is done, lunch breaks, lighting, the rest rooms, potholes in the parking lot—anything that concerns workers and can be handled by joint effort. Once such procedures are instituted, the manager–employee dialogue begins to expand. Soon equity in general becomes a topic.

A similar example is General Motors' Fisher Body Plant Number 2 in Grand Rapids, Michigan. The 2,000 employees have been organized into six teams, each a kind of "business on its own" with its own maintenance, scheduling, and engineering people. Early in the 1970s, when this unusual approach was launched, everyone on salary joined in decision-making about how to meet the team's objectives. But now hourly paid employees, too, are being included in decision-making. Much is experimental, and many problems remain to be solved, but the general drift of things is quite clear. What is especially significant is the organizational motive. According to one senior GM spokesman, "The point isn't to improve productivity. It's to improve the quality of work life."

As employees get more and more in the habit of "governing" their work and making the rules, it is a shorter and shorter step to deciding on rights of a civil liberties nature. They ask, "If it is appropriate for us to decide on a change in lighting or a method of requisitioning supplies, may it not also be appropriate to blow the whistle on an improper order given by a boss or to criticize a department head's insensitivity to our desire for discretionary coffee breaks?"

Quality of work life has a long way to go in this country because employee expectations keep rising. For a long time to come, they will spark employee willingness to talk back to management when things don't seem right.

Rise of Dual Loyalties.   Another long-term generator of dissidence is the rise of competing loyalties. No longer has the employer organization a dominant claim on the allegiance of many an employee. The corporation or agency must share its employees' loyalties with other objects of their affection.

This is most noticeable in the case of what the census calls "professional and technical workers," who more than doubled in number between 1960 and 1980. Scientists, engineers, computer specialists, accountants, social scientists, and other professionals belong to associations that encourage certain values and norms of their own. These values sometimes conflict with the expectations of an employer organization.

For example, Frank von Hippel of Princeton University points to the code of the National Society of Professional Engineers, which states that the engineer "will use his knowledge and skill for the advancement of human welfare." Moreover, when his duty brings the engineer into conflict with the demands of an employer, the code instructs him to "regard his duty to the public welfare as paramount."

In fact, among professionals there is a growing conviction that acts of dissidence, honestly and thoughtfully taken in the public interest, may be not only permissible but obligatory. In 1975, an ad hoc committee of the American Association for the Advancement of Science reported on the changing requirements of scientific freedom and responsibility. The committee concluded that more than a right is involved in the release of facts that are in the public interest, regardless of timing. Experts possessing such information *should* release it, the committee stated, "even though they might prefer to remain silent."

This philosophy is incompatible with the textbook philosophy of management control, with its corollaries of secrecy and obedience once the organization commits itself to a course. It destroys the notion of competition and the pursuit of profit as a game with rules that must be honored by all participants. Broadly speaking, the professionals tend to be more interested in effectiveness than in efficiency. They prefer to see an employer corporation doing the right thing inefficiently than the almost-right or wrong thing efficiently. To the traditional manager, this attitude is exasperating and even intolerable when it leads, as it often does, to questioning a company decision after it is made. Once management arrives at a decision, the manager insists, all must assume it is right (at least, until the decision-makers themselves change their minds). Otherwise teamwork is impossible. By contrast, professionals are trained to believe that no finding ever becomes "right" by fiat.

What is more, profesionalism tends to spawn new varieties of voluntary societies, which, alongside the primary professional associations, encourage values that may conflict with employer fealty. The Union of Concerned Scientists, the Municipal Finance Officers Association, societies for energy conservation, anti-nuclear groups—one could go on and on, for there are hundreds and even thousands of them. The now-famous monkey-seizure case at the government-funded Institute of Behavioral Research in Silver Spring, Maryland, in 1981 is one of many examples. Alex Pacheco, the employee objector in this case, was a master's student in zoology at the University of Maryland. He also was a founder of an animal rights society called People for Ethical Treatment of Animals. Becoming distressed over the egregiously unhappy lot of the monkeys in the laboratories, Pacheco turned for help to a scientist friend who belonged to the Humane Society, and that friend in turn solicited the help of three other scientists. To the acute consternation and embarrassment of officers of the Institute of Behavioral Research, Pacheco and the four scientists succeeded in bringing in the police, who raided the labs and spirited away seventeen monkeys. This event then sparked new proposals for animal protection legislation in Congress. The case, believed to be the first of its kind in the country, typifies the *kind* of challenge of employer prerogatives that is encouraged by dual professional loyalties.

Judges Who Smile on Dissidents.   During most of our history, the courts have sided with employers against whistleblowers, employee critics, and other kinds of dissidents. The majority still do—some of them automatically, it seems. For instance, in 1979 an Indiana appellate court sided with a company that fired two employees for reporting to a senior manager that their supervisor was soliciting and receiving kickbacks from suppliers.[8] And in 1978 an Iowa court sided with a company that fired an employee for writing a letter (based in part but not in whole on misunderstandings of fact) critical of the firm's business policies.[9] In these cases, like many hundreds of earlier ones, the judges assumed that an employee served "at will"—since he or she could leave any time, the employer could fire him or her any time—and that any reason, short of one expressly prohibited by law, or no reason, was sufficient to justify discharge.

The first big crack in the common-law rule came in 1968, when the majority of the U.S. Supreme Court ruled that a public-school teacher had a limited right to criticize the local school board.[10] A string of similar cases

[8] *Martin* v. *Platt*, 386 NE 2d 1026 (1979).
[9] *Abrisz* v. *Pulley Freight Lines, Inc.*, 270 NW 2d 454 (1978). For other decisions favoring the traditional common-law rule, see my book, *Freedom inside the Organization* (New York: Dutton, 1977), pp. 3–4, 99–100, 219–220.
[10] *Pickering* v. *Board of Education*, 391 U.S. 563 (1968).

followed. Today federal employees have a variety of openings in the law for suing their employers for unjust discharge. In state law, however, the situation continues to favor the employer. (A startling example is the case of James Rittenhouse, described in Chapter 2.)

Corporate employers shrugged off the Supreme Court's 1968 decision because the setting was a public organization, but in 1974 a U.S. district court decided that a factory inspector had a right to criticize his employer's labor-relations policies in a local newspaper; so much of the factory's production was for the Department of Defense, said the judge, that a "governmental presence" made it subject to the same rule as public schools were.[11]

Still, few corporate attorneys and executives paid much attention. The factory inspector's case was an aberration unlikely to be repeated, management was advised. But like cracks in a basement wall, the fissures in the common-law rule widened. In 1975 a trial court in California decided in favor of an electrical engineer who was fired after pointing out that a computer console manufactured by his employer did not conform to the state's safety code.[12] The case was not appealed, however, so it acquired no precedential value. Once more defenders of the common-law rule breathed with relief.

Then in 1978 a major rupture happened. John C. Harless, an officer of a West Virginia bank, had been fired in 1976 for protesting his bank's practice of overcharging certain types of customers. Taking the employer bank to court, he was greeted with the customary defense: Since he was a nonunion employee and no special statute was involved, any reason or no reason sufficed for sacking him. The West Virginia high court disagreed, ruling that exceptions to the traditional rule had to be made when the public interest and public policy were involved.[13] For the first time a major court had turned its back decisively on a rule that had held sway for centuries in the United States and England.

Since then, other courts have come to the aid of employee critics and conscientious objectors. Judges appear to be most comfortable with the justification that public policy (especially if articulated in a relevant statute) is served by reinstating the dissident or allowing the claim for damages. For instance, a New Jersey court ruled in favor of an x-ray technician who contended that she had been discharged for refusing to perform illegal catheterizations.[14] Again, when a fifteen-year sales veteran of Atlantic

[11] *Holodnak* v. *Avco Corporation*, 514 F. 2d 285 (1975). For a complete account, see pp. 68–75.
[12] *Murray* v. *Microform Data Systems, Inc.*, Superior Court, Santa Clara, Calif., No. 337237 (1975). For a complete account, see pp. 106–110.
[13] *Harless* v. *First Fairmont National Bank in Fairmont*, 246 SE Reporter 2d 270 (1978). For a complete account, see pp. 54–60.
[14] *O'Sullivan* v. *Mallon et al.*, 390 A. 2d 149 (1978).

Richfield was fired for refusing, as ordered, to threaten gas station owners who didn't cooperate in fixing prices, the Supreme Court of California ruled in his favor.[15] And when an employee alleged that his discharge was the result of his refusal to cooperate with management in violating the antitrust laws, a federal court came to his rescue, ruling that an employee should be protected and supported in an effort to comply with the law.[16]

But public policy is not the only justification judges are finding for rescuing dissidents. In a case that legal beagles consider significant, a middle manager with five years of employment with Blue Cross in Michigan was fired; he sued for damages, and won a decision from the Michigan Supreme Court.[17] In effect, the court said that if, as in this case, the employee had been given verbal assurances of job security by superiors, and referred to written discharge policies in the company manual that protected him from arbitrary dismissal, the superiors could not change their mind and show him the door.

Of course, for years unions have defended—successfully—members who were discharged for flimsy or spurious reasons. In 1980, for example, a worker at Honeywell accused his bosses of racial bias in denying him promotion to the position of electrician. Finally he vented his anger by writing accusations on the walls in the men's lavatory. When management suspended him for ten days, the union and then the National Labor Relations Board upheld his right to write graffiti constituting, in the board's phrase, a "public airing of his grievance."

The umbrella of protection afforded by the unions protects only about one employee in five, however, and among the many people not protected are most professionals, technical workers, secretaries, salespeople, information specialists, and supervisors.

The beginnings of a more benign judicial attitude toward whistle-blowers, conscientious objectors, and other dissidents have not gone unnoticed by employees—or their employers. The likelihood that this court attitude will spread during the 1980s is another reason that dissidence will continue to increase.

Support from Solons.   In state legislatures there is a growing conviction that laws should be enacted to protect at least some employees who talk back to their supervisors or disobey directives. Alan F. Westin of Columbia

---

[15] *Tameny* v. *Atlantic Richfield Co.,* 164 Cal. Reporter 839 (1980).

[16] *McNulty* v. *Borden, Inc.,* 474 F Supp 1111 (1979).

[17] *Toussaint* v. *Blue Cross,* 79 Mich. App. 429 (1977). A similar decision was rendered three years later in *Voorhees* v. *Shriners' Hospital for Crippled Children;* see Robert Coulson, *The Termination Handbook* (New York: The Free Press, 1981) pp. 173–176.

University, director of the Educational Fund for Individual Rights, believes that such statutes will spread because they can be written so as to put the burden on the judicial system rather than requiring a new state agency to investigate complaints and monitor performance. In this sense, Westin says, they give "more regulatory bang for the buck." Such a philosophy is consistent with the new political winds of the cost-conscious 1980s.

The first statute of this type to be enacted was Michigan's Whistleblowers' Protection Act, which took effect in March 1981. Representative Perry Bullard was the prime mover behind this legislation. In the California, New York, New Jersey, Wisconsin, and Pennsylvania legislatures, similar legislation is being prepared. New Jersey's bill, introduced in June 1981 by Senator Matthew Feldman, favors employee critics who are penalized for expressing valid complaints about the workplace. If the state court finds that the dissident was expelled in vengeance for an honest and apparently valid complaint, the employee may be reinstated and awarded damages, and the employer firm can be fined a maximum of $20,000.

In all states where such legislation is fermenting, egregious incidents reported in the media are a major factor creating legislative concern. For instance, Perry Bullard found support in the Lansing legislature for his bill because a Michigan chemical company that had sold contaminated animal feed (mixed by error with a fire retardant) had issued a gag order forbidding its employees to report inside information to government investigators. Similarly, Feldman's bill introduced in New Jersey was supported by many solons who remembered the unfortunate case of A. Grace Pierce, erstwhile director of medical research for a pharmaceutical company in Raritan, New Jersey. In 1975, after refusing to test a new diarrhea drug on infants and elderly people because it contained high levels of saccharin, then feared to be a carcinogen, Pierce was removed from her position; soon after that, as her superiors hoped, she resigned.

At the federal level, the much-heralded Civil Sevice Reform Act of 1978 was sold to public employees in part on the promise of greater protection for critics of fraud, mismanagement, and wrongdoing in their employer agencies. President Jimmy Carter's assistants were especially concerned with the demonstrated powers of an agency to retaliate against a whistleblower, civil service regulations notwithstanding. To protect the critic against reprisal, the 1978 legislation created the Merit Systems Protection Board and its Office of Special Counsel. Despite the hopes of many legislators on Capitol Hill and the endeavors of earnest officials in the new agencies, the act has been little short of a disaster. In its first two and a half years of operation, the board failed to uncover a single prohibited practice of retaliation. Moreover, as pointed out by the Government Accountability Project of the Institute for Policy Studies (which provides legal counsel to federal whistleblowers), the board succeeded in establishing new legal ground rules making it virtually impossible for whistleblowers to save their jobs through the Office of Special Counsel. This neat trick was executed by requiring the Special Counsel attorney to prove that the agency official who signed the papers directing dismissal of an employee critic had direct personal knowledge of the act in question. In effect, all an unscrupulous agency management has to do is be sure that a "hatchet man" did the work out of sight of the official signing the discharge papers. Provisions requiring the critic to endure a public fact-finding by the board *after* the lengthy process of investigations by the Special Counsel's office, along with a limitation on the critic's rights to legal fees, put new dampers on employee talk-back.

Conceivably, however, this reversal of employee rights could be short-lived. In the summer of 1981 the Merit Systems Protection Board released a study of whistleblowing that soon became a local best-seller in Washington. The study showed that large numbers of federal employees knew of instances of fraud, abuse, and wrongdoing in their agencies but were afraid to speak out or report it. Many members of congress and senators began thinking, "If we *really* want to improve the efficiency of federal agency operations, should we not make better use of such an excellent reservoir of firsthand information as the agency work forces themselves?"

At a more modest level of achievement is legislation barring the discharge of employees who irritate their superiors by serving on juries, filing workmen's compensation claims against the employer firm, or asserting other legally authorized employee rights that a superior happens to frown upon. Close to half of the states have passed laws of this type. The fact that the great majority of enactments have come since 1978 suggests how much momentum has been gathering.[18]

Related to whistleblower statutes are employee privacy laws. In one sense, a privacy law is the opposite of a whistleblower law: It deals not with information or views purposely communicated to superiors but with information *not* intended to be given to them. In other senses, however, privacy legislation is in the family of employee rights laws along with whistleblower protection, for it concerns the civil liberties of employees and their rights to certain measures of dignity during working hours.

The first major piece of legislation protecting employee privacy was the Federal Privacy Act of 1974, which set forth a code of fair information

---

[18] For those interested in pursuing this aspect of the law, two key court cases are *Nees* v. *Hocks*, 272 Or. 210, 536 P. 2d 512 (1975) and *Sventko* v. *Kroger*, 69 Mich. App. 644, 245 NW 2d 151 (1976). In *Nees*, the court ruled in favor of a woman fired for serving on a jury; in *Sventko*, the bench rescued a man dismissed for filing a workmen's compensation claim against the employer firm.

practices for federal agencies to follow (e.g., allowing an employee access to information in his or her personnel files and affording a means of contesting and correcting inaccurate information there). The 1974 act also created the Privacy Protection Study Commission to examine the possible need for similar rules in the business sector. Since then, about a dozen states have passed statutes similar to the Federal Privacy Act.

Unlike the whistleblower laws motivated in part by legislative anger over cases of unjust discharge, the privacy laws are the result mainly of social and technological trends. In the 1960s and 1970s many old barriers concerning employee dress, life-style, sexual preference, and political belief were swept away. To most Americans it no longer seemed appropriate for superiors to learn about a subordinate's views on racism, homosexuality, and other matters now considered to be legitimate personal choices. As for technology, in the decades following World War II the whole "classic balance of privacy," as Westin calls it, was turned upside down. Electronic listening devices, polygraphs, personality tests, television monitors, and computerized data systems gave employers fabulous new powers enabling them to assume, if they desired, the role of Big Brother and to turn employee workplaces into animal farms à la the famous nightmare of George Orwell. As a fear of invasion of privacy came over much of the workplace, legislators—and, as we shall see later, a good many corporate leaders—responded by saying, in effect, "We don't want it to happen here."

The pro-employee ferment in legislatures, like the other trends described, is bound to keep the dissidence ball rolling. Surely the movement will not be consistent; instead, it will be jerky, failing here, succeeding there, stalled temporarily over there. The important thing, though, is that it ensures that employee civil liberties will be talked about. The more they are talked about, the more awareness grows; the more awareness grows, the more both subordinates *and superiors* edge toward meetings of the minds on new bounds and measures of propriety. The case is somewhat like that of the miner in Pennsylvania who was asked by a reporter when he became conscious of unnecessary hazards to health and safety in the mines. He answered, "When I read about it in the newspapers."

TIME FOR A NEW MODEL

Since there is no known way of suppressing or draining dissidence from the workplace, organization leaders need to think of their prerogatives in fresh terms. They need to switch to a new ideal of the "good" organization. They need to turn in the model of the past hundred years for a new model. The outmoded model was influenced by engineering and technology; the "good" organization was seen as a smooth-running mechanism. Perhaps that was inevitable in a period when technology was seen as the cure for everything. We know that technology has no magical powers.

Recognizing that the engineering model is obsolete, we must look to a different kind of pattern, one that, while emphasizing productivity and output, also allows for dissidence, cacophony, and heterogeneity. Such qualities, though they make any good engineer shudder, are quite natural. No flower runs like a machine. As it grows, various cell groups conflict with each other, often wastefully; colors run into one another; stems don't always grow straight; leaves often are not identical. We need to change the terms with which we describe organizations. Instead of thinking of organizations as running or humming, we might better think of them as growing or living; instead of referring to modules, subsets, or units of organizations, it might be better to refer to groups, branches, or limbs. The phrase *human resources* is a better one than *human assets* or, worse, *human capital*, and rather than "manipulating" and "structuring" people we might do better to think of management as "leading" people and "creating conditions for growth." Even the word *efficient* now has outmoded connotations, for it is primarily a mechanical and engineering term; *effective* is a much better word, for it allows for a good result to be different from the best possible mathematical ratio between input and output. A rigid, totalitarian company may be efficient for a while but it cannot be effective for long because it doesn't nurture the heresies, minority viewpoints, and creativeness that keep an organization innovative and adaptive to changing conditions.

The mechanical, engineering view of employees has stayed in our system like a nonbiodegradable poison. "What," wrote Thomas Hobbes three centuries ago, "is the heart but a spring, and the nerves but so many strings, and the joints but so many wheels, giving motion to the whole body?" Everyone now knows this notion is spurious, yet it underlies many organization practices. Fair pay, decent lighting, clean rest rooms, clear work instructions—these are the heralded "motivators" to get the job done. The agency or corporation as a whole is seen as a huge machine that, in Hobbes's words, is "sub-divided into an infinite number of lesser machines." Clockwork man, clockwork woman.

Yet the power of totalitarian managers to command a taut ship is the power to impose boredom, tedium, staleness, stasis, and, of course, fear in the ranks. Someday a good research group should study boredom as an instrument of management control. From the standpoint of the totalitarian administrator who wants a smooth-running, friction-free department, nothing beats boring supervision, boring management pep talks, boring control systems, boring-looking offices, boring memoranda, boring bureaucracies— but what is their effect on employee consciences? Do they so dull and stupefy that nobody cares any more, or fears to care, when financial statements are doctored and defective products are knowingly approved for sale and corners are cut in the law? Perhaps, as sociologist Robert Coles has suggested, the bored and alienated person comes almost to welcome disasters, unsettling surprises, stupid leadership acts—anything to break the monotony of keeping a tight mouth and doing as you are told.

A person is a passionate being, Erich Fromm pointed out. Human nature needs stimulation. Men and women tolerate boredom and monotony badly, and if they cannot take a genuine interest in life, they are capable of perversion and destruction. Historians may someday write that the best reason for civil liberties was that they made life more interesting. Years ago Max Frisch wrote a play about some men who organized what they expected to be a perfect factory, completely efficient and harmonious. But conflict arose anyway and the employees went on strike. One executive sighed, "We hired workers and human beings came instead."

For the organization, the short-run costs of a more democratic, biological model are slower, less "smooth" decision-making, extra supervisory training (to develop skills in conflict resolution and participation), and more administrative headaches of certain types (but offset by fewer headaches of other types). The reward for the organization: full membership in a democratic society and an employee staff that exercises a broader range of discretion, is more expressive, and finds more "wholeness" at work. Job satisfaction, finds Jonathan Freedman of Columbia University, basing his conclusions on a series of surveys, is almost as essential to overall happiness as love and marriage are. In *Doctor Zhivago*, Boris Pasternak has his main character chastise a "reformed" Soviet party member in these words:

> Your health is bound to be affected if, day after day, you say the opposite of what you feel, if you grovel before what you dislike and rejoice at what brings you nothing but misfortune. Our nervous system isn't just a fiction; it's part of our physical body, and our soul exists in space, and is inside us, like the teeth in our mouth. It can't be forever violated with impunity. I found it painful to listen to you, Innokentii, when you told us how you were re-educated and became mature in jail. It was like listening to a horse describing how it broke itself in.

THE "GOOD" ORGANIZATION

In the decades ahead, the "good" organization will not resemble the taut ship idealized in the past. The "good" organization will be one that accepts tension, accommodates certain kinds and qualities of dissidence, and makes daily use of procedures and mechanisms for resolving conflict.

This will not be an organization that tolerates the chronic complainer, the lazy employee, or the gadfly who wants to debate routine decisions made by bosses. Such toleration does not enhance employee dignity. But the "good" organization will be one in which every employee has some say in the planning and control of his or her job, in which every employee enjoys rights to privacy and freedom of activity after working hours, in which every member has a qualified right to speak out against actions or policies that seem immoral, unethical, or irresponsible, and in which every member has a right to a prompt and fair hearing when he or she feels wronged by a superior.

One of the philosophies of such an organization is that tension and conflict have a basic value. Littlefair expresses this value in terms of an analogy.[19] A sailboat, he observes, makes headway because of the opposition of its sail to the wind. If this opposition is firm, the sailboat makes good speed. Of course, the opposition must not be too strong, for then the boat may keel over. On the other hand, if the opposition is too weak, little or no progress is made. The setting of sail against wind must be done with judgment. The analogy applies to human relationships, Littlefair argues, because a certain amount of opposition is valuable for individual growth and development.

The moral of the analogy for organizations is clear. If employees are to gain the fullest from their association, they and their managers must be willing to differ, to guard their self-interests, to recognize conflict. If they do not oppose each other enough in these ways, their relationships become static. If they oppose too much, conflict will get out of hand and upset operations. Proper judgment must be used so that the amount of difference and conflict will continue within a reasonable range. Integrity and goodwill are important ingredients, too; nothing is gained from the tensions created by malice or petty feuding.

If managers and employees are aware of their differences and are concerned about them, they will feel tension. This tension is a prerequisite of being able to respond intelligently to conflict and profit from it. Of course, the employees must also be able to live with the tension and not be overwhelmed by it. This in turn means that they cannot be neurotic misfits excessively prone to anxiety and distrust. We are talking, in other words, about what might be called healthy tensions; that is, the stresses created by the need to accomplish, to feel productive and creative, to overcome the inevitable hurdles imposed by production, marketing, negotiating, financing, and other necessary functions.

In the good organization, ways are sought to bring tension and conflict

---

[19] Littlefair, op. cit., pp. 103–105.

into the open. Dissidence and dissonance are useless if unrecognized. As the head of a fast-growing British electronics firm once commented on his own actions at board meetings, "I usually endeavor to bring out something controversial so that at least one member of the board will get hot under the collar about it. *If we can each of us do this without fear* then I think we are creating a very powerful team relationship." [20]

This leader wanted board members to put their conflicts on the table, and he wanted them to feel that there was no danger in so doing. He wanted tensions treated matter-of-factly, as a problem that everyone was fully capable of handling.

The general atmosphere desired by the British executive was, I suspect, very much like that which was found some years ago in one branch of the Office of the Assistant Secretary of the Air Force. The researchers noted that a superior was often described by a subordinate in words like these: "You can always talk back to him if you want to," or, "You can always tell him what you think even if he doesn't agree with you." [21]

Still another example was set by Alfred P. Sloan, the first great chief executive of General Motors. As I have it from Peter Drucker, Sloan called a conference to consider a very important technical change under consideration for GM cars. Apparently his own leanings in favor of the innovation were known. At any rate, he asked for the individual views of the people at hand, and they took turns, one after another around the table, saying why they thought the innovation was a good idea. When all had spoken, Sloan said, "Gentlemen, let's think about it some more tonight and meet again tomorrow. If no one has arguments against this, we're not in a position yet to decide."

Later in this book we will look in more detail at the policies, procedures, and mechanisms of the good organization.

WHAT WILL BE GAINED?

Organizations that encourage more openness, civil liberties, and human dignity in the workplace will be rewarded in many ways. And so will American society.

First, judging from past experience, corporations and public agencies will gain by making fewer mistakes. There will be fewer cases of utterly unnecessary boo-boos due to the muzzling and gagging of employees who see

[20] The Solartron Electric Group Ltd. (A); a case copyrighted by l'Institut pour l'Etude des Méthodes de Direction de l'Entreprise, Lausanne, Switzerland, 1959. (Italics added.)

[21] John D. Glover and Paul R. Lawrence, *A Case Study of High-Level Administration in a Large Organization* (Boston: Division of Research, Harvard Business School, 1960), p. 68.

pitfalls and potential disasters looming. During the 1970s the U.S. economy witnessed blunder after blunder by companies and government agencies—the General Services Administration's linkups with favored contractors in Boston, the Ford Pinto gasoline tank disasters, the DC-10's faulty cargo hatch, and payoff scandals at Gulf Corporation and other companies, just to name a few. All might have been averted had the organizations been more responsive to warnings from the workplace.

Speaking on this point several decades ago, Zechariah Chafee, Jr., had this to say:

> A sailor related that he was once on board a vessel with a passenger who had made the same voyage. This passenger told the captain about a rock ahead which was hidden beneath the waves, but the captain would not listen to him. When the passenger kept on talking about that rock, the captain had him thrown into the sea. This energetic measure put an end to all remonstrances, and nothing could be more touching than the unanimity which reigned on board. Suddenly the vessel hit the reef and was wrecked. They had drowned the giver of the warning, but the rock remained.
>
> I was recently reminded of this story when an American general was threatened with demotion for saying in public that the Soviet air force was superior to ours. A spate of assertions that it was inferior immediately broke forth. Which side was right is beyond my ken, but I am sure of one thing. It is wrong for American generals to assume that what they say will lower the number of Soviet planes.[22]

Second, as discussed earlier, organizations should gain from more *esprit de corps* and *élan vital* in the work force. When employees have a recognized right to speak up on matters of conscience and equity, when they are entitled to fair hearings in cases of conflict, when they enjoy rights to privacy, when they participate in decisions and plans that affect their ways of working—then, if past experience repeats itself, the likelihood of high morale increases.

Third, corporations and government agencies will benefit from the excitement and "noise" generated by civil liberties. The very clamor and confusion that the totalitarian manager wishes to avoid is what many an emotionally healthy subordinate needs and enjoys. "Speech is civilization itself," said Thomas Mann. "The word—even the most contradictory word—preserves contact. It is silence which isolates."

I think of a case that used to be taught in courses on organizational

[22] Zechariah Chafee, Jr., "Freedom of Speech inside an Enterprise" (Address given at Radcliffe College, June 11, 1955).

behavior at many business schools: One work group in a large company has set all kinds of records for productivity and quality. But the supervisor of this group is unorthodox (or so he is perceived by many other managers). He insists on letting the operators set the atmosphere and "climate" of work. So they argue freely with him and with each other, and the work area often is noisy and messy, because that is the way they like it. This situation comes to the attention of senior management. An industrial engineer, an "efficiency expert," is assigned to review the procedures of the group. The industrial engineer is horrified. Too noisy! Too many people interacting! Too confusing to have operators debating changes in their methods! But the supervisor defends the way things are done. "Yes, I know it's noisy and confusing and that there's lots of chattering and debate among the operators," he says. "However, this is the way they work best. It doesn't interfere with my job of setting goals and managing output and costs. Besides, look at our performance—the best in the company!"

Fourth, corporations and public agencies will gain in public confidence. When an organization receives a low rating in a public opinion poll, its failure often is the result more of what people in the street do *not* know about it than of what they do know. Its management has disenchanted the public because of its secretiveness. Its decision-making processes are mysterious, the noise of its internal conflicts is muffled. All that is visible to the public is the outcome and the output.

During the famous demonstrations against the planned nuclear power plant at Seabrook, New Hampshire, late in the 1970s, I talked to several groups of demonstrators. One message that came through loud and clear again and again was their objection to the secrecy with which problems in the proposed plant seemed to be shrouded. They viewed it as an American version of the Kremlin style of policymaking. One demonstrator used an analogy of a wrestling match going on under a rug. From the movements and upheavals of the rug you could see that a lot was going on, but you couldn't tell what until the fight was over. The indignation of the demonstrators at Seabrook was fueled repeatedly by leaks from engineers and technicians on the staff who felt that they could not vent their worries to their superiors, and so talked instead in hushed tones with outsiders.

A ship, said Chafee in his Radcliffe address, is symbolic of any closely integrated organization, such as a factory, a church, the State Department, the Army. "All the members are, as we say, in the same boat. They lead a life of their own apart from the rest of the world, just as all those aboard a ship are cut off from the shore when the last gangplank is hauled in." Yet the crew and passengers must not behave as if they had no relationship with their society, as in the tragic case of the Dreyfus affair when the French Army ignored the elementary principles of French justice and acted as if it existed solely for itself.

Democracy has been called an ideology opposed to silence. It is the ideology of discourse, debate, and interchange. At least part of the disillusionment and cynicism about business that creeps into the outlook of many professional and technical employees comes, I believe, from the discrepancy between life in the corporation and life outside. By the time you've got your degree, society has invested quite a bit of time and money in you. You have been taught by many public-school teachers whose salaries are paid by taxes. You have used public buildings built and maintained out of public funds. You have used expensive equipment in colleges and institutes financed by years of private fund-raising and tuition fees or by state taxes. You have taken the time and the energy of many college instructors whose salaries come out of tuition fees, investment income, donations, or taxes.

Throughout this educational process you are taught to think independently, to question freely, to speak articulately. You are taught to value facts, evidence, and the scientific method. You are taught to evaluate an idea on the basis of its merit, not its sponsor. Presumably, society also values such qualities or it would not create and maintain all these facilities for your education.

And then you take a job in an industrial or public organization and, unless you are lucky, presto! All those values and attitudes may screech to a stop or even be reversed. Not your mind but your obedience may be cherished now. The freedoms and civil liberties that schools, religious institutions, and the community impressed on you are turned inside out and upside down. It is as if the organization were betraying the educators and donors who fed it with talent. The organization is too free to go its own way, society seems to complain from time, and in particular it is too free to go its own way in secrecy. It is as if the organization had a life of its own and didn't have to heed the rules everyone else must follow.

Now, the gains that have been decribed do not come without a price. Decision-making may take longer (as is supposed to be the case in Japanese companies). Supervisory training must be more sophisticated and expensive because administrators need to learn how to deal more openly with subordinates and encourage more participation, by no means an easy task. The outspoken conflict, dissonance, and cacophony in the organization are upsetting to some employees, especially those who have been brought up in rigid, autocratic settings and are uptight about "noise" and uncertainty. In addition to the dissidents, the harried administrator may have a batch of stiff-necks and worrywarts to deal with.

None of these price tags should be dismissed from consideration. From time to time, they will loom large in management thinking, just as they have in every organization that has accepted a shift in the balance of employer–employee rights. But what is purchased with these price tags is enormous. It is *viability*.

2

WHERE PREROGATIVES ARE STRONG AND RIGHTS ARE WEAK

In business an administrator used to have a fairly free hand to deal with employee talk-back, protests, argument, activism, lassitude, and incompetence. If the administrator felt sympathetic or uninclined to be hardnosed, he or she could put up with the resistance; otherwise, the troublemakers could be demoted, transferred, or discharged. The situation was much the same in state government agencies and other types of public organizations. Even in numerous colleges and universities the superior's hand was largely unfettered. In the federal government, it is true, civil service regulations restricted the manager's right to deal with nettlesome subordinates, but, as we shall see in Chapter 6, an ingenious and determined superior could get around most restrictions—at least, if the managerial climate was conducive.

Now that attitudes are changing and restrictions are increasing, administrators must be more discriminating. No longer is it enough for them to know what they *want* to do. Nor is it enough to sense clearly what they *can* do in the light of legal and other restrictions. Today superiors also need the wisdom to understand what they *should* do for the sake of economic and social values. Lacking such judiciousness, they may get their organizations into trouble even though their actions are legally in the clear. In short, the administrative task has become more sophisticated. "Professional" management has taken on a larger meaning.

Now, in some cases what a professional administrator should do is pretty much the same today as it was a century ago. These are the cases in which, now as then, prerogatives have to be strong because that is essential to effective management. If the prerogatives aren't strong, administrative power will be crippled, the organization will not move efficiently, and important work will not get done on time. In a certain range of decision situations, therefore, a professional, humanitarian, rights-conscious administrator can be as hard-nosed and arbitrary as anyone, depending on his or her temperament.

Where and when are a manager's prerogatives necessarily strong and a subordinate's rights weak? Let us consider five areas.

RESISTANCE DUE TO INCOMPETENCE AND UNCOOPERATIVENESS

It is the administrator's job to deal promptly with subordinates who cause trouble because they are incompetent, lazy, uncooperative, vindictive, or disloyal. This must be done for the sake of efficiency and economic survival; it is consistent with laws about management and industrial relations; and it accords with what our society expects of a boss. In fact, many liberal observers of organizations feel that managers are not tough enough in dealing with incompetence and uncooperativeness. Too easy, too uninclined to do what they think is right, too willing to turn the other cheek, such managers make other employees suffer, impede the organization, and cause society to suffer through the lowering of standards needed to reinforce family and community values. In short, dignity in the workplace is a function not just of respect for employee rights but also of the assertion of management prerogatives.

There is no single "right way" to deal with incompetent and uncooperative employees. Administrators must do it in their own manner and style, which can vary from quick and rough to gentle but firm. Of course, an agreement with a union may require "progressive discipline," as it is called, and company policy may require certain forms of counseling, but subject to formalities like these, the boss's judgment prevails, right or wrong. The rationale is simple: No other way works reasonably well in a competitive economy. Every effort that I know of to make life easy for employees who don't contribute, from permissive civil service rules to ill-fated experiments in "golden rule management," has proved disastrous.

For the sake of concreteness, here are a few examples of problems in this area:

"There are two types of employees," goes the saying,"those who resent authority and those who pay no attention to it." An employee whom I shall call Chris seemed to fall alternately in both groups. For every three times she followed instructions she didn't follow them once. Perhaps her supervisor could have been clearer, perhaps she could have motivated Chris in some clever way—I just don't know. But clearly the supervisor had to let Chris go soon, which was exactly what she did.

The assistant operator on a machine got very irritated because of a pile of cartons stored near his workplace. Again and again he roared his displeasure at his supervisor, but the supervisor either couldn't or chose not to correct the problem. One day, before finishing his shift, the operator took a broad-tipped marking pen and scrawled obscenities on scores of the cartons. The supervisor fired him, and the arbitrator (the plant was unionized) ruled in favor of the supervisor. The operator could have used a less upsetting way of venting his grievance.

A technician in a hospital operating room was often absent, shirked unpleasant duties, and in other ways interfered with effective operations and morale. Her bosses kept looking the other way, either because they hoped she would improve or because they lacked the gumption to level with her and give her an ultimatum. Had they penalized her, their decision would have stood, and it would have done the technician little good to file a grievance (the technicians were organized). The supervisors paid for their sins when the technician threatened one day in the lunchroom to denounce a management decision in the local newspaper. Unable to stand it any longer, the supervisors now fired her. After filing a grievance with the National Labor Relations Board, she was reinstated on the ground that writing an antimanagement letter in the press was a protected legal right. For some time she had a kind of immunity from discipline because supervisory action would have been seen as retaliation.

A customer representative for a power company submitted two fraudulent expense accounts for reimbursement. One was for meal expenses not incurred; the other, for meals that were not reimbursable under company rules. Although the employee had a good performance record, he was dismissed when the improprieties were proved. Because neither the corporate financial office nor public policy was served by overlooking such dishonesty, the boss had just cause for his actions. (When management's action was upheld in court, its case was bolstered by the fact that the employee had received a prior warning about excessive expense accounts.)

After suffering pain, an employee went to a company doctor and later had an operation by a surgeon recommended by the doctor. The operation was a failure; the pain persisted. The employee went to another doctor of his own choosing and had another operation, which afforded some relief from pain. The employee then sued the first surgeon for malpractice; he also sued the company because its agent, the doctor, had recommended the surgeon. The employee, who was a manager, was fired by the president as soon as news of the suit was publicized. Believing that the suit would upset other employees and cause bad publicity for an employer that was acting in good faith, the president acted within his rightful prerogatives. (When the employee sued the company for dismissal, the court held in favor of the company.)

DISAGREEMENTS OVER EVERYDAY DECISIONS AND PRACTICES

Administrators have no obligation to put up with the subordinate who interferes with or obstructs their management because he or she doesn't agree with what has been decided or simply doesn't like the superiors. No way has yet been found to run an organization efficiently if employees down the line try to substitute their thinking for their superiors' judgment. Even in the worker democracies in the plywood companies in the Pacific Northwest, a foreman or supervisor is normally entitled to cooperation and compliance, whether or not his or her subordinates think the decision is the best one. If the subordinates believe the supervisor is unfair or out of line, they can resort to other procedures without upsetting current operations. As the old saying goes "One tiger to a hill."

Some capable managers are able to put up with argumentative subordinates. It is within a manager's prerogative to do this if he or she can still manage the work effectively. But it is also within a manager's prerogative to penalize or get rid of the obstructionist any time the manager wants to. I am told by the liberal and employee-conscious head of a New York engraving firm that he once fired his best salesman because the man constantly complained and ranted. In cases of this sort the old rationalization is entirely appropriate: "If you don't like it here, you don't have to work here."

Here are some examples of the justifiable exercise of a boss's prerogatives to "call 'em as I see 'em":

The editor of a trade publication decided to run a controversial article on business ethics. An assistant editor assigned to work on the article first kept putting the work off, then resorted to outrageous deletions and unreasonable demands of the author for new material. The assistant editor was fired for just cause.

After a new dean took over in a midwestern college, he asked most of the administrators from the former regime to stay on. They did. One of these administrators, however, developed a strong dislike of the dean. The subordinate bad-mouthed his boss in lunch conversations with associates, at cocktail parties, and in sessions with students. When the dean heard about this, he asked the administrator to leave. This was his prerogative. The fact that the subordinate was capable was irrelevant. Also irrelevant was the possibility that the dean might have chosen instead to sit down in private with the subordinate and induce him to correct his ways. Others might have had the patience to do this, but that fact did not oblige the dean to do so.

A director of management information services disagreed violently with her superior's decision to buy new equipment from supplier X instead of supplier Y, which happened to be favored by the subordinate. Although she worked hard and effectively on the changeover to the new machines, she talked incessantly with other employees about what an egregious decision her superior had made. "He doesn't know what he's doing . . . he's stupid . . . the company shouldn't have a person like him in that spot . . . we'll pay for this stupidity later on, just you watch." Realizing that these harangues were bound to affect the cooperativeness of other employees, her superior transferred her out of his division. An able person, she did well in her next assignment and even had the satisfaction of hearing via the grapevine that she may have been right in her criticisms of supplier X. But that fact did not curb the prerogative of her indignant superior.

An able but hot-tempered accountant whom I shall call Pete became incensed about his company's air-pollution and safety policies. Although they met legal requirements and were defended by top management, Pete felt the company could and should do better. Nobody paid much attention to his comments—the company atmosphere was fairly open and permissive—until one day when he went to the city council to vent his criticisms. It so happened that a contract between the company and the city was up for renewal, and Pete's accusations jeopardized the contract. The president of the company had to send two top spokespersons to plead the company's case and save the sale. At the same time, Pete was fired. Although his superiors did not doubt his sincerity and concern for the public welfare, they could not forgive him for public disloyalty to the company.

OBJECTIONS TO ADMINISTRATIVE DISCRETION

Administrators also need fairly wide discretion to make special rules and arrangements to expedite work and supervision. So long as these rules are reasonable and honest (and not, for example, used to disguise illegal discrimination or abusive retaliation), subordinates have no grounds for complaint. Here are two examples:

A federal agency decided that employees must fill out time report forms called program activity records. The form would be used to help management learn how much time was being spent in various activities of the agency. That information, in turn, would be used to allocate administrative costs. When an employee called the forms demeaning, degrading, and insulting, and would not fill them out even after being given an explanation by the supervisor, the objector was fired. Suing the agency for reinstatement, the employee lost. In a 1981 decision, the U.S. Circuit Court of Appeals upheld management's right to require such reporting if it had a legitimate purpose. The decision is a sound one in administrative theory.

An employee diagnosed by a psychiatrist as having manic depression was involved in two unpleasant incidents or flare-ups with supervisors. Although prior to these incidents the employee had worked for the company for three years without special problems, her supervisors told her, in effect, "Every week after this we want you to verify, in a note to the personnel director, that you kept your appointment that week with your psychiatrist. If any week you fail to do this, you are automatically fired." Furious, protesting that the rule made her feel like "a time bomb ready to explode," the employee went to her union steward. The steward affirmed management's right to impose such a requirement. The employee then wrote to columnist Ann Landers early in 1982. After checking with Chicago attorney Lowell Sachnoff, Landers wrote the employee and also confirmed management's right to make the rule. Most management authorities would, I believe, agree. In fact, the employee probably should feel lucky to have such understanding supervisors.

COMPLAINTS ABOUT PAY, WORK, AND EQUITY

If managers are to manage effectively, they must make a whole host of decisions concerning the tasks and rewards of subordinates—work assignments, reporting systems, job titles, promotions, demotions, transfers, pay, bonuses, vacation policies, and so on. They must make these decisions as their own best judgments dictate; often they must decide quickly, under pressure, and with imperfect information; they must be willing to take chances and make mistakes.

When they make mistakes—or, rather, when subordinates *believe* they make mistakes—the subordinate should have some good recourse. Some capable systems for this purpose are described in later chapters and include employee assistance offices, employee councils, open-door procedures, and others. But superiors and subordinates must leave it up to *these* bodies to correct injustice and judge what is equitable rather than delude themselves into thinking they can always perceive equity themselves. Subordinates must not expect their superiors to be perfect, and, above all, bosses must not try to be perfect. As Benjamin Selekman used to remind executives at Harvard's Advanced Management Program, "Sin bravely." You were born a sinner, you were trained a sinner, and you will always be a sinner, Selekman told them, so do the best you can, do it courageously, and don't presume too much about yourself.

In short, it is a manager's prerogative to make the everyday work decisions as he or she thinks best and deal appropriately with employees who are made unhappy. Some managers are better than others at dealing with objectors to their judgment, thanks to understanding and training, but in any case they must enforce compliance in order to get the work out.

Here are a few brief examples of the proper exercise of managerial prerogatives:

A librarian at a large accounting firm felt she was overworked and underpaid. One day she sent a sharp memorandum about work and pay policies to the firm's partners. According to *White Collar Management*,[1] the memo resulted in a sharp reprimand from the personnel manager. The firm's policy, the personnel manager reminded the librarian, was to take complaints to the immediate superior and not go over the boss's head to the top. Ignoring this admonition, the librarian sent five more complaining memos to the main office. Angry, the head of the regional office fired her. Although she was competent, dependable on the job, and sincerely convinced that she was overworked and underpaid, she was insubordinate in violating the well-known rule of the firm. When she sued the company in a District of Columbia court, she lost.

An employee in a freight company in Iowa wrote a "To Whom It May Concern" letter to the executive vice-president arguing that another employee in the company had been treated unjustly. (The other employee had taken a maternity leave of absence, requested a part-time position when the leave was over, and been offered only a full-time position, which she could not accept.) Finding the letter full of erroneous statements, half-truths, and hostility, the executive vice-president fired the letter-writer. In his opinion, there was no way the company could have faith in such an alienated and hostile worker. When the employee sued

[1] *White Collar Management*, June 1, 1979, pp. 1–2.

the company, she lost.[2] The decision was sound. The vice-president's action was not malicious or abusive; it simply reflected the senior's judgment that such a hostile letter could not have been written by one who had made a sincere, intelligent effort to ascertain the facts and be helpful. (It was unfortunate, of course, that the freight company lacked its own fair hearing procedure, for if it had, the hostile employee probably wouldn't have risked going to the courts to vent her spleen.)

INDICATIONS OF WRONGDOING

When managers receive tips or evidence of dishonesty, fraud, or other types of wrongdoing, they are entitled and sometimes obligated to investigate and determine if the suspicions are justified. It does not matter if the suspicions turn out to be unjustified and if, in conducting a probe discreetly and in good faith, investigators ruffle a few employee feathers. For example:

Learning of a cash shortage and deciding, by process of elimination, that the culprits must be two employees in particular, a department manager called the employees to his office and accused them of the crime. They insisted on their innocence. The manager then called in the police to investigate. The two employees were exonerated. When they sued the company for slander, however, the Illinois Appellate Court ruled in favor of the company (421 N.E. 2nd 409, 1981). The judges noted that management used no strong-arm tactics, made the accusations only in the presence of management people and the police, and ordered the investigation with reasonable motives. Management had the right to be mistaken.

Naturally, administrators have no right to make an accusation or investigation maliciously or recklessly, or to broadcast their suspicions to people who do not need to know about the probe.

USING PREROGATIVES WISELY

The necessity for the prerogatives just described would never be disputed if managers exercised them with consistent prudence and goodwill. The logic of the case is so clear, and the need so obvious, that one may wonder why these principles are ever questioned. The reason, unfortunately, is a good one: Some managers use their prerogatives viciously, vindictively, and greedily.

[2] *Abrisz* v. *Pulley Freight Lines, Inc.*, 270 NW 2d 454 (1978).

Even so, employee alienation probably would not be such a problem if management established systems for due process so that injustices could be corrected promptly. But most organizations lack fair hearing procedures, or, if they do have them, fail to support them. As a result, aggrieved employees must go to court and suffer months and usually years of almost intolerable waiting and expense for a decision by outsiders who know little about the unique conditions and "climate" of the conflict.

Let me cite two instances in which, as a result of malicious action, managers may have contributed to an undiscriminating backlash against all prerogatives, including the just and necessary ones. In the first case, a veteran employee of Korvettes was discharged after thirteen years of service during which he received frequent promotions and salary increases. In the findings of fact by a New York court, he had been a model employee. The company did not dispute this. Why, then, did it fire the man? Because, it admitted, his rights in the corporate pension plan would vest if he were kept on the payroll much longer. In the litigation, the company's only defense was that it was legally entitled to fire a nonunion employee whenever it wanted to. An indignant New York court decided that, although this rule had been in operation for two centuries, the time had come to make an exception to it. The judges wrote,

> To allow an employer to avoid the vesting of rights in a pension plan after thirteen years of service by a model employee, under the guise of the employment-at-will doctrine, does not sit well with this Court. Such behavior not only suggests the employer never fully intended to comport with the spirit of the Plan, but also that it sought to avoid its obligations thereunder by systematically terminating its employees at will prior to the vesting of their rights under the Plan. Accepting plaintiff's allegations as true, as we must, defendant here has clearly violated New York's policy favoring the integrity of pension plans to protect the interests of the participants in such plans. If ever there were a case to invoke the doctrine of abusive discharge, this is it. Courts cannot hide in ivory towers ignoring the economic and social realities of modern society, for it is that very society we are here to serve. As that society changes, so must our thinking. We are convinced New York courts would recognize the abusive discharge doctrine on the facts of this case.[3]

How many employees, one wonders, were turned against management in general when the grapevine reported this case of executive action?

[3] *Savodnik* v. *Korvettes, Inc.,* 488 F. Supp. 822 (1980).

The second example involves two employees, Liz Hirsh and Patti Schiffer, in the health clinic of Boston University. They were fired in 1975 by clinic director Wilbur Hemperley for complaining (with other staff workers) about surveillance of employees, harassment of a female medic, and what they considered unreasonable time limits on patient care. After employing legal maneuvers, they got reinstated late in 1977. As part of their reinstatement, the trustees were forced to sign a statement that the administration would no longer "take adverse personnel actions" against them or interfere in their right to collective activity (such as participating in a staff meeting critical of work conditions).

Undismayed, management devised another approach. It ordered the construction of a cubicle for Hirsh and Schiffer to work in. The cubicle had walls separating them from the nurses and people in the lounge area. New rules were written forbidding the two "troublemakers" to leave the cubicle for any reason whatever, whether to go to the bathroom, escort a patient, or take a record to a doctor. Their work load was doubled or tripled by requiring them also to do their own filing and other chores not formerly required. In addition, they were kept under constant surveillance, and their work area was searched, they asserted, every evening after they left for home. They alleged that Hemperley told them they erred in not "following the chain of command," and that he once remarked, "In World War II you would have been shot for your insubordination." [4]

In 1978, only three months after the two dissidents had been reinstated, the administration retaliated. Overly impatient to get rid of the two, and prematurely losing confidence in its strategy, it fired them again. The two clinic workers sued the university and obtained an out-of-court settlement for $101,500.[5] This and other abusive acts of the administration, widely reported in the *Boston Globe, Esquire,* and other publications, created ill will not only for the Boston University regime but also, by association, for university management in general. One wonders how many indignant employees or students who learned of the episodes sometimes thought, in effect, "If management is like this here, it must be like this everywhere—to hell with management!"

The Case of the Cashiered Health Commissiner

We come now to the extraordinary story of James F. Rittenhouse.[6] In addi-

---

[4] Liz Hirsh, "What Really Happens at the Health Clinic," *Daily Free Press* (Boston University), February 24, 1978.

[5] *Daily Free Press,* January 24, 1979.

[6] The data for this account are taken from an interview and correspondence with Rittenhouse, his master's thesis, court records, and local newspaper stories.

tion to the unusual and, indeed, almost comic legal insights that the story gives us into the common-law rule, it raises some interesting issues concerning the prudent limits of management's prerogative to fire an employee who "rocks the boat."

Born and raised in western Pennsylvania, Rittenhouse was graduated in 1956 from Washington and Jefferson College, where he majored in biology. After college he served a couple of years in the U.S. Army, then worked in Pittsburgh, and next moved to Cleveland, where he lived for about fifteen years. In Cleveland he served as a public health representative for the Ohio Department of Health, specializing in organizing mass immunization programs (measles, rubella, polio, etc.), epidemiology investigations, and surveillance of communicable diseases. It was this work in public health that had led the Board of Health of Painesville, a town of about 20,000 people in northeastern Ohio, to hire him as their new health commissioner. It is in Painesville that our story begins.

A bearded, intensely individualistic person who took a great deal of pride in his work, Rittenhouse took up his duties at city hall on October 1, 1972. He inherited a staff of three employees: a nurse, a sanitarian, and a registrar of vital statistics. The Board of Health, to which he reported, legally was an independent group beholden to no one but the electorate; in actuality, however, its five members needed to work cooperatively with the city manager. Partly because of this, the city manager had come to exercise considerable power over affairs in the health department.

Rittenhouse was not protected by civil service rules and received no contract for a specified term of years; he was what the law calls an *employee at will*. In fact, for about six months he served conditionally without the permanent title of health commissioner. If he thought about the insecurity of his job, he did not worry much about it, for he was confident of his qualifications and ability. Also, he must have reasoned that he could not help but breathe fresh life into the department. For about a year, since the previous commissioner had been let go after an emotional breakdown, the department had been without a head, and morale was poor. There was an obvious need for rejuvenation, and he appeared to be the person for the job.

What no one took into consideration, apparently, was the inevitable clash between a proud and independent-minded health commissioner and a very assertive, hard-nosed city manager. The two men irritated one another repeatedly, and in time their relationship became malignant.

The city manager, who had been in power for about two years, was Kenneth McDonald. A bright, energetic, ambitious official in his mid-thirties, oval-faced with a receding hairline, McDonald had already become a controversial figure in city hall. In his master's thesis, which analyzes some of the problems to be described here, Rittenhouse wrote,

I was asked [by other employees] if I had noticed the figure "1" which rested on the city manager's desk. I had not yet noticed such a figure, having not been in his office more than once or twice to date, but on the next opportunity I made a point to observe it. It was a metal figure about three inches high in the shape of a cardinal number "1" mounted on a round pedestal. Several explanations were given to indicate its significance, both of which seem appropriate in retrospect. First, the manager apparently informed certain people that he had been first in his class, presumably in graduate school at Fels Institute, where he received a degree in urban management or something similar. The other interpretation was that he was "number one" at city hall and that he did not want anyone to have any doubts about this position of eminence. When at some point in time one of the department heads decided to openly exhibit a figure "2" on his own desk, a scene ensued that let the culprit know that he was out of line and not at all funny.[7]

For all of McDonald's undoubted abilities, he reportedly was held in less than high esteem by some officials. For instance, Rittenhouse reports that one day he was asked by McDonald to join him at a meeting with some township trustees, county commissioners, and others—all people who were not subordinate to the city manager, and therefore not obliged to please him. Shortly after the meeting began, reports Rittenhouse, McDonald made a remark that irritated one of the other officials. Leaning toward McDonald, the official cried, "Don't give us any more of your ———!" It looked as if fists might fly until another official jumped forward and calmed the belligerents.[8]

It seemed to Rittenhouse that subordinates, too, held a jaundiced view of McDonald. "To the very last person I can think of, right from department heads clear down to clerks and typists who had any dealings with the city manager," Rittenhouse tells me, "they all feared him, they all had nothing but intense dislike for him, and they would repeat that they feared him and disliked him not just occasionally but frequently." For example, says Rittenhouse, the grapevine reported that one day, without notice or warning, McDonald sent a city policeman to the home of the city engineer, at 10 P.M., to notify the startled employee that he was fired. Again, the grapevine reported that an inspector in the building department, in an effort to resolve a personnel problem, brought one of the workers to the city manager's

[7] James F. Rittenhouse, "A Case Study of Governmental Executive Behavioral Pathology and Its Effect upon Personnel and the Community" (Master's thesis, Kent State University, 1974), p. 22.
[8] Ibid., pp. 81–82.

office. After the problem was disposed of, McDonald reprimanded the inspector for bringing a "common worker" to his office.

If McDonald caused Painesvillians so much pain, how was it possible for him to stay in power for several years? Rittenhouse quotes from Wayne Milburn, the city's law director, as saying, "Everybody knows that Ken McDonald is a ———, but he got the city out of financial trouble and he gets things done." This feeling, Rittenhouse believed, was shared by a good many people.

All of this might have been only of incidental interest to Rittenhouse but for one fact: Apparently McDonald felt compelled to control various operations in the health department, and the Board of Health appeared willing to let him intervene even though this area was outside his legal jurisdiction. Time after time, Rittenhouse found himself being treated as if he were McDonald's subordinate, and the Board of Health made few efforts to shield its commissioner.

A revealing incident took place in April 1973. Rittenhouse sent a memorandum to the city manager with a proposal for solving a sewer problem the city was worrying about. McDonald responded the next day with a caustic note. "The comments you have made in your April 17th memorandum," replied the city manager, were "in your inimical style which combines bad taste with a lack of factual knowledge." McDonald sent copies of this reply to everyone who might have any interest in it, including the five members of the Board of Health. Smarting, Rittenhouse went to Charles Johnson, a thirty-year veteran of the Board of Health and a local mortician. What did Johnson think of the city manager's response? Rittenhouse hoped for at least a little sympathy. But Johnson answered funereally that the health commissioner somehow would have to work out his problem with the city manager. Johnson offered no suggestion concerning how the difficulties might be cured.

Was the real trouble Rittenhouse himself? Was he failing to do his job well? Two pieces of evidence bear on this question. First, the Board of Health decided to award him the permanent appointment of health commissioner in June. It did this after delaying a couple of months (his permanent appointment was scheduled to be confirmed in April), and after some behind-the-scenes efforts by McDonald, Rittenhouse thinks, to thwart the confirmation. So the five board members had plenty of time, and some incentive, to find serious faults in his performance, but they didn't. Second, when the Board of Health found itself head-to-head against Rittenhouse in a court case sometime later, it could not prove bad performance. "Any mistakes he [Rittenhouse] made were viewed as minor," concluded the judge, reviewing the evidence. The board did produce a memorandum describing alleged failures in the health commissioner's work but the judge tossed the memo aside as spurious.

So Rittenhouse, although working diligently and intelligently, was left exposed by his superiors to the city manager's blunt needle. For instance, soon after he reported to work at city hall, Rittenhouse was summoned to the city manager's office. Was he the same James F. Rittenhouse, he was asked in a dramatic tone, as the James F. Rittenhouse who had signed a certain letter to the editor in the local newspaper? He was indeed, answered the health commissioner, recognizing the clipping placed before him. It was his letter criticizing President Richard Nixon's public comments on terminating the Vietnam War, and also criticizing the editor for taking the presidential comments at face value. Well, said McDonald, the letter was a serious mistake; it was an egregious exhibition of engagement in partisan politics; besides, it had embarrassed McDonald in front of friends at a football game. He would have to ask the Board of Health to review the matter, McDonald said. So he asked the board and certain other city officials to do that, and a special meeting was called. The consensus, Rittenhouse reports, was that he was entitled to any opinions he chose, but he was not at liberty to express them in the public media. In vain Rittenhouse protested that his letter was not partisan, since in it he had also criticized former President Lyndon Johnson.

Again, about six months after he had been on the job, Rittenhouse was called into the city manager's office and told he had insulted one of the town's most important citizens. That person was Frank Stanton, owner of the local Ford agency. Rittenhouse had complained to the car dealer about the repair work done on the health department's automobile. A large hole had rusted in the trunk, allowing carbon monoxide fumes to seep into the car, and two repair efforts by the agency had failed to stop up the hole. In a letter to the Ford Motor Company in Detroit, Rittenhouse had complained of the service his department was getting. Ford headquarters wrote Stanton about the trouble, and Stanton in turn buttonholed McDonald and demanded an apology. So ulcerated was McDonald that he told Rittenhouse, when they met in the city manager's office, that this problem, too, would have to go to the Board of Health. Another special meeting was called. The board directed that a letter of apology should be written to the unhappy auto dealer. He was an influential citizen and friend of some of the board members, and his brother was a U.S. congressman. The letter of apology was written by McDonald and signed by Johnson, then head of the Board of Health.

In June, when Rittenhouse was awarded his permanent appointment, all direct communications between him and the city manager ceased. They communicated for a while through the Board of Health. In ensuing months, however, the situation eased somewhat and they began talking again.

An important break came in late fall: McDonald resigned and left

Painesville. The new job he took, as city manager of Oak Lawn, Illinois, paid about $5,000 more than he had been getting in Painesville. He made the decision in November and left officially on December 12.

This event promised a remission of the health department's pains, and in a way it did. In February, for instance, a number of officials and department heads (including Rittenhouse) got together to see if they could start developing feelings of "trust." Unfortunately for Rittenhouse, however, McDonald's successor as acting city manager was Robert Wooten, the finance director. Wooten had been quite compatible with McDonald, faithfully carrying out his directives and sharing many of his views. Soon it became clear that the Wooten–Rittenhouse relationship would be almost as difficult as the one with Wooten's predecessor. And every time Rittenhouse stood up to Wooten, as with McDonald, he also challenged indirectly the Board of Health, which was influenced by Wooten and delegated some of its tasks to him.

Within days after McDonald's departure from city hall, Rittenhouse made the decision that would change the rest of his life. As part of a thesis he was writing for a master's degree in public administration from Kent State University, he decided to draw up a questionnaire about McDonald and send it to about two dozen officials and acquaintances who had known him well.

In the covering letter, he explained his purpose and promised complete anonymity to the respondents. The questionnaire itself was divided into three parts. The first part asked for a general assessment of the former city manager along with "any specific incidents involving yourself and others." The second part asked for the respondent's opinions about McDonald's greatest achievement and greatest failure, and then asked the respondent to circle any of about a hundred adjectives and nouns that were felt to "be a reasonable description of the city manager." These words ranged from *modest* and *wisdom* to *unjust* and *liar,* with a preponderance of the former type, and with the kind and unkind words mixed together on the page so that no bias was obvious (except possibly a bias in favor of McDonald). The third part of the questionnaire contained a series of twenty-one statements about the former city manager, ranging from "The manager is a good leader" to "The manager is likely to blame others for his own mistakes," and the respondent was asked to indicate agreement or disagreement with each of them.

Rittenhouse conceived of the questionnaire as a means of furnishing objective data to supplement the more subjective opinions and impressions that made up the main text of the thesis. He realized that there was some risk in sending it out, and both his wife and a few friends worried about the possible repercussions. However, he thought that with McDonald gone, and the difficulties of his regime already being worked out, the Board of Health members and other city officials would not object strongly.

But he did not ask permission of the board to send out the questionnaire, nor did he alert any member to his plan. He regarded it as a scholarly project that was of no direct concern to anyone but his thesis adviser and himself. "I was not going to make this information public," he explains, "because I did not want to cause any more difficulties at city hall than had already occurred, especially since the city manager had left the prior month." He told the members of his staff what he was going to do, and of course he also called his thesis adviser at Kent State and obtained his approval of the idea.

He dated and mailed the questionnaires on New Year's Day, 1974. One of the respondents made a copy for the Board of Health to see and also phoned McDonald at his new abode in Oak Lawn. Within days McDonald retained an attorney in Painesville to go to Kent State and talk with Rittenhouse's thesis adviser. (Rittenhouse learned about that conversation in due course from the thesis adviser.) Presumably, McDonald also called one or more members of the Board of Health and made no bones about his displeasure.

Wooten, on learning of the questionnaire, drafted a memo addressed to department heads asking them not to answer the questions. (Rittenhouse was never able to obtain a copy of this memo but apparently it contained a veiled threat that the department head's job would be jeopardized by answering and returning the questions.) But the acting city manager never sent this memo out; when he showed it to the city coucil for approval, the council members, according to newspaper reports, told him not to send it.

The response to the questionnaire from respondents was useful to Rittenhouse but not what he had hoped for purposes of his thesis; only eleven of the two dozen people answered. As for the response from the Board of Health, that was disastrous. In retrospect, Rittenhouse thinks that the members may have believed that the thesis, pointing up their failure to intercede in and manage the difficulties between McDonald and Rittenhouse, would make them look bad.

At any rate, the board members made an assumption that put them on a collision course with the health commissioner. They assumed that he had no right to gather and present data that might embarrass them as officials. They assumed, in short, that his rights as a citizen to free speech stopped at the office entrance. In contrast, Rittenhouse proceeded on the assumption that a manager in state government did have a limited right to speak out. Although he recognized restrictions on the right (notice, for example, that he waited until after McDonald had left Painesville, ending the managerial relationship with the board and Rittenhouse), he assumed he did not have to obtain his superior's *agreement* with what he said if the speech fell within the restrictions.

A meeting of the Board of Health was held on February 13. While the health commissioner and his wife had been away the preceding evening, a member of the board, Dr. Albert Bringardner, an obstetrician and gynecologist in private practice, had called the Rittenhouse home but had not told the son Brian what he wanted to talk about. The message was communicated starkly on February 13. A few minutes before the board meeting was to begin, Bringardner asked Rittenhouse to step out into the hall with him. There the doctor said that the board was going to fire Rittenhouse at the meeting. The two men walked back into the meeting room and sat down, and presently the session began. Lester Nero, the city manager elect (who would succeed Wooten) was there along with the regular board members; so was Celia Kendall, a reporter from the *Telegraph*, Painesville's newspaper.

The board went routinely through the agenda. When the last scheduled item was finished, board member Harold Heckman, a retired employee of Ohio Bell Telephone who was then a real estate salesman, took the scalpel in hand. From under a pile of his papers he produced a copy of the questionnaire Rittenhouse had mailed. Various members remarked that in their opinion the document "was loaded" and the health commissioner "had no right to send out such a document." Rittenhouse argued that it was not loaded, that in fact there were more positive choices in it than negative ones. Furthermore, he argued, the first section was open-ended and asked the respondent to state his or her opinions in the person's own words. Bringardner ventured the opinion that the question of bias depended on who the respondent was. Rittenhouse insisted that wasn't right. Then Bringardner moved that Rittenhouse be dismissed. Donald Holland, a dentist in private practice, seconded the motion. The board voted unanimously in favor.

The board gave Rittenhouse a month—until March 15—to stay on the payroll and hunt for a new job. Soon after the meeting he hired an attorney from the American Civil Liberties Union, Albert L. Purola. With the attorney's advice, he asked the board to put in writing its reasons for firing him. It complied. The letter listed five reasons for firing the health commissioner, none of which had to do with the questionnaire. One reason concerned Rittenhouse's letter of complaint about the hole in the health department's car; others had to do with his alleged mishandlings of requisitions or requests; the last one concerned his poor communications with McDonald.

Rittenhouse and his attorney filed a lawsuit in the U.S. district court in Cleveland to prohibit the board from firing him. His right to send the questionnaire, Rittenhouse argued, was protected under the First Amendment to the Constitution. In retrospect, he wishes he had also brought criminal charges against the board. "The reason I did not," he says, "is that my wife implied she would divorce me if I did such a thing. She was afraid of the social implications of bringing criminal charges. Also, she did not want me to press the board too hard because Dr. Bringardner was on the staff of the Lake County hospital where she worked as lab supervisor, and conceivably he could get her fired from her job if we pressed too hard."

Judge Frank Battisti, who presided at the court where the suit was filed, ordered the Board of Health not to fire Rittenhouse until the case could be tried. So Rittenhouse stayed on the job after March 15.

In the meantime, the case was taking a bizarre turn. For reasons of its own, the Board changed its assumptions about Rittenhouse's rights as a manager. It apparently decided it would look bad if it challenged the health commissioner's right to say anything, however indirect or scholarly, with which it disagreed. One can only speculate on the reasons—talks with neighbors, perhaps, or conversations with other town employees. Whatever the reasons, the board concluded that it had to devise a new rationale for firing Rittenhouse. The questionnaire would not hold up as its motive, and an unexplained firing would be interpreted as a discharge motivated by the questionnaire. In short, the Board became fearful of challenging Rittenhouse's original premise that his right to send out the questionnaire was constitutionally protected. Because of this temporary loss of courage, the Board would lose the first round in its legal contest with the commissioner.

The hearing was on March 25. Three of the five board members were there to testify, and the testimony consumed much of the day. The board's reason for firing Rittenhouse, the members testified, was that he had not been able to maintain a healthy relationship with city manager McDonald. When he took the liberty of sending out the questionnaire, the board had felt it could stand no more. But its case seemed shaky. "Prior to February 13," testified Heckman, "we really had no—wouldn't have come up—his dismissal wouldn't have come up." The judge would not permit Rittenhouse to testify to the merits of his performance as health commissioner, nor would he allow his attorney Purola to cross-examine the board members about their allegations of poor performance. Battisti wanted the case cleansed of that issue. The only issue he wanted to see debated was the role of the questionnaire in the board's decision.

Nine days later, on April 3, Battisti handed down his decision. "Although the Court finds some previous friction existed between the ex-city manager and Rittenhouse, which in turn caused some concern within the Board of Health," he wrote, "that friction had been eased to the Board's satisfaction by January 1, 1974. In addition, although Mr. Rittenhouse may have failed to perform certain duties of the Commissioner without fault, any mistakes he had made were viewed as minor and did not form the basis for his dismissal on February 13, 1974. . . . the Court finds that the motivating factor or catalyst behind the Board's dismissal of Rittenhouse was the circulation of the questionnaire about the ex-city manager, McDonald." The questionnaire, he ruled, was an exercise of constitutionally protected free speech, and therefore was not a valid reason for dismissal. Rittenhouse must keep his job as health commissioner—at least, as long as the questionnaire was the real reason for firing him.

But the judge's suture was to be short-lived—as indeed it may have been intended to be, in view of the fact that the last statement of his opinion practically told the board how to do the operation over again legally. The very next day Wayne Milburn, Painesville's law director, told a reporter of the *Painesville Telegraph* that the judge's decision made it illegal only to fire Rittenhouse because of the questionnaire. The decision, said Milburn, "specifically did not preclude them from firing him—only firing him for the wrong reason. *I assume they will fire him again.*"

If they did, thought Rittenhouse and Purola, the act would surely be seen by Judge Battisti as contempt of court. Purola wrote Johnson a letter urging the board to forget the poisoned past and start fresh. This and other pacifying efforts did no good. "To see the salve doth make the wound ache more," says Lucrece in *Romeo and Juliet*. The Board had seen how it could legally amputate its health commissioner, and that vision made his continued presence more cancerous than ever.

On April 15, Johnson called a special board meeting at his home. The board members told Rittenhouse they wanted him to resign. Heckman complained about the letter Rittenhouse had sent to Ford Motor Company. Holland sighed "that things aren't like they used to be." Bringardner moaned that Rittenhouse had taken the board to court. Bringardner also accused the health commissioner of not getting along with the new city manager (he must have been referring to Rittenhouse's relationship with Wooten, since Rittenhouse was getting along fine with Lester Nero, now the new permanent city manager). And so on.

But the health commissioner refused to tender his resignation.

So on April 24, at another special board meeting, with members of the public and the press in attendance, the board again fired Rittenhouse. When asked the reason, the members refused to give one.

After Rittenhouse and Purola filed a contempt-of-court charge against the board, the same people found themselves facing each other in court again. But this time things went differently. After about an hour of testimony, Judge Battisti ruled that the Board of Health had not acted in contempt of court and that its firing of Rittenhouse was valid. He said, "The Board is not required to show the cause of the plaintiff's discharge. On the contrary, the plaintiff has the burden of showing that the Board discharged him for reasons which inhibit his First Amendment rights. This he has not done." He went on to explain that since no reason was given publicly by the Board, and since in court it had denied Rittenhouse's claim that the questionnaire was the reason (as proved in the first trial), the discharge was legal.

Rittenhouse wanted to keep suing the board, but he and his attorney disagreed on money matters and parted ways. Studying law in his free time, Rittenhouse decided to argue his case by himself. He made trips to Kent State University, fifty miles away, to do his legal research. Suing for libel and slander in a local court of common pleas, he lost on the ground that his claims had been ruled upon in the last trial (the so-called doctrine of res judicata). Next he appealed to the Ohio Appellate Court. This court ruled in his favor on technical grounds and gave him a chance to argue his side again in the local court. He did that, lost (victimized again by res judicata), and appealed again. As this is written, his legal actions against the city continue.

Some of his friends stealthily disappeared from his presence rather than risk "guilt by association." He and his wife were divorced, and he thinks the trauma of fighting for his job was the main reason. They are still on good terms, though, and talk regularly by telephone. He is happily remarried. Economically he did not fare so well. In vain he tried to get other jobs in public administration, even as far away as Florida and Alaska. His falling-out with the Painesville authorities seemed to doom his applications. Finally he got a job in a nearby machine shop as an inspector. Gone were his savings, his pension, and the cash value of his life insurance. In 1980, however, his fortunes improved as he took a position as assistant personnel director of the city of Cleveland.

━━━━━━━

The Rittenhouse story raises interesting questions for managers, subordinates, and legislators. For instance,

> What were the legal prerogatives of the Board of Health? Should Judge Battisti have decided, as the U.S. Supreme Court did in 1969 in the case of *Pickering* v. *School Board*, that an employee of a government agency may have a constitutionally protected right of free speech? (For a discussion of the *Pickering* case, see the opinion of the court in *Holodnak* v. *Avco*, reproduced in the Appendix.)
>
> How wisely did the Board of Health use its prerogative to fire Rittenhouse? Might it have approached the need, as it saw it, in a more productive manner?

Does such a use of management prerogatives encourage unionization of municipal employees?

As for the dissident employee himself, might he have used more effective tactics after he found out he was in trouble with the Board of Health?

When does permissiveness toward subordinate employees compromise the dignity and effectiveness of their superiors?

In a situation of this sort, should the organization, too, be seen as possessing rights? If so, how were the organization's rights affected by the actions of management and the dissident?

In what ways is a community affected by retaliatory and nonretaliatory actions against an employee objector?

Light on these questions—and in some cases answers—will be forthcoming in later sections of this book.

MANAGERS STILL CAN MANAGE

If you are a manager, you do not have to allow subordinates to question or dispute your judgments on everyday problems, such as what sort of new equipment to buy, how many people to assign to this task and how many to that, how much money to spend on advertising, what salary increases to award, what inventory control system to use, and so forth. Also, as the Rittenhouse case vividly demonstrates, you do not have to hear subordinates out on the quality or ability of top management.

If you *want* subordinates' opinions on such matters, fine. Most business school professors, management training instructors, and textbook writers will bless you. But you do not *have* to allow subordinates to speak up or put their contrary views in writing—unless, of course, that is required by your superiors, company policy, or agency regulations. The law gives you a fairly free hand. As we shall see later, sometimes the law says, in effect, "If you contract with an employee to treat him or her in such-and-such a way, we may hold you to the terms of that agreement," so you should check if any such agreements were made by management. In actuality, however, such contracts are infrequent. As we shall also see later, the law may say, in effect, "You can fire or penalize an employee who hassles you *except* in certain instances, such as when you are using an everyday business decision as a cover-up for firing a person protected by the employment laws or collective bargaining laws."

Moreover, with only occasional exceptions in the corporate world and some exceptions in state governments, you are free to fire employees who are uncooperative, incompetent, or antagonistic. Indeed, if you don't you may soon get in trouble with *your* superiors. In the federal government there used to be notorious exceptions to this rule, and there still are, but in 1978 the Carter Administration made a serious attempt to give managers a freer hand to deal promptly with incompetents and malcontents. Here again, though, your own organization may have policies that must be observed. For example, some companies give employees who have served faithfully for a certain number of years, such as five or ten, a kind of tenure. In such a case, your wish to dispatch the troublemaker may be subject to review by senior managers, the personnel department, or possibly the chief operating officer himself or herself.

In short, the familiar dictum that managers must manage still means that they can demote, transfer, penalize, and discharge in most cases where they are only trying to get the day-to-day job done in a suitable, ethical, and legal manner. As we shall see presently, those qualifications are very important. But quantitatively, if not qualitatively, the restrictions are not nearly as impressive as the powers.

While the right to talk may be the beginning of freedom, the necessity of listening is what makes the right important.

WALTER LIPPMANN

3

WHERE PREROGATIVES
AND RIGHTS ARE
IN UNEASY BALANCE

In a second area where employee dissidence occurs, managerial prerogatives are strong, but not as strong as in the area discussed in the preceding chapter. This second area involves challenges of the efficiency, legality, and desirability of operations authorized by management. During most of our national history, management had a rather free hand to throw off these challenges. It could transfer the employee challenger to another part of the company, humiliate him or her, or demote or discharge the trouble maker. This power is being pruned. What is happening is very significant because the employee challenge in this area is very potent.

Of course, management's prerogative to run the organization efficiently or wastefully, legally or illegally, is not limited by employee action alone. It is limited by several other countervailing powers. For example, the board of directors can shine a red light and either force executives to change directions or throw them out in favor of a new team. As a practical matter, however, relatively few boards exercise such a discipline over management. Some management authorities hope that boards can be induced to become more proactive, and there are many signs that some change already has taken place, but this road is going to be a very difficult one.

Another check on management's prerogative is government. For government officials, there are agencies like the General Accounting Office, as well as legislators; for corporate executives, agencies like the Department of Justice and the Securities and Exchange Commission. But watchdog agencies and legislators work under severe constraints, including time and lack of inside knowledge, so they succeed in challenging a management team only now and then.

Still another possible check is the stockholder. However, stockholder suits have proved to be an inept source of discipline; only on rare occasions do stockholder activists score. Theorists see competition as a restraining influence on corporate waste and inefficiency, and indeed it may be. Unfortunately, however, competition is only as effective as a company's competitors, who may be ineffective; also, its effects may be long delayed.

In short, the power of employees to speak out against wasteful or illegal practices probably is the most important check we know of on management. In an age in which employees are willing and able to protest faulty operations, management's prerogative to fire at will or penalize an insider comes close to being the same thing as its prerogative to direct operations wastefully or illegally. The approximation may be closer in business than in government agencies, because business is less exposed to the policing effect of watchdog legislative committees and media reporters. But even in state and federal agencies, our cases suggest, the approximation is fairly close. The Rittenhouse story in the previous chapter is one such case; the Painesville board had a fairly free hand to authorize egregious management, if it chose, as long as it could dispatch an employee complainer. Other such cases will be presented later in this book.

If the most important check on waste and illegality is employee action, and if, as seems to be happening, management loses some of its prerogative to put down employees who complain of waste and inefficiency, then organizations stand to gain in terms of economic efficiency. How much they gain depends on the tradeoff between decision-making speed and the quality of employee challenges. That tradeoff, in turn, depends on the quality of mechanisms for handling challenges promptly and fairly. If the mechanisms are poor, the resulting noise and commotion of protest will impede swift, bold decision-making, and valid challenges may be swallowed up in the noisiness. But if the mechanisms are good, the organization can respond promptly to challenges proved valid, and groundless or inaccurate challenges, when heard, will burst like soap bubbles. This effect can be observed readily in organizations with efficient hearing procedures. One example was given at the beginning of this volume—the employee who, complaining of a senior's impropriety, was able to get a prompt hearing, avoid dismissal, and see the offenders penalized instead of finding himself on the street.

Now, there are several good reasons for keeping management's prerogatives in this area fairly strong:

1. Managers see actions and policies in terms of the "big picture"—the larger context of long-range plans and aspirations. What may seem wasteful or ineffectual to the employee who is aware only of the immediate situation may be seen by management as a necessary cost of getting from one stage of operations to another. The temporary inefficiency may be known to be a small cost for a larger accomplishment. For instance, when a publishing company switches from hot type to cold type, in the short run there may be confusion, duplication, and error; to the would-be whistle-blower, the scene is ripe for protest. But to the planners, the immediate costs may be realized as a small price to pay for the long-term gains.

2. Management has—or should have—the best and most detailed knowledge of an operation. In the example just given, managers alone might have a well-documented picture of cost savings in printing and distribution in places far from the scene of the whistleblower.

3. In addition to being poorly informed, employee challengers may be driven by malice, publicity, or other undesirable motives. In such cases, the longer they create commotion, the more damaging the effect on the morale of other employees.

However, there are also several good reasons for restricting managerial prerogatives, for providing checks and balances in the form of legitimized employee protest:

1. Sometimes the managers themselves are motivated by greed, malice, or other undesirable emotions.

2. Even managers with the finest intentions may fall into errant ways, or be blinded to the errant ways of colleagues or favored subordinates.

3. In large organizations, it may be close to impossible for a senior executive to appreciate what is going on everywhere in the operations managed. The effects of decisions may be subtle; subordinates may be skilled in covering up malignant operations. As one senior executive once put it, "The only way I can avoid mistakes is by having subordinates warn me." The best source of early warning, of course, is the person working at the scene.

With these prefatory observations in mind, let us turn to specific types of employee talk-back that superiors cannot deal with as arbitrarily as in years past.

CHALLENGES OF PERCEIVED ILLEGALITY AND WASTE

Statistically, most complaints and allegations of management inefficiency or illegality must be off the mark. They reflect frustration and envy more often than accurate, disinterested perception. Nevertheless, since an important minority of these complaints do come from subordinates with firsthand knowledge, the trend is in favor of giving the complainant some standing at the expense of the superior's traditional prerogative. This trend is the result of the efforts of several groups of people.

The *American public*, as indicated earlier, is sympathetic to the right of a critic to sound off if the criticism is substantial. Whether this sympathy springs from compassion for the underdog, chronic suspiciousness of top management, a belief in the principle of civil liberties, or some combination of these motives, no one knows for sure. In any case, the majority of Americans believe that a true whistleblower deserves some kind of a break—at least, until proved wrong. A case in point is James Morrissey, the white-haired retired seaman who for many years has been blowing the whistle on leaders of his union, the National Maritime Union. When Morrissey has charged union leaders such as Joseph Curran and Shannon Wall with raiding the union till for personal benefit, battled them in court, and spoken out against them in the press, in many quarters he has been hailed as a hero. Clyde Summers, a University of Pennsylvania law professor and specialist in labor law, probably echoes the majority sentiment when he asserts that rebels like Morrissey help to keep the union bureaucracy from going completely sour.[1] Morrissey has succeeded in getting more national attention than most dissidents, of course, but the same generous reservoir of public sympathy that he has drawn from has nourished thousands of other rank-and-file rebels.

Employees generally give a dissident the benefit of a doubt if his or her criticisms are not self-serving. Although the dissident may be given a wide berth by employees who fear that bosses will find them guilty by association, and in some cases may even be threatened physically by fellow workers (as in Morrissey's case, for example), he or she usually has the sympathy of other workers. Dissidents fortunate enough to have unique status or prestige may have almost instant credibility. For instance, Robert M. Stronach, who in the 1970s blew the whistle repeatedly on his employer of thirty-four years, Narragansett Electric Company, was a vice-president in the organization and, because of his status, was believed by almost everyone.

Many *courts* are tending to be sympathetic to employee critics of management waste and impropriety, as the *Tameny, McNulty,* and *O'Sullivan* cases already mentioned illustrate. To elaborate on the last, Frances E. O'Sullivan was a hospital nurse who, when asked to perform catheterizations, refused on the ground that she was not properly trained to do so. When she was dismissed, she took the doctors and the hospital to court for

---

[1] *Wall Street Journal,* July 13, 1981, p. 1.

breach of contract. In court, the defendants pleaded that she had no right to sue because she was an employee at will, but the Superior Court of New Jersey broke from tradition and held that she had indeed stated a valid cause of action. Since both the public interest and the law (i.e., the Medical Practice Act of New Jersey, forbidding catheterizations by unlicensed nurses and physicians) were involved, the judges thought that an exception to the traditional common-law rule should be made.[2]

It must be emphasized again, however, that such holes in the common-law dike are still small, management's prerogative remains strong, and the inside critic of illegality or inefficiency has a heavy burden of proof. A case in point is *Martin v. Platt*.[3] In 1974 two employees of Magnavox reported to the president that a vice-president was soliciting and receiving kickbacks from suppliers. The two whistleblowers were sacked. Whether their allegations were sound was a question the Indiana Court of Appeals did not bother with, for it felt that the boss's prerogative to fire for any reason or no reason should not be disputed. Though that case probably would have gone the other way in a number of other states, and might even go the other way in Indiana today, it is a reminder that the old rule still has some standing.

In addition, *labor arbitrators* customarily protect union members who speak out against perceived illegality and inefficiency. This protection is far from being automatic, however. For example, an arbitrator is not likely to rescue an employee who vindictively bad-mouths management in public, speaks so vehemently in the shop that worker morale is threatened, or in other ways appears to abuse the freedom.

Finally, *chief executives* are becoming more sympathetic to the employee critic of waste and wrongdoing. They believe that such an attitude may serve the cause of employee morale as well as help to keep superiors on their toes. Impressive statements of this philosophy have appeared in magazines like the *Harvard Business Review, Dun's,* and *Personnel Administration.* One may wonder why it has taken so long for chief executives to take this stance. The answer probably is that they used to believe that top-down pressure on managers and supervisors was enough to assure honesty and efficiency. Once upon a time it may have been.

In *King John* Shakespeare has his hero observe, "How oft the sight of means to do ill deeds makes ill deeds done." Most smart executives can see ways to cut corners here and there, or make an end run around this law or that regulation, and the temptation indeed may be irresistible. What will block it? As we shall see in the following two accounts, one involving a bank and the other a state agency, the only thing that stands between the perpetrator and success may be an observant subordinate.

[2] *O'Sullivan v. Mallon et al.,* 390 A 2d 149 (1978).
[3] *Martin v. Platt,* 386 NE 2d 1026 (1979).

The Case of the Beleaguered Banker

Banking was not John C. Harless's first choice of a career, partly because he may have believed he lacked sufficient education for advancement.[4] After graduation from high school in Rivesville, West Virginia, he attended Fairmont State College for one semester, then went to Cleveland for a year and worked as an apprentice machinist. Giving up on that career idea, he returned to Rivesville and, after holding various construction and sales jobs, went to Fairmont and took a position in a small loan company that was willing to educate him in retail credit financing. He learned on the job, he went to seminars, and he took courses offered by the National Retail Credit Association. After five years, he was promoted into management.

Shortly after this promotion, he made two fateful contacts: a vice-president of the bank across the street, the First National Bank in Fairmont, and a director of that bank, a man who also happened to be a county judge. These two contacts led to a job offer in the bank, which he accepted.

Happily, Harless began learning all he could about a new world of deposits, loans, interest rates, service charges, federal and state regulations, and organization. He wanted to learn everything he could, and First National helped him. It sponsored his attendance at seminars of the American Institute of Banking. It paid his expenses to attend a course on computer operations conducted by IBM in Pittsburgh. He was promoted to office manager of the consumer credit department. And then, as he continued to learn and benefit and win the respect of the bank's staff, it sent him to a three-year resident program in banking at the University of Virginia in Charlottesville. The bank officer who recommended him for the university program was vice-president Aubrey B. Wilson..

It was Harless's habit to observe and question. For some time he had suspected that the bank was overcharging certain customers, and that his mentor Wilson was involved. However, he himself was not directly involved, and for obvious reasons he didn't want to go out of his way to force the issue. Unhappily, in June 1975 Wilson put an end to his innocence. It appeared to him that Wilson had succumbed to "the sight of means to do ill deeds." According to testimony in court later on, the vice-president was authorizing the illegal withholding of part of the rebate due customers who had prepaid an installment loan, calling the sum a service charge. It was illegal, Wilson admitted, but he wanted Harless to do it anyway. Harless says that Wilson told him, "Add $50 or $100 to the charge, whatever you think you can get away with."

Harless protested. He talked to other employees of the bank. He returned to Wilson with a reply that forced the senior officer's hand. "I'll do it

---

[4] The data for this account, which is mentioned also in Chapter 1, are drawn from court records, local newspaper articles, and an interview with John Harless.

only if you give me written authorization," Harless said. He knew, as Wilson knew, that a written order was out of the question. Late that June, Wilson fired the manager whom he himself had recommended and in whom First National had spent so much training money and effort. Harless's halcyon days at the bank were over.

However, a week later, Harless received a letter from Wilson telling him to return to work on July 3. What accounted for Wilson's change of heart? Harless thinks the letter was sent under pressure from members of the board. Harless also believes that a board member had reminded Wilson that one officer of the bank could not unilaterally fire another officer—that only the board itself could fire an officer.

But none of this made Wilson happy about the reinstatement. The dismissal, he told Harless, would be treated as a one-week suspension without pay. He also told Harless that he had the backing of the board in the overcharging practice. If you complain again, Wilson told him, you'll be fired for good.

Back in harness, Harless was once again the workhorse that the bank wanted, but not the servile subordinate that Wilson wanted. The illegal overcharging was continuing, and Harless went in September to J. Harper Meredith, the county judge with whom he had become acquainted while at the small loan company. In the judge's chambers he reported that Wilson was trying to force him to overcharge customers. (In court later, Meredith denied this conversation.) Harless says that Meredith promised to look into the matter and, if the illegal practice existed, to stop it. But shortly thereafter, says Harless, the judge called him to report that an auditor could find only trifling overcharges. Harless says he argued that this was not the case. He had verified accounts showing larger overcharges, he told the judge.

Shortly after this, according to the court record, telltale documents began to disappear. Harless believes that Wilson instructed certain employees to get rid of records showing illegal overcharges and withholding of proper rebates. In court later on, Wilson denied giving such an instruction. Someone gave it, however, and Harless was able to rescue some of the incriminating records from trash cans.

Apparently this purging of the files continued for several months, which suggests that there were quite a few incriminating documents to be gotten rid of. In court four years later, Beverly Daniels, an employee who got fired presumably for knowing too much, testified that files were thrown away at Wilson's direction as late as December. After the purging, the files were put downstairs in the bank building where, like Bluebeard's corpses, they would remain silent forever.

Of more immediate concern to Harless than the files was his demotion. In October, soon after his talk with Judge Meredith, he was told that he would no longer serve as office manager but would work as a clerk in the

Federal Housing Administration department of the bank. In his harassment of Harless, Wilson was indefatigable, Harless recalls:

> I was transferred to the FHA department to do clerical duties such as type FHA reports, type loan agreements, and do various other types of clerical duties and reports. Every chance Mr. Wilson got when we were alone, he kept reminding me how he had the power to ruin my career and see that I was never able to obtain a job in any other bank or to advance in First National Bank. Mr. Wilson would call employee meetings. Everyone was to attend but me. He would advise the employees not to talk or associate with me during or after working hours. As though to keep ridiculing me, Mr. Wilson would continuously pass around memos to all the employees to remind them that if he should have to leave the office for any reason, I was not in charge. He advised them not to go to me with their problems or to obtain any approvals from me on their work. In February of 1976, Mr. Wilson saw one of the young women who worked at the office with my wife and me at one of the local shopping malls, and the following day he dismissed her.

The hazing of Harless continued into the winter, spring, and summer of 1976. Early in the summer, however, he took another action that would bolster his cause; he retained a local attorney to help him. The attorney, Ross Maruka, went to Judge Meredith with a list of about a dozen accounts of egregious overcharging. But the months dragged on, and in October Harless still had received no response from the board or any relief from Wilson's harassment.

Now he decided to get in touch with a local federal bank examiner. At their meeting he disclosed numbers, dates, and then hard facts about the overcharging. Soon the examiner, reporting the evidence to the comptroller's office, was sent to First National to verify the allegations. After investigating, he told Harless that his allegations were essentially correct and that the overcharging was serious. Auditors from the Pittsburgh office of Ernst & Ernst came in and made a long list of overcharged accounts. The bank made some 441 refunds, Harless says, but not all of the customers on the list got their due.

On November 1, both Harless and Wilson were summoned to the boardroom by a committee of officers who had been appointed to investigate the illegal practices. At this session one of the directors said that the committee realized that overcharging had indeed been going on and would be stopped.

Wilson now admitted the overcharges, but protested that he didn't know they were illegal. Judge Meredith answered that ignorance of the law was no excuse, and instructed Wilson not to come to board meetings (a privilege Wilson had enjoyed in the past) and not to try to fire Harless. Harless was reinstated as manager of the consumer credit department, and the judge told him to inform the executive vice-president right away if Wilson caused him any more grief.

For a few minutes, Harless was happy with everything. But when he returned to his office, Wilson threatened to get even with him. Back in his old job, Harless found the people in his department helpful and friendly. Only Wilson seemed to want to hassle him.

Around the middle of November, two federal bank examiners appeared. They had been assigned to investigate the illegal practices. In a couple of weeks, two officers of the bank, executive vice-president Patrick L. Schulte and auditor Charles E. Hawkins, began a series of interviews with various employees to dig up as much evidence as possible. When they came to Harless, they emphasized that the interview was confidential—their main purpose was to find out about refunds still due. Harless disclosed all he knew. He had retrieved some of the records thrown into the wastebaskets and garbage cans, he said. They asked if he could produce them. Yes, he guessed he could. He gave the incriminating records to Hawkins.

On December 30, Harless was called to Schulte's office and told he was fired. Harless asked why. The board had decided that no reason should be given, the executive vice-president answered. Even after Harless's attorney contacted the board and the bank's attorney, no reason was ever given orally. However, a couple of years later Harless's lawyer, then David L. Solomon, told reporter Peggy Edwards, who faithfully reported the many twists and turns of Harless's story in the *Fairmont Times–West Virginian,* that the minutes of the board meeting noted the dismissal decision was based on "personal possession of bank records and supplying false and misleading information to regulatory agencies."

What must have happened is that the directors who wanted to oust Harless were briefed by legal counsel and told that it was quite unnecessary to offer a reason for firing him. Indeed, the law made it undesirable to do so in a case like this, counsel might have explained. Perhaps counsel quoted the often cited rule of the U.S. Supreme Court's decision in 1884 in *Payne* v. *Western & A.R.R. Railroad*—employers "may dismiss their employees at will . . . for good cause, for no cause, or even for cause morally wrong, without thereby being guilty of legal wrong." One can imagine a scene something like this:

DIRECTOR: What we really want to fire him for is causing a hell of a lot of trouble, to say nothing of the money he's cost us.

COUNSEL: I realize that.

DIRECTOR: To be blunt, he's a pain in the neck.

COUNSEL: You don't have to explain.

DIRECTOR   (with dollar-thin smile): You mean to tell me we don't have to give a reason?

COUNSEL: That's essentially correct.

DIRECTOR   (with unbelieving smile): Not to Johnny himself?

COUNSEL: That's right.

DIRECTOR   (more smile): Not to the bank staff or the press?

COUNSEL: That's right, sir.

DIRECTOR   (beaming): Not even to the bank examiners?

COUNSEL: To no one, no reason at all.

So Harless was on the streets looking for work. When he applied for unemployment pay, the reason he gave for getting sacked was that he had refused to engage in illegal overcharging and had reported the wayward practice to the feds. This statement was sent to First National, and in due course it was returned without being disputed. So he was at least able to start drawing jobless pay without having to hassle for it.

"After contacting nearly every bank in a three-county area, and being treated very rudely by them," Harless says, "I gave up and went to work for Consolidated Coal as a laborer in a deep coal mine. In April of 1977, several of the banks I had applied to advised me that Mr. Wilson had contacted them before I had ever applied for a job, and advised them that I was a troublemaker."

In court two years later, an officer of a bank in Morgantown testified that he had been called by Wilson and told that Harless was nothing but a troublemaker. However, Wilson has denied such a conversation.

The hazards in Harless's way multiplied. In *The Merchant of Venice,* Shakespeare writes: "You take my house, when you do take the prop / That doth sustain my house; you take my life, / When you do take the means whereby I live." Although Harless was able to hold on to both his house and his life, the months that followed his discharge took a heavy toll. "He could not sleep, eat, he wouldn't associate with his family," his lawyer was to report later on. "For nine months he was broken in spirit and body."

But he got help from family and friends. Some help also came from his old friends at the bank, who kept him informed about goings-on there. Fear of losing their jobs kept them from seeing him publicly, however—perhaps they remembered the swift dispatching of the young employee seen with the Harlesses at a shopping mall some time earlier. Also, they would not sign depositions for him confirming the practice of overcharging.

Although hampered in his efforts to find a satisfactory job and vindication, Harless was not handcuffed. He possessed an important advantage, and he made the most of it: his case was based not on his opinion against the bank's, or his judgment against Wilson's, but on hard, factual, often quantitative evidence. The fact that he could recite numbers, names, dates, and places could not fail to impress interviewers. His break came at a bank in Morgantown. It was Central National Bank, a newly chartered bank scheduled to open its doors in the fall of 1977. Since it did not have a track record, as Harless puts it, it had a hard time luring qualified people from secure jobs in banks with standing. Nor could it pay generous salaries. Of course, none of these disadvantages bothered Harless.

Back when he had been with the small loan firm, he had gotten to know one of Central National's directors. That helped his cause. Another director of Central National happened to have been a victim of First National's illegal overcharging. He met several times with the directors and explained in detail what had happened at First National. He assured them that he had not blown the whistle without first discussing the problem with the First National board and trying to solve it quietly inside the bank.

Central National hired Harless in September as second man in charge, with the title of cashier. Like a tenacious ghost, however, Wilson continued even then to haunt him. Various directors of Central National, says Harless, told him that Wilson had called them to say what a troublemaker he was and to predict he wouldn't be able to handle the job. But these last-ditch efforts at revenge failed, and on July 1, 1978, Harless was promoted to chief executive officer.

In the meantime, however, Harless was head to head with First National on a different front. In the spring of 1977, about four months after being fired, Harless sued the bank, Schulte, and Wilson for $1,250,000. As presented by his attorneys David Solomon, a former prosecutor for Monongalia County, and Morgantown lawyer S. J. Angotti, his case alleged that he had been maliciously fired and blackballed for objecting to illegal overcharging practices; he sought $750,000 in compensatory damages and $500,000 in punitive damages. The action came before Marion County circuit court judge Fred L. Fox II. Judge Fox ruled against Harless, on the basis that an employee at will has no cause of action against an employer for arbitrary dismissal. However, Fox sent the case to the West Virginia Supreme Court of Appeals for review, and the high court agreed to hear it.

In July 1978, Justice Thomas Miller, speaking for the Supreme Court, ruled that Harless was entitled to recover damages in a trial. Although acknowledging the long-standing rule, Miller pointed out that public policy was firmly on Harless's side. In a case like Harless's, he said, the old rule needed to be reformed. "Where the employer's motivation for discharge contravenes some substantial public policy principle," he ruled, "then the employer may be liable to the employee for damages occasioned by the discharge." [5]

So in September 1979, the case was tried before Judge Fox (who, incidentally, shared the Sixteenth Judicial Circuit with Chief Judge J. Harper Meredith, the director of First National) and a jury. Bitterly fought, the trial brought Harless face to face with those who had hamstrung him at First National, including Wilson and Schulte (the latter was relieved of being a defendant, however). Wilson testified that Harless's allegations were spurious. It was Harless who was in the wrong, Wilson claimed—for trying to protect a guilty employee. When he tried to correct the troublemaker, Wilson claimed that he was berated and told to get off the plaintiff's back. He "would sit at his desk. He wouldn't do anything unless he was told to. He stared off into space. He had a chip on his shoulder." Thus testified the vice-president. As for the allegations that Wilson had ordered illegal overcharging, the vice-president called them ridiculous, and he further denied ordering the destruction of incriminating records.

Harless, on the other hand, kept hammering away with fact after fact and number after number, many of them confirmed by the actions of the accounting firm, the bank examiners, and witnesses.

On September 20, 1979, after four hours of deliberation, the jury returned a verdict for Harless and awarded him $125,000 in compensatory and punitive damages. Significantly, Wilson was tagged with a larger share of this amount than the bank was. The jury ordered Wilson to pay $10,000 for the act of firing Harless, $40,000 for "outrageous conduct causing emotional distress," and $25,000 for the blackballing.

_____

What is the lesson of the Harless case for managers? It does not say that you are no longer free to manage as your predecessors could years ago. It does not say that you are no longer free to dispatch a troublemaker. It only says that you cannot manage with abandon. You had better look out if the real troublemaker, from a legal standpoint, is yourself or your colleagues. The courts and the public want you to manage efficiently and make a profit. However, in an ever larger number of states (though by no means every one) judges and legislators do not want you to manage at the expense of the law, and if you try to make an end run by getting rid of conscientious

[5] *Harless v. First National Bank in Fairmont,* 246 SE Reporter 2d 270, 275 (1978).

objectors or muzzling them by intimidation, the judges will not take your side.

"We Invited You into Our House, and You Took an Axe to the Furniture"

With no axe to grind, though with youthful idealism, Michael Nelson entered Barbara Sugarman's house on July 21, 1975.[6] Of course, it was not a house in the literal sense; it was the Office of Volunteer Services of Georgia's Department of Human Resources. Sugarman was the official head of the household, created a few years earlier by the governor of Georgia at the time, Jimmy Carter. In converting a number of old departments into "divisions," Carter had had to build a new bureaucratic level. On this level were erected units like the Office of Volunteer Services.

Nelson entered with enthusiasm. He was going to help the government clean up poverty and misery. A graduate of the college of William and Mary who had gone on to earn a master's degree in political science at Johns Hopkins, he had been influenced by what he calls the "moralistic tone" of the campuses in the late 1960s and early 1970s. "I wasn't involved in the student Left," he says, "but everyone in college then learned to regard politics in terms of good guys and bad guys." Though his salary was as low as his ideals were high, this didn't bother him. With no family responsibilities, he could live on $2,500 a year—and besides, it was just for a year that he was visiting.

Working out of an air-conditioned office in suburban Augusta, Nelson encountered some people who reinforced his idealism. For example, he worked with two dedicated state officials, one a volunteer coordinator for regional institutions for the retarded, the other the head of the local regional mental health center. In addition, in Barbara Sugarman, the boss, he saw an executive who was extraordinarily persuasive and winning when dealing with other state officials, though he perceived that her household staff was less than enthusiastic about her.

Sugarman would describe how she had gotten to know Rosalynn Carter, taken her around to different mental hospitals, and gotten her seriously interested in mental health, a cause she would support when the Jimmy Carters moved to the White House. Sugarman was the first head of the Office of Volunteer Services, and later on she would be promoted to a government position in Washington.

Nevertheless, Nelson soon became disillusioned. "It did not take long for

---

[6] The data for this account are drawn from Michael Nelson's article, "Whistle-Blowing in Carter Country," *Johns Hopkins Magazine,* November 1976, and an interview.

me to realize that what I was doing had about as much to do with fighting poverty as that chair you are sitting in," he says. He wrote in his alumni magazine, "I was the quintessential paper-shuffling, pencil-pushing bureaucrat. I worked in an office with other paper-shuffling, pencil-pushing bureaucrats. All except the boss. He did not have anything useful to do either, but he had so many friends in the state capital that he did not have to pretend to." It was like a house where everyone is so busy reading and passing notes back and forth that nobody gets dinner on or tends the leak in the roof.

Of course, he didn't work inside all the time. Carrying the imposing title of Area Volunteer Resources Coordinator, his assignment was to drive around a seven-county area, visit local welfare offices, encourage them to use volunteers, and send weekly reports to Atlanta. But he didn't find these visits very useful, either.

"On a typical day I would drive out to, say, Lincolnton, a Plains-style metropolis, to 'confer' with John Ludwig, the head of the local welfare office. 'John,' I would say, 'why don't you use some volunteers here?'

" 'Because I don't need 'em, Mike,' he would tell me. 'I got too much paid help already.'

"Then on to antebellum Washington [Georgia]. 'Mrs. Beckum,' I would ask, 'how about using some volunteers here in your office?'

" 'Why I already do, Mike. We've got old Mr. Pollard, he drives the children to clinic, and Betsy Blanchard,' and so on.

"After a few weeks of this it began to sink in: what I was doing—and I did it fairly well, I was told—served no useful purpose at all! If local DHR offices needed volunteers, they went out and did the one thing most likely to startle an Atlanta planner out of his shoes—got them all by themselves. If they did not have any use for volunteers, they were not about to go get some just because I came around. I was the living, breathing embodiment of fat in government. If I owned a briefcase, the only thing I would have thought worth putting in it was a peanut butter and jelly sandwich."

Nelson began looking around for a transfer. Finding an opening in the Georgia Legal Services Program, a worthwhile federal–state program assisted by the national Volunteers in Service to America (VISTA) program, he packed his suitcases and left the Sugarman household.

At Legal Services, where he represented Medicaid clients, the problem was just the opposite of the problem at Volunteer Services. Though inexpensive medical aid for the poor was much needed, cutbacks were being planned because of pressure from the governor's mansion to economize. Since Nelson's work occasionally brought him into contact with high officials in the Department of Human Resources, he was able to complain about the proposed cutbacks at the policy level. The officials retorted that there was no money in the budget. No state agency was improving itself, they said.

No agency? Well, in fact, there was one—the Office of Volunteer Services. It was getting a big boost in funding—specifically, more than a doubling of its appropriation, from $220,000 to $470,000.

Nelson could hardly believe it. Legal Services, which really helped the poor and didn't have enough, was getting cut back, but Volunteer Services, his old organization that accomplished nothing, was getting an enormous increase! He knew that Sugarman was intensely loyal to Jim Parham, commissioner of the Department of Human Resources (also, a protégé of Jimmy Carter), and he knew that Parham reciprocated that loyalty—but this was a little much: Could government be so perverse? He recognized it could be inefficient. He realized it could bog down in red tape. But he was not prepared to find it so "off-the-wall crazy"! This was like deciding to add a new wing to an eighteen-room house where an old couple sat rocking all day, and taking space off a two-room house across the street where eighteen people lived.

Nelson decided to sit down, analyze why the Office of Volunteer Services shouldn't get an increase, and send his written analysis to a half-dozen key legislators. It was January 1976—late in the cycle to be doing this. Ordinarily, in fact, it would have been too late, for Sugarman's bonanza had been made a part of Governor George Busbee's fiscal program and had cleared the Georgia legislature's appropriations committee. However, Nelson knew that the legislators were frantic to hold the line on the budget, and for that reason they just might listen to him.

In his analysis, Nelson pointed out that Volunteer Services was hampered by poor staff morale, clogged with paperwork, dishonest (it forged data in its performance reports), poorly administered, and poorly conceived. He advised the legislators to check around for themselves.

It was too late to discuss his letter first with his old boss Sugarman or with Commissioner Parham. Such a discussion wouldn't have done any good, he believed—as Zorba the Greek said, "You can knock forever on a deaf man's door." But he sent copies of the letter to Sugarman and Parham.

This letter was a precocious and risky step, and Nelson knew it. For one who had lived in Sugarman's house, and who still lived in Parham's house, it was the worst type of table manners. He would be classified with the Goops described in Gelett Burgess's poem:

> The Goops they lick their fingers
> And the Goops they lick their knives;
> They spill their broth on the tablecloth;
> Oh, they lead untidy lives.

Only in this case he was spilling the broth not only on the tablecloth but all over the floor of the legislature.

None of the risks deterred Nelson. Once the idea came to mind, he says he just sat down and began drafting the letter. "I'm a person who believes that often you should follow your impulses," he explains, "because I don't believe most impulses are impulses at all. I think they tend to be what comes forth from a lot of sifting and sorting of information in the back of your mind." Besides, he says, he didn't have very much to lose. His salary wasn't substantial enough to be important. Also, his commitment was for only one year. Finally, he wasn't constrained by the need for a regular paycheck to pay the bills and fulfill family obligations—the kind of pressure that gives many employees a powerful incentive to be "good" houseguests when they see wrongdoing that should be reported.

Reaction to his letter from the capitol was swift. Chairman Joe Frank Harris of the House Appropriations Committee directed his staff to contact Nelson for more details. Nelson sent them a point-by-point critique of the annual report that Volunteer Services had sent to the governor; his critique showed, among other things, that the numbers had been grossly inflated under orders from the top. The official report was so bad that it didn't even disguise this chicanery very well—Nelson had little trouble pointing it out. He confined his remarks to the financial reporting and wrote in terms of costs and benefits; he didn't volunteer a lot of seamy information that he had acquired from Volunteer Services staff about matters that had been swept under the beds and rugs.

Reaction to his letter from the heads of the agency house also was swift. They hit the roof. They told the solons, according to one Nelson confidante, that his critique was "absolute and outright garbage." (Apparently this was mild language by top officials' standards. When Nelson wrote his story for *Johns Hopkins Magazine* a year later, Parham sent the magazine editor a letter that attacked Nelson so intemperately that it could not be printed. As Nelson remembers the essence of the letter, it warned that, though the young whistleblower might picture himself as a David fighting Goliath, he was really a Judas.)

But the timing was just right. The legislators were searching everywhere for places to make cuts in the budget. And Nelson had credibility. He had worked in the Office of Volunteer Services; he also had a fine academic background. The letter not only got to the right people at the right time in just the right stage of the budget proceedings, but it also came from the right source.

On February 10, Harris and other legislative leaders met with Governor Busbee. They persuaded him to remove the entire budget increase for Volunteer Services. They also persuaded him to launch a long-term study of whether this agency should be funded at any level.

Nelson's letter had been sensationally successful: Many veteran legislature watchers will tell you they've never seen a simple one-stroke coup produce such quick and decisive results.

So Nelson and his friends celebrated. However, the jubilation was short-lived. Parham called Nelson's new boss at Legal Services, John Cromartie. He also called the head of VISTA. Angrily Parham demanded that they throw Nelson out.

Obediently Cromartie called Nelson. "I have to fire you," he said. "Parham says he won't support Legal Services if I don't fire you, and we can't get along without his support."

Nelson went out and walked the streets of Atlanta for several hours. What should he do? He decided to go to Parham and plead his case. He called Parham's office. Parham said to come over. When Nelson got there, Parham shook his hand and asked him to sit down—"not warmly, but politely," Nelson recalls. Nelson told him he knew how angry he was, and said he supposed that if he were in Parham's position he'd be angry, too. But the work he was doing for Legal Services was useful work, Nelson said. Telling Cromartie to fire him was not going to do Parham or anybody any good.

First, Parham denied that he had threatened to withdraw his support from Legal Services if Cromartie wouldn't fire Nelson. Then Parham said, "I feel that we have invited you into our house, and you took an axe to the furniture."

Nelson felt stunned by this unusually frank expression of the bureaucratic mind. Was he hearing things? It wasn't Parham's house, or Cromartie's, or Sugarman's, or any other state official's. It was the *taxpayer's* house.

However, as the old saying goes, "Your boss may not be right, but he's the boss." And so Nelson was evicted. It was like the old story of the father who points his wayward daughter into the night and commands, "Don't darken my doorway again." Then and there, pleading does her no good.

But there was a possible solution—VISTA's appeal process for aggrieved employees. Nelson decided to try it. He learned that it involved half a dozen stages or layers and a lot of letter-writing and discussion. In his first official consultation, an informal talk, the official's main effort seemed to be to get him to resign quietly. It was tempting to do so. But no, Nelson said to himself, he wasn't going to give up that easily. Next began the written communications part. He found that there were complicated rules concerning when an aggrieved employee had to file, what the nature of the written complaint must be, and so on. Fortunately, one of his telephone calls to

Washington, D.C., brought him into contact with a helpful woman in one of the employee relations offices there. Deciding Nelson had a case, she gave him encouragement and careful advice. She told him how to avoid missing the filing deadline, how to make sure the appeal went to the right person and address, whether to certify or register the letter, and so on. "There were a lot of technicalities on which they were hoping to trip me up in the appeals process," Nelson remembers. "She guided me through it, and without her I don't know what would have happened."

As he negotiated one stage and level after another, the state was bringing charges against him. One was that he had violated VISTA's prohibition about moonlighting; he had written a piece for the Op-Ed page of the *New York Times* on the subject of the New Jersey Turnpike and had been paid $150 for it. This was an impermissible violation of the house rules, the bureaucrats pointed out. Another charge—this one vague and worded in the most general terms—was that Nelson had acted in a manner detrimental to VISTA.

The hearing examiner dismissed the moonlighting charge as trivial. He dismissed the second charge as unsupported.

About a week before Nelson's year was up, he was informed that he had won his appeal. The good news was sent begrudgingly, however, and had he been a long-term employee it might not have come to him at all. The hearing examiner had recommended to the regional director in Atlanta, Paul Jones, that Nelson be reinstated. The director wrote Nelson that he didn't agree with the decision but that, since Nelson had only a week to go, he would let it slide.

Following his eventful year in Georgia, Nelson moved to Washington, D.C., and became an editor of the *Washington Monthly*. After earning his doctorate at Johns Hopkins in 1978, he went to Vanderbilt University as assistant professor of political science. Reflecting on the general problem of government employees who want to speak out, he observes:

> "Whistle-blowing" is an all too rare phenomenon in American bureaucracy. The disincentives are powerful. A bureaucrat who "goes public" to expose waste or malfeasance has few legal protections against dismissal. Even if not actually fired, his on-the-job effectiveness will surely be destroyed beyond repair. He becomes, after all, the "traitor" who "took an axe to the furniture." It is a rare and courageous person who would risk all this for the sake of principle.

> Yet clearly our system requires the kind of information about how bureaucracy operates that only insiders can provide. Executive agencies now spend more than a third of our gross national product every

year, and employ one-sixth of our work force. As scholars from Max Weber to Francis Rourke have pointed out, their very size, complexity, and power make them all but impossible for elected officials to penetrate and control. Unless "whistle-blowers" can bring problems to lawmakers' attention when they arise inside agencies, democracy inevitably breaks down.

Nelson believes that his own experience points to a good way to cope with the problem. Student interns, visiting academics, "dollar-a-year men," and short-term, low-salary volunteer workers like himself have little to lose by speaking out, he argues. They could be looked to as watchdogs, as observers who get a good chance to see from the inside what is going on. They would not serve as "spies" for the public for they would not be *expected* to report wrongdoing. But once acquiring a conviction that wrongdoing exists, they would not have strong personal reasons *not* to speak out. Though the bureaucracy might see them as malcontents, they would not feel in jeopardy.

Of course, as Nelson points out, there is a danger in such an approach. People with nothing to lose may "sound off at every real and imagined shortcoming and cause chaos in government." But he doesn't see this possibility as a serious one: "People who intern initially have, as I did, a favorable orientation to their agency." In addition, the burden of proof falls on the whistleblower, not on the officials impugned. "Surely the greater danger," he says, "lies in a runaway bureaucracy whose errors go unchecked because those inside it are cowed into silence."

CRITICISM OF MANAGEMENT POLICIES

In still another area management prerogatives, no longer dominant, rest in uneasy balance with employee rights. This area involves employee criticisms of a corporation's or public agency's policies. A group of computer programmers puts up signs protesting the corporation's activities in the Mideast, or a scientist in a government regulatory agency blasts top management for being too soft on violators of agency regulations. What many an executive would *like* to do in such a case is show the critic to the door. In view of this instinctive reaction, and also of the law's haziness, one might expect managements to give short shrift to dissidents. In actuality, however, many managements do not. In fact, some corporate house organs, including those at American Airlines, Dow, and Bank of America, regularly publish employee criticisms of organization policies. There is no evidence, so far as I know, of retaliation against the writers. Furthermore, labor arbitrators generally are sympathetic to employee critics of organization policy. In everyday practice, if not in theory, management's prerogative is becoming limited.

This does not mean that managers have to put up with anything that can be labeled "free speech." Far from it. The sorehead, the newcomer who blasts organization policy without having been around long enough to know the pros and cons of the policy, the headline hunter who uses inside knowledge of an organization's errors to catch the attention of a TV talk-show host or a newspaper reporter—these and other types may be dealt with harshly in the most enlightened organization. But the wise manager will carefully weigh the pros and cons of retaliation before dispatching or reprimanding the critic who thoughtfully and knowledgeably disagrees out loud with a top management policy.

Although few judicial landmarks exist, more are likely to be established in the next ten years. One case that may provide helpful guidelines is pending in California. As reported by Alan F. Westin, in 1979 seven black employees of the Zellerbach Paper Company in Los Angeles wrote an angry letter to the Los Angeles Board of Education protesting an award made by the board to Zellerbach's personnel director. The award was for progress in affirmative action. The employees accused the personnel director of being a racist, said that the company was being sued for violating the equal employment opportunity laws, and expressed shock and dismay over the egregious award. About two weeks later, without any warning, the seven critics were told they were fired and ordered to be off the plant grounds in fifteen minutes. Each was given a letter stating that his disloyal conduct was intolerable and that the company's reputation had been damaged by the false assertions made in the letter. With the assistance of the American Civil Liberties Union, the employees sued the company.[7]

Where is the dividing line between wise and unwise retaliation in this area? The two accounts that follow, which are representative of many that might be given, suggest that the prudent manager takes into consideration a variety of factors, including the general tone of employee relations, the form of the irritating criticism, its possible damage to the organization's image and goodwill, and the dissident's apparent motives.

The Case of the Wrathful Writer [8]

Michael Holodnak drafted the article in anger. "Most union members resent being treated like kindergarten children by the company," he wrote of

---

[7] See Alan F. Westin, Whistle Blowing! (New York: McGraw-Hill, 1980), pp. 157–158.

[8] This account is based on court records and an interview with Michael Holodnak.

his employer, the Avco-Lycoming Division of Avco Corporation. He was no more charitable toward the union leadership, Local 1010 of the United Auto Workers of America. "The Sunday monthly meetings . . . have long been regarded by the members as a futile way of achieving effective policies in the plant," he wrote. "All the members keep doing is changing officers in the hope of some day stumbling upon some that will truly represent them."

From time to time his fury turned darkly to sarcasm. "Despite the fact that the company has a stupid, incompetent, and irresponsible management that has arrogantly sabotaged the grievance procedure," he accused, "the union members must continue to kiss the company's posterior for the privilege of living." He turned his wrath even on the arbitrators in labor disputes. "The most recent example was the firing of the twenty-two so-called 'hard core of miscreants,' " he wrote. "From his Heavenly perch the 'impartial' Arbitrator, backing up the company, pronounced his God-like opinion upon us poor sinful mortals while praising the pure-as-the-snow 'patient company' to the high heavens."

He chided union and corporate officials for imploring employees to be "reasonable." The American people weren't "reasonable" when they rejected President Lyndon B. Johnson's pleas to unite in the war against North Vietnam, he argued. George Washington wasn't "reasonable" in challenging British domination, nor was Galileo "reasonable" in challenging the Church's concept of the universe.

"The point is that nothing has ever been accomplished by so-called 'reasonable people,' " he stated. "Actually, it's unreasonable to tell us that we must be 'reasonable' to all the official insanity that exists around us."

He mailed the article to the *AIM Newsletter,* published in New Haven, Connecticut, by the American Independent Movement. The article came out several weeks later. The issue went to about 750 readers.

In his early forties when he wrote the article, Holodnak had grown up in Bridgeport, Connecticut, attended public schools in Bridgeport, and gone on to Bridgeport State Trade School to learn toolmaking. In World War II he had served as a radio operator on B-29s. Restless, he had pursued a variety of occupations in civilian life after the war. He had sailed to Europe as a merchant seaman. He had worked as a salesclerk. For a couple of years he had owned a truck and hauled freight. For four years he had driven tractor-trailer trucks. From time to time he had returned to the vocation for which he had first been trained, serving in small jobbing shops as a tool-and-die maker.

All this time he kept training himself in still another vocation. He wrote letters to newspapers. He wrote short stories. He began thinking about writing novels—later he would try his hand in that direction, too. When he sat down at his desk at home to vent his criticisms of Avco-Lycoming, therefore, he was testing a familiar skill. As Shakespeare admonished in *Twelfth Night*, "Let there be gall enough in thy ink; though thou write with a goose-pen, no matter."

Holodnak had been stewing for some time. First as a tool-and-die maker, later as a small-parts inspector, for five years a shop steward, he had worked at the Avco-Lycoming plant in Stratford for nine years. A zealous union member, he had never hesitated to join protests or picket lines. Although, until he sat down to write the article for the *AIM Newsletter*, he had never spoken out publicly against policies and conditions at the plant, he had gritted his teeth numerous times over the activities of management and union officials.

One morning at work about two weeks after writing the letter, Holodnak received a terse written notice from management. He was ordered to report to the company labor-relations office for a "disciplinary hearing." As was customary, he went to the hearing accompanied by union officials, in this case shop steward Frank Guida and committeeman Joe Mezick. When he reached the labor-relations office, he found several stony-faced management officials waiting.

One of them, William Ashlaw, showed Holodnak a copy of his article in the *AIM Newsletter*.

"You write this?"

"Yes."

Ashlaw picked up a copy of the plant conduct rules and read Rule 19, which testily prohibited the making by an employee of "false, vicious or malicious statements concerning any employee or which affect the employee's relationship to his job, his supervisors, or the Company's products, property, reputation, or good will in the community." Then Ashlaw read several paragraphs from Holodnak's article.

"You believe those things?" Ashlaw asked.

"Yes."

Ashlaw turned to another management official present, the company security officer. "What about the American Independent Movement, which publishes this thing," he asked the security officer. "Is it on the Attorney General's subversives list?"

"No," said the security officer.

Ashlaw wheeled back to face Holodnak. He said, "We're going to have to let you go for violating Rule 19."

Mezick defended Holodnak. The article wasn't all that bad a violation, Mezick argued. It wasn't all that different from other attacks on the company that had been printed, such as the union's leaflets. This wasn't a church group but a rough-and-tumble factory manufacturing nose cones, helicopter engines, constant speed drives for fighter planes, and other items of military hardware for the government. Read in that context, Holodnak's criticism wasn't vicious or unusual.

Unimpressed, Ashlaw told Holodnak, "I want your badge."

Holodnak gave it to him. Ashlaw said, "Don't come back."

At about 11 A.M. Holodnak marched out of the plant. Although he did not know it, he would never again work in a factory, there or anywhere else.

He got in touch with George Johnson, an attorney for AIM. Johnson advised him to go through the customary grievance procedure and, if he got nowhere on that route, resort next to arbitration. Holodnak took this advice. When, as expected, the grievance procedure produced no change in results, he contacted the union and requested an arbitration hearing.

To represent him at the hearing, Holodnak called on Edward Burstein, the attorney at Local 1010. At the time this seemed like a smart step, though an unusual one, since in most cases committeemen represented complaints at arbitration proceedings. Johnson tried to help. Early in July, before the hearing took place, Johnson spoke with Burstein on the phone and offered his assistance on the Holodnak case. What neither Johnson nor Holodnak realized at the time was that Burstein had little more sympathy with Holodnak than the company managers had. So, although Burstein thanked Johnson for the offer of help, he never talked with him again. In fact, Burstein never even got around to meeting Holodnak until the arbitration hearing.

On the appointed day in July, Holodnak arrived at the Howard Johnson Motor Inn in West Haven. He got there early, as did Burstein; during the course of their ten- or fifteen-minute meeting Burstein read the controversial article for the first time. A feeling of dread must have come over Holodnak as he witnessed the other man's unpreparedness.

They went into a fairly large conference room, where tables were arranged in a horseshoe pattern. On one side sat the company officials, including the legal counsel, the director and assistant director of industrial relations, two other labor-relations officials, and a security official. On the opposite side sat the union people, including Burstein, the president and vice-president of Local 1010, and several othrs. Holodnak sat on the union side. The arbitrator, Burton Turkus, sat at the table joining the two sides. A court stenographer sat at a small table inside the horseshoe.

When the proceedings began, Burstein asked which rule Holodnak was accused of violating. Rule 19, management answered. Burstein then said that Holodnak's right of free speech was at stake. Although this argument was potentially explosive, Burstein tossed it aside later. When arbitrator Turkus asked him if he was attacking Rule 19 as an infringement of the First Amendment to the Constitution, Burstein said no. Rule 19, he admitted, was a "fair and reasonable rule" and did not infringe on the right of fair speech. The practical effect of this admission was devastating. It looked as if Burstein were taking the sword to his own client.

Burstein didn't argue, as he could have, that Rule 19 was vague and easily susceptible to overly broad interpretation. Nor did he argue that the authors of the rule could not have intended it to apply to conduct like Holodnak's.

One of the company representatives got out his stick and began poking. What was Holodnak's personal background? What were his political and social views? What books had he read, what candidates did he support for political office, what opinions did he have about "corporatism"?

Even the arbitrator, normally considered to have the neutral and objective role of impartial umpire, began poking at the victim. Did Holodnak travel to Cuba in 1960 and had he written articles in favor of Fidel Castro? He had. Did not that reflect on his motives in writing the nasty article in the *AIM Newsletter?* "Emphasis throughout the proceeding," noted Judge Lumbard several years later, "seemed to be on instructing Holodnak on the mistake of his ways." When Holodnak defended himself by claiming that, yes, he did believe the union wasn't doing everything it might, the arbitrator told him to come off it. The arbitrator's obvious bias, when reviewed years later by the courts, was astonishing.

"Well, don't you know, as a fact, when you wrote this article," the arbitrator accused, "that you have here a very militant and zealous union that seeks the protection of the rights of its membership and seeks to endorse all Company obligations under the contract? Didn't you know that when you wrote the article?"

Holodnak, according to the stenographer's record, answered: "Well, I didn't say that they didn't enforce it. I'm pointing out the shortcoming here. I know there are some good things they do, a lot of good things."

So the arbitrator got out a longer and sharper stick to poke with. The record reports he said (the italics are added): "Well, *certainly* when you wrote the article, you *knew* there was *no* shortcoming, that this was not a supine Union that sat by and allowed the Company to do whatever it wanted; *you knew that* when you wrote it."

In the words of the district court opinion later, "The arbitrator seemed compelled to convince Holodnak that he was wrong."

As for Holodnak's caustic criticisms of the company, neither his counsel nor anyone else, strangely, thought to remind the session of some of the statements printed in leaflets distributed by the union. In one, the union had called company officials "the Mickey Mouse managers of Stratford's Disneyland." In another circular, a union writer had snarled that the plant supervision was "the political cesspool of mahogany row." Another union circular had crucified general foremen as "brainless." The grievance pro-

ceedings were put down as a "weekly farce." Contrasted with such vi-
tuperation, Holodnak's complaints seemed rather mild, yet this fact in his
favor was overlooked

After the members had completed their badgering, the inquisition broke
up and the counsel for the company and for Holodnak went home to write
their postarbitration briefs. Burstein, in his brief intended to take Holodnak's side, got in some more licks at his client.

"It is said, 'A little knowledge is a dangerous thing,' " wrote Burstein
with distaste, "and so it is with Michael Holodnak—that which he knows is
but a scintilla of what he doesn't know." Burstein's hostility and revulsion
increased by the word. "Testimony throughout is replete with examples of
this man's superficial knowledge, which because it was gleaned informally,
is oftimes wrong and even childlike in its naiveté." After this series of knees
to the groin, Burstein gave his client a soft pat on the back. He argued
briefly that there was no evidence of falseness or maliciousness in Holodnak's comments. He also alleged that Avco had in effect waived any right to
discharge an employee for violating Rule 19.

The outcome of the hearing was a foregone conclusion. It came in December from arbitrator Turkus—a one-sentence decision in favor of the
company.

Holodnak wandered into the dark woods of a new destiny. In vain he
sought a new job. After a while he gave up. Arthritis was invading his hip
joints. He applied for social security disability benefits and veterans' pension benefits. His hip joints became so arthritic that he had to resort to
crutches in order to walk. In 1972 surgeons at the West Haven Veterans
Hospital replaced the destroyed joints with artificial parts.

In the meantime, however, he had decided to take Avco-Lycoming to
court if he could. Had George Johnson been available, he would have been
Holodnak's choice, but Johnson had left Connecticut to teach in Boulder,
Colorado. Someone put Holodnak in touch with Eugene N. Sosnoff, an able
attorney in New Haven. Sosnoff listened as Holodnak told his story. He
agreed to take the case on a contingency basis (there was no way Holodnak
could have paid an attorney for time and expenses).

A two-day trial without a jury began in the U.S. district court on April
29, 1974, with Judge C. Edward Lumbard presiding, in Bridgeport. Holodnak was present along with his counsel. He was suing Avco and Local 1010
for close to $80,000 in damages with interest, and counsel fees of $50,000.

Lumbard took umbrage at the arbitrator for his partiality during the
proceedings at the Howard Johnson Motor Inn, and at Holodnak's attorney
for a poor defense. He then proceeded to reason that Holodnak's right of
free speech under the First Amendment to the Constitution had been violated. An employee in a government agency had a limited right to criticize

management, under the *Pickering* line of decisions by the U.S. Supreme Court,[9] Lumbard noted, and Holodnak enjoyed the same privilege because so much of Avco-Lycoming's output was produced under contract with the U.S. military. Wrote Lumbard:

> Beverly Warren, Avco vice-president and chief operating officer at the Stratford plant, testified that approximately 80% of the work done at the plant at the time of the plaintiff's discharge was defense-related and primarily directed toward producing aircraft engines, missile nose cones, and constant speed drives for the military. Nearly all the land, buildings, machinery, and equipment at the Stratford plant were owned by the government. The Department of Defense maintained a large task force at the plant to oversee operations, assure contract compliance and guarantee quality control.[10]

Lumbard noted that Holodnak's criticisms had to do with management's labor-relations policies, an area traditionally protected. "It is noteworthy that even in private enterprise where the guarantees of the First Amendment do not apply, federal statutes have given employees the right to speak their minds on labor relations." Lumbard went on to quote from a 1940 decision by the U.S. Supreme Court: "Free discussion concerning the conditions in industry and the causes of labor disputes appears to us indispensable to the effective and intelligent use of the processes of popular government to shape the destiny of modern industrial society." He also quoted the freedom-embracing opinion of another federal court: "Under the First Amendment there is no such thing as a false idea. However pernicious an opinion may seem, we depend for its correction not on the conscience of judges and juries but on the competition of other ideas."

Lumbard awarded Holodnak damages of slightly more than $9,000 for back pay and $10,000 in punitive damages. He decided against giving Holodnak his job back. "Holodnak's physical condition, observed at trial," wrote the judge, "makes it doubtful that he is physically capable of returning to doing the work he had been doing." The amount of the fee to be paid by Avco and the union to Holodnak's attorney was left to fact-finding and later determination.

The district court's decision was appealed to the Second Circuit Court of Appeals. In 1975 the decision was affirmed except for the award of $10,000 in punitive damages. When the company appealed to the U.S. Supreme Court, certiorari was denied.[11]

---

[9] See David W. Ewing, *Freedom inside the Organization* (New York: Dutton, 1977), pp. 100–101.
[10] See p. 15 of *Holodnak v. Avco*, Civil Action No. B-15, U.S. District Court, Conn., 1974; also see *Holodnak v. Avco*, 381 F. Supp. 191 and 514 F. 2d 285 (1975).
[11] Certiorari denied, 96 S. Ct. 188 (1975).

Whether Judge Lumbard's decision becomes an isolated opinion or historic precedent, only time will tell. But without question it has been discussed and cussed in many a library, office, and home study. Numerous American corporations do as much work for the federal government as Avco-Lycoming did, and thousands more produce a substantial, though lesser, amount of products and services for government agencies. If Avco-Lycoming comes under the umbrella of the First Amendment, why not a company doing, let's say, 60% of its work for the government? If that company is under the umbrella, why not a corporation producing 45% of its services for public agencies? Avco's lawyers were aware of this possibility when they appealed Judge Lumbard's decision to the circuit court. His decision, they argued, should be overturned because it would "constitutionalize" a great many companies "that sell notable portions of their products . . . to the government."

How to Get Peeled in Orange [12]

When managers and dissidents come head to head over company policies and philosophies, the outcome depends partly on where they are. In this heterogeneous country, the uneasy balance between prerogatives and rights tips erratically from state to state.

Louis V. McIntire graduated from the University of Southwestern Louisiana in 1944, served in the U.S. Navy for two years, and got his doctorate in chemical engineering from Ohio State University in 1951. Five years later he went to work at the Sabine River Works of the prestigious E. I. du Pont de Nemours and Company in Orange, Texas. In a couple of years he was promoted to the position of research supervisor; a year later he was promoted to senior research engineer. In the ensuing years he worked on polyethylene processes and ionomers at the plastics plant. He received regular salary increases and other forms of recognition for his work. By 1972, after sixteen years with the chemical company, he was earning approximately $24,500.

However, the energetic and freethinking McIntire was not what managers would call a "good company man" (although they did not realize this at first). Interested as he was in promotion and prestige in the company, he also saw himself as a campaigner for members of his profession. A liberal Democrat, McIntire got interested enough in politics to run in the 1972 Democratic primary for the U.S. House of Representatives. He took a two-week leave of absence to campaign. His speeches did not endear him to his corporate superiors. The damage was not reduced when he failed to win the nomination. Scientists and engineers were paid generally like production

[12] This account is based largely on newspaper articles.

workers, he maintained, but they didn't have similar legal rights. For instance, they didn't have the protection of the National Labor Relations Act (which forbade, among other things, unfair and arbitrary dismissal). He took a sour view of perceived inhibitions on speech in the company, feeling that they oppressed professional employees. He saw those working behind the corporate wall as exempted from the protection of the First Amendment to the Constitution, and this made no sense to him.

Still, he might have survived but for another action. That was to collaborate with his wife Marion on a novel that budded with criticisms of the management of large industrial corporations like Du Pont. The novel did not describe or libel anyone in the Du Pont organization. Neither on the jacket nor in the text was McIntire identified as an employee of Du Pont. Nor were there any references to Orange, Texas. But clearly the mood of the book was heretical to many managers and supervisors in the plastics plant. The McIntires expressed their views, as the phrase goes, "with the bark off."

The title of the novel was *Scientists and Engineers: The Professionals Who Are Not*.[13] It dealt with an imaginary chemical corporation, LoChemCo, which had life-or-death powers over its scientists and which harvested their ideas without proper recompense. A restless, inquiring scientist named J. Marmaduke Glumm argued that technical employees should form a national federation to push legislation favoring members. Said Glumm at one point: "It is a peculiar paradox that workingmen with little bargaining leverage have more actual job security than we do." The story also sprouted with such contentions as that employee contracts gave most of the rights to the employer, and that favoritism and intracompany politics governed advancement more than technical proficiency did.

Including a number of drawings by Dick Murphy, the novel was 208 pages long. The McIntires began writing it on weekends in 1968. In 1971 it was published by an unincorporated company in Louisiana that he set up for that purpose. About 2,000 hardcover copies were printed in August 1971. In his 1972 primary campaign, McIntire had 9,000 paperback copies printed for distribution as campaign material.

"It wasn't a money-making proposition," McIntire told a reporter of the *Wilmington Evening Journal*. "We published it to point out a problem." The problem was not Du Pont in particular. In fact, he told the reporter, "Du Pont is probably one of the better companies in its treatment of people." But large organizations in general, the book implied, expected blind obedience and loyalty from scientists and engineers.

After the Democratic primary in May 1972, McIntire returned to work.

---

[13] Arcola Communications Company, Box 2101, Lafayette, La. 70501.

He was greeted with the enthusiasm accorded a lemon in a candy factory. He claims that a supervisor suggested that he leave Du Pont for his own benefit. Early in August he received a tart letter telling him, "August 31 will be your last day on the Du Pont salary roll."

He protested his discharge. His attempt to persuade management was useless. Presumably he was describing the futility of his effort when, four years later in Boston, addressing a section of the American Association for the Advancement of Science convention, he described the dissident's typical humiliation in these words:

> You are called into top management's office. This usually results in your standing alone and facing two or more management people. Your immediate supervisor is usually absent. Top management says your performance is not good. You protest that it is good. The management people suggest you might be better off somewhere else and that you should leave the company quietly. They always point out that if you leave quietly, you can expect good recommendations. They also state that if you do not leave quietly and "voluntarily," then— "Well, you know what that means. . . ." You ask for management to give you their position in writing. Management refuses to give you anything in writing.

In vain he tried to land another job. His hopes were squashed repeatedly. He became convinced that he had been blackballed by Du Pont.

He talked to the Houston law firm of Combs & Arthur, which agreed to represent him in a suit against Du Pont. One of his claims was that his First Amendment right of freedom of speech had been impinged. The Texas court threw this claim out right away. McIntire's other claims were that he had not been paid by Du Pont for his inventions ($5 million), that he had been blackballed ($5 million in damages), that he had been denied due process ($5 million), and that he had suffered because of denial of a fair hearing ($5 million damages). In the lengthy legal rhubarb that followed, all $20 million of these claims were thrown out by the court.[14]

When it became apparent that he would have difficulty finding another job in a chemical company, his wife took a position teaching in an elementary school. He began offering his services as a technical consultant. In addition, he made speeches whenever he could to technical societies and other groups. He developed a practice as a consultant, which he maintains today. He continues to be a legal thorn in the side of his old employer,

---

[14] *Louis V. McIntire* v. *E. I. Du Pont de Nemours & Company,* 165 Judicial District Court, Harris County, Texas: No. 954,904.

however, for he is suing it for preempting technical processes he invented before he was fired.

_____

Why do organization leaders fear the printed word? They know the power of advertising. They know the power of publicity. They know the power of dramatization in books, movies, and plays. Even when hostile words are not directly critical of them, they fear the indirect influence on public opinion. If the soil becomes unhealthy, they say, even the largest tree is affected. Look how excessive zeal for government regulation undermined the once-thriving railroads, for instance.

The defense made by employees like McIntire is as follows: "We're not trying to destroy the corporation. We don't nurture a dream of vines spreading over the employee parking space and of the headquarters building greening like an Incan temple in the jungle. We simply think our way for the corporation is better." And McIntire in particular would defend: "I didn't criticize a Du Pont product. I didn't blemish the company's reputation for safety and technology. I only urged greater bargaining power for scientists and engineers, an idea which, in my opinion, would help the company to thrive."

The conflict between the irreverent, freely inquiring spirit of the scientific mind and the more committed, more channeled spirit of the managerial mind is likely to be with us for some time. Our organizations in business and government are becoming increasingly technological. Between 1960 and 1980, the number of professional and technical workers in the United States came close to doubling; the growth in the number of managers and administrators was great, too, but nowhere near as spectacular as the growth of technical employees. What is more, the professionals are becoming increasingly "professional"; their allegiance to their disciplines and professional associations is becoming ever greater, overshadowing more than before their allegiance to any employer.

And so the seeds of conflict are present when managers and scientists come together in an organization. The managers tend to feel committed to the concept of the organization—not necessarily to its precise form, but to its present pattern. On the other hand, the scientists are likely to feel no such commitment to any organization pattern, only to the process of inquiry and knowledge.

The details of the McIntire case are unlikely to be repeated. But the conflict it represents is verdant and growing, and his style could become a familiar one in the years ahead. The effect on management prerogatives seems obvious: They will become more judgmental, and they will call for increasing skill and sophistication. Ironically, the professionalism of scientific employees is forcing more professionalism in management.

REDUCING UNCERTAINTY

From four accounts of employee objection—stories that are going to be repeated again and again in the 1980s—we see that the out-of-bounds markers for managers are being moved in on some fairways of administration. How much they are being moved in, however, is far from certain. It is as if the markers were obscured by trees and hills, and judges and solons, crouching out of sight, were changing them while managers are in the act of swinging. What can you as a manager do to reduce the uncertainty?

First, you can double-check the effect of your proposed action. No matter how much your superiors and colleagues endorse it, is it illegal? As we saw in the Harless case, if it is, you could be getting into trouble. Is it wasteful or inefficient? If you are an administrator in the federal government or a state government, watch out, especially these days when legislators and the media love to criticize poor public administration. If you are a corporate executive, however, you probably can get away with it if your superiors and the directors automatically side with managers against subordinates, or are in complicity with you. The stockholders won't be happy, or your customers, but it is hard for them to do more than make noise.

Second, if the objector is talking about waste, inefficiency, or irresponsibility, appraise the person's standing. If the objector belongs to a union, look out. Even if the union doesn't back the person well, as in the Holodnak case, arbitrators may come to the objector's rescue; if arbitrators don't, the courts may. But if the objector is an engineer, scientist, or other type of worker not protected by a union, then you probably are free to be as autocratic as you want if top management does not object. The McIntire case is a good example. Your decision may not be wise in terms of the corporate future, stockholders, or the well-being of the economy, and journalists as well as management authorities may cry foul. But you can get away with it. Many managers are doing so, as our estimates in Chapter 1 suggest.

The big question, of course, is this: How do you view your responsibilities as a manager? If you see them as being tied in with public service and the economic future, you will get one answer. But if you see them as related only to your power to do as you want, you may get another answer.

4

WHERE PREROGATIVES ARE WEAK AND RIGHTS ARE STRONG

We come now to the opposite end of the prerogatives–rights spectrum. Beginning with the areas where managerial prerogatives are strong and the rights of employee subordinates weak, we went next to the areas where the two tend to teeter, depending on the circumstances of the case. Now we turn to areas where the balance is in favor of employee rights at the expense of prerogatives—if not always legally, almost always in terms of long-range organizational interests. These areas have to do with such concerns as public welfare and safety, the sanctity of the individual, ethical and moral standards, and legal codes.

Why are prerogatives weak and rights strong in these areas? What is the rationale for favoring the employee critic, the conscientious objector, the activist at this end of the spectrum? One reason is simply that the dangers employees resist, if real, are of immediate, personal concern to the public and employees. "It isn't the stockholder or the organization that might be hurt, but *me*," says the worried observer.

A more complex reason is the tendency of the economic system to blind managers to dangers that should be perceived, to desensitize them to hazards that worry nonmanagers. "When we didn't meet our growth targets, the top brass really came down on us," a marketing official of H. J. Heinz

Company told a *Wall Street Journal* reporter late in 1979, when the company was suffering from a profit-juggling scandal. "And everybody knew that if you missed the targets enough, you were out on your ear." [1]

Most managers are quite familiar with top-down pressure to perform, to "get results at any cost, don't bother us with how." From time to time the obsession may dominate decision-making. Unable to meet top management's profit goals by any other method, some harried managers resort to deceptive bookkeeping, misdating invoices, transferring sums from one account to another. Others attempt shortcuts in quality control or research spending. Still others violate contracts with suppliers or resort to stealing secrets from competitors or bribe prospective buyers. "A certain amount of tension is desirable," observes Harvard Business School professor Paul R. Lawrence, "but at many companies the pressures to perform are so intense and the goals so unreasonable that some middle managers feel the only way out is to bend the rules, even if it means compromising personal ethics."

In 1972, Harvey Copp, a Ford Motor Company manager in charge of engine emission testing, brought to the attention of top management the fact that test results of the company's 1973-model engines were being manipulated. Unauthorized maintenance was being done on engines undergoing federal certification tests. Copp emphasized that he didn't feel top executives at Ford condoned the tampering, only that they had created the environment for cheating by putting the squeeze on the testing department. Top management wanted middle-management people to see to it that the engines got certified. If the middle managers failed, said Copp, the company would not have been able to meet its ambitious production and earnings objectives for the year. As management consultant Harry Levinson observes, "There's a tendency for top management at many companies to keep pushing for the numbers without bothering to ask their managers how they got them. And when top management doesn't ask, lower management figures anything goes as long as they're meeting their targets."

CONCERN FOR SAFETY, HEALTH, AND WELFARE

On issues involving the safety of products in the hands of users, the unwanted side effects of medicines and drugs, and similar risks, senior managers are much less free than in the past to do what may seem expedient or self-serving. The freedom was first curtailed sharply in unionized companies; a well-known example is that of a steel company worker who refused to dump hazardous wastes into the Cuyahoga River in Ohio, was

[1] *Wall Street Journal,* November 8, 1979.

suspended by his boss, and rescued by the union-supported grievance procedure. Next the freedom was curtailed by professional associations such as the American Chemical Society and the American Association for the Advancement of Science, which encouraged their members to observe the profession's code of conduct and discouraged corporations and public agencies from penalizing professionals who objected to a dangerous practice or procedure. The media have effectively pruned the prerogative still more through exposés of public-be-damned and employees-be-damned practices—and the perennial threat of such exposés. In their efforts to professionalize management thinking, the business schools have been notably successful in convincing administrators about the wisdom of self-restraint.

But the most important force curtailing management's prerogative is the concerned employee. Outside pressures on management have only a mild effect if subordinates are unwilling to speak up, resist, call on outsiders to help, and risk their jobs and chances for promotion. Without this willingness, reporters don't get the story until it is too late. Professional groups don't learn about the abuses in time to exert pressure. Union grievance procedures lie unused. Management training falls on deaf ears. Judges don't get many cases to decide.

It must be emphasized that the managerial prerogative to decide a safety or health question arbitrarily is far from dead. It is very much alive, as indeed it must be if public and corporate organizations are to function. Much of the time managers see the risks better than their subordinates do; much of the time, too, they can weigh the risks better than anyone else can, in particular, better than "crusaders," missionaries, and fanatics can. So the prerogative lives. Our point is simply that it must be exercised with great care and restraint, or the organization suffers. When an intended decision is challenged by a dissident on safety or health grounds, the wise manager practically never refuses to consider the objection; if necessary, the challenge is heard and weighed at the expense of deadlines, short-term profits, the manager's personal advantage, and other pressures.

For an exceptional illustration of an employee challenge, let us turn to a story that took place in the 1970s in the steel industry.

The Case of the Insistent Salesman [2]

Nobody seems to be quite sure why salesman George B. Geary was invited to the meeting in Pittsburgh in 1965, but he was, and it changed the rest of his life.

The meeting was called by Henry Wallace, then the vice-president of

[2] This account is drawn from court records and an interview with George Geary.

sales of U.S. Steel Corporation. He invited about a dozen managers from the sales, metallurgy, and production areas. Geary was the only nonmanager who attended. A veteran salesman, he had been brought up in Pittsburgh, graduated as a petroleum engineer from the University of Pittsburgh in 1948, served as a petroleum engineer for Creole Petroleum, and gone to work for U.S. Steel in 1953. Perhaps he was asked to the meeting because he wasn't a manager and could offer a different quality of opinion from the rest, one that would be respected because of his background and talents.

As Geary quickly learned, the meeting was important. It concerned a strategic move Wallace wanted the company to make, what some would have called corporate gamesmanship. An important customer, A. O. Smith Company, had threatened to drop U.S. Steel as a supplier unless the steelmaker made good on a failure in some steel plate it had supplied. A. O. Smith, which had bought the plate for fabrication into line pipe, considered the failure to be not its fault but U.S. Steel's. In a series of meetings, U.S. Steel people had held the position that the plate was not at fault, and A. O. Smith threatened to retaliate by scrapping U.S. Steel as a supplier and giving its business to another company. If it did that, U.S. Steel would lose sales of 5,000 or so tons per month.

To stave off that possibility, Wallace proposed a counterthreat. If A. O. Smith scratched U.S. Steel, he wanted to be able to warn that U.S. Steel would start manufacturing and marketing S-95 oil well casings. This casing, used in deep oil wells, was a profitable business for A. O. Smith, the sole manufacturer, and the thought of having to contend with a giant competitor ought to be a very unpleasant one.

What Wallace wanted to know was this: Could he tell the A. O. Smith people that U.S. Steel could get its own S-95 casing on the market in three months? If his counterthreat were to work, it had to be dangerous and imminent. Everyone at the meeting agreed that this could be done—everyone except Geary. Geary didn't think there was a chance that U.S. Steel could gear up in such a short time. He told the meeting that it would take three months just to decide how to make the new casing, another six months to test it, and still another three months to produce it—about a year altogether.

Strangely, although this was not what Wallace wanted to hear, he ended up agreeing with Geary. He decided to tell A. O. Smith only that his company would, if it lost the Smith business, go on the market with a competitive casing, without announcing when this retaliative move would happen.

Wallace liked Geary's realism. He also approved of the speed with which his able sales engineer worked. The next day Geary wrote out a procedure for the development of an S-95 casing, including such steps as how to obtain samples of A. O. Smith's product for laboratory analysis. Geary personally arranged for procuring those samples from the field.

The samples were obtained and the testing began, because, just as Wallace had feared, A. O. Smith gave U.S. Steel the shaft and cut it as a supplier. And as Geary had predicted, the development work dragged. It dragged and it dragged—slower even than Geary had predicted. Geary was promoted and assigned to work in Houston, Texas, under Ted Brissman as assistant manager of oil country tubular products. Geary lost interest in the casings project. Relatively few employees, in fact, were aware of its existence. It was closely controlled by top management.

In Texas, Geary's work went well. About two years passed since the meeting with Wallace. Then one fateful day Brissman announced to Geary that U.S. Steel soon would have its new S-95 casing ready to market. Moreover, it was going to be Geary's job to sell it. In fact, Brissman said, Geary was to have sole responsibility for personally contacting prospective customers and soliciting orders.

Geary was wary. Although his knowledge of the casings project was rusty, he doubted that U.S. Steel could make the product because the company lacked the equipment, and the process was patented by A. O. Smith. "Could you show me the test results?" Geary asked. Brissman produced a mill test report on eighty-four samples. He would only let Geary look at the report, not keep it. But what Geary saw confirmed his suspicions. In the eighty-four tests there had been three failures—a failure rate of 3.6%. Now, maybe that would be acceptable for hula hoops but it was not acceptable for a casing in deep oil wells, where a failure could be both dangerous and expensive. "This casing isn't good enough," Geary told the boss. "It's got to be 100% reliable, not 96%—this failure expectancy is much too high. No one will buy it on the basis of these tests."

The next day Geary called on W. C. French, vice-president of sales for the Southwest. Geary described his fears about the reliability of the new casing. Also, he said, he didn't think that the intended price was right. French, who had been aware of the development project, listened. "George," he said, when Geary was through, "I'm not your boss and can't tell you what to do. But this program comes from a very high source, and like in the Navy, I would follow orders."

Geary went back to Brissman. Instead of refusing to take the new selling job, as intuition told him, he let Brissman persuade him to try it.

But there's no rest for the wary, and Geary's worries kept nagging him. About six weeks later, when the McKeesport, Pennsylvania, mill was near ready to produce the initial rolling, he went to that city and confronted the chief metallurgist and his assistant. The casing didn't meet the specifications, Geary argued. They claimed that it did. Look at your own test results, Geary insisted. His arguments were too compelling for them—they not only agreed but promised to put their reservations in writing to management.

It was a victory for Geary, marred by one ominous note. "I hope it doesn't happen," said the assistant metallurgist, Richard Stripay, to him, "but if you keep on this way you're fixing to be fired." The possibility hadn't occurred to Geary and, though he remembered the warning later, he didn't give it much thought then.

The next day he went to Pittsburgh and, refreshed by his success at the mill, tested his mettle again. He requested a thorough review of the entire casing development program. However, this time his arguments made scarcely a dent. Neither the general manager, Art Elbert, nor the managers at lower levels were willing to bend. "Everyone," says Geary, "was fearful of touching the project because it was the brainchild of Henry Wallace, vice-president of sales."

Why didn't Geary give up at this stage? Certainly he had done more than his duty, as most employees would define it. Also, there seemed little point in attempting further resistance; the people in power seemed determined to forge ahead. Yet the iron-willed Geary kept fighting back. For one thing, he was the one who had to sell the new casing, and naturally he didn't want his reputation stained by a blunder stemming from a vendetta inspired by Henry Wallace. For another, he was mindful that none of the managers involved were engineers or knew anything about drilling an oil well. He was an engineer with that knowledge, and it made him feel a sense of obligation. An accident was waiting to happen.

Through the whole ordeal, Geary kept noticing that no one in management was attempting to prove him wrong. "They were not capable of discussing the subject," he recalls. "The only desire of everyone associated with the project was to satisfy the instructions of Henry Wallace. No one was about to buck this man for fear of his job."

Geary returned to Houston. He arranged another meeting with French and once more argued against the casing project. Impressed, French got on the telephone with the brass in Pittsburgh and suggested that they arrange a meeting there and listen to Geary. They agreed, with the result that Geary was back in Pittsburgh the following week, trying to weld his case again. The consensus of the meeting was that production should be stopped. It looked as if Geary had finally won.

But his joy went into a blast furnace. After he got back to Houston, Brissman came down from Pittsburgh and demanded that he resign or be fired. When he refused to resign, he was fired. The date was July 13, 1967, one month short of what would have been his fourteenth anniversary with U.S. Steel.

"I went to Bill French that same day," Geary remembers, "and he asked what he could do for me. I asked him to save my job, and he replied, 'Except that!' Of course, he had been well primed in advance of the firing, and had obviously concurred."

Two weeks later, Geary, unable to get a new job immediately, filed in Pennsylvania for unemployment benefits. To his astonishment and dismay, he found U.S. Steel opposing his claim. Goliath, having dispatched David, was pursuing his ghost. When the Bureau of Employment Security granted Geary's application, the steel-fisted company appealed. Two hearings were then held, one in Houston and a second in Pittsburgh, with U.S. Steel each time represented by lawyers determined to deny benefits to Geary. On the appeal, the company's expensive effort paid off. However, when in turn Geary appealed to the Board of Review in Harrisburg, his claim was reinstated. The Board of Review was unimpressed by U.S. Steel's contention that Geary had lost his job because of "willful misconduct" and therefore should be disqualified from receiving unemployment pay. The board wrote in its opinion:

> No company places a man in the position held by the claimant and pays him the salary received by claimant [nearly $20,000 a year, in 1967 dollars] simply to have him quietly agree to all proposals. The claimant did not refuse to follow orders but, in fact, agreed to do as instructed despite his opposition to the program proposed. Although he may have been vigorous in his opposition and offended some superiors by going to a vice-president, it is clear that at all times the claimant was working in the best interest of the company and that the welfare of the company was primary in his mind.

Why would such a large and profitable corporation go to so much trouble to save itself a few dollars (a slight increase in its unemployment pay contribution because of Geary) and spite the salesman who had worked for it for fourteen years? Possibly Geary has the answer. "My mistake," he says, "was not going to Wallace the same day I received the assignment from Brissman to sell the casing. I knew the instructions came from Wallace, and also that he had picked me for the job. But instead of attacking the problem head-on, I let myself be persuaded by Brissman. I subverted it gradually and embarrassed many people instead of just one."

Calling on prospective employers for a new job, Geary had no luck. Repeatedly he was turned down. "The problem," he believes, "was that U.S. Steel blackballed me, and neither the other steel companies nor anyone who did business with U.S. Steel would hire me. I had any number of promises from many companies, including a personal promise from the president of one, but they all reneged after checking back with U.S. Steel, though I could never get anyone to admit he talked to U.S. Steel."

In 1969 Geary, having found a lower-paying job, convinced Paul Titus, a Pittsburgh lawyer, to sue U.S. Steel for him. Titus, who had successfully handled a case for Geary's brother against an oil company, agreed to take the case on a contingency basis. Because of U.S. Steel's "wrongful and abusive discharge of plaintiff," Geary's brief alleged, his "good reputation and the goodwill which he had in the oil and gas industry was seriously damaged." He claimed damages in excess of $100,000 for the loss of remunerative employment and another $500,000 in "punitive and exemplary" damages.

In both the Pennsylvania Court of Common Pleas and the Superior Court, in 1971, the decisions went against Geary. Unwilling to buckle under, he appealed to the Supreme Court of Pennsylvania. In March 1974, in a 4 to 3 vote, the Supreme Court upheld the steel company.[3] The reasoning of the majority was bolted onto the traditional common-law rule about employer prerogatives. Many lawyers were astonished by the closeness of the decision. Only a dozen or so years earlier, the decision would have been a lopsided victory for the company, 6 to 1 or perhaps a unanimous 7 to 0. That the old common-law rule survived by only one shaky vote was astonishing. What was more, the minority opinion of the court, delivered by the much-respected Justice Roberts, was a cogent appeal to reason. For example, Roberts' opinion stated;

> His [Geary's] suggestion that the unsafe steel pipe be withdrawn from the market to protect both the public from danger and his employer from liability was in complete harmony with his employer's best interest.

> When he correctly recognized that the defective steel pipe had strong potential for causing injury and damage, he immediately notified his superiors. His reward for loyalty was dismissal. Of course, had Geary not informed his superiors of the defective product, he may well have deserved discharge for his failure to do so.

> The manufacture and distribution of defective and potentially dangerous products does not serve either the public's or the employer's interest.

> The time has surely come to afford unorganized employees an opportunity to prove in court a claim for arbitrary and retaliatory discharge.

[3] *Geary v. U.S. Steel Corp.*, 319 A. 2d 174 (Pa., 1974).

It is far too late in the day for this Court to indulge itself by fictionalizing that the doctrine of freedom of contract justifies insulation of an employer's arbitrary and abusive exercise of his power of discharge.

What is the significance of the Geary story for management prerogatives? It signifies that a superior is, or soon will be, no longer free to sweep aside opposition to a decision involving the safety or health of users and employees. There are four reasons for this change:

1. *Employee Morale.* The impact on other employees of dispatching a conscientious, intelligent objector like Geary is enormous. As discussed earlier, a superior cannot make consistently good decisions without understanding the pros and cons of each idea. Subordinates will not present the pros and cons if the question in their minds becomes "What does the boss want us to say?" rather than "What do I think is right?"

2. *Image of Organization.* It does not take many newspaper write-ups of a case like Geary's to form an image in the public mind of an arbitrary, totalitarian management system. This does *not* mean that the employee critic's opinion has to control, only that he or she should continue to be respected in the organization. In the account just given, for instance, Wallace was under no compulsion to agree with Geary, only to keep this devil's advocate on the payroll. For that he would have won public respect, not lost it.

3. *Profit and Loss.* In a substantial number of cases, critics like Geary are right. By continuing to listen to them, the professional manager increases the chance of being persuaded to change his or her mind when the facts call for that. The organization profits thereby. In the case just described, for instance, it appears that Geary was right; had his counsel been taken, the corporate bottom line should have benefited. Several years after Geary was discharged, U.S. Steel began marketing the very S-95 casing manufactured by A. O. Smith that Steel had tried vainly to compete with. It sold the rival casing through its wholly owned distributor, Oilwell Supply. (The deal was made possible because A. O. Smith had been acquired by Lone Star Steel.)

4. *The Law.* In a few short years prior to the Pennsylvania Supreme Court's decision, the law on retaliatory discharge came close to being turned around. This is an indicator of how fast judicial opinions can change in an age of ubiquitous public anxiety and concern over the effects of technology. Suppose the case were to come up to Pennsylvania's high court

today? I would predict that Geary would win, for Justice Roberts' approach to the problem has been gaining legal ground steadily in the industrial states.

VIOLATIONS OF PERSONAL INTEGRITY AND LIFE-STYLE

A superior's prerogative to manipulate the reputation of an employee or control subordinates' life-styles also is being cut back sharply. This prerogative, like some of the others, once was assured by the senior's ability to fire and penalize at will. Today, however, the senior does that at his or her own peril. He or she runs a strong risk of disapproval from peers as well as from subordinates, the community, and the media. For instance, bitter satires of companies that want their employees to conform to rigid dress codes have appeared in the student newspapers of many business schools. The companies that were pilloried lost goodwill in a place where they generally hate to lose it—happy hunting grounds for young management prospects. Again, there is a growing conviction in the management community that an employee should be able to inspect his or her personnel file and contest any piece of information found there—for example, hearsay or a vindictive note from a supervisor.

As a result of these and similar pressures, the day appears to be drawing to a close when a superior could bandy about a subordinate's reputation or issue a very arbitrary edict concerning clothing, political affiliation, exercise, outside activities, or other such personal preferences. Again, this is not to say that the superior is powerless. Far from it. In numerous companies and agencies it is still permissible for a senior to stuff a disliked subordinate's file with damaging and inaccurate information that other supervisors can see but the subordinate cannot. In numerous companies and agencies superiors still issue edicts against women wearing trousers and men wearing turtleneck shirts, even though those personal preferences have no apparent relationship to sales or public relations. What is more, in the most enlightened organizations a superior continues to have considerable discretion over such matters. For example, in one very rights-conscious bank that I know of, superiors still set dress standards *within "reasonable" limits*. And I know of no organization where the managerial grapevine, which influences many judgments about subordinates, is not influenced more by superiors' opinions, right or wrong, than by subordinates' opinions.

During the past couple of decades, judges and arbitrators have been reinforcing social norms and legalizing, so to speak, the curtailment of management's prerogative. The following account, involving the same state court system as the Geary case, suggests the general drift of opinion.

The Filching of a Good Name [4]

Early in 1974 William Berg took a job at Consolidated Freightways as a supervisor in a Pittsburgh terminal. The father of four children, he was happy about his job and looked forward to a long partnership with Consolidated. His past employment record presented, like most people's, a picture of ups and downs in job fulfillment. After an honorable discharge from the U.S. Army after World War II, he had enrolled at Penn State University, studied dairy manufacturing, and married while in college. After college he worked at various dairies, became assistant plant manager in one, went into selling, then became a supervisor at a freight company. Consolidated was his second employer in the trucking industry.

On the night of September 27, while working as assistant supervisor on the night shift, Berg went looking for Frankie Mann, the yard hoestler for Berg and sometimes dock hand for the night supervisor. Hearing a truck moving in the terminal yard, and thinking that Mann was driving the truck, Berg moved toward the entrance door of the building. There he came across Mann. Berg asked who was moving the truck. Mann replied, "No one was moving a truck. We've been ripped off." When Berg asked by whom, Mann reportedly replied, "I am not going to tell, they'll get caught." Berg said that if Mann wouldn't tell him about it, he would call the FBI. When Mann wouldn't, Berg called the Pittsburgh branch of the FBI and reported the incident. Berg advised the FBI that he had no idea who was ripping off the terminal, but if he did learn, he would immediately report to Consolidated and the FBI.

On October 3 the FBI came to the terminal and interrogated Berg's supervisor for three hours. They also questioned several dock hands. Berg was given no information about these discussions. The supervisor drove off with the FBI; the dock hands were sent back to work under Berg. At the end of the shift Paul Ray, the terminal manager, called Berg to his office. The security head of Consolidated was present with Ray. The two set upon Berg, suggesting that a major theft had transpired which Berg should have known about. Berg's rebuttals were ignored; he was told that if he did not resign he would be fired. Ray explained that Berg was "losing control of the men." Upon resignation, Berg says he was promised a good recommendation and an extra week's pay (neither of which he later received). Berg didn't know why he was being fired and was given no reason beyond the statement about losing control. He was concerned about the fact that he was terminated following the uncovering of the theft; he feared he would be viewed as guilty by association because he had been fired.

[4] This account is drawn from court records, correspondence with Mr. and Mrs. Berg, and local newspaper stories.

As FBI records later showed, neither Ray nor the FBI checked on the freight Ray had reported stolen until October 11. Of three shipments reported stolen, two were found complete except for a few pieces. The third shipment was not located. (Berg did not obtain this information until after his trial by using his privilege under the Freedom of Information Act.) The dock hand suspects were continued for the next six months as Consolidated employees; the night supervisor, after a good recommendation from Ray, got another job. However, Berg was on the streets without an explanation for his dismissal.

Berg learned that he was given a good recommendation, as promised. When he asked another supervisor what he had told the FBI when interviewed, the man reportedly replied, "I was an undercover agent." The man was disturbed that Berg had lost his job—that wasn't supposed to have happened. When Berg and his wife Bernice questioned the FBI, they were told that the supervisor was a suspect in the theft case.

In vain Berg tried to get Consolidated's corporate headquarters in California to review his dismissal. He learned of scandalous stories being told to dockworkers as to why he had been dismissed. He telephoned an attorney and was told, "You might as well forget a suit. An employer can fire you for any reason if you are not in a union."

Former co-workers were calling Berg to ask what had happened. He had no quick reply. He borrowed money from his seventy-five-year-old mother-in-law to save his home. In addition, since Consolidated had cut off certain dental claims he had filed, he had to proceed to small-claims court to receive the payments due him.

For many months the family lived off his unemployment compensation and earnings from odd jobs. He and his wife began reading up on the law and contacting attorneys. After Stanley M. Stein agreed to represent them on a contingency-fee basis, they sued Consolidated Freightways and Ray in the Allegheny County Court late in 1974. He alleged that the defendants had defamed him by accusing him of criminal dishonesty and had made it impossible for him to get work in another trucking company.

Midway through the proceedings, Consolidated offered to settle with him for $7,500; he turned down the offer since the company would not also give him a letter of recommendation stating that he was trustworthy. In May 1978 he won a jury verdict for $40,600. Waving the *Geary* decision, the company and Ray appealed to the Pennsylvania Superior Court. When that court affirmed the trial court's decision, the defendants appealed to the Supreme Court of Pennsylvania. Early in 1981, that court, too, held in Berg's favor.

When Consolidated sent its check to Berg, the following words were typed at the bottom: "For an unjust dismissal."

In *Othello,* Shakespeare has Iago say,

> Who steals my purse steals trash; 'tis something, nothing;
> 'Twas mine, 'tis his, and has been slave to thousands;
> But he that filches from me my good name
> Robs me of that which not enriches him,
> And makes me poor indeed.

DISAGREEMENTS OVER ETHICAL ISSUES

A third sector where prerogatives are weak and rights are strong is the handling of disagreements over the ethics, propriety, and wisdom of a management decision. Although managers are entitled to expect subordinates to comply with a superior's decision and follow through on it, they are not entitled to dictate subordinates' personal views about the matter, whether expressed inside or outside the organization, as long as the expression is not destructive. Although there is only hazy legal support for this position in the corporate world, it is well supported in other ways.

First, federal civil service rules have long recognized the right of a subordinate to free speech on questions of ethics and responsibility. Since the U.S. Supreme Court's *Pickering* decision in 1969, the federal courts have affirmed such a right, at least in the limited number of cases brought before them. Of course, neither civil service officials nor the judges want the right to be used as an excuse for disobedience, slacking off on the job, or needlessly upsetting other employees.

Second, arbitrators have generally recognized the right of an employee in a unionized company to express an opinion contrary to that of management, in words or action—again, so long as the expression is not vindictive or destructive. When subpoenaed, employees can testify under oath against their employers; a worker in a General Motors plant is free to drive a Ford (though he or she is not free to work weekends for a Ford dealer, which is seen as disloyalty); a subordinate is free to work for a community organization that takes an opposing position to top management's on the morality of a war or the ethics of school desegregation; and so on.

Third, employee morale stands to gain from a limited right of free speech. There is bound to be a lot of cynicism about the organization in the heart of an employee who, instilled with the norms of a democratic society, finds that the work atmosphere is totalitarian.

Fourth, and perhaps most important, capitalism has no future if it is seen as amoral, neutral to ethical concerns, and uninterested in societal values. Companies and public agencies must not be concerned only with "where the bucks are." If their leaders generally agree—and I believe they do—that organizational prosperity depends in the long run on a strong moral and ethical societal fabric, then every company and agency is obligated to contribute to that fabric. The fabric cannot last long if organizations are holes in it. Just as an organization gratefully takes ethically concerned employees from the community, so it must give them back.

These general principles are easily stated, but specific questions and cases can be extraordinarily difficult to resolve. There is no good way of formulating when a subordinate's disagreements become tantamount to disloyalty and obstructionism. Midway through the 1970s, three engineers of General Electric Company, which was building nuclear reactors, quit their jobs in order to publicize their views about the dangers of nuclear power plants. Was it necessary for them to resign? A company official told the press the answer had to be yes. Was he right? Even if we grant, for the sake of argument, that the engineers were right and that society needed to be alerted, were they justified in taking good salaries and fringe benefits from their employer if they sought to put an end to the employer's business?

For an unusual illustration of opposing views of employee free speech, and of the bizarre results such a conflict may lead to, let us turn to a drama that took place in Florida.

The Case of the Talkative Town Water-Tester [5]

When the city of North Miami Beach hired Glenn Greenwald as a chemist in the public utilities department in 1973, he was paying off a $3,000 loan that had helped him get through college, studying technical books at night, and hoping he could soon get into scientific research. A twenty-three-year-old bachelor, he was living the frugal life. With his long hair flowing and shirt open, he often jogged or biked to work from his small apartment, not only because he believed in physical fitness but also to save on bus fare.

He was only the second chemist hired by North Miami Beach. The first one, whose place he took, had gone on into teaching and academic research. Greenwald appeared to have the same kind of inquiring scientific mind that his predecessor had. Some years earlier, while attending North Miami High School, Greenwald had been a finalist in a science contest sponsored by the Westinghouse Company. He had then been called one of the top forty young scientists in the country. His two bosses in the city department, Raymond Van Loon and Michael Estok, considered him to be very smart.

---

[5] This account is based on official records of administrative hearings, local newspaper stories, and an interview with Glenn Greenwald.

One of his jobs was to test the city's water supply. He would take samples, test them for purity and drinkability, look into complaints, report problems to his superiors, and recommend corrective action if he thought any was needed. For example, he would test to see if the level of chlorine, used as a disinfectant, was high enough. Sometimes he would take water samples back to the laboratory to measure the amount of coliform bacteria, associated with pollution. He would look at the color of the water and taste it.

After working the usual probationary period of six months, Greenwald was given a permanent job and a merit increase in pay. The recommendation, signed by Estok and Van Loon, stated, "Mr. Greenwald has taken an enthusiastic interest and concern in achieving the best water quality possible. He performs well in routine chores and has shown a profound interest in learning the complete water treatment process."

Greenwald's good fortune continued for another four months. Then, one Tuesday late in August, he happened to be taking routine water samples at the home of the Cohen family. He noticed that the free chlorine level was too low; there was only what testers called a "trace" (.05 parts or less per million). The water didn't look and taste right, either; there was a muddiness or turbidity about it. He took some samples back to the lab for testing, and that evening he ordered a routine nighttime flushing of water in the area of the Cohen home. By chance, the flushing, which means the fire hydrants are opened to flush out the old water and any sediment, was not done that night.

The next morning, Wednesday, Greenwald discovered that the overnight test of the water samples showed a positive and too high coliform count. Returning to the Cohen home he made some more tests, which confirmed that the water wasn't right. There was still only a trace of free chlorine, the combined or residual chlorine level also was low, and the taste, color, and appearance of the water weren't right. He took some more samples back to the lab for coliform testing. He wouldn't be able to get the results of that test until the next day but he believed that something should be done to correct the situation.

Unable to find his supervisor, Estok, he approached the department head, Van Loon. "I think we ought to have a daytime flushing," Greenwald recommended. "That water could make them sick." He explained that he had no conclusive evidence but "just a strong feeling." Daytime flushing was avoided if possible in the city, for a variety of reasons, but Van Loon, who trusted the young chemist's judgment, agreed and ordered it to be done. Greenwald then left for the Cohen residence to observe the procedure.

Only minutes later, Estok learned what had been done. Disturbed, he raced off after Greenwald, found him at the Cohen house, and said, "What's going on here?" Greenwald told him about the tests but Estok, unconvinced, threw cold water on his reasoning. A daytime flushing shouldn't have been ordered in an affluent area of the city, he said. Not that it caused any harm—it didn't—but all the splashing around could get a few people worried and start a flow of telephone calls to the department or complaints to the city hall.

They argued. There was no reason to panic, Estok claimed. Two more samples had yet to be taken; also, there was some residual chlorine, not a complete lack of it. According to Estok, Greenwald accused his superior of trying to hide facts from the public. "You're wrong!" Estok cried. "And under no circumstances are you to make a public announcement until the proper number of samples are taken and the results prove positive."

But it was too late for Estok to stop the flushing procedure. Around midmorning the neighborhood water lines were flushed. As the fire hydrants poured water into the streets, it became apparent that a heavy sludge was in the system. Resampling after the flushing, Greenwald found the chlorine levels to be higher but not high enough to meet the standard. He took more samples for a coliform count at the lab.

Back at the office, he was ordered to appear at a 3 P.M. meeting with Estok and Van Loon. You have "outdone yourself this time," Estok told him. Greenwald knew he was in hot water.

At the afternoon meeting, Estok and Van Loon began by telling Greenwald that he was an excellent and conscientious chemist. However, they said, he should look for a job elsewhere—perhaps at a health agency. He was too health-oriented and research-oriented for the job; he was spending too much time *looking* for bacteria in the water. Besides, he was immature. Another thing they didn't like was his jogging to work. What might people be saying? As if that weren't bad enough, they understood he was using a city shower after jogging or biking to work. In addition they thought his appearance wasn't right—he was too much of a "free spirit."

Possibly of the greatest importance to Estok and Van Loon, they may have *thought*—the evidence on this point is not clear—that Greenwald had leaked word of the danger to residents in the Cohen neighborhood. To them, that would have been rank insubordination. They resented even that he had talked about the positive test cultures in front of the office secretaries.

"Am I being fired?" Greenwald asked.

Van Loon said no, that he wanted to think things over and would tell Greenwald the next day what their decision was. In the meantime, however, wouldn't Greenwald consider submitting his resignation. If he did, they promised, he would not lose two weeks' sick pay due him. A meeting was scheduled for the three of them at noon the next day.

Before the Thursday noon meeting, however, some fateful events occurred. Around 9 A.M. on Thursday, the coliform tests taken Wednesday before the flushing showed the presence of eleven large coliform colonies in the Cohen water system. This finding, in addition to the findings of a low level of free available chlorine and excessive turbidity, made Greenwald very uneasy. He worried even though the samples taken after the flushing showed no problem, and even though the samples taken at neighboring houses looked okay. He told Estok about the high coliform count and left to make some further tests at the Cohen premises.

At the Cohen residence at 10 A.M., Greenwald began taking water samples again. While he was doing this, fifteen-year-old Franklin Cohen, observing with interest, asked him why he was sampling so much.

"I'd known the guy for a long time," Greenwald recalls. "First I told him I was just making another check of the water. Then I thought again, and I thought I shouldn't have to lie for my job. I told him there was a problem Tuesday with the water."

In his conversation with the teenager, Greenwald emphasized that the bacteria had shown up only in tests made Tuesday. He said also that he had drunk the water then and was feeling fine. When the Cohen boy said the family normally drank distilled water, not water from the tap, Greenwald said it would be a good idea to keep on doing that—distilled water only—and not to brush their teeth or wash dishes in tap water until he was able to call back in a few hours after getting further lab test results.

At noon, Greenwald found himself facing two implacable superiors. He told them that he enjoyed his job and would not resign, particularly since his initial suspicions about the water had been confirmed. He touched again on his belief, as he recalled later to a reporter, that "there was a danger of cross-connection with the drinking water being contaminated by some source at the house, maybe from the washing machine." In this respect he clashed head-on with Estok and Van Loon, who held that the water department's responsibility ended at the meter, that all any of them had to worry about was getting good water to the property. Greenwald felt that their responsibility ended at the consumer's mouth.

The young chemist's pleas did no good. Van Loon told him he was fired. Greenwald then questioned Van Loon about how he was going to handle the situation. He told him about a chemical analysis made of the samples taken just that morning, after he returned from the Cohen house, showing the water was still below standard. He also told Van Loon of his talk with the Cohen boy.

Hearing Greenwald admit candidly, right there in front of him, that he had told a resident about the water pollution, Van Loon was furious. He had already fired the rash young chemist for other reasons, he said; now he was firing him for insubordination.

Greenwald packed his personal belongings, as ordered, and left the laboratory. A couple of days later he received a written notice of removal from the city manager, Harvey M. Rose. "Pursuant to the recommendation of your department head, Raymond Van Loon, Director of Public Utilities, you are hereby removed from the Civil Service effective 1:00 P.M., Thursday, August 24, 1977," Rose began. Reasons given included Greenwald's violation of Estok's order not to notify the residents of the water problem, his use of improper techniques of analysis (the authority given for this allegation was Estok, who was not a chemist), and the allegation that he had "hit the panic button." "It is regrettable that a specialist, such as yourself, must be disciplined in so harsh a manner," wrote Rose. "However, under the circumstances, and the possible damage that your rash actions could have caused, we are left with no alternative but to confirm the recommendation of Mr. Van Loon."

About a month later, Greenwald's predecessor, who had gone into academic research, conducted a test of the North Miami Beach water supply that indicated dangerous contamination. This report made a major splash in the media and threw a scare into the community, especially when the 70,000 residents were instructed not to drink city water. A rumor started that pesticides had been dumped into the water—by a saboteur, by Greenwald.

Greenwald can only guess how this rumor got started. "What I gather from various people who knew something about it," he says, "is that the public utilities commission sat around and said, 'We've got to do something—it's sabotage. You know, that chemist who made all the trouble—he has long hair, he rides a bike. Yeah, he must have done it, that hippie did it.' They didn't give my name but they spread the rumor around—an ex-chemist, a disgruntled, recently fired employee, dumped the pesticides in. Well, who else could it have been but me? There was only one fired chemist in the employ of North Miami Beach—in fact, only two chemists of any type, the first one having left for Florida International University. It was on the air and in the papers."

Greenwald happened to be in Tallahassee when the rumor was spread. He was looking for a job and also hoping to persuade some people in the state's Department of Natural Resources to look into his firing. "When friends called to say the police were looking for me, that the water was contaminated, I couldn't believe it! I thought it was a joke! I wanted to come right home, but I waited a couple of days to see what the real story was."

The police questioned him and read him his rights. Greenwald was scared. Fortunately, his able attorney, Maurice Rosen, kept the police at bay, offering proof that Greenwald had been in Tallahassee at the time the alleged sabotage was committed. Help came also from his friend Jim Kukar, who happened to have some connections in the state's public utilities department.

After a tense waiting period, Greenwald was able to relax. City officials announced that the cause of the contamination was actually industrial garbage, which had seeped into the water because of a faulty valve in a city plant.

Now it was Greenwald's move. He prepared to file and appeal his firing to the Civil Service Board of North Miami Beach. He says that he received an offer, from the city, of having his record cleared and being sent a couple of weeks' termination pay if he would drop his plan to appeal. He can only surmise why the city was so anxious to avoid an appeal. From bits and pieces of information gathered by Rosen, who had numerous pipelines to city hall as a result of having served earlier as a city attorney, he gathered that city officials were unnerved at the thought of more complaints and bad publicity about the water supply. Although the water had been improved in recent years, it "was still not up to par, it didn't taste good," Greenwald recalls. There was talk of the Dade County water authority annexing the North Miami Beach water department, which would dry up a profitable source of revenue for the city as well as cause a loss of jobs.

Although tempted sorely by the city's offer, Greenwald decided to turn it down. "I thought about it, and I know I'm taking a chance of ruining my career," he explained. "But why should I sneak around and settle for a compromise?"

Greenwald's case went to the board in November. Early in the trial the question of his performance on the job came up. Production of the ratings would be an obvious point in his favor, for they would show that up to the fateful days in late August he had been in excellent standing. What did the records say? Estok, who had to answer the question, squirmed. They weren't available, he said. "They're gone, and I don't know where they are."

Arguing Greenwald's side of the case, Rosen said he should have been given a medal, not a discharge, for warning the Cohen family. The order to keep quiet about the danger was unreasonable, he insisted. He asked the members of the board to put themselves in Greenwald's place. Knowing the family, could they have gone around concealing the knowledge Greenwald had, hiding from them the possibility that there might be something wrong with the tap water? Would secrecy have been moral and responsible?

Rosen produced various experts who testified in Greenwald's behalf. An assistant chief of the county sanitary engineering division stated that Estok was wrong and Greenwald was right about the amount of residual chlorine that should be present in a sample to ensure freedom from coliform bacteria contamination. An engineer in the state environmental resources department testified that Estok and the city attorney were wrong in their belief that North Miami Beach was responsible only for bringing safe water to a resident's property line, and not for problems in the home that might be contaminating the water. City officials did not understand the state law, he said.

For the city, attorney Joseph Nazzaro had a different assortment of arguments. For one thing, he emphasized Greenwald's testimony that he was not sorry for what he had done, that he would warn the Cohens again, if the situation were to repeat itself. In his summing, Nazzaro stated, "There was something strange about this employee when he testified. He is a sampler, a tester, who goes out in the field, and yet, as you've noticed, when he attempted to raise the mike, he took out a handkerchief and later he used the back of his hand, as though he was afraid of bacteria. . . . Maybe he used a handkerchief when he was taking samples and contaminated the water. . . . To allow this sampler to tell people or warn people indiscriminately can cause great harm and fear in the community." [6]

But the city *wanted* health-oriented employees, said William Dresback, one of the seven members of the board, when they convened later to review the evidence and vote. "He was only looking after our best interests. Do we want someone who is concerned mostly with giving his superiors what they want?"

Others on the board took a different view. "I can't understand the man saying, 'I'll do it again,' " Gennaro Romano, another member, told the *Miami News*. "What the hell do we need bosses for?" Recalling that day, Greenwald feels that Romano's attitude was typical of one prevailing in city management. The creed was "My city, right or wrong," with the city being represented by management.

The board voted against Greenwald by a majority of five to two.

As he was entitled to do under the nation's Safe Drinking Water Act, Greenwald appealed to the U.S. Department of Labor. An administrative law judge, Samuel A. Chaitovitz, heard both sides of the argument. On the merits, Chaitovitz had little sympathy with the city managers. "As the facts clearly establish," he ruled, "it was simply out of concern and regard for the public safety that Mr. Greenwald approached his supervisor, the department head, and told him of his findings and intuitive suspicions. To punish or discriminate against a chemist for recommending a procedure which, at

---

[6] *Miami News*, December 2, 1977.

worst, would be a precautionary step, would be to demand that all subordinates at all levels remain silent if so instructed until harm has occurred or is imminent." The judge also cited a section of the Safe Drinking Water Act that prohibits retaliation against an employee who tries to carry out the regulations. He thought that Greenwald acted prudently both in requesting the flushing of the mains and in notifying the Cohen boy of the danger.

Despite these findings and convictions, Chaitovitz could not ignore a lapse in procedure: The law, said the judge, required the dissident to appeal to the Department of Labor within thirty days of discharge. Greenwald had not appealed until December, nearly three months after his firing. Therefore the judge felt the appeal had to be dismissed. (Strictly speaking, Chaitovitz only recommended thus to the U.S. Secretary of Labor. However, such recommendations almost always were accepted, as this one was.) [7]

For many months Greenwald looked for employment in vain; doors closed on him when it was learned he had been fired for being a "troublemaker." He went hungry, he lived off friends and relatives, he was unable to pay his bills. After several makeshift jobs, he moved to California, and in 1979 he got a part-time job at the University of California at Santa Barbara.

The Greenwald story has an important moral for managers: Don't deal autocratically with subordinates who object to the public hazards that may be caused by your action. Don't do this even if your colleagues support you. Because if the objector goes public, the chances are great that a hue and cry will result. If Greenwald's organization had been a private corporation instead of a municipal agency, it is unlikely that management would have received less abuse from the media or more sympathy from the judges. In these times when people walk around with chronic nagging fears and suspicions about the effect on their health of pollution, radiation, toxic wastes, and other hazards of products and services, it simply does not pay to challenge the media, legislature, or courts.

LEGAL PROHIBITIONS

Next, managers have no prerogative to penalize employees whose actions are protected by federal and state statues. Here we shall list only the highlights of legislative curbs; more detailed and definitive treatments can be found in other texts.[8]

---

[7] *Greenwald* v. *City of North Miami Beach,* U.S. Department of Labor, Case No. 78-SDWA-1, March 15, 1978.

[8] See, for example, *Employee Termination Handbook* (New York: Executive Enterprises, 1981).

Protests of Unfair Labor Standards and Practices.   An employee cannot be fired or penalized for protesting an employer violation of the Fair Labor Standards Act, which sets forth minimum wage levels. The same goes for an employee who criticizes the company or gives court testimony against it concerning unfair labor practices as set forth in the National Labor Relations Act, which proscribes a great range of arbitrary management actions, from illegal work orders to maintaining unsavory working conditions. Supervisors, although members of management, are protected in certain cases; for instance, superiors in management cannot retaliate against them for refusing to commit unfair labor practices or for attempting to prevent their employers from committing unfair labor practices.

Organizing Activities.   Perhaps the best-known restriction is on penalizing employees or prospective employees for trying to persuade workers to have a union. In 1979, over half of the more than 17,000 charges brought against companies by the National Labor Relations Board were for this reason.

Safety and Health.   Under the Occupational Safety and Health Act, it is illegal for managers to penalize an employee for going to the government to complain about unsafe or unhealthy working conditions—or for complaining to management about such hazards. Among several other acts with similar provisions, the federal Energy Reorganization Act may be the best known. It was to this act's protection that Michael Cotter appealed in 1981 after being fired by Consolidated Edison. The New York power company claimed that it fired Cotter, a veteran of twenty-two years with the firm, for threatening a foreman. Cotter claimed that his dismissal resulted from his complaining after safety hazards at the Indian Point 2 nuclear plant in Buchanan, New York. At the U.S. Labor Department hearing, Cotter's viewpoint prevailed.

In addition, the U.S. Supreme Court has ruled that management has no right to penalize an employee for refusing to perform a dangerous task.

Race, Color, Religion, Sex, National Origin.   Title VII of the Civil Rights Act of 1964 and the U.S. Code make it illegal for a manager to discharge an employee because he or she happens to be, let us say, a Mexican American, a Jew, a woman, or a Russian. Employees who believe they were victimized on such grounds can go to the Equal Employment Opportunity Commission (EEOC) for reinstatement and back pay. In addition, contractors for the federal government must take affirmative action to protect members of racial, religious, and ethnic minorities as well as women employees.

In legal theory, the aggrieved employee has the burden of proof. In actuality, if the EEOC happens to be in an aggressive mood, the manager had better be sure that he or she has warned and counseled the errant employee—what industrial relations people call progressive and corrective discipline—before writing out a pink slip. If the boss sees a prospect of an EEOC suit, one good way of obtaining advance protection, or "putting a board in your pants," as veteran observer Raymond W. Miller calls it, is replacing the troublemaker with another employee who happens to be a Mexican American, Jew, woman, or Russian.

As for gays and lesbians, they are not protected by Title VII, as this is written, but by a variety of state laws. Many observers feel that Title VII protection will be extended to them later in the 1980s.

Sexual Harassment. It is illegal for managers to harass subordinates sexually or to permit sexual harassment in the plant or office. The definition of *sexual harassment* is far from complete, but in general the courts are emphasizing firing or threatening to fire an employee who resists sexual advances, or refusing further promotion to such a person.

Age. Supervisors cannot fire employees between the ages of forty and seventy because they are "too old." The Age Discrimination in Employment Act of 1967, amended in 1978, is the protective statute. The unhappy employee may go either to the EEOC or a state court. The best protection, if the boss sees a prospect of a suit, is to make sure an objective, systematic evaluation procedure is used to decide that the employee can't perform the job in a satisfactory manner.

Handicaps. In companies having contracts to sell to the federal government (directly or via a prime contractor) $2,500 or more of services, materials, or products, administrators are not free to fire subordinates because of physical or mental impediments if those subordinates can be helped in some reasonable way to do the job, or if the job can be altered to suit the person's abilities in some reasonable way, or if a transfer to a different task can be accomplished without hardship to the employer. The protective statute is the Rehabilitation Act of 1973. Personnel experts believe that the act is most likely to be applied to employees who develop a handicap *after* being hired by the contractor company.

WRITTEN PERSONNEL POLICIES

Managers may be limited by the terms of personnel policies of the company or agency, especially written policies. For instance, if a personnel manual states that an employee may be fired only for reasons X, Y, and Z, a supervisor cannot dismiss a subordinate for reason A, or for no reason. This appears to be the rule in many states.

A frequently cited case was decided in 1980 in Washington State. One evening Juanita Voorhees, who had been working at the Shriners' Hospital for Crippled Children for six years, playfully tossed a few drops of water at a patient. The patient tossed some back; she repeated. She wiped up the water, and everyone laughed—everyone, that is, except the supervisor, who reported the incident in nonhumorous terms. Voorhees was fired for gross violation of her duties. When she took the hospital to court, she cited its written personnel policies, which stated that an employee could be let go for any reason during a probationary period, but after that was a "permanent" staff member. The judge of the state's Superior Court decided this provision meant she could be discharged only for just cause, and that such a cause did not exist. The hospital's claim that it could fire a nurse any time it wished was repudiated.

Commenting on such provisions, the American Arbitration Association's president Robert Coulson believes that they will make employers more cautious about what they print in employee manuals. Coulson writes,

> Until recently, these booklets were not viewed as contracts. Employers usually accentuate the benefits of employment. Little thought has been given to protective language. Now some employers may protect themselves by including a statement that they have the right to discharge any employee with or without cause. Others may stop publishing such booklets or hand the entire problem over to their lawyers.[9]

The Supreme Court of Michigan made similar rulings in 1980 for an employee of Blue Cross–Blue Shield (described in Chapter 1) and an employee of Masco Corporation. Though receiving a "just cause" promise orally when he was hired, without any written confirmation, the latter collected $300,000 from Masco.[10]

NONCOMPLIANCE WITH CODES

Finally, there is a growing feeling among managerial and legal observers that a manager is not entitled to penalize an employee for speaking out

[9] Robert Coulson, *The Termination Handbook* (New York: Free Press, 1981, p. 175.
[10] See *Ebling* v. *Masco,* 408 Mich. 579. (The Michigan court decided this case jointly with the *Toussaint* v. *Blue Cross* case.)

against a perceived violation of a legal regulation or statute. In Michigan this attitude was legislated in 1981. Similar laws are being considered in the legislatures of other states. But even if a whistleblower law is not on the books, and even if the whistleblower is not protected by a union (which generally can be expected to come to the employee's aid in such a case, along with arbitrators), the managerial prerogative may be limited. On the bench, there is increasing impatience with managements that dismiss or discipline employees who object to violations of the law. The media can often be counted on to publicize the action of such a management. Many professional societies pledge their members to uphold the law rather than employer edicts, if the two must come into conflict. And the executive community itself is progressively less tolerant of using managerial prerogatives to subvert the law.

A related attitude is that an employee's courtroom testimony is not grounds for dismissal or other reprisal. Some states have laws to this effect. Many companies and agencies have policies against penalizing an employee for testimony under oath. For some time unions have protected employees who might have been penalized for this reason, and the federal civil service rules accord such protection.

Nevertheless, in all sectors some executives persist in retaliating against the employee who gives testimony they don't like. For instance, in January 1982 U.S. district court judge Robert E. Keeton ruled that Mary Jane England, commissioner of Massachusetts's Department of Social Services, was in contempt of court for holding an employee's testimony against him. In the summer of 1981, Ronald Newcomb, an area director in the department, had testified that the agency had not provided sufficient foster home and child welfare services for thousands of children. Returning on September 8 to his desk after a vacation, Newcomb was given his choice of resigning or being fired immediately. After his resignation, the Juvenile Law Reform Project, a state organization, sued the department, claiming that by forcing Newcomb's resignation England intimidated other employees and made them fearful of testifying in the project's class-action suit against the department. Judge Keeton, having earlier ruled that the department could not take reprisals against employees for their testimony, therefore found the commissioner in contempt.

An instructive case comes from an advanced technology manufacturer in California. The fact that the case was not appealed means it lacks precedential value, legally speaking. On the other hand, the same fact suggests that the company realized it was bucking the odds in trying to uphold its prerogative.

The Case of the Chancy Computer Console [11]

In Marvin Murray's mind, the problem was as clear and uncomplicated as Ohm's law about voltage and current. The company that employed him, Microform Data Systems, was making a computer console that could be dangerous for the telephone company operators who used it. The console was the main part of a new directory-assistance system in which a telephone operator, using a keyboard, got names, numbers, and other listed data quickly and accurately from microfilm. The trouble was that there was no one switch for cutting the power—no common circuit breaker—in all three power cords running to the machines. If something went wrong with the equipment and the operators panicked, Murray realized, they might not succeed in shutting down the machines. Compounding the risk, the cabinet doors were not safety interlocked, and twist-lock power plugs were used.

Just to be sure, Murray checked with the state's department of industrial safety. Yes, the equipment indeed violated the state safety regulations, he learned. In addition, it violated the national electrical codes.

Ordinarily, the rest would have been simple. Let management know and get a pat on the back for saving the company from a lot of potential trouble with customers. It was not a question of his business judgment against management's, or of his technical opinion versus other engineers' opinions. It was a simple question of fact: The consoles were hazardous and illegal. They could be corrected, and should be immediately. Murray could see how to make the corrections.

In reality, however, the rest was anything but simple. For Murray's superiors didn't want to hear any bad news about the equipment. The company was growing fast, it was planning for much more growth, it was experiencing the usual stresses and strains of a fast-growing company, and it was up against some of the toughest competition in the country. There were enough problems, they thought, without Murray coming in with a bothersome one that should have been taken care of long ago. Besides, the consoles were already being sold, and nobody had complained yet, had they?

Murray had not been on the job long for the company. Raised in New Mexico and California, he had married and gone into the U.S. Navy at the age of nineteen, served for three years, and entered the University of California at Berkeley. He had received his engineering degree in 1959, bringing it home to a wife and four children.

He had worked for a series of companies in California, including IBM and, for eight years, Lockheed. He had gotten divorced from his first wife

---

[11] This account is based on judicial records, an interview with Marvin Murray, and local newspaper articles.

and remarried, in the process acquiring a stepdaughter. In May 1974 he had started working for his present employer, Microform Data Systems. Microform was a highly charged, fast-growing firm that had sparked the interest of numerous investors and businesspeople. Since its founding in 1968, sales had leaped year after year—from hundreds of thousands of dollars to $1 million, and then to $9.3 million by 1974. There was no sign sales wouldn't keep on leaping (as indeed they did for four more years).

Hired as a project engineer, Murray was to give technical support to marketing and sales personnel, analyze the requirements of customer companies, design special equipment for them, and perform a variety of other tasks. His salary exceeded $21,000, a generous one for a young engineer in 1974.

Increasingly concerned about the safety problem as he checked into it more, Murray wasted little time in deciding to take action. He did not stop to confide in family or personal friends because, as he says, "I am somewhat of a loner." Yet he was well aware of the risks involved. For one thing, the technical director of the company, Bram Kool, was known as a difficult man to work with. From the talk of other employees, Murray had gathered that Kool was capricious and arbitrary in his dealings with people. "It was generally assumed," says Murray, "that if you wanted to get your job done, your best bet lay in keeping Kool from knowing what you were doing until it was finished." Yet Murray was neither awed nor intimidated by Kool. "I had found out very early," he recalls, "that veracity was not one of his long suits, nor was technical competence."

What made Murray willing to take the risks was his knowledge that the console was already in use in several customer companies, including Southern New England Telephone Company, New York Bell, Illinois Bell, and GT&E Company in Southern California. As the owner of some 3,000 shares of Microform stock, he was more sensitive than many engineers might have been to the possible effect on the company of lawsuits from injured users. In addition, he was far from sure that the company president knew about the danger; a company's top executive, as any veteran observer knows, can be efficiently insulated by his lieutenants from bad news in the shop. "I wanted to make sure," he says, "that either the president or the chairman was aware of the situation."

Finally, of course, he knew, as any thoughtful engineer must, that public concern is a professional obligation of engineers. The Code of Ethics of the National Society of Professional Engineers requires an engineer to put first the safety, health, and welfare of the public.

In the summer of 1974, Murray discussed the safety violations with his boss, Jerry Tennant. They agreed not to document the charges—at least, for a while. One reason for delaying was that a new design for the telephone assistance system was under way; another was that they wanted to avoid creating undue publicity.

However, in January of the following year Pacific Telephone and Telegraph Company, an important customer, found out that some installations of the equipment were violating the state's codes for wiring buildings. Tennant changed his mind. He instructed Murray to go ahead and document the violations—there was no time to lose. So Murray did that in a memorandum to his boss, and he sent a copy of the memo to Kool.

However, while this memo was being typed, and before it could be sent out, a meeting was held to review the design of the console and other equipment. Murray was there along with Tennant, Kool, and some higher-level managers. Murray told them about the violations of the safety code and said he was documenting the problems. Kool blew a fuse. Pacific Telephone was an expert in the business, wasn't it? It wouldn't have accepted the equipment if it violated the codes, would it? What did Murray think he was saying!

The fact was, Murray pointed out, that the equipment *was* faulty. All one had to do was look at it and compare it with the national and state electrical code requirements. As for Pacific Telephone's reaction, there was a widely held feeling among company engineers that, although the Bell System engineers at the labs in Murray Hill, New Jersey, were tops, the technical people in the operating companies sometimes were not. From time to time, Murray said, they acted as if they had an I.Q. "about one point above that of a duck."

Kool was unswayed. He didn't see how Murray could be right and all the other engineers wrong, and he didn't want to have such a problem flashing around in his mental circuits. He wanted to get on with the job as he wished to conceive it.

At a meeting soon after, Murray again raised his concerns. He suggested what kind of device could be installed on the directory-assistance system to make it safe and in compliance with the law. None of these words soothed Kool.

Kool called Tennant in and, according to Murray, asked Tennant to fire him. Tennant refused. Kool then made a swift organization change, transferring Tennant to another department. Now Kool had Murray reporting to him directly—right where he wanted him.

About two weeks later, Kool fired Murray. It seems likely that he pulled the plug in retaliation for Murray's complaints. Of course, Kool denied this motive. Murray was not fired, Kool told a reporter for *Electronic Engineering News*. "He was laid off for lack of work." You see, he explained, the system repackaging job was complete and Microform no longer needed Murray on its payroll. However, as indicated earlier, there was no lack of work at Microform in those days, Murray was not hired to work on the directory-assistance system alone, and it seems more than a coincidence that the discharge came soon after the argument.

Murray went job hunting. When he explained to potential employers how he had lost his job at Microform, they shied away from him. For nearly a year he searched in vain.

His second marriage, which had been subjected to considerable strain while he had been at Microform, burned out. "My wife was a hospital nurse," he recalls, "and apparently a very good one, and she could of course get a job any time she wanted, anywhere. She didn't understand why it was difficult for me to do the same. She felt that I was not really looking for another job. She said I should even take an hourly technician's job—she couldn't understand why companies don't offer engineers jobs as technicians." With the youngest of their children finishing high school and preparing to go off to college, he and his wife began going their separate ways.

Finally he got a job on a project at Food Machinery Corporation. When this project was completed and the staff disbanded, he made a good connection at Memorex in Santa Clara. For several years now he has worked for that company as an engineer. With his life becoming more orderly, he happily remarried in 1979.

While all these marital and employment changes were taking place, Murray was the spark in a significant legal development. Shortly after his firing from Microform, he happened to read about the whistleblowing case at San Francisco's Bay Area Rapid Transit (see Chapter 5). Learning about attorney Matthew Quint's role in that case, he contacted him; Quint agreed to take Murray's case. First he and Quint tried to settle with Microform, but the company was not interested. Then they filed a suit against Microform, asking $17,500 for breach of contract, $75,000 in damages for the aftermath of the firing, and $500,000 in punitive damages.

Shortly before the case was tried in front of a jury, the attorneys for Microform moved for a summary judgment. In effect, they were saying, "Look, there's no case to argue here. Murray has no rights." Legally, they were counting on the traditional common-law doctrine that a company can fire an employee for almost any reason it wants. But the Superior Court in Santa Clara surprised them. The common-law rule didn't make sense, the court reasoned, if it led to the violation of a public policy, and having safe appliances was indeed a public policy in California, as the safety codes made clear. The reason the old common-law rule didn't make sense was that it would discourage engineers like Murray from calling attention to safety defects and looking out for the public interest, as required.

So the case went to a jury for argument, and after relatively short deliberation, the jury found in favor of Murray, awarding him about $20,000.[12] (In the court's opinion, Murray was not eligible for the punitive damages because an employment contract was implied.)

Engineers, civil liberties enthusiasts, and others were jubilant. *Electronic Engineering News* wired the story in on the front page of its October 11, 1976, edition. "Certain to have far reaching importance is the September 15 ruling by a Santa Clara jury that an engineer may not be terminated if he objects to the design of unsafe equipment," the story began. Rejoicing, Quint told the press, "This is, to my knowledge, the first time in California, or anywhere in the United States, that an engineer has been protected in such a retaliatory termination."

Microform's management was less radiant. "We feel," Finance Vice-president Hugh Kelly told a reporter dejectedly, "that we have every right to discharge an employee." This lugubrious reaction notwithstanding, Microform did not appeal the verdict.

CAVEATS AND IMPLICATIONS

The new balance of managerial prerogatives and employee rights is portrayed in Exhibit 1. To the left on the spectrum are the areas discussed in Chapter 2 where prerogatives are strong and rights weak; in the middle, the areas discussed in Chapter 3 where prerogatives and rights are in a kind of rough balance; and to the right, the areas discussed in this chapter where prerogatives are weak and rights are strong.

How much harm may be caused by the weakening (deterioration, some would call it) of prerogatives at the right-hand end of the spectrum? From the standpoint of the public, none. The net result clearly is a public gain, not loss. What about the stockholders? In the long run, little seems to be lost, for sooner or later the management team that takes chances with the law, personal integrity, and public safety is going to run afoul, and the costs then will be larger the longer the violation has been going on. For the short-run investor, the answer may be different, for before management's chickens come home to roost, the stockholder may have sold out and bought into another corporation.

In any event, some implications for managers seem clear. First, take time to learn what laws may protect your subordinates if they protest or criticize your decision, or leak the action to a government agency. For a given indus-

---

[12] *Murray v. Microform Data Systems, Inc.*, Santa Clara Superior Court No. 337237 (October 1976).

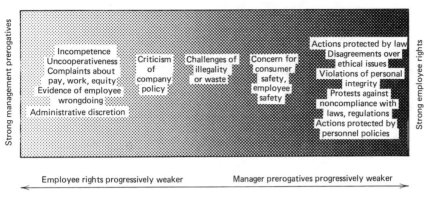

Strong management prerogatives

Strong employee rights

Incompetence
Uncooperativeness
Complaints about
pay, work, equity
Evidence of employee
wrongdoing
Administrative discretion

Criticism
of
company
policy

Challenges of
illegality
or waste

Concern for
consumer
safety,
employee
safety

Actions protected by law
Disagreements over
ethical issues
Violations of personal
integrity
Protests against
noncompliance with
laws, regulations
Actions protected by
personnel policies

Employee rights progressively weaker   Manager prerogatives progressively weaker

EXHIBIT 1

try, the laws are not numerous, and little study time is required for a problem area that can, if you run afoul of it, cause considerable anguish.

Second, don't try to "manage" the reputation of a subordinate. Though your action may seem tempting and convenient from a narrow administrative viewpoint, it runs directly against the grain of employees who increasingly believe they have a right to be treated with dignity and respect, even if they have no right to a job.

Finally, don't try to extend your authority and executive power into ethical issues. Even though you may be better informed than most citizens and possess worlds of insight and understanding, people outside your administrative world are not going to accept your claims. Argue your position, speak your mind, present your case as persuasively as you can, but don't expect anyone to be persuaded because you are a manager. If you can persuade them, you must do so as an equal.

> Men are never so likely to settle a question rightly
> as when they discuss it freely.
>
> THOMAS MACAULAY

5

THE THIRD DIMENSION

In one part of Homer's *Iliad,* Agamemnon, who is the commander of the Greek forces in the Trojan War and called "king of men," leads his armies to Troy to get back the beautiful Helen, who had been abducted. The Greeks besiege Troy for ten years. In the tenth year, Agamemnon steals for his concubine the daughter of Chryses, the priest of Apollo. The priest walks in anguish by the surf and prays to Apollo for her return. Apollo answers his prayers by visiting a deadly plague on the Greeks.

Baffled, Agamemnon convenes a council of his top warriors and advisers. What should they do? The plague has gone on for nine days and has been taking a terrible toll. The best Greek fighter, Achilles, urges that some prophet be called on to disclose the cause of Apollo's rage. Agamemnon agrees. The prophet Calchas stands up. First he wants to know if there will be any penalty for speaking candidly. He says to Agamemnon:

> First give thy faith, and plight a prince's word
> Of sure protection, by thy pow'r and sword.
> For I must speak what wisdom would conceal,
> And truths invidious to the great, reveal.
> Bold is the task, when subjects, grown too wise,
> Instruct a monarch where his error lies. . . .

Achilles assures Calchas that no one will hurt him. So the prophet divulges his revelation: Apollo is punishing the Greeks for the kidnapping of Chryses' daughter. The plague will spread, says the prophet, until Agamemnon returns the girl to her home without exacting a ransom.

Agamemnon is furious. "With a gloomy frown," the chauvinist Greek commander starts from his shining throne. "Black choler" fills his breast that "boils with ire," and from his eyeballs flash "the living fire." He denounces the whistleblower—"Augur accurst!" he cries. Nevertheless, he feels bound to heed the prophet's advice and send the girl home as recommended.

But Agamemnon hasn't risen to power without learning how to make a good trade. He demands another woman for the one he's returning. One of his comrades must give up a concubine, the king says; Achilles would be a good choice.

Now it's Achilles' turn to rant and rave. He tells the king,

> What cause have I to war at thy decree?
> The distant Trojans never injured me. . . .

This makes Agamemnon angrier still, and his rising anger makes him lustier. His ship will take the kidnapped daughter back to her native land, he decrees, and as compensation he'll have Achilles' concubine in her place. Achilles will "curse the hour thou stood'st a rival of imperial power," Agamemnon tells the dissident warrior.

Achilles pulls his sword half out, and a free-for-all seems imminent. Old Nestor tries to smooth things over but the king puts him down. Fortunately, however, Achilles has a change of heart and agrees to give up his woman. He'll not fight for her, but neither will he fight for any woman, not even the treasured Helen, object of the Greek invasion. "No more Achilles draws his conquering sword in any woman's cause," he avers. The conference breaks up, and in the days that follow, Achilles sulks in his tent. Morale sinks.

Like a good middle manager, Achilles did what top management requested, and did it well. For his successes he was well rewarded. But also, like middle managers today, he was the one who paid the price when the realities created by top management didn't check with the promises. When what Agamemnon had *said* he wanted—to know how to stop the plague—didn't accord with what he really wanted, Achilles, who relied on the statements, was the one who paid the price.

In government agencies and corporations today, this phenomenon is familiar. Middle managers are probably the most likely members of the hierarchy to confront the ethical dilemmas created when top management sends the word out that company objectives must be met. If a government agency is under pressure from the administration to cut costs, or if the industry is in a recession, the goals become tougher and tougher to meet, and the probability of ethical conflicts intensifies. As many observers have noted, when a middle manager feels that his or her job or the organization's survival is at stake, he or she is going to be tempted to sacrifice some of the standards of conduct that the leaders have promulgated.

Unlike the leaders, middle managers often have little say in the setting of goals. And unlike production-line workers, maintenance employees, and others, middle managers are unlikely to be protected by a union from a superior's wrath if they put ethics ahead of results. Their future depends almost solely on their ability to serve up what headquarters demands.

In consequence, examples like the following occur with almost monotonous regularity:

Aware that Dorsey Corporation's aging glass-container manufacturing plant in Gulfport, Mississippi, was falling behind other corporate plants in productivity, the manager became fearful that the plant would be closed, throwing him and 300 other employees out of work. He was under constant pressure to raise production. A *Wall Street Journal* reporter was told by his wife that he knew that "as long as he kept production up, he and his men had a job. But when it fell, that was it." Secretly, the manager began altering production and cost records. In time he was able to inflate the value of the plant's production by 33%. The janitor was ordered to destroy the real records. The fabrication was caught by company auditors when the janitor showed them the actual records, which he had hid behind a chicken coop. The company had to revise two years of earnings reports downward, and of course the manager was fired.[1]

At a large Chevrolet truck plant in Flint, Michigan, managers were instructed to limit the speed of the assembly line to the speed agreed upon in General Motors' contract with the United Auto Workers. At the same time, however, plant managers were under pressure to produce better results than seemed possible if the agreed-upon speed was kept. "At Chevrolet, we're given a production goal each week that's predicated on the assumption that everything will go perfectly," a manager told a reporter. "The problem is that on an assembly line, nothing ever does. There's always a conveyor breakdown or high absenteeism or something. As a result we were constantly missing our targets, and the bosses were putting pressure on us to do something about it. We tried to explain our problems to higher-ups in the company, but we were told, 'I don't care how you do it—just do it.' So the managers arranged the installation of a secret box in the supervisor's office that could be used to override the control panel governing the speed of the assembly line. When the plant began meeting the difficult production goals, the managers won praise from their superiors. (If headquarters had wanted to,

[1] *Wall Street Journal*, November 8, 1979.

one plant manager claimed, it could have detected the fraud from discrepancies in the reporting, but it asked no questions.) Unfortunately for managers at all levels, the union discovered the cover-up, sued the company, and won $1 million in back pay for workers who had been working faster than they were supposed to.[2]

There is no easy solution to problems like these—and perhaps no complete solution at all—but one thing is clear: Organization leaders exacerbate the problem by penalizing middle managers for talking back. If they allow and encourage candid two-way communication, they sacrifice their prerogative to order that results be obtained in a soldierly, no-talk-back manner. This prerogative naturally makes life at the top easier and quieter. But something important and precious can be purchased by giving up that prerogative: a more spirited, energetic, creative middle-management group. If top management truly wants to serve the best interests of the owners, in the case of corporations, or of the public, in the case of public agencies, that gain is well worth the price.

The third dimension in modern management is frank two-way communication between managers and subordinates. It is policies and procedures that allow employees to vent their complaints, air their grievances, object to orders that would force them to act unethically—all without prejudice to their opportunities for promotion, pay raises, and interesting assignments. It is, in short, the "legalization" of certain types of dissidence. It is civil liberties. For unless subordinates can act in the workplace in ways similar to those learned in schools, family life, community organizations, and religious institutions, their work lives can have no wholeness. They leave their personalities and individualities, so to speak, behind them in the parking lot when they enter the building.

Exhibit 2 is a schematic portrayal of the three dimensions of management today. The first dimension, the best-known one, is *economic performance*—profit (or budget attainment, in the case of public agencies), productivity, growth, the "bottom line." This dimension calls on managers to plan, organize, and control efficiently as well as to match employees to tasks in a productive and rewarding manner. The second dimension, also familar, is *compliance* with the many laws, codes, rules, and regulations that govern the workplace. Even if it succeeds temporarily in getting good economic results, the corporation or agency won't succeed for long if it flaunts labor laws, health and safety regulations, environmental restrictions, and industry codes. Nor will managers succeed personally in the long run if they fail to observe the particular policies and rules set forth by top man-

[2] Ibid.

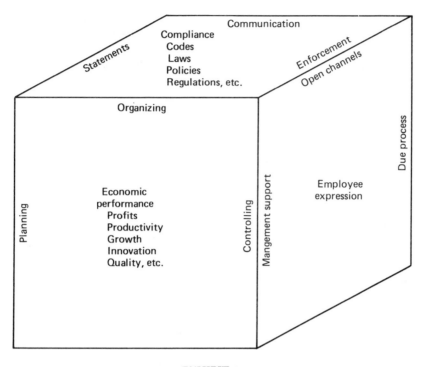

Communication

Compliance
Codes
Laws
Policies
Regulations, etc.

Statements

Enforcement
Open channels

Organizing

Due process

Economic
performance
Profits
Productivity
Growth
Innovation
Quality, etc.

Controlling

Mangement support

Employee
expression

Planning

EXHIBIT 2

agement—expense account guidelines, production quotas, equipment purchase rules, investment policies, regulations concerning nepotism, vacation rules, and so forth. The third dimension, the new and unaccustomed one, is the authorization and support of candid *communication from subordinates*. In a very general way, such communication is comparable to what we are used to calling civil liberties in community life. As in the community, there must be mechanisms for expressing complaints and concerns over the heads of immediate superiors who may not want to hear them, and for getting prompt, fair decisions in case of conflicts or persecution from those superiors.

A two-dimensional organization cannot stand today. It is like a piece of cardboard with width and height but no depth, or like a room with only one wall. The third dimension is necessary for the satisfaction of employees and for the long-term survival of the organization itself.

The surest way to kill the sense of wholeness for middle managers and other employees raised in typical American communities is to instruct them, "Just give us results, we don't care how," and "Directives are right if they come f:om someone higher up than you are." Sooner or later these instructions translate into "The truth doesn't count" and "Ethics is for ministers and scout leaders to worry about." Self-fulfillment and one's sense of "rightness" about a job and work situation cannot be manufactured by bonuses and letters of commendation from the chief executive. What often are the most exciting and exhilarating questions for an employee—ethical problems, conflicts of viewpoint with the boss, puzzles, tough assignments to "do right"—must not be banned from discussion on the grounds that "We want you to get the job done; don't tell us how you do it."

Many people have their favorite stories of the horrors of two-dimensional organizations. An example is the BART story.

The Engineers Who Went off the Track [3]

Judging from what people said, the event was carried out like an execution, only the three victims were marched out from offices instead of cells, and they fell to a legal discharge instead of a discharge of bullets. Holger Hjortsvang and Max Blankenzee were the first ones to go. On March 2, the security chief and a guard appeared suddenly at Hjortsvang's office. The security chief ordered Hjortsvang out and left him momentarily in the custody of the guard. The security chief then went to Blankenzee's office with another guard and ordered him out. All this happened quickly, and apparently took the two men by surprise. The two were marched by the guards and the security chief to the office of their superior, where they were given a choice. "Do you want to resign or do you want me to fire you—now?" Neither man volunteered to resign, so the superior told them they were fired. They were marched back to their offices under custody and ordered to remove their personal possessions and leave. The offices were locked behind them.

They got Robert Bruder the next day, March 3. By telephone he was ordered to accompany his supervisor, John Fendel, to the office of Earl Tillman at headquarters. Fendel drove Bruder there—a twenty-minute ride without conversation. Tillman issued the order without even saying hello. He said, "You can resign or be dismissed—take your choice. Now." Bruder refused to resign so he was fired on the spot. He was ordered not to set foot in his office again.

The year was 1972. The place was Oakland, California. The organization was the San Francisco Bay Area Rapid Transit District, better known as BART, an enormous commuting system then under construction and about 30% completed. The general manager who orchestrated the discharges was

---

[3] This account is drawn mostly from more than 100 articles in the *Contra Costa Times*, the majority written by Justin Roberts.

Bill R. Stokes, a persuasive, savvy administrator who had been in command for nine years and knew how, as the saying goes, to "push the buttons of power." Hjortsvang was a systems engineer who lived in Walnut Creek and had worked for BART for several years. Blankenzee, a computer systems engineer who lived in Milpitas, had served in the organization for about a year. Bruder, who had worked for BART for several years, was an electronics and electrical construction engineer who lived in Concord. Hjortsvang and Blankenzee made up half of the crucial group assigned to monitor the computer systems being designed by Westinghouse to control train and yard operations.

For the three engineers it was to be a long day's journey into spite. But if they were to pay dearly for the acts leading to their "execution," so was BART. What dictated the "mini-massacre" of March 2 and 3? Let us turn the clock slowly backward.

On Tuesday, February 28, two days before Hjortsvang and Blankenzee were marched out of their offices, Stokes told reporters that there were "no plans in any way, shape, or form" to fire the employees (their identities were then unknown) responsible for an outside consultant's report criticizing BART's planning. This explains why Hjortsvang and Blankenzee later were caught by surprise. Being identified by Stokes and his aides was not unexpected, but his statement on Tuesday sounded reassuring to the engineers; they weren't ready for what happened. In addition, the statement had been preceded by another reassuring pronouncement from L. A. Kimball, BART's assistant general manager for administration, who had said that there were "no plans about" to fire anyone involved with the critical report.

Going back a few days earlier still, we find Stokes himself urging the unknown engineers who reportedly were critical of BART plans to come to his office and thrash things out.

In other words, a series of friendly sounds had emanated from the head office, and although the three engineers might well have suspected that only lip service was being paid to the let's-talk-it-over principle of good personnel relations, there was also some ground for wishful thinking. Unfortunately for them, that ground would crumble.

In the meantime, however, Stokes's aides were grilling employees in an effort to identify the critics. Why were they so anxious? Turning the clock back more, on Friday, February 24, the board of directors was in session. This meeting produced a victory for Stokes because a hostile report, which precipitated the meeting and threatened Stokes's leadership, was beaten down. The report was made by an outside consultant from Palo Alto, Edward A. Burfine. The gist of the report was that BART badly needed better coordination—better systems engineering and control—or the commuter system being built would turn into an unholy mess. In fact, Burfine gloomily predicted the possibility of three breakdowns an hour if the planning was not improved. After Stokes, his aides, and friendly directors scoffed at the report, baring faulty assumptions and various errors in it, the board voted, 10 to 2, to forget it.

With this triumph in his pocket on Friday, February 24, one might have expected Stokes to relax and forget the existence of a few critics on his staff. But Stokes apparently looked at his 650-employee organization (due to double in a year's time) as if it should function without friction or hesitation and as smoothly as a perfectly running automated train. And if it haunted him that the organization might not actually be functioning so smoothly, it also haunted him that the train system seemed to be running on square wheels. There had been reports of slippage and failure in the Westinghouse-made signal reception equipment, and alarming signs of failure in the automatic train control equipment. Construction was behind schedule. Nasty rumors about failures in the Westinghouse equipment in the train cars were circulating.

Because he wasn't an engineer and couldn't evaluate these reports technically, Stokes's uneasiness on February 24 increased. Moreover, in the back of his mind was a challenge to the legitimacy of his power that had rankled for almost ten years, since a report in the *Contra Costa Times* in September 1963. That report disclosed that Stokes had been named general manager, but that the BART board was less than delighted about it. In fact, several of the directors were reported as being outraged. It was also reported that John M. Pierce, the former general manager, had been gotten out of Stokes's way by a ruse. A clique of directors, some reporter claimed, had induced Pierce, who also was not an engineer, to take a lower position in the organization (as district comptroller) on the promise that an engineer would be picked for the general manager job.

On February 24, therefore, Stokes believed he had to prove himself, to repudiate the notion that an engineer, not he, should be directing this enormously complex and innovative engineering project. At the board meeting that day, only one director, Daniel C. Helix of Concord, seemed to know the answer to the question on everyone's minds: Who paid and helped Burfine to make the study? Helix would not say. Stokes damned the report as "the most unethical thing I have ever seen." The critics should have come to him directly, he insisted. Tapping the table, he stated that his door was and always had been open to employees with questions or problems. But there was a note of defensiveness in his manner. Why? And why could he afford to be so scathing in his denunciations?

Two days earlier, on Wednesday, February 22, the engineering committee had held a meeting. Stokes's lieutenants on this committee had studied the Burfine report, in consultation with Westinghouse experts and others, and had found little technical merit in it. In fact, Westinghouse's vice-president Woodrow Johnson, who attended the session, rallied the shaken by announcing that his company was making astonishing progress in solving the radio signal problems confounding everyone. All train control problems on the Alameda County line should be solved by mid-April, he predicted cheerily. "I believe we are at last to the point where all our major problems are behind us." Johnson's prediction would turn out to be ludicrous.

Helix was apprehensive. Were the fears of the engineers a phantom? Later in the day, some of the directors on Stokes's side chastised Helix for having leaked the report a month earlier. His action was "irresponsible," some claimed. Why had he felt it necessary to throw egg in BART's face? Well, Helix answered, he had talked to several engineers about the problems in the trains, and he believed that they had tried in vain to bring the problems to the attention of their bosses. In fact, he added, they feared they would be terminated for being critical.

It embarrassed Helix to acknowledge that any staff engineers were in cahoots with Burfine. But this much he had to admit because several weeks earlier Burfine had said that several engineers helped him. Burfine also had admitted making the study in one day. If Burfine made the study in only a day, and if the report was so bad, then why was the BART management so disturbed?

About two weeks earlier, on Wednesday, February 8, another engineering committee meeting had been called. At this meeting Helix wanted to ask a series of embarrassing questions but the committee would not let him. But how did Helix, who was not an engineer or computer expert, get onto this line of embarrassing questions? He revealed that Burfine had given him an analysis. Everyone in BART was shocked. But the *Times* had gotten wind of the report; besides, Helix was a director. So there was no chance of sweeping everthing under the rug. Helix, however, would not say anything more about the report. He let top management seethe. This was a shrewd step from Helix's standpoint, for it postponed the day of discrediting the report. From the standpoint of the engineers, however, Helix's questioning was a tactical blunder.

Why was Helix more confident in the analysis of an outside consultant than in the conclusions of BART's own staff? The answer lies in a meeting held several weeks earlier, in mid-January, with the three staff engineers. They had requested an opportunity to talk in confidence with him.

After introducing themselves they explained why they had come to Helix. First of all, they knew he was critical of BART's approach to planning and organizing and willing to stick his neck out. Appointed to the board in

October 1971 by the Contra Costa Mayors' Conference, he had been questioning top management ever since then. But that was not the only reason, Blankenzee explained. The three of them were worried about the planning that was taking place. They had expressed concern to their bosses but the bosses answered, in effect, "Don't rock the boat, we're not interested." The three of them worried that if they continued to raise the question with their supervisors, they would be labeled troublemakers.

As professional engineers and members of the California Society of Professional Engineers, Bruder said, they felt obligated to blow the whistle. Both the California Society and its parent organization, the National Society of Professional Engineers, make it an obligation of members to inform their superiors about perceived flaws in technical specifications that may endanger users or the public.

At this closed-door meeting, Helix grilled the engineers, asking how hard they had tried to alert their superiors to the problems, whether they had really made it clear that the three of them, among the leading experts on the staff about computer control problems, feared the results of what was going on.

Hjortsvang had copies of memos he had sent to his superiors in 1969, 1970, and 1971, each mentioning serious shortcomings in the planning. His primary concern was that the BART staff was not properly overseeing the work of the prime contractor, the engineering firm of Parsons, Brinkerhoff, Tudor, and Bechtel. BART simply was not on top of the job, Hjortsvang believed, and the prime contractor was not being called to account for mistakes and deviations it was allowing in the construction work being done by Westinghouse. But the memos apparently had been filed and forgotten, for Hjortsvang heard nothing more about them.

Blankenzee said that five months previously he had asked management for a chance to explain what was wrong in the computer system, and how the problems could be corrected. But he, too, got no answer. Blankenzee also had copies of memos he had sent to his two superiors, one the superintendant of maintenance engineering and the other the superintendent of the power-and-way division. Though the memos pointed to flaws in the computer system for controlling trains, Blankenzee's superiors had acknowledged them orally and had done nothing further about them.

Bruder reported that he had repeatedly been told to accept, as completed, jobs that had not actually been completed by the contractor.

In sum, the engineers impressed on Helix that it was safety that they were most concerned about. They feared that the shortcuts and sloppy work were likely to cause failures in the automatic train control system. The errors were piling up because BART had not been overseeing the design and construction. To put it in another way, BART was going directly from design to construction and operation without any "systems engineering," the modeling, monitoring, and checking of technical interrelationships in a complex project.

There was concrete evidence of the engineers' fears. For instance, some years earlier, the Westinghouse equipment had failed to function as planned; when the company made modifications, the changes had not been charted and specified so that BART engineers could check them at a later time. As a result, BART engineers and technicians were unable to fix certain equipment that failed to work, because there were no drawings of the modified circuits. Earlier still, in 1966, at the Concord end of the Contra Costa test track, a test train car shot off the track and into a sand pile, for reasons unknown.

Helix listened thoughtfully. He knew that he was not the only director who was uneasy about what was going on. In 1969 director Wallace Johnson, an engineer and former mayor of Berkeley, had sent to fellow directors a report on peculiarities he had noted in BART staff reports and procedures. The word *peculiarities* was delicately tactful. For instance, one of the items was a progress statement from the prime contractor, dated July 11, 1969, that a station in Lafayette was 39% complete. When Johnson drove to the site, he found no construction whatever had taken place.

Helix began to formulate a plan of action. With the help of one or two such colleagues, he could commission an outside consultant to sit down with the dissident engineers and put together a critical analysis. Armed with that, maybe he could get somewhere. For a heretic like Helix, it was a delicious thought, even though it would propel him down a dangerous track.

In the minds of the engineers, as they sat in the private meeting, there was not much light at the end of the tunnel. Why were they so sure they had to take the risky step of bypassing their bosses, their bosses' bosses, and Stokes himself? Why had they no hope of being able, with sustained gentle persuasion, to catch the attention of their supervisors?

One day weeks earlier they had left copies of an unsigned memorandum on the desks of many engineers, middle managers, and senior managers. The memo contained a summary of various design and construction problems and it called for an organizational change so that BART could assert more effective control over the work of contractors. The reason they distributed the risky memo was a combination of frustration over management inaction and fear for themselves. From the preceding months, incidents like these were fresh in their minds: [4]

[4] The following incidents are drawn from the research and write-ups of a team of scholars at Purdue University: Robert M. Anderson, Robert Perrucci, Leon E. Trachtman, and Dan E. Schendel. See, for instance, their paper "Whistle-Blowing: Professionals' Resistance to Organizational Authority" (San Francisco: American Sociological Association, September 1978). Also see the same authors' book, *Divided Loyalties* (West Lafayette, Ind.: Purdue University, 1980).

Hjortsvang warned his supervisor about the poor design of Westinghouse equipment, and urged him to do something about the lack of test scheduling. The supervisor shrugged the problem off. In Hjortsvang's terms, the supervisor's attitude was, "Hey, thank God it's not our group that's stuck with that problem; it's downstairs or in operations, not in our shop."

Blankenzee, latest of the three to come to BART but quick to catch on to the design faults, worried aloud to his supervisor. The supervisor told him to stop worrying and suggested that Blankenzee not criticize Westinghouse so much "for your own good."

A senior engineer with whom the three dissidents had talked said he didn't want any part of their action. He said that he had four kids, would be retiring soon, and didn't want to jeopardize his security.

A manager (whom we will call Bill) was concerned enough to go to the group head and report the engineers' fears. Unfortunately, the group head didn't like bad news to go from his shop to the offices of higher-ups, and told Bill to forget the reported troubles and go back to work.

A chilling thought occurred to Hjortsvang, Blankenzee, and Bruder: If the control system turned out to be as disastrous as they believed it to be, the blame might be put on their shoulders, not Westinghouse's. It might be said one day that they were the ones who were asleep at the switch.

But why was the BART organization so hell-bent on speeding into a dark tunnel with warning lights flashing? Top management, and lower echelons inculcated by top management, seemed to be driven by a blazing sense of mission. Where did it come from?

In the early 1960s, BART was conceived, a dream that stirred not only Californians but urban planners and transportation experts all across the country. BART was to be the first regional rapid transit system to be constructed in the United States since the beginning of the century, when Philadelphia's transit system was built. Trains and ticket sales were to be almost completely automated. Under computer control, the trains at rush hours would travel speedily only one and a half minutes apart. They would be able to zoom up to 80 miles per hour in only forty-five seconds. When completed, at a projected cost of about $1.5 billion, the system would extend for 75 miles in three counties and would include a tube linking San Francisco to Oakland. About 200,000 passengers per day would be carried—not far below the volume of the nation's largest commuter line, the Long Island Railroad—yet only about one-sixth the number of employees on the L.I.R.R. would be needed, thanks to the powers of modern computers.

It was a dream of results, not methods, and that may have been one of its

THE THIRD DIMENSION 125

shortcomings. Those entrusted with managing the dream became obsessed with time tables and technology. The human side of planning and building received much less attention. In terms of Exhibit 2, the organization was conceived mostly in two-dimensional terms.

What happened after the mini-massacre of March 2 and 3, 1972?

For a few days after the firings, nobody but insiders knew about it. Then one evening Bruder, who knew Justin Roberts of the *Contra Costa Times* because two of their children went to school together, called up the reporter and said he would like to talk with him. Roberts, who already was suspicious that something was awry, lost no time in arranging a meeting. Bruder gave Roberts the details, and on March 7 the story of the firings broke in the *Times*. Asked on March 8 if the dismissals were true, Stokes answered, with the skill of a poker player who holds four aces but casually looks as if he has only two pair, "I'll have to check with my people. This is strictly a personnel matter." He added, "We must respect employee rights to things in this case."

Stokes's casualness did not mislead everyone. A week after the purge, state senator John Nejedly asked BART to explain the firings. He said that he wanted to make sure that the dismissals were the result of incompetence, not the engineers' criticisms of planning. "I would guess there was no simple coincidence like that," said Nejedly, possibly with tongue in cheek, "but I want to make sure. If it is the case that the firings were the result of critical remarks by BART staff engineers, then it is certainly regrettable. Public access to information would be greatly curtailed if one is unable to discuss anything with the staff on an informal basis without the threat of reprisal over them."

There now began an extraordinary transformation of professional opinion about the firings. Although Justin Roberts and the *Contra Costa Times* deserve credit for guiding the metamorphosis, much of the credit must go simply to the facts of the case as disclosed by the engineers and confirmed by a series of independent inquiries and investigations.

On Sunday, March 12, the California Society of Professional Engineers met in Oakland with the engineers. Their case, as they narrated it, appeared convincing to society officials, including its president, William F. Jones. The next day, Monday, Jones called Stokes three times to discuss the affair with him. Each time, says Jones, he was told that the general manager was on the phone, in a meeting, or otherwise unavailable. Wouldn't he like to talk instead with David Hammond, assistant general manager and chief engineer? Somewhat reluctantly, Jones agreed and waited for Hammond to call back. When he did, and Jones explained why he wanted to talk to

Stokes, Hammond replied (according to Jones), "This is an internal matter. What has it got to do with you?"

His voice rising, Jones answered that the society was interested in the well-being of its members as well as the safety of the automatic train control system. Jones warned Hammond that if society officials could not confer with Stokes, they would be forced to resort to legal action.

Under those circumstances, replied Hammond, he would explain to Stokes. Fortunately, none of the society's officials held their breath waiting for Stokes to call. They waited impatiently until Friday. On Friday they learned that, because of the threat of litigation, top BART officials felt unable to meet with them.

About two weeks later Jones announced that the society had decided to fight. "Evidence is mounting," he said, "that the public will be grossly endangered if this system is put in operation. I have instructed the society's attorneys to take appropriate action." The firm of Malone, Dennis, Schottky, and Pearl in Sacramento was to handle the legal controls and switches.

Under the chairmanship of Gilbert A. Verdugo of the society's Diablo chapter, an investigation was made. The resulting report by Roy W. Anderson supported the engineers' claims of mismanagement and led to several subsequent investigations by the California state senate. An attempt to censure the Diablo chapter failed.

Meantime, another professional society, the Western Council of Engineers, got interested. It, too, started an investigation, and this investigation, too, indicated that the smoke came from a real fire.

Next, the prestigious Institute of Electrical and Electronics Engineers, the world's largest engineering society, got interested. Stephen Unger of Columbia University, with strong support from IEEE's president, spearheaded the effort. The IEEE's inquiries led it to join with Hjortsvang, Blankenzee, and Bruder in 1973 when they sued BART. The IEEE board commissioned an amicus curiae brief, which was widely regarded as an excellent analysis and presentation.

The queue of authorities backing the short-circuited engineers kept lengthening. In the second week of April, at a meeting of the BART board, Thomas L. Follett, a lecturer in the Department of Computer Science at the University of California, decried the approach BART was taking. Top management, he alleged, was failing to build up a strong enough staff—engineers like Hjortsvang, Blankenzee, and Bruder—to monitor the design of the train control system, especially the computer controls. He said he found it deeply disturbing that there was so little documentation about the control system—he hadn't even been able to find minimal descriptions for use by a class he was teaching at Berkeley. He decried the cheery optimism of the

Westinghouse vice-president, Johnson. He warned the board, "You are obviously headed for more delays, more public embarrassments, or worse."

In November, A. Alan Post, an analyst for the California state legislature, posted a report highly critical of BART planning. The problems were more serious than people realized, Post concluded. What disturbed state senator Nejedly and others almost as much as the findings was that Post had had to obtain his information by a special probe because top BART executives would not cooperate with him.

In December, W. H. Wattenburg, a scientist, told a hearing board of the state Public Utilities Commission that there were serious faults in the digital equipment for controlling the trains. Wattenburg's testimony was followed by a report from Raymond R. Gentry, an official of the PUC; Gentry described more than a hundred malfunctions in train operations discovered in a two-day study.

While one after another the experts released their testimony, a personnel survey inside BART showed that morale was sagging in the ranks. As for life out on the tracks, it was hazardous. In April 1973 Helix took a fully automated ride on a BART train (a test ride, for the system wasn't yet open to the public). At first the train wouldn't start, then it stopped without warning; next it couldn't be started again because the doors wouldn't close.

In June, management decided to order two new and unbudgeted computers to help run the trains; it concluded the main computer was unable to do the job as planned. Long series of tests had made it clear that the main computer designed by Westinghouse couldn't function as planned because it received so much false electronic information from the tracks. The signals sent to one pair of tracks had a habit of radiating to adjacent tracks. The engineers called this problem *cross talk*. The cross talk between the tracks was sending conflicting simultaneous signals to the computer and was making efficient train control impossible.

The tale became grimmer and grimmer. After the official opening of the system, trains went off the track, unplanned expenditures had to be authorized, a track foreman was killed, trains had to be removed from service, new brakes had to be designed to take the place of those installed, trains kept overrunning the terminal platforms, and so on. In 1979 the director of a state transportation agency received a list of more than fifty safety hazards. A disastrous fire in the transbay tube that year led Justin Roberts to refer in the *Contra Costa Times* to BART trains as "rolling time bombs ticking their way to prospects of another disastrous fire."

The year after being fired, the three engineers sued BART; San Francisco attorney Matthew Quint, who later took Marvin Murray's case (see Chapter 4), prepared their case. Before the arguments were scheduled to be heard early in 1975, the management of BART proposed an out-of-court settlement for $75,000, which the engineers accepted.

The BART story is an awesome reminder to managers of the reality of the third dimension. It is there whether you want it or not; it *has* to be there in an organization of human beings. Even in the Soviet Union it is there. The only way to get rid of it is to eliminate people and substitute machines to supervise, coordinate, and do the work. You can reduce the third dimension to the smallest amount possible, as the heads of BART did, at least as perceived by Hjortsvang, Blankenzee, and Bruder. This may work if management's plans and programs are perfectly designed and if events transpire without a hitch. But if anything happens, as it did at BART, to make the third dimension loom larger in your scheme than you wanted it to, you are in trouble.

The BART story also bears on the themes of earlier chapters. It shows how employee expression, as it edges toward the right-hand end of the spectrum in Exhibit 2, takes on a meaning different from expression at the left-hand side. The three engineers were objecting to actions that could endanger the public and employees. This kind of resistance registers far differently in the public mind from resistance to practices that are, for example, only inefficient or poorly planned.

Finally, the BART account raises interesting questions about the tactics of both employee objectors and their supervisors. But this is a matter that we will deal with later in this volume.

SIMPSON AND SAMPSON RIDE AGAIN

To review the accounts of dissenters at BART and other organizations is to be impressed with the righteousness with which management often persecutes dissidents. In the 1970s Martha Mitchell was silenced for the good of the country, as President Nixon's aides saw that good. In the 1920s Billy Mitchell was court-martialed for the good of the Army, as his superiors saw that good. In the BART case, Hjortsvang, Blankenzee, and Bruder were sacked for the good of the rapid transit project, as Stokes and others conceived of the project. Seen as troublemakers who in no way can serve a constructive cause, the dissidents are out to foul things up, management tells itself. They throw sand into the gearbox. To use the legend of the old cowboy movies in the 1920s and early 1930s, when the good guys always wore white hats and the bad guys always wore black hats, the dissidents wear *very* dark hats.

One may be reminded of a beautiful fable published several decades ago by Munro Leaf, author of many books for children. The fable, entitled *Simpson and Sampson*,[5] begins in the castle of a medieval baron, where identical twins are born. They are named Simpson and Sampson. As they grow to manhood, they continue to look almost exactly alike. When the time comes for them to become knights, the baron and baroness decide that something must be done to tell them apart. They put Simpson in shining silver armor and give him a beautiful white steed. He rides forth to right the wrongs in the world. But they outfit Sampson in black armor and give him a powerful black charger. Sampson sallies out to sully what was good and turn right into wrong.

However, the results are not what was anticipated. When Simpson gallops to a place and tries to right a wrong, he fouls up. His efforts to help the peasants only make them worse off. But just the opposite results from Sampson's adventures. Though he sets out to annoy the peasants and make trouble, his ventures make things better; the villagers become happier than they were before.

From the standpoint of the organization, it is clear who today's Simpsons are. They are the intelligent, well-meaning, loyal, cooperative men and women who carry out the leaders' decisions without fussing or arguing. They are pleasant to work with. They don't rock the boat or make waves. They are team players.

On the other hand, it is painfully clear who the Sampsons are, at least from their superiors' standpoint. They are the dissenters. Just as a program gets moving, they find something wrong with it, and they won't shut up. Just as everyone seems to have reached agreement, they put their fingers on a fact that is wrong, or on an unexpected consequence, or on an untenable assumption. They are irritants, gadflies, thorns in the side, boat-rockers, wave-makers. The fact that originally they were on the superior's side makes their defection all the worse. "The man who used to be with you and suddenly wobbles off the line is doubly your enemy," Nikolai Lenin is supposed to have declared. "You must hit him first of all."

Why is it that the Simpsons in corporations and government agencies, despite their good intentions, may succeed in doing wrong?

One explanation may lie in their tendency to emphasize goals at the expense of methods. Riding forth to right the wrongs, the Simpsons are passionately committed to their worthwhile causes. It becomes natural for them to see any obstacle or dissent as a wrong. Thus, at BART the thing that was foremost in top management's mind was meeting the schedule for construction. This goal became an obsession. As the board goal was divided

---

[5] Munro Leaf, *Simpson and Sampson* (New York: Viking Press, 1941).

into subgoals for different departments to meet, the effort became more obsessive. The word went out: "Get the job done. We're not interested in excuses. *Get results!"*

But, of course, goals are not separate from methods. Good goals become contaminated by nasty methods. BART's ambitions and loftly goals became dirty when quality, precision, and safety considerations were shunted aside. Nixon's legitimate interests became a cover-up when Martha Mitchell and others were hushed.

A more elegant explanation of the failures of many Simpsons is cognitive dissonance. This fancy label, coined by social psychologists, refers to the tendency of people who believe strongly in a notion to reaffirm it vigorously at the very time it deserves most to be questioned because of fresh facts and perceptions. The original and classic study of cognitive dissonance was made by Leon Festinger. The study concerned a sect of midwestern millennialists who predicted the end of the world at a certain date. Assembling on a hilltop at the appointed time, they waited confidently for the hour of judgment. But the hour came and passed with nothing happening. Did the millennialists walk down the hill and in disillusionment decide they were wrong? Not at all. They trooped down the hill and stepped up their proselytizing efforts! They insisted that their calculations, not their premises, must have been in error. Cognitive dissonance was very much in evidence at the top management level in the BART story and other accounts given in this book.

Turning now to the Sampsons in corporations and public agencies, why is it that their "wrong" efforts may lead to improvement?

One reason may be that the Sampsons live closer to the everyday facts. Their information is not filtered by subordinates and reports, as so often happens at the upper levels. Their perceptions are not influenced by five-year plans or profit goals or grandiose schemes. For instance, Hjortsvang, Blankenzee, and Bruder personally saw or analyzed the equipment failures. However, when management superiors were apprised, they learned of the problem secondhand—from a paragraph in a report, or a number in a table of statistics in a memo, or an item of conversation relayed over the lunch table in the executives' dining room. Moreover, the paragraph or the number or the conversational item related to a large store of other and probably inconsistent information in the executive's mind, such as other secondhand information indicating that things were all right. Therefore it was easier for superiors to rationalize the distracting facts out of existence by considering them anomalies, reporting errors, or the work of biased minds.

In short, although organization leaders have the advantage of a larger and grander view of the operation, the dissident has the advantage of seeing a deviant or unpleasant fact in raw, unvarnished, undiluted form. If this fact then happens to be a significant one, the dissident is the one wno has the inside view of the future. His or her actions may slow the project down and cause deadlines to be missed to enable a revision of goals or policies, but such actions may be necessary to put the project on a more promising track. In "wronging the rights," the Sampsons produce gains and improvement in the end.

In 1973 the judges of the U.S. Court of Appeals, Fourth Circuit, ruling in favor of Delores S. Canaday, a clerk not protected by civil service rules and fired without being given a fair hearing, made the following comment:

> The Constitution recognized higher values than speed and efficiency. Indeed, one might fairly say of the Bill of Rights in general, and the Due Process Clause in particular, that they were designed to protect the fragile values of a vulnerable citizenry from the overbearing concern for efficiency and efficacy which may characterize praiseworthy government officials.[6]

Viscount John Morley once remarked, "Where it is a duty to worship the sun, it is pretty sure to be a crime to examine the laws of heat." This would seem to apply to the Simpsons. So too would Judge Felix Frankfurter's statement: "I don't like a man to be too efficient. He's likely to be not human enough."

As for the Sampsons, the sages also have some maxims for them. "Truth always originates in a minority of one," said Will Durant, "and every custom begins as a broken precedent." And Josh Billings observed: "As scarce as truth is, the supply has always been in excess of the demand."

---

[6] *McNeill* v. *Butz*, 480 Fed. 2d 323 (1973).

The right to be let alone is the most comprehensive
of rights and the right most valued in civilized man.
                                        LOUIS D. BRANDEIS

6

THE BREAKDOWN OF
MANAGEMENT BY FEAR

$\equiv$ Authoritarian managers harbor no illusions that they can control outsiders—a Ralph Nader, a Jane Fonda, a Robert Heilbroner—but they seem to believe that they can intimidate insiders when they want to. This is where they go wrong. More and more Americans are dissatisfied at living only vicariously with heroes who stand up to authority, as most people lived in centuries past. More people now want to do the challenging themselves. They want to conduct their own confrontation with the mayor or the corporate vice-president. They want to risk their own security in a conflict with management policy. They want to feel the pain, if pain must be felt, in their own limbs and bankbooks. The late Abraham Maslow put it this way:

Self-actualizing people are relatively unfrightened by the unknown, the mysterious, the puzzling, and often are positively attracted by it. . .

They do not neglect the unknown, or deny it, or run away from it, or try to make believe it is really known, nor do they organize, dichotomize, or rubricize it prematurely. . . . They can be, when the total objective situation calls for it, comfortably disorderly, sloppy, anarchic, chaotic, vague, doubtful, uncertain, indefinite, approximate, inexact, or inaccurate.[1]

[1] Abraham Maslow, *Toward a Psychology of Being* (New York: D. Van Nostrand, 1962), p. 130.

One is reminded of the end of Aldous Huxley's *Brave New World,* where the savage cries out that he does not want bland comfort and security. He would rather suffer, rather take risks. Or the Book of Jeremiah, where, after first vowing that never again did he want to become involved and feel pain, Jeremiah realizes that it is better after all to go on caring and suffering the woes of being human.

The authoritarians continue to assume that the rewards they can pass out will motivate subordinates to keep their questions and scruples to themselves. The rewards can be great, and often may work, but they don't work as often or as thoroughly as they used to. Although everybody may have his or her price, the price of buying out a would-be employee critic is becoming very high, and there are getting to be too many challengers to buy out. There are not enough promotions, pay raises, better-work spaces, larger bonuses, budget concessions, and more generous travel allowances to go around.

In a speech in Detroit some years ago, Jervis C. Webb, the head of Jervis Webb Company, narrated a personal story that captures the spirit of today's employee activist:

> I can remember as a youngster, when I visited my grandmother, a very strong Scotch woman who was, in those times, pretty well fixed. I was sitting in her drawing room with her when I first arrived for the visit, and she opened her purse and pulled out a brand new ten dollar bill. Almost in the same motion she pulled a little notebook out of a cubby hole in her desk and started to write. She offered me the ten dollar bill and I said, "What are you writing?" She said, "I'm merely putting down your name and ten dollars." Being a spunky little kid I threw the ten dollars back on her desk and walked out on her. It seemed to me that she wanted me to do something for her, like be good for money.

If Webb had not succeeded in management, he would have fitted perfectly the mold of today's employee activist, who is not willing to "be good for money."

So we have a paradox in the organizational world. Many managements of corporations and public agencies are applying reward–punishment schemes that were built for authoritarian control and are now outmoded, ineffective, and inapplicable to most of today's employees. A large number of these managements, though failing to recognize psychological, sociological, and cultural changes, have adjusted well to technological and marketing changes, rethinking their roles and reorganizing to meet new conditions. The abilities exercised so skillfully on the economic and legal dimensions of enterprise are missing on the third dimension, employee individuality. If organization leaders were to do half as much innovative thinking about discipline and punishment as about, for instance, marketing in the new legal environment or investment in modern technology, they might solve much of the problem. It would become apparent that punishment in the old authoritarian sense of humiliation, retaliation, and embarrassment is as outmoded as the eight-cylinder gas-guzzling car. It is outmoded because it makes the victim less effective, resentful, a drain on the organization. The employee who doesn't fit, who can't contribute, and who can't be trained to fit and contribute should be dismissed. Otherwise the American economy will not be able to compete and produce as it must. But the capable people should be instructed and treated with respect, whatever their transgressions, or they may not grow in capability.

Management's prerogative to dismiss the noncontributor is still strong. But its prerogative to dismiss the critic of inefficiency, immorality, or inequity is not so strong any more. So management must find ways to live with the able activist and the intelligent critic. If it does not, it cannot have a productive work force. If, employing the old forms of punishment, it cannot get rid of the employees it does not like, but whom society and the law like, then it will exacerbate its problems by continuing to use the old forms.

A FIEND'S MANUAL OF PERFIDIOUS PUNISHMENT

The trouble with the old forms of punishment is not that they are simpleminded or crude. In fact, they may be ingenious. The trouble is that, since the punished employees are entitled by law or personnel policy to stay on, the organization becomes a kind of purgatory. If the punished stay on, their influence is demoralizing; if they leave, they usually take with them needed talents—or, worse, haunt the organization in court. It is time to take a satirical look at the ruses and devious schemes used by autocratic administrators as substitutes for the diminishing prerogative to fire outright.

The Brown-Shoes Stratagem. Comedian George Gobel is credited with the remark, "Have you ever had the feeling the world is a tuxedo and you are a pair of brown shoes?" Giving an employee critic or objector such a feeling may be seen as a sure way of getting him or her out of the organization without legal pain. The stratagem is especially popular among authoritarian administrators who possess a streak of sadism, for it enables them to extend the pleasure of humiliating an unwanted employee.

Not long ago the marketing heads of a textile company became disenchanted with a young researcher. Although his findings were proving of exceptional value to the department and often led to great increases in sales, he was winning more fame than his seniors had won for articles published in marketing journals. Naturally they were resentful. Because of a company policy protecting employees with high performance ratings, the seniors dared not fire the prodigy outright. So they began a concerted effort to make him feel out of place. Important memos he wrote to management got "lost" and were not answered; his secretarial help was mysteriously reduced; his requests to attend professional meetings were turned down; "mistakes" were made in his salary checks, and so on. As might be expected of a person of his intelligence, in no time he got the message and left the company.

Of course, there is a hitch in this stratagem: It penalizes the stockholders. Such costs, however, are viewed as minor details by the gratified autocrats.

The Yo-Yo Trick. If at first the brown-shoes stratagem doesn't work, the ingenious authoritarian accelerates the tempo of humiliation using such devices as the artful yo-yo trick.

The approach was used successfully by the Food and Drug Administration in the early 1970s. Until its revamping later on in response to public outcry, the FDA executed many of these roundabout approaches brilliantly. The target was Alice Campbell, a highly capable medic on the staff who had argued against the safety of a new antidepressant drug that her superiors wanted to approve so it could go on sale to the public. After Campbell audaciously presented an unfavorable review of the drug and wrote a report on its clinical toxicity, her superior handed her an official letter of reprimand. When she asked him about the letter, he refused to discuss the charges, an act that, though required by personnel procedure in the bureaucracy, was conveniently overlooked by his peers. She hired an attorney, filed a formal grievance, and was scheduled for a hearing on September 20, 1973. Two days before the hearing, the superior rescinded his letter of reprimand and the hearing was canceled. The distraught Campbell asked, "What about the $1,500 I spent on my lawyer's fee?" Personnel officials answered sadly that she had no recourse.[2]

In this and other ways she was inoculated with the feeling that she was seriously mismatched in the FDA. She left the next summer after finding another position, and after her story had circulated well enough to discourage many employees.

One agency official I know, who considers himself the very model of a

[2] *The Whistleblowers*, Committee on Governmental Affairs, U.S. Senate (Washington, D.C.: U.S. Government Printing Office, 1978), p. 149.

modern manager, says he accepts the sinner's resignation with words like "profound regret" and "your leaving will be a loss to us all." He may even send a handwritten note of best wishes to the dissident at the farewell lunch. *He* thinks he's fooling somebody.

The Blow-Smoke-in-Their-Face Routine. Robert A. White, a veteran construction estimator in Oldsmobile's plant engineering department in Lansing, Michigan, apparently fell into disfavor with his superiors for an illegal reason—his age of fifty-five years. Sans firing prerogative, the superiors chose wily indirection. They moved his desk into an aisle where, White later testified, "No one ever had sat in all the years I'd been working there." Then a man who smoked foul-smelling cigars was seated next to White.

Getting the message, White chokingly resigned in 1978. But he did not disappear from the scene; he made some smoke of his own. He sued General Motors for age discrimination, then added the charge of abusive retaliation. After listening to the testimony, a Wayne County Circuit Court jury deliberated for an hour and awarded him $20,000. The *Detroit Free Press* circulated the story to other employees and the public at large on October 6, 1981.

The Fly-in-Amber Method. Unfortunately for authoritarian supervisors and stockholders or taxpayers, not all victims of managerial displeasure are able to leave as forthrightly as our construction estimator did. For instance, family obligations or community ties may make it worthwhile for them to stay on despite the harassment. For stubborn employees in this category, the ingenious autocrat may select another method: neutralization.

For twelve years prior to 1972, the FDA made remarkably clumsy attempts to fire John Nestor, a physician whose cautious approach to the approval of new drugs irritated top management. By 1972 it was too late to force Nestor to resign. However, the FDA saw another way out of its problem. "Applying true brilliance," as Howard Cosell might say, it transfixed the nettlesome Nestor in an obscure division where he could bother no one.

Later on, to be sure, a team of investigators under the leadership of New York University law professor Norman Dorsen failed to see the wisdom of this strategy and was openly critical in a report completed in 1977. They stated, "The payment of a substantial federal salary for almost no work is intolerable." This observation must have seemed naive and erroneous to Nestor's former superiors. *They* were able to go on their happy, prophylactic way without criticism from Nestor. They didn't sign his paychecks—the taxpayers did. And of course they weren't alienated by gossip on the employee grapevine—only Nestor's colleagues were.

The "Now You See a Job, Now You Don't" Ploy.   In the autocrat's bag of tricks, this one is unusual in its directness. To exorcise the dissident spirit, simply abolish the job. Thus when Paulette L. Barnes, after being promised a promotion in the Environmental Protection Agency, resisted the sexual advances of her boss, management declared the position she had held superfluous. Presto! No reason existed under the civil service rules for Barnes to stay on, and superiors were able to retaliate even though lacking a prerogative to fire her outright. Or so they thought.

Barnes took the EPA to court. In a moment of weak judicial resolve, as her rebuffed superiors saw it, the local U.S. Court of Appeals decided in her favor. Thereafter the superiors would have to carry on under a cloud.

A similar ploy was used at the Ellis Fischel State Cancer Hospital in Columbia, Missouri. In late 1977, an overly eager health physicist named Clifford W. Richter learned that some seeds of iridium-192 that had been implanted in a cancer patient's body had been overlooked and left in the body when the patient was discharged. Knowing that the error required reporting under federal law, Richter reported the lapse to the Nuclear Regulatory Commission. About a year later, Richter had the gall to report that another iridium seed was missing (this one later was found on the roof of the hospital).

An embarrassed superior decided that enough was enough. Undeterred by the fact that Richter's performance ratings had been excellent and that only three months before his first report to Washington he had been recommended for a $10,000 raise because of his accomplishments, the superior first warned the dissident about his treachery, then notified him that his job as chief physicist was abolished. All might have gone well for the autocrat had the Department of Labor, after hearing the case, not ordered in 1979 that Richter be reinstated on the staff, with back pay.[3] (The decision was based partly on a provision in the Energy Reorganization Act of 1974 stating that institutions licensed by the Nuclear Regulatory Commission to use radioactive materials for cancer therapy may not fire an employee for reporting violations of the rules.) So management lost face and following. A caustic write-up in the March 1980 issue of *Science* did not enhance the hospital's public image.

The Make-Them-Think-They're-Coming-Unbuttoned Tactic.   If despotic officials have time to spare, they can borrow some useful concepts from gamesmanship and psychiatry. One beauty of this approach, from their standpoint, is that it leaves no outward manifestations; everything takes

---

[3] The order was affirmed in *Ellis Fischel State Cancer Hospital v. Marshall*, 629 F. 2d 563 (1980).

place in the dissident's head. A showcase example comes from Foggy Bottom.

According to information released by the U.S. State Department a few years ago, a young black, Walter J. Thomas, filed a racial discrimination complaint while serving in the Peace Corps. Certain superiors were not pleased. Later he applied for a position in the foreign service. After he passed his physical, his earlier indiscretion caught up with him. He was ordered to take the exam again. During the second exam the doctor harassed him with so many questions that he flunked for "hypertension, hyperuricemia, elevated fasting blood sugar" and other impairments. When word got around, the effect on other young employees was not good, but presumably some senior administrators rubbed their hands together in glee.

Reflecting on another agency's defenses against unruly employees, one autocrat said, "First we drive the dissident crazy. Then we tell people not to listen to him because he's crazy."

The Promotion-to-Nowhere Plot.   A breezy means of punishment, though somewhat costly in terms of overhead, is to promote the unwanted employee into the wild blue yonder. Soon after she began speaking out against waste and ineffectuality in the division where she worked, a staff person whom I shall call Dorothy caused her superiors to put their heads together. Because of her brilliant track record with previous employers, the autocrats decided wisely that outright firing might bring the case to the attention of top management. So they promoted her to the position of director of management information services. She protested, "But there aren't any management information services to direct." Quickly the boss replied, "That's just the point. It's your job to create them." Of course, when she made valiant efforts to plan computer services, create a data base, and institute other standard programs, no one cooperated with her. Removed from the scene as effectively as a fat pitch batted out of the stadium by Reggie Jackson, she turned in her resignation within a year. The experience served as a cogent warning to other able employees: "You can only improve on saying nothing by saying nothing often."

The Mushroom-Farming Scheme.   Still another sophisticated scheme of authoritarians appears to have been developed by officials knowledgeable about the mushroom business. Mushrooms are grown in cool dark caves in a rich nitrogenous soil and, when they grow to size, harvested. Similarly, officials keep the dissident in the dark, embed him or her in manure, and, as soon as a head is raised, cut it off. The more indirectly and impersonally this is done, the more effective. For example, the notification of the chopping off might come by means of the grapevine or from a lower-level employee.

A well-executed example is the case of Marion Bryant, who joined the FDA in 1967 after teaching internal medicine at the University of Michigan and New York University and serving as chief of cardiology at Bellevue Hospital in New York.[4] After six years with the FDA, it became apparent that Bryant would not approve a new drug simply because his superiors and the manufacturer desired him to. It was painfully obvious to his superiors, if not to him, that beheading time had arrived.

Bryant later told the Dorsen team how he had learned that he was to be transferred out of the way to a new area: "An administrative clerk-type abruptly entered my office without knocking or inquiring if it were convenient for her to enter. She interrupted a conference between Dr. John O. Nestor and myself. Without preamble, she informed me that my office equipment would be moved within a few days to the offices of the Generic Drug Staff. Needless to say, this came as a most abrupt and profound shock to me. . . ."

Bryant asked the clerk under whose orders she was acting. She told him, and he went to that official to ask what was going on. The official appeared suitably embarrassed over the incident, but management stuck with its decision to make the transfer. When Bryant finally did get an official notification of the move, management's memorandum was addressed to "Employee."

Unfortunately for the art of cutting down dissidents, the FDA was later exposed, came under a fresh management, and began demonstrating serious interest in methods of due process for employees.

A variation of the mushroom-farming approach was employed by Edward J. Daly, the tough-talking chairman of World Airways. Instead of beheading the would-be dissident, Daly believed in paralyzing the person. Apparently certain up-and-coming executives in the airline made some ill-advised statements to reporters about the grounding of the DC-10 in the summer of 1979, and also about a strike of employees who were members of the Teamsters Union. Daly promptly issued a memorandum to all subordinates, particularly those feeling a tendency to be precocious. "No one, absolutely no one," he stated, was to make any statement of any sort to the media. "I will determine what response if any is to be made," he ordered. The reason for such restraint was that "the majority of senior vice-presidents . . . have no more than a 20% awareness of the overall intentions of

[4] See *Investigation of Allegations Relating to the Bureau of Drugs, Food and Drug Administration* (Washington, D.C.: Department of Health, Education, and Welfare, April 1977), p. 497. The study was made by seven experts under the direction of Norman Dorsen, professor of law at New York University.

the company." But this was not all. He wrote that anyone violating the instruction "will wish that he or she had been in hell twenty-four hours before the act of commission." In addition, the indiscreet employee "will be answerable to me on an eyeball-to-eyeball basis, and this experience will be in lieu of and worse than purgatory." [5]

With a delicate touch of understatement, the airline's senior vice-president told a reporter that Daly's memorandum was "something that strikes home very solidly."

The Anonymous Note Trap.   In August 1979, Rita Ward, an energetic and efficient employee of Boston's Metropolitan District Commission, happened to be walking by a photograph of MDC commissioner Guy A. Carbone. The photograph was one of several that Carbone had ordered to be placed in the Somerset Street headquarters of the MDC. Ward noticed that someone had taped a photo of a gorilla over Carbone's framed picture. "Who's that?" she inquired. A fellow employee answered, "It's the commissioner." Reportedly Ward quipped, "It looks more like his wife." [6]

Ward was not employed under the protection of the city's civil service regulations (she was a counselor on retirement and death benefits). Accordingly, as soon as word of her faux pas was passed up the line to Carbone, via an anonymous note, he fired her. "She verbalized an attitude that was demonstrated in her work," he explained. Though the troublesome Ward confessed afterward that the commissioner's wife was "really a beautiful woman," she was not pardoned. Other MDC officials anonymously criticized Carbone's act as being "like chopping a kid's hand off when you find it in the cookie jar, instead of just slapping it," but of course such demoralization did not impress the autocrats. Their dictum was that the rooster that crows the loudest is the first to be invited to the chopping block.

The Saw-off-the-Limb Ruse.   Perhaps the best example is offered by Joseph Heller in *Catch-22*. Lieutenant Scheisskoft is shaking in anguish because his aviation cadets are marching atrociously in parade competitions at cadet school in Santa Ana, California. Clevinger, a brilliant and perceptive cadet, feels a compulsion to inform the lieutenant where the fault lies, though his friend Yossarian tells him not to be an idiot. Scheisskoft gets the cadets together and implores them to help him:

"I *want* someone to tell me," Lieutenant Scheisskoft beseeched them all prayerfully. "If any of it is my fault, I *want* to be told."

---

[5] *Wall Street Journal*, August 8, 1979.
[6] *Boston Globe*, October 26, 1979.

"He *wants* someone to tell him," Clevinger said.

"He wants everyone to keep still, idiot," Yossarian answered.

"Didn't you hear him?" Clevinger argued.

"I heard him," Yossarian replied. "I heard him say very loudly and very distinctly that he wants every one of us to keep our mouth shut if we know what's good for us."

"I won't punish you," Lieutenant Scheisskoft swore.

"He says he won't punish me," said Clevinger.

"He'll castrate you," said Yossarian.

"I swear I won't punish you," said Lieutenant Scheisskoft. "I'll be grateful to the man who tells me the truth."

"He'll hate you," said Yossarian. "To his dying day he'll hate you." [7]

Clevinger falls into the trap despite Yossarian's warnings. Although his recommendations turn Lieutenant Scheisskoft into a parade winner, Scheisskoft loses no time in lodging charges against him—high treason as well as indiscriminate behavior. The three-officer Action Board finds him guilty and sentences him to fifty-seven punishment tours.

═══════════

Of course, this mildly acerbic commentary on the ways and successes of the autocrat contains nothing new. The strong man has long been able to devise methods of circumventing the obstacles raised by blundering idealists. A contributor to the *Wall Street Journal* noted that biblical sayings sometimes are proved in business. For instance, tell the boss what you honestly think of him, and the truth will set you free. And a century ago Mark Twain observed that this country has three unspeakably precious things: freedom of speech, freedom of conscience, and the prudence to practice neither.

Unfortunately for the fiend, perfidious punishment is a two-edged sword. Although it may kill dissidents, it also may kill organizations.

THE BOOMERANG EFFECT

Probably no specter worries the authoritarian manager more than the possibility that scientists, technical people, clerical workers, and other em-

---

[7] Joseph Heller, *Catch-22* (New York: Dell, 1961), p. 71.

ployee groups will become unionized. But probably no management approach creates the right conditions for unionization better than management by fear—or, as an executive in a company so managed once put it, management "by sheer terror."

Decades ago, autocratic managers laid the groundwork for unionization of blue-collar workers by letting them become fearful of employment insecurity. However, white-collar workers, engineers, and scientists generally did not turn to union cover because they felt uncomfortable with the personalities and tactics of union organizers. This situation might have been prolonged indefinitely but for two factors. First, the sophistication of union leaders has increased enormously. Second, new conditions in industry give even the best-educated employees an incentive to unionize that did not exist in generations past. If the fear of job insecurity is not enough, that fear plus fears of injury and sickness may be. In short, a kind of double jeopardy is growing in many workplaces.

The workplaces most affected are those involved with new technologies—chemistry, nuclear power, transportation, and so forth. For it is in such organizations that resentment of despotic authority will combine with a psychological condition called *ressentiment*.

As coined by European social scientist Max Scheler, and discussed by opinion analyst Daniel Yankelovich, *ressentiment* refers to massive, pent-up anger. Scheler used as examples the terror in revolutionary France, the Shanghai uprising of 1927, and the unrest in Germany in the 1920s and 1930s that paved the way for Hitler. Since *ressentiment* is destructive, and often self-destructive, it does not apply to many uprisings. For instance, the American Revolution, fought to create a government that would protect human rights, was not tainted by *ressentiment*.

Although *ressentiment* has not been noticeable in U.S. political life (not even, according to Yankelovich's studies, during the Vietnam War), traces of it may be visible in economic events. One example could be the burning of black ghettos in Watts, Detroit, and Washington, D.C., in the 1960s. The mass demonstrations against the proposed nuclear power plant in Seabrook, New Hampshire, in 1977 and 1978 provide another example. The demonstrators didn't agree on an alternative to nuclear power. They were divided in a hundred ways on the solution to the power shortage, and even on whether a solution was needed. They just wanted the construction to cease and desist. If there was a prevailing attitude, it was "Stop the world, I want to get off!"

Although *ressentiment* is not yet in flame anywhere in the U.S. economy, in technologically advanced sectors it nevertheless is a real and present danger. Here and there it may be approaching combustibility. As Scheler described it, *ressentiment* is the product of two critical conditions. First, people's bitterness and fear must concern the perceived threat of personal harm. Second, they must feel it necessary to act out the hostility because it can't be talked out in councils of action. *Ressentiment,* says Yankelovich, "refers not only to an intensity of negative feelings in relationship to authority but to—and this is of the essence—feelings that are bottled up, suppressed, prevented from overt expression." [8]

Are these conditions present anywhere? In some advanced-technology sectors, the fear of harm is personal. In the atmosphere where employees work, there is no sense of detachment or remoteness from the dangers of the chemicals, products, technology, or unethical practices. If the worry is cancer from exposure to petrochemicals, it is "my bladder" that is in danger. If the worry is about the instruments for blind flying, it is "my plane" that will go down. If the worry is about pollution, it is "my air and water" that are threatened.

In addition, the fear may be accompanied by a feeling of helplessness to influence the decision-makers. Speaking out invites retaliation, in authoritarian organizations. Moreover, in the case of the corporation, the organization is private property, isn't it? Isn't it accountable not to the community or to the employees but to anonymous stockholders? How do you get to the corporation president? Who is on the mysterious board of directors that elects the president—aren't they mostly out-of-state bankers and lawyers? The agency administrator may seem just as remote. He or she tends to avoid confrontation with rank-and-file critics, finding this a nasty business that may soil an executive's reputation. When he or she is seen, it is through a glass darkly—in the back of a limousine leaving a downtown office, in a commuter train with a briefcase sitting in his or her lap like a pencil box, or behind a distant desk in a steel-and-glass office building.

The feeling of helplessness is compounded by the invisibility of the menace. A product defect often cannot be discovered until after an accident occurs. Cancer caused by exposure to petrochemicals may take ten or more years to become apparent. At Seabrook, one group of demonstrators wrote a letter to newspaper reporters from their makeshift prison. "Radioactivity is a silent and invisible killer," they wrote. "You cannot see it, hear it or taste it." The atomic process is a mystery to all but a few experts; even its "ashes" are invisible.

Such a situation is perfect for union organizers. They can point to nearly countless occasions in which a union has given employees an influential voice on issues of safety and hazardous working conditions. They can point to case after case where the grievance procedure has saved the job of an

---

[8] Daniel Yankelovich, "The Status of *Ressentiment* in America," *Social Research,* Winter 1975, p. 764.

employee fired or suspended for criticizing safety hazards and poor working conditions. And if an alarmed corporate leader pleads that unionization will destroy needed decision-making powers, could angry, worried employees care less?

In the account that follows, we witness the power of a technological hazard to force a professional employee to run great personal risks in challenging management. The account also demonstrates the job-saving power of a professional union in such a case.

Fear of Flying (without Proper Instruments) [9]

Dan Gonzales Gellert was born in New York City, but as a teenager in World War II he lived in Budapest. It was not the right time for his family to be there; he spent two years in a German concentration camp. On the last day of his imprisonment, something happened that made a profound impression on him.

Walking through the camp one day, he noticed that the gate was open and that a man in uniform was coming toward him. The man reached into his pocket for something. Assuming it was a gun, Gellert hit the ground. But what the man pulled out of his pocket was a Hershey candy bar. He was a British pilot. He and other Allied officers had come to liberate the prisoners, not punish them.

Two years later, Gellert was back in the United States. He attended Harvard Business School and Stanford Transportation School. He taught courses in management, meterorology, and aeronautics in Florida. He became a commercial airline pilot. After fifteen years of flying, in 1963 he joined Eastern Airlines and flew nine more years before the events that put turbulence in his own career, Eastern's, and the lives of many other people. That turbulence has continued to the time of this writing.

In the summer of 1972 he was going through flight training school for Eastern's new airliner, the Lockheed 1011. His roommate was in a simulator, that is, a mock-up of a cabin having controls and instruments responding to those controls to indicate the effect on an imaginary plane in flight. The roommate's automatic pilot and flight engineer instrumentation disengaged, with the result that the simulator—the plane that the roommate presumably would have been flying if all this were for real—crashed on its landing approach.

Now, in days of old such an error was acceptable. It is said that the flying regulations of 1920 of the United States Air Service included the rule "Do

---

[9] This account is drawn from the *Civil Liberties Review*, September–October 1978, pp. 15–19, and from court records, newspaper articles, and conversations with Dan Gellert.

not trust altitude instruments." (Other rules on the list included "Never leave the ground with the motor leaking" and "Pilots should carry hankies in a handy position to wipe off goggles.") But not in 1972! So Gellert reported the episode to the flight operations people.

"You might say that they had created their own monster," he reflects, "because, through my safety training, I was able to spot a serious design problem in the 1011 aircraft." The defect involved the complex interaction between the crew and the automatic pilot and related instrumentation. About ninety seconds before reaching ground level, about 2,000 feet above the ground, the automatic pilot could disengage without sufficient warning. If he was distracted, the pilot could fail to realize that he was not maintaining the proper altitude. Some years later a Florida judge would describe the difficulty as follows:

> The "altitude hold" (an automatic control device designed to maintain a set altitude level) could become disengaged silently upon inadvertent application of pressure on the wheel control column. . . . By design the "altitude hold" was to disengage upon application of 15 to 20 pounds pressure on the control wheel column. When the "altitude hold" was "on," that fact was shown by a lighted indicator on the control panel, called an annunciator. When the automatic hold became disengaged, the annunciator light on the panel would go out. Such an inadvertent disengagement of the altitude hold was experienced by Gellert on two occasions.[10]

After studying the problem in 1973, the National Transportation Safety Board (NTSB) reached a similar conclusion. "It is possible, therefore," concluded the board, "to disengage altitude hold without an accompanying 'CMD DISC' warning appearing on the captain or first officer annunciator panels. The normal indications of such an occurrence would be only the extinguishing of the altitude mode select light on the glare shield and the disappearance of the 'ALT' annunciation on both annunciator panels." [11]

When Gellert reported the incident, the management official said, "We'll look into it." Gellert said, "You'd better, before we kill a bunch of people." Apparently, however, no corrective action was taken.

There was no rest for the wary. In the fall, flying a 1011 after leaving the training school, Gellert says he noticed that the automatic pilot tripped off a number of times without warning and without triggering an alert light on the instrument panel. On another occasion, after dropping a map and bend-

---

[10] Associate Judge Charles Carroll in *Gellert* v. *Eastern Airlines*, District Court of Appeal of Florida, Third District, April 17, 1979; Case No. 78-352, pp. 2–3.
[11] NTSB Aircraft Accident Report, File No. 1-0016, June 14, 1973, p. 13.

ing over to retrieve it, he accidentally deactivated the automatic pilot. But no warning light showed on the instrument panel, nor did a warning buzzer go off.

Unfortunately, Gellert's early warning was prophetic. Several months later, on December 29, 1972, an Eastern L-1011 crashed in the Florida Everglades. The lives of 103 people were lost.

Immediately Gellert wrote to the top three executives in the company—Frank Borman, then vice-president of operations; Frank Hall, chairman of the board; and Samuel Higgenbottom, president of operations. His letter was a two-page evaluation of the L-1011's automatic pilot system.

"Then I just sat back and waited," Gellert recalls. "It wasn't until February that Borman replied with a letter, pointing out that it was sheer folly to say that any one safety procedure could prevent all accidents. I realized I had to do something else."

So he sent his two-page evaluation to the Airline Pilots Association and the NTSB, which was conducting hearings on the crash in the Everglades. The NTSB called him to testify. Although colleagues warned him he'd be sorry, he went to the hearings and told what he knew.

In June 1973, when the NTSB's analysis was released, pilot error was blamed for the crash, not the instruments. Gellert believes this report on probable cause was slanted purposely in order to take the pressure off Eastern and the aircraft's manufacturer, Lockheed. Also, with the crash being attributed to pilot error, only what the law calls compensatory damages had to be paid to the relatives of the crash victims, not punitive damages, which are larger.

Although Gellert's suspicion of collusion cannot be proved, he cites this additional piece of evidence: The day after the December 29 crash, the head of L-1011 flight training, Thad Royall, and an NTSB official named Turner went into a flight simulator and flew the same pattern as had the doomed aircraft. With instruments simulating every move, they did exactly what the crew had done. And they "crashed" at almost exactly the same spot in the Everglades.

It so happened that Royall had been one of the officials Gellert had notified when first bringing the problem to management's attention. Royall and Turner, says Gellert, decided to keep this astounding simulator incident quiet. In March, Royall attended a meeting with Borman and other airline executives. There Borman decided not to change the design of the 1011 because "the Federal Aviation Agency had approved it." But in July, after the NTSB released its findings, Gellert says that management decided quietly to modify the automatic pilot design.

Up on the wing, however, life was not to be as healthy as it was in flight simulators and operations offices. In December 1973, Gellert was flying a

1011 when the automatic pilot tripped off twice. The second time this happened Gellert and the copilots were approaching an airport. Their great plane, with its sky-blue stripes and enormous *Whisperliner* label on the rear jet, broke through the clouds about 200 feet over houses, whereas the instruments said the altitude was 500 feet. Putting on a burst of power, the crew averted tragedy and made the runway safely.

Gellert wrote a twelve-page petition to the NTSB; he sent a copy to Frank Borman. He knew that solo fighter interceptors get a lot of return fire, but he didn't yet know how bad it could be.

Eastern demoted him to copilot. In Gellert's view, the reason was spurious, trumped up, contrived. He wrote a letter of protest to Borman. Before receiving Borman's reply, which took some time to arrive, he applied for an FBI job in Eastern Europe, where he could use his childhood knowledge. The FBI made him a good job offer. He was thinking about it seriously when Borman's reply came: He was grounded.

Gellert was furious. Never had a passenger or crew member complained about him. Never had he even blown an aircraft tire. He wondered what Eastern would do to him next. It appeared to him, as Gellert's lawyer Ellis Rubin was to observe sometime later, that the company had "begun an organized campaign to run him out of the airline or make it so tough that he'd have to quit."

He turned down the FBI job offer. He felt that accepting it would indicate that his grounding was justified. "I decided to remain with Eastern and salvage my reputation," he says. "I decided the only way to protect myself from further action was to file suit against them." He brought the suit in his home state, Florida. (Eastern headquarters also was in Florida.) In addition, he took advantage of the grievance procedure supported by the union of airplane pilots. As a result, in seven months he was flying again.

But his flying days were to be interrupted once more. To backtrack a little first, after the NTSB had made its report on the December 29 crash, Gellert had petitioned it to reconsider some of its findings. Also, he had written a lengthy letter to the Federal Bureau of Investigation and to Borman, attaching to his letter to Borman a copy of his letter to the FBI. The letter to Borman, dated May 23, 1974, contained such paragraphs as the following:

> Information that I have indicates that you were in the close proximity of the person that was utilized to convey certain threats etc. in this matter on a flight between JFK/MIA prior to the NTSB hearing. Since the possibility exists that you personally have been compromised by this situation and since you had me pointed out by Captain Furr during the hearing and still refused to discuss the matter so that we

could have laid it out to rest oh so long ago; the inference I am drawing [is] that you are involved in this matter and without going the legal
route many more illegal activities will take place and the whole incident will continue to get more complex.

I am beginning to understand the awesome power that you and your
team can bring on me or anyone else that brings matters to attention
that you don't want surfaced. The economic pressure, and the ability
to tamper with one's aircraft is a powerful force. Most of us including
myself resist going outside the company with matters such as this, but
I just cannot let something as flagrant as this continue.

Apprehensive about Gellert's state of mind, Borman instructed the senior
vice-president in charge of industrial and personnel relations to have
Gellert examined for mental stability. There followed a confusing series of
medical diagnoses. First, Eastern's medical director, Dr. Serrano, received
the psychiatrist–neurologist's conclusion that the "construction, tone, intent
and implications of the letters indicate to me that there is sufficient reason
to suspect a mental disorder in this man." Interviewing Gellert a short time
later, Serrano arrived at a diagnosis of paranoia and concluded that it was
unsafe for Gellert to fly. He wrote,

Because of his, if you will, monomania, I do not believe that this man
would be completely safe to fly aircraft at this time. Men who are
primarily preoccupied with such matters [i.e., Gellert's concerns about
equipment, his relations with management, and so on] let everything
else go and become completely concerned with their cause: Seeking
justice for themselves. It seems amply clear to me that this 24-hour-a-
day job is not compatible with clear headed, relaxed flying of an
aircraft in conjunction with other crew members.[12]

Accordingly, in August Gellert was put on sick leave pay and grounded, but
it was agreed he would be reevaluated a few months later.

Next, a psychiatrist selected jointly by Gellert and Eastern's medical
staff, a Dr. Giffen, examined Gellert in December. This doctor concluded
that it was safe for Gellert to fly again, and Gellert returned to the cockpit in
January 1975.

But the game of "now you fly, now you don't" wasn't over. Dr. Giffen
testified in the fall of 1975, during a lawsuit Gellert had brought against
Eastern, that he had not seen the letters to the FBI and to Borman when he
had made his December examination. Now that he had seen them, Giffen

---

[12] *Gellert v. Eastern Airlines*, op. cit., p. 4.

agreed that they showed a tendency to paranoia. Therefore Gellert was grounded again.

The next year Gellert agreed, after an arbitration hearing concerning his grounding, to take still another medical examination. The psychiatrist found him qualified to return to duty. Once more, therefore, he returned to the cockpit.

Gellert's conviction that he was being harassed by management was fortified by another unfortunate incident. Hearing about a position that was open to serve as captain on certain flights from New York City, he mailed an application for a change of pilot duty. He feels certain that the envelope he used for the application had a return address and his name, but management alleges that his name was omitted along with other necessary information. (His application, by the way, was one of nearly 2,000 that were processed.) In any case, in about two months a letter addressed to "Occupant" at his address came, stating that his application didn't contain much necessary information. Believing this to be untrue, and that someone in the executive suite was sabotaging him, Gellert went into a fresh series of mental acrobatics. In the judge's phrase later, "he suffered intense mental distress." [13]

His suit against Eastern came to a head in September 1977. He asked for $1.5 million in damages for mental distress, some of it intentionally inflicted (for instance, the first grounding and the handling of his bid for the New York-based flights), and some of it occasioned by management retaliation to his criticisms of airplane safety. (Several other charges were dropped during the trial.) His case was well-argued, and he himself was a personable and convincing plaintiff; obviously the jury was impressed.

During a recess in the trial an interesting exchange took place. Gellert happened to meet Frank Borman, now president of the airline and testifying in its defense, in the corridor. "Mr. Borman," Gellert recalls telling the chief executive, "you're making me a millionaire—*and there's not a damn thing I can do about it.*" His point was that the company, by refusing to deal fairly with him, had forced him to go outside to sue it. Borman, says Gellert, looked at him without answering and hurried down the hall.

The jury found for Gellert, and the judge awarded him the $1.5 million he asked plus an extra $100,000. The unprecedented extra, Gellert thinks, reflected the judge's anger at Eastern for its attempt to discredit its pilot. After the verdict, one of the jurors walked up to Gellert and shook his hand. The juror said he was proud there were airline captains who would sacrifice their careers for the sake of air safety.

[13] Ibid., p. 5.

After the verdict, Gellert says that management grounded him again in an effort to "starve me out." He says that officials swore they would not recommend him to other employers or even answer letters requesting references. He claims management also wanted him to sign a letter relieving it of any liability, which would mean he would give up his claim to the $1.6 million in damages awarded. Of course, he did not comply with that request.

For a short time, Gellert flew high. But then a series of reverses struck and, legally at least, he lost altitude. The trial judge, petitioned by Eastern to set aside the decision on legal grounds, agreed to do so. There was not, he ruled, an "under-lying tort" as the law required. Gellert and his lawyer appealed this ruling. In April 1979 the Third District Court of Appeal of Florida upheld the trial judge's ruling, thus killing Gellert's hope for receiving the damages awarded. One may not "recover damages for intentional infliction of severe mental distress which is without physical contact, and which is not incidental to or consequent upon any separate tort or other actionable wrong," the appellate court stated.

In 1978 Gellert lost again in court. He had filed a $12 million lawsuit charging named officials of the airline with "civil conspiracy to force me out of employment." Again the jury decided in his favor, and again the verdict was set aside. He appealed the ruling but lost.[14] He appealed again and, as of June 1982, expected to win a reversal. In 1980 he won a $235,000 verdict against the airline for defamation of character because of a prejudicial article written by an Eastern official in the magazine *Brevard Today*. Also, in a grievance proceeding he was awarded a substantial sum of back pay that had been withheld by Eastern. Moreover, as this is written he is prosecuting a major lawsuit for libel against Eastern in the federal courts.

Let us consider the broader implications of the Gellert story. What does it tell us about the potential appeal of a union to professional and technical employees? Is it likely that engineers, scientists, accountants, and other groups of knowledge workers will be stirred to support unionization in their organizations? Suppose management were to establish its own procedures for due process. How good would they have to be to induce someone like Gellert to use them in parallel with, or possibly in place of, the union grievance procedure? What kinds of top management commitment would be necessary to make a due process procedure appealing to employees?

These are just a few of the questions raised by the Gellert saga. In the meantime, he flies some of Eastern's largest planes as senior pilot. More

---

[14] *Gellert* v. *Eastern Airlines, Inc.*, District Court of Appeal of Florida, Third District, July 31, 1978; Case No. 78-352.

than once, he tells me, he has noticed the chief executive officer among his passengers.

GHOSTS OF THE FOUNDING FATHERS?

On April 19, 1976, at Old North Bridge in Concord, Massachusetts, shortly before President Gerald Ford came by, one of the youthful demonstrators of the People's Bicentennial Commission shouted, "The American dream is dead!" And so it might have seemed to a person who saw the large corporation as the contemporary counterpart of King George III, for there was and is no practical way of abolishing the large corporation. Later, the demonstrators reflected sadly on their futile efforts to arouse public opinion. Seeing that their words had sparked no lightning and realizing that their "revolution" had succeeded at most in creating a storm in a wash bowl, they may well have wondered if the revolutionary spirit of 1776 wasn't dead. The fervor of the patriots, some say, has passed from our society to other societies.

If the American dream is defined in terms of human dignity, however, the spirit of the patriots lives on. In the third century of our independence, we are seeing a remarkable new fervor for individual rights. There are differences from the first revolution. Today's rebels fight with words, not guns, in plants and office buildings, not battlefields, and run the risk of economic, not physical, death. Though this fervor cannot be called a revolution, surely it is a movement—some would call it a peaceable rebellion— and though it is not dramatic it is terribly earnest.

In the eyes of the ill-conceived People's Bicentennial Commision at Concord, the "new monarchy" to be abolished was "America's giant corporations." But this is not what employee dissidents challenge. What they object to is not power per se but employer prerogatives that diminish civil liberties and the dignity of the individual. Those prerogatives bear little relation to size or volume or legal form. They may be exercised in a small organization as well as in a large one, by a public agency as well as by a private corporation. What today's dissidents challenge is the power of *any* organization to deny any of its members the kinds of rights that are established in the Bill of Rights of the Constitution—especially freedom of conscience, privacy, and due process, and a qualified right to speak up.

"The colonists didn't believe they were creating a whole new social order," Pauline Maier of Harvard University once noted. "They felt they were restoring the ancient rights of Englishmen which had been infringed by royal power." Nor do today's dissidents think of themselves as "creating a whole new social order." In their minds they are fighting for the principles (if not the exact form) of the Bill of Rights during working hours. They do not see why those principles should not apply so far as practicable to the workplace.

How might the rebels of 1776 and today's dissidents regard each other if they could meet face to face? The possibility of such a confrontation brings to mind a haunting short story, "The Other," written by Jorge Luis Borge. In the story, Borge describes a mysterious encounter between his graying present-day self, more than seventy years old, and his self at the age of twenty. The younger self is sure he's dreaming; the older self is sure he's not. Between the two selves there is strangeness on the surface but deep familiarity beneath. If dissidence is thought of as generic, today's dissident is some 200 years older than the self of revolutionary times. In Borge's terms, how would the older self regard the younger self?

To begin with, there are striking similarities. For example, each would sense in the other a certain animal vitality, a psychic energy, a "get up and go" power, a self-starting capacity. No dissident ever used up all his or her energy in performing the regular work tasks assigned. There has to be something left at the end of the day for scheming, planning, fact-finding, looking into the law, special errands, writing letters, making urgent telephone calls, lying awake.

In each other they would also recognize a willingness to go first. The dissident doesn't wait until there's a group. He or she doesn't say, "I can do nothing alone." He or she asks, "If I don't do it, who will?" This leads at once to triumph and tragedy. The triumph is that a candle is lit. The tragedy is that, like the early Christians, the dissident may get thrown to the lions.

Both the older and younger selves tend to be middle-of-the-roaders or conservatives, not flamethrowing radicals. He or she almost always believes in rules of order, property rights, stability, thrift, private investment, industriousness. The classic dissident of 1776 was Roger Sherman of Connecticut, the only patriot who signed all four of the basic documents of the American Revolution (the Continental Association, the Declaration of Independence, the Articles of Confederation, and the Constitution). Sherman was considered a paragon of Yankee virtue; he was self-controlled, serious, frugal, pious, industrious. Similarly, the dissident of today is likely to be considered by peers as hardworking, family-loving, and property-conscious, not as a hothead. "I began as a conservative Republican, firmly entrenched in the middle-management echelon of big business," says Dan Gellert, the subject of the story just given. "Now I am labeled as a whistleblower. I never wanted to be a whistleblower, but my professional ideals and my conscience would allow me to be nothing else." Other dissidents would make similar statements.

What about the differences between the rebels of today and of revolutionary times?

For one thing, today's version is taller, heavier, and better dressed. Also, today's self does not have the calloused hands and weathered face of the younger self of 1776. Then the majority were farmers. Today half of the work force, and considerably more than half of the dissidents, are professional, technical, managerial, sales, and other white-collar employees. Furthermore, the great majority of dissidents today are city slickers. In only four decades the proportion of people in U.S. metropolitan areas has risen by nearly half, from 52% in 1940 to about 75% today. For whistleblowers and other employee critics, the percentage of city workers is probably nine out of ten or more. Two centuries ago, by contrast, many dissidents came from rural areas.

In addition, there is an important sex difference. Many of today's dissidents are women, whereas only a few of the rebels of 1776 (the known rebels, that is—the histories were written by men) were women. The proportion of women in the work force has risen dramatically. Among American women between the ages of thirty-five and forty-four, well over half are in the work force today, as compared with only 40% in 1950 and half that much earlier in the century. These women tend to be rights-conscious and articulate.

Today's and yesterday's rebels also differ in amount of formal education. Most of the leading patriots knew how to read and write, and some of them had studied and absorbed the major English treatises in philosophy and law, but none of them possessed the funds of scientific, social, and economic information that today's dissidents take for granted. In fact, as noted earlier, the steadily rising percentage of employees with college educations contributes importantly to the rise of dissidence in organizations. With years of training in raising questions, challenging conventional wisdom, and thinking independently, these people do not make "good soldiers."

Another difference is charisma. Today's employee dissidents do not have the power to capture the public imagination that a raucous Samuel Adams had, or that the men of the Boston Tea Party or the minutemen had. As playwright Tennessee Williams once noted, "Man is by nature a lover, a hunter, a fighter, and none of these instincts are given much play at the warehouse." To catch the historian's or dramatist's fancy, it seems, one must be violent and risk death, but the typical employee dissenter is not so inclined.

In fact, about the only white-collar dissident to achieve literary or dramatic fame so far is Thomas Stockmann, the fictional subject of Henrik Ibsen's famous play An Enemy of the People. Medical director of the Municipal Baths in a town in southern Norway, Stockmann discovers that the water in the baths is poisoned by refuse and waste leaking into the pipes that lead to the reservoir. The poisons are dangerous to bathers and are making some of them ill. Stockmann speaks up but his brother Peter, mayor of the town and chairman of the Baths Committee, learns that the expense of correcting the pipe system will be great. Moreover, the job will take two years. Resistance to Stockmann grows and solidifies. Peter tells him that he must not make his discovery public but let the news be handled privately by town officials. "Nothing of this unfortunate affair—not a single word of it—must come to the ears of the public," Peter declares. When Stockmann refuses to hush up, Peter warns him, "As an officer under the Committee, you have no right to any individual opinion." Amazed, Stockmann answers, "No right?" Peter says, "In your official capacity, no. As a private person, it is quite another matter. But as a subordinate of the staff of the Baths, you have no right to express any opinion which runs contrary to that of your superiors." Confident he will prevail because right is on his side, Stockmann goes to the newspaper editor. To his chagrin, he is rebuffed. The editor tells him, "It would mean the absolute ruin of the community if your article were to appear." At a town meeting, he is hooted down and declared to be "an enemy of the people." He is fired from his job at the baths, a petition is circulated urging no one in town to employ him, and he loses his medical practice. But all this adversity, instead of weakening him, only makes him more stubborn. He is "the strongest man in the world," he avers to his family as the curtain falls.

The often-observed tendency of employee dissidents to stiffen when beaten down, as Ibsen's hero did, rather than weaken, is an enigma to many administrators. How is it possible, they ask, for an employee with a comfortable income, trained for advancement, and surrounded by industrious and friendly associates to reject so much security and prospect of reward? In vain they search for ties with communist organizations, radical groups, or bizarre cults.

At Seabrook, New Hampshire, in 1978, the demonstrators were not prepared for the physical ball game Governor Meldrim Thomson, Jr., decided to play, but when they saw what was coming—being dragged to overcrowded "meat trucks," days of stewing in makeshift prisons—they were undeterred. Official accusations of subversive connections became a joke. The administration's retaliation seemed to galvanize the rebels, and ultimately the stubborn resistance played a part in the state–industry decision to shelve the nuclear power project.

Few employee rebels better symbolize dissidents' willingness to flout managerial prerogatives, peacefully and legally, than does the subject of our next account.

The Case of the Irreverent Reporter [15]

Al Louis Ripskis, a slender, mustachioed, mild-mannered bachelor who often comes to the office in blue jeans, works officially on the ninth floor of the Department of Housing and Urban Development in Washington, D.C. His job—officially, that is—is analyzing programs that HUD is interested in. Although his position in the hierarchy is modest, and he is classified as GS-13, hardly a supergrade, his name is probably known to more people in and about Washington than any of the top officials at HUD.

The reason is that Ripskis works in a second and unofficial capacity. He is the editor, publisher, printer, treasurer, marketer, and cleanup man of a multigraphed eight-page bimonthly journal called *Impact*.[16] *Impact* is one of the few examples of a nonunion-supported, nonmanagement-supported free press in the American organizational world. With a publishing life of more than a decade, it is the longest lived of any such periodical. Ripskis uses *Impact* to criticize, satirize, cajole, prod, and second-guess (and sometimes commend) the higher-ups of HUD and other government agencies.

"God save us from the incompetents," Ripskis says. "There are a bunch of incompetents messing things up, and yet they've got the power to keep you silent and from criticizing them." One of his favorite quotations comes from the great scholar of bureaucracy, Max Weber: "It is horrible to think that the world could one day be filled with nothing but these little cogs, little men clinging to their jobs and striving toward bigger ones. . . . It is such an evolution that we are already caught up in, and the great question is therefore not how we can promote and hasten it, but what we can oppose to this machinery in order to keep a portion of mankind free from this parceling-out of the soul from this supreme mastery of the bureaucratic way of life."

Born in Lithuania before World War II, Ripskis was the son of an outspoken farmer, teacher, and political activist. When the Soviet rulers began shipping relatives to Siberia, the family fled to Germany and spent four years in a displaced persons camp. He remembers that his family and another family of four shared one room and one blanket, which was draped over a clothesline in the middle of the room. After this ordeal the Ripskises found their way to Chicago Heights, Illinois, and a series of cramped apartments. He remembers stoking stoves manually, chasing rats away, and shivering in cold basement rooms. To help pay the bills, he worked for a while in steel, chemical, and tile factories and learned "how to earn a dollar the hard way."

---

[15] This account is drawn from correspondence with Al Ripskis, newspaper articles, and issues of *Impact*.

[16] P.O. Box 23126, 475 L'Enfant Plaza, Washington, D.C. 20024. (Subscriptions are taken out by individuals as well as by organizations.)

Life for him improved when he went to the University of Illinois. After graduation, things improved again when he took a job in the Public Housing Administration. There, in the early 1960s, he felt he could play a hand in housing reform and urban progress. In 1965, when HUD was created, he joined its staff in Washington.

During his first seven or eight years as a federal employee, Ripskis had smooth sailing. He drew choice assignments and earned glowing performance ratings; he advanced from the apprentice junior executive grade of GS-7 to GS-13, enjoying faster promotions than most of his colleagues did. It looked as if he were going to steer his way right to the top of his division. As a member of a key task force called Social Concerns of HUD, he relished the conviction that the organization would help to develop public housing that met the needs of family life-styles and behavior patterns rather than just space and cost standards.

At the same time, however, he was beginning to feel a riptide of frustration and impatience over the work HUD was doing. He began questioning and doubting more. When a reorganization plan appeared to jeopardize his career, he and a few others filed suit against the department with the help of Jay Thal, the editor of an employee-produced newsletter called *Quest*. In this publication Thal, Ripskis, and others aired a variety of liberal and sometimes radical views.

In 1972 the smooth sailing abruptly ended. His colleague Thal was ordered to proceed to Alaska to study the Alaska State Housing Authority. To one who grew up, as Ripskis had, in an atmosphere of family fears of deportation to Siberia, the order seemed like an all-too-familiar form of punishment. The assignment was supposed to be temporary, but who believed it?

Ripskis took over the helm for Thal in order to keep *Quest* going. He was conscious of the possible consequences of sailing outside the approved channels, but he felt enraged over the treatment of his old friend. In his very first issue, he published an article that, to his superiors, must have seemed the equivalent of hoisting the Jolly Roger.

This issue recounted the famous flagpole affair. Until 1972, *Quest* reported, HUD had a forty-five-foot-high flagpole in front of its building. Then the new Department of Transportation, right across the street, had the audacity to erect seventy-five-foot flagpoles—two of them. Peering out from his captain's cabin, HUD Secretary George Romney choked and sputtered. Tear down HUD's flagpole, he cried. Raise two new splendid eighty-foot flagpoles in its place! The order was carried out swiftly at a cost to the taxpayers of $26,000.

The *Quest* article was picked up by the Associated Press. "Who's got the taller flagpoles?" the AP story asked. "The Department of Housing and Urban Development, that's who!" After having fun with the facts of the incident, the AP story mentioned that "the flagpole caper was disclosed by an employees' underground newsletter at HUD called *Quest.*" No less delighted with the caper than the AP editors had been, NBC News televised the story the following evening. Within a few days, the story appeared in newspapers all across the country.

The reaction in the captain's cabin? Reporter Florence Isbell put it succinctly: "The Secretary was not amused." Isbell reports that Ripskis received no more challenging assignments from senior officers. "His office space got smaller and smaller; and his performance appraisals dropped." [17] He conscientiously applied for every available higher position he heard of but more to satisfy his sense of justice than out of any expectation a promotion might be given him. None was. Ripskis is at the same grade level today he was then—GS-13.

Despite the overnight fame he had brought *Quest,* Ripskis decided to abandon this ship and build his own. *Quest* was interested in all sorts of government issues, and it sought to provide an open forum for viewpoints. Ripskis was interested in a more focused publication, one that would concentrate more on HUD. Using a network of "monitors" in the organization, he would concentrate all his journalistic energies on bringing about change in this one place.

He christened his new publication *Impact* and launched it in the fall of 1972. The copy for the printer was typed by volunteers; about 2,500 people received copies of the first issue. "Dear Fellow Co-Worker," Ripskis wrote. "The department we work for has been sullied by scandals, waste, mismanagement and corruption to the point where Romney himself has admitted that HUD is acutally contributing to urban decay rather than reducing it." In the issue he reported a series of familiar bungles and described a few new ones.

Then, as today, Ripskis stood on the sidewalk by HUD's front door and handed copies out to employees as they came in the morning and left in the evening. Although he uses the mails to send copies to subscribers and others (who comprise the majority of readers), he says he likes to "show the flag" and taunt the powers that be. It is a risky life. One of the people he handed an early issue to was Secretary Romney himself. A few minutes later, Ripskis recalls, guards came out and told him to leave or face arrest. He left. However, he reappeared the next month to hand out extra copies of the new issue.

How does this pesky, unarmed little boat manage to stay afloat in the midst of so much managerial firepower? Ripskis's old friend Jay Thal was

[17] Florence Isbell, "Dissidents in the Federal Government," *Civil Liberties Review,* September–October 1977, p. 73.

chased out of sight, why not him? *Quest* sank from view with scarcely a ripple in 1973; why not *Impact?* Columnist Nicholas von Hoffman wrote: "How long Al will be with HUD is a guessing matter." But the years have gone by, and the bridge at HUD has seen several changes in command, and Ripkis still darts back and forth. How come?

Like a sailor who has been warned repeatedly about the high dangers of mutiny, Ripskis knows how vulnerable he is. When the Nixon administration was in power he once remarked, "There haven't been any reprisals yet, and if they do send me to Guam, it won't be until after the election." They didn't—but other elections are coming. Being a realist, he knows that he plies dangerous waters in any political climate, whether Fordian, Carterian, Reaganomic, or some other kind.

He has seen the ominous little signs, such as the assignments to smaller offices, the rejection of applications for new positions. He knows the petty things superiors can do to a dissident. Since he began editing *Impact,* for instance, his "writing ability" ratings in his annual performance appraisals have plummeted from the highest mark possible, 10, to a miserable 3. But penalties of this sort are petty annoyances. He can live with such irritations. Why hasn't a burst of machine-gun fire finished him off? It turns out that his charmed life has not been pure happenstance. Artfully, he has chosen his tactics.

To begin with, there is the civil service code. It helps enormously. Yet it has failed to protect many other dissidents. Why has Ripskis survived? Part of his secret, he believes, lies in the furor he created at the outset. "If they decide to fire you at the start," he told writer Helen Dudar, "it's hard to reverse the bureaucracy once it gets rolling. But I started muckraking and kicking up a lot of publicity, and I became well known, so the department knew it would be bloody if they torpedoed me."

Another part of the secret is his connections. He has built liaisons with people in the consumer movement, Washington newspaper reporters, and many others. *Impact* goes regularly to a number of media people, members of House and Senate staffs, and government union officials. All of these people know they can quote him by name. He is not one of the anonymous sources in the capital city who leak stories to reporters and solons. Therefore, any time HUD turns on him, the outside world is going to know about it. The waves that would be created would be greater than any that *Impact* could make.

Of course, as Isbell points out, "that delicate balance could change if Ripskis were to latch on to some really horrendous scandal." It is interesting to speculate what a "horrendous scandal" would be, since, as we shall see presently, Ripskis has been anything but gentle in his choice of exposés to date.

Still another part of his secret is that he runs a very tight ship during office hours. He does none of the writing or marketing of *Impact* on HUD time. If he peddles *Impact* in front of the building for so much as five minutes during regular working hours, he logs that time against his annual leave.

Moreover, he draws a line between information he gets as *Impact*'s editor and information he harbors in his regular office duties as project analyst. He says he gives a wide berth to information acquired in the course of his regular duties. Nor does he withhold from the organization any data he acquires because he edits *Impact*. Once he found a copy of an explosive memorandum in his office in-basket. Obviously it was sent to him for use in the publication. He told his superiors promptly that he would show them a slightly smoke-screened version from the one his source supplied, if they wanted to see it. Thus he protected himself as well as the source.

Again, if an informant wants to discuss a sensitive subject with him, he will not do it in the office or even on the office phone. He'll make a date with the person to meet at his apartment, or he will call the person back from an outside booth. Reporter Dave Rothman, at the time a free-lancer in Washington, was impressed with Ripskis's "bureaucratic prudence." Rothman wrote that, even at Ripskis's apartment, the two of them talked "as if James Lynn were personally snooping on us through a ceiling mike." According to Rothman, one government official remarked to the *Federal Times* in 1974, "You can be sure they're going to be watching him very closely— not only HUD but the Civil Service Commission, and who knows, even some of the investigative arms of government."

As for out-of-pocket costs of *Impact*, which were about $3,000 a year in 1977, according to Ripskis's estimate, and surely must be much more than that now, he bears them all himself. In addition he benefits from volunteer work in producing each issue. Most of the writing, though, he does himself. He runs a few articles anonymously because the HUD employees who drafted them would have to walk the plank if their identities became known. Some of his material comes from stringers in HUD field offices.

What kinds of stories appear in *Impact*? The following samples come from the first page of the September–October 1981 issue:

Impact has finally been permitted to review the draft Rand Corporation consulting study entitled, "Rental Housing in the 1970's: Searching for the Crisis." It is a snow job. . . . This report will undoubtedly find a friendly court within Reagan's HUD. It comes within an inch of announcing a surplus of rental housing. Get that? . . .

One has to give HUD's Policy Development and Research (PD&R) due credit for its audacity, brazenness, and gall. While President Reagan has declared war on government waste, PD&R has decided to do just the opposite—to continue wasting taxpayers' money with abandon, just as it has been doing in the past. But PD&R is no longer content with doing it quietly; it is now advertising it—or to be more precise, flaunting it. PD&R is announcing this waste in HUD press releases [describing a new project on water conservation].

Now if anybody in PD&R had bothered to mosey over to the HUD library (which by the way is conveniently located on the same floor as PD&R) and looked under "water" in the card catalogue, he would have found over five full drawers (or 44½ inches of drawer space) of 3 by 5 cards listing books and other references on the subject. To further help PD&R's personnel: they might want to check more specifically under the subtopics "water conservation," "water resource-research," Department of Interior's Office of Water Research and Technology, Senate's Sub-committee on Water Resources, EPA's Water and Waste Management office, and GAO reports. . . .

Some years ago *Impact* ran an article under the headline, *"A HUD Official, His 'Mistress' and Taxpayers' Money."* The article asserted that for two years a highly placed official had been cruising around the country with his "female assistant," charging their good times to the federal expense account. *Impact* warned HUD readers that it knew of similar sinners but wouldn't keelhaul them in its pages so long as the officials didn't charge the government for their happy hours. ("I consider my first loyalty to the taxpayers who pay my salary," Ripskis says, explaining his publishing philosophy.)

Here are some other examples of stories that Ripskis has floated in *Impact*:

In 1979 HUD installed enormous glass security doors at the entrance of the Secretary's office. The doors were a half-inch thick and nine feet high. The Secretary, said Ripskis, "already has two huge, thick, wood doors leading to her suite which the Crusaders couldn't break through." Although the General Services Administration had proposed white lettering on the doors at a cost of $136, HUD decided instead on gold-leaf lettering at a cost of more than $1,000. Total cost of the doors: $58,000 (including more than $4,000 for paperwork and $3,313 for two desk-sized counters that, *Impact* reported HUD officials as admitting, would not be used). Their practical value? GSA officials reportedly said the doors were useless because HUD refused to keep them closed and manned by full-time guards.

When the dangers of lead poisoning from paint were being publicized, *Impact* assailed HUD for failing to enforce restrictions on the use of lead-based paint. HUD was said to be playing "the old game of appearing to implement the letter of the law while violating its spirit."

In the summer of 1979 *Impact* barged out with a report that rocked much of Washington and even made waves overseas. The story reported the results of a survey of sexual attitudes of bosses. More than 160 female employees in HUD responded that, in their experience and observation, promotions and pay raises often hinged on willingness to go to bed with the boss. Some 30% of respondents reported cooperating with their bosses' sexual demands; the remaining 70% said they had refused. In the write-up, Ripskis emphasized the finding that 80% of the females who "cooperated" were (or believed they were) rewarded on the job. But those who refused often reported becoming subject to reprisals (or what were believed to be reprisals). For instance, they were frozen in their jobs, verbally harassed, or given poor assignments. The major television networks reported Ripskis's findings; radio stations all over the country wanted interviews with him; many newspapers featured the story (the *Washington Star* referred to him as "resident whistle blower and part-time father confessor at Housing and Urban Development"); and overseas the *Daily Telegraph* of London joyfully printed a write-up of the survey. Next Congressman James Hanley of New York, chairman of the House Sub-committee on Investigations, asked the Merit Systems Protection Board to initiate a survey of the whole federal work force, asking the kinds of questions that Ripskis had asked. Hanley also arranged for his commit-tee to begin hearings on the subject.

Not all *Impact* stories are critical of HUD. In one issue Ripskis congratulated management on its efforts to help the handicapped. "Certain bathrooms have been remodeled (and very attractively, we might add) to accommodate people in wheelchairs," Ripskis wrote. "Attempts have been made to place braille numbers next to the floor buttons in elevators. Showers and locker rooms have been provided for those who are into exercising."

Ripskis is convinced his publication has done a lot of good. Not only has it saved taxpayers a lot of money, he believes, but it has had a healthy policing effect and nudged some management people to act on a variety of important public needs. Increasingly he finds reporters using his material and giving it additional circulation and impact in large publications. In the

meantime, employees keep directing a steady current of ideas and materials
to him.

LOYALTY: GENUINE OR COUNTERFEIT?

Like the Gellert story, Ripskis's experience symbolizes the gradual
breaking down of management by fear. It is hard to imagine a federal
employee of 1890 or 1925 challenging an enormous federal agency as bra-
zenly and publicly as Ripskis has done (even had there been equal civil
service protection then). What is more, Ripskis's efforts have drawn enough
publicity to guarantee that other potential whistleblowers will note not only
what he has dared to do *but how*, especially how to exploit an advantage of
some sort. In an increasing number of situations, the would-be critic has
some kind of protection. If it is not civil service, it may be an organization
policy; if not that, it may be a watchful press; if not that, it may be union
organizers waiting hopefully for some egregious management mistake to
dramatize their cause. Whatever the protection, employee critics like
Ripskis are showing that there are deft ways to exploit it, to gain the maximum possible cover from it.

In short, employee objectors of today and tomorrow are taking advantage of a know-how that was not available in years past. For the management that would continue to rely on management by fear, it seems that a
dwindling supply of sand is left in the hourglass.

In addition, there is the question of what Herbert Simon has called the
"limits of identification" in employees' regard for an organization. If management by fear breaks these limits down, it attacks some of the values that
make professional employees tick. Kenneth E. Goodpaster, a visiting professor at the Harvard Business School, makes the following pertinent
observations:

Perhaps no thinker has explored the depths of the virtue of loyalty
more than Josiah Royce, whose turn-of-the-century reflections contain
the following observation: "All the recognized virtues can be defined
in terms of our concept of loyalty. And this is why I assert that, when
rightly interpreted, loyalty is the whole duty of man."

Royce's conviction was that loyalty held the key to all of ethics and
morality, and he defended this conviction not only in obvious contexts, like family and country, but also in less obvious contexts, including business.

But there is an insight in Royce's treatment of the subject that has special contemporary relevance, and that links the two concepts of corporate loyalty and business ethics. As he applauds loyalty to a cause or a company as essential to both an indivdual's personal fulfillment and to his or her moral development, he imposes a constraint that carries enormous force: loyalty is self-defeating when the cause destroys or ruins the loyalties in *other* lives.

If loyalty is a value, it must recognize itself in others and face up to its moral impact. Conscience, according to Royce, requires us to keep *some* distance from our causes and our companies. Otherwise, loyalty corrupts.

This insight, that loyalty can be twisted from its course, is readily understood by most of us: Watergates (either in the public sector or in the private sector) haunt us from the last decade, and remind us of loyalty run amok; middle managers who "blew the whistle" often have suffered abrupt dismissal, while those who kept quiet have suffered in other ways.

The point is that loyalty in harness with conscience is a truly admirable human resource, either for individuals in organizations or for organizations in the larger society. But once decouple the two and we all are in for it.

So the chief executive officer . . . who said, "When it comes to establishing loyalty, I have yet to find a substitute for fear," might give the matter some more thought, however tough-minded his or her management philosophy.

Loyalty born of fear is plainly counterfeit. And a corporate culture that fosters this brand of loyalty is surely doomed to sacrifice whatever measure of freedom its enterprise may currently command. . . .

American individualism can create a climate in which the organization comes unglued for lack of allegiance, of loyalty. But in our enthusiasm for "rekindling" corporate loyalty, and despite the dismay of some over what appears to be a new breed of not-so-loyal managers, we should at least allow for the possibility that loyalty, either blind or imposed by fear, may be more a liability than an asset.[18]

---

[18] *Dallas Morning News,* June 2, 1981.

7

WHAT TO DO
WHEN THE
WHISTLE BLOWS

In view of the changing balance of management prerogatives and employee rights, how should managers respond to criticisms form subordinates, claims of wrongdoing, and protests against a management decision? If you had been the manager involved in the accounts of dissidence described in previous chapters, how might you have reacted? What might you have done to avoid the mutually destructive imbroglios that resulted from the stubborn refusal of either side to give in?

After talking with many managers involved in whistleblower cases, and after studying numerous cases, I am convinced that a large number of the hassles that damage both sides could be avoided. Both the responsibility and the best opportunities to avoid internecine conflict belong to managers. This is not only because they have more power and prestige than dissidents do but also because, as administrators, they can be expected to have more perspective, more wisdom, more "cool."

In coping with a dissidence problem, your guiding principle is simple: Aim to keep the conflict from becoming an "I win, you lose" affair and instead approach it as a "We both can win" situation. An excellent translation of this principle into everyday practice is the book, *Getting to Yes*, by Roger Fisher and William Ury.[1] The authors draw from their experience with the Harvard Negotiation Project, an informal group of experts in

[1] Roger Fisher and William Ury, *Getting to Yes* (Boston: Houghton Mifflin, 1981).

Cambridge, Massachusetts, who explore bargaining issues, as well as from their personal experience in political, industrial, and domestic bargaining situations. As might be expected, therefore, the principles of what the authors call "principled negotiation" (as contrasted with position bargaining, the "I win, you lose" approach) are drawn from the experience of a good many negotiators and authorities over the years. They are not new inventions. Because the book is readily available to administrators who want to look into these questions in more detail, I shall follow parts of Fisher and Ury's scheme in the pages that follow, developing it in terms of manager-subordinate conflicts in particular rather than as they do, in terms of conflicts in general. For specific examples, cases earlier described in this book will be used.

NEGOTIATING TO WIN (FOR YOU AND THE DISSIDENT BOTH)

There are four main steps to a "We both can win" outcome. Let us examine each in turn, reflecting on how they might have helped in some of the cases described in earlier chapters.

1. *Separate the Issues from the People Problem and Deal First with the People.*

Suppose you are an airline executive and a pilot begins to make noise in the way Dan Gellert did. In a confrontation with him, your conversation might proceed bumpily, hitting one air pocket after another:

YOU: What's going on here, Mr. Pilot? It was bad enough when you complained about the automatic hold equipment to the vice-president but now you've gone and written the National Transportation Safety Board.

HE: Mr. Manager, if the pilot accidentally presses the wheel control column, the automatic hold can disengage—

YOU: Mr. Pilot, you had training in how to use this equipment, and your instructors showed you how to avoid that problem. The other pilots aren't complaining. I read your letters, and I've listened to my engineers, and I'm convinced the equipment is safe. Are you disputing my judgment?

HE: Mr. Manager, I've flown the 1011 myself and—

YOU: I know, you told us all about that, and the Safety Board, too. Are you saying we don't know our job?

He: No, sir, I'm saying no such thing, only that—

You: Now listen, Mr. Pilot, we're paying you to fly these planes in the best way we know how, and we're doing everything we can to make them as safe as possible. What kind of fools do you take us for? Do you think we're going to sit by while you go around writing letters to everybody that the equipment is unsafe? We won't have it. We'll speak with one voice on this issue, thank you—there'll be one hell of a lot of confusion if we don't. As of now, Mr. Pilot, you're grounded. Good day.

After a meeting like this, if you're dealing with a Dan Gellert, you can be sure you're flying right into a thunderhead. The dissident isn't going to see your concern with safety as passionately as you do. He or she isn't going to be as impressed as you are with all the reports and testimony you have carefully weighed. The one thing he or she is sure to remember from this meeting is that you swung like Jim Rice at a waist-high fastball, threatening his or her job future by the grounding order. What that dissident is sure to try to do next is knock *your* pitch out of the park when the chance comes.

It would be far better to avoid any evaluations or judgments, making an opening statement something like this: "Mr. Pilot, you complained about the altitude hold in a letter to the vice-president, and then you sent a copy of the letter to the National Transportation Safety Board. Naturally we're concerned." Encourage the dissident to tell his side of the story. Listen as actively as you can, avoiding words that prejudge his behavior, asking open-ended questions that invite him to detail his fears and criticisms. Questions that begin with "What" or "How," and requests that begin with "Tell me" or "Would you describe," work best. From time to time restate the dissident's views in your own words. "So what you're afraid of is that a pilot might accidentally push the wheel," you might say, or "In other words, you believed that the vice-president didn't pay any attention to the first letter you wrote."

This approach is to be preferred because personalities become entangled with issues, in emotional situations like whistleblowing. You may want to attack the issues, but you do *not* want to attack the people. When Mr. Manager reacts to Mr. Pilot's fears as if they were ridiculous, he treats the employee himself with contempt.

In your own mind, the accident that Mr. Pilot fears may be unreal. But his *fears* are real. Demolishing the factual basis of the fears does not necessarily demolish the fears. Anyone who has raised a child who was afraid of the night knows this. It isn't just the night that the child is afraid of, but the fear of not being protected and of being left alone.

Just as you encourage Mr. Pilot to express his fears and concerns, so should you tell him your own. You're afraid of the bad publicity. You're afraid the criticism will lead to a chain reaction, igniting groundless complaints from other employees. You're concerned that your leadership will be questioned. And so on. As long as this kind of expression takes place frankly and honestly, without either side blaming the other, it will help solve the first-stage problems. Though the dissident may be too emotional to talk this way at first, after a while he or she is likely to react positively to your good example.

A common mistake of seniors is to dismiss some concern expressed by the subordinate because, in their own minds, the problem is not serious. For instance, Mr. Pilot may let it slip that he's afraid of being penalized by assignment to the Washington–New York shuttle run or to a back office. Though in your own mind you know that this is not a serious possibility, don't wave it aside as foolish. That's the same thing as treating Mr. Pilot as foolish.

Involve the dissident as early as possible in ways to work out the conflict. He's afraid the altitude hold will fail again; you're sure it won't. "How shall we go about resolving the disagreement? Any ideas, Mr. Pilot?" Surely he's going to feel more confidence in a process that he himself might have suggested or has had a hand in approving, than in one that you and your colleagues work out in private.

It is important not to ask the dissident to agree to something that suggests that he or she is backing down. Try to frame any proposal you offer in terms that won't make the employee a loser. Don't propose that if Mr. Pilot will retract his criticisms, all will be forgiven. Don't ask him to have faith in management's judgment and forget it. Don't insist that he wait until the next technical bulletin comes out, which contains an article proving how sound the altitude hold equipment is. Ideas like these say, in effect, "Your fears aren't substantiated. We know better." Instead, you might steer him in the direction of making constructive suggestions—perhaps a study of the whole cabin system, pilot training in the use of the altitude equipment, or ways to modify the cabin to avoid accidental pressure on the steering column and disengagement of the altitude hold. Once the two of you get your minds working in this direction, you're on your way to unfreezing yourselves from position bargaining—that is, from a debate where one wins at the expense of the other.

Throughout, keep encouraging the expression of feelings. Fears that seemed too difficult to express at first may surface later in the discussion if you can win the dissident's trust. Keep coming back to your own concerns, if you feel that the dissident is hiding some private concerns: "You know, the people on our side feel miffed that you didn't follow up and come to us personally when your letter was unanswered. When you sent a copy to the

NTSB, we were really embarrassed. Some of the others think you're going to write the board again, or publicize all this in the union's bulletin. Personally, I think they're overreacting, but that's their feeling just the same."

Making your own feelings more explicit not only encourages the dissident to do the same but underscores the seriousness of the problem, the depth of your concern. "Well, to tell the truth, Mr. Manager," confides Mr. Pilot after a while, "there's this guy in operations control. And you know, I went to him about this way back in March—a couple of us were worried about it then—and you know what he tells me? 'You goddam pilots think you know everything, just because you get paid so much.' And before he got through, he was saying something about my ancestry, too." Now, you'll be violating his confidence if you rush out and blame the person he named, but you can suggest that something might be gained by getting the operations controllers and pilots together to work out some of their distrust of one another, or by top management's paying a little more attention to the needs of operations controllers for more indoctrination and training.

Strive to avoid giving any impression that your response to the dissident is a routine that you learned in some management training school. Don't let your eyes suggest that you're listening just to make the dissident feel better. Interrupt occasionally to ask, "Do I understand correctly that you're saying that the vice-president never answers those letters himself anyway?" or "Excuse me, but you just said some operations controllers were spies for management. How do you mean that?" Don't worry about how far off base you think the dissident is. Put these questions or rephrasings in his or her own words. And remember that listening sympathetically does not mean you agree with the employee critic, only that you take him or her seriously.

At the end of the discussion, often it is wise to try to sum up. "Let me see if I've got the point of what you're saying. You're saying that there's no way for that equipment to be operated without an occasional accident due to pressing the steering column. It seems to me also that you're saying that operations doesn't really care what the pilots think about the manufacturer's tests." State such impressions positively—from the dissident's viewpoint, not your own or management's.

Finally, Fisher and Ury offer this counsel:

In many negotiations, each side explains and condemns at great length the motivations and intentions of the other side. It is more persuasive, however, to describe a problem in terms of its impact on you than in terms of what they did or why: "I feel let down" instead of "You broke your word." "We feel discriminated against" rather than "You're a racist." If you make a statement about them that they believe is untrue, they will ignore you or get angry; they will not focus on your concern. But a statement about how you feel is difficult to challenge. You convey the same information without provoking a defensive reaction that will prevent them from taking it in.[2]

2. *Focus on the Employee's Interests and Desires, Not on the Position Taken.*

If you concentrate on the position taken by the dissident, you may run into an impasse. Don't get hung up on the merits of the person's arguments. Instead, ask yourself what the person is trying to achieve, what gain he or she is after. Understanding the person's interests in challenging management or talking back is much more likely to help you make some progress than focusing only on the position taken.

But how can you do this? The dissident may not oblige by coming out and candidly telling you. One good approach is to put yourself in the other person's shoes and ask, "Why" Suppose you have a Louis McIntire sitting opposite you. Why have this chemist and his wife gone to all the work of writing a novel criticizing the way management treats scientists and engineers? Is their motive to put public pressure on companies like yours to recognize the rights of professional people to bargain with top management? And if that is so, what kinds of management unfairness is he most concerned about? Pay? Unfair discharge? Perhaps, as you're sitting there listening, it will become clear that one of these is his real interest.

One useful mental procudure is to ask yourself (*a*) what the dissident thinks you want him or her to do, and (*b*) why the person chooses not to do it. For instance, suppose you believe Mr. Chemist realizes how much you want him to get that antibusiness book off the market—to expunge it, if possible. If Mr. Chemist sees that, why doesn't he oblige? Does he see this issue as one on which he has a right to speak out just as a person has a constitutional right to speak out against a government action? "If I do what the company wants and take the book out of circulation," you may see Mr. Chemist thinking, "I sell out to management, I'll be criticized by other scientists as pro-management. Professionals like me will look weak, and our superiors will scoff at us for doing nothing. But if I refuse to comply with management's obvious wishes, I uphold the rights of professional people to speak out, I will be praised by my colleagues, others will be encouraged to do what I have done, we'll get publicity and public support, we'll gain more respect and recognition by executives . . ."

Perhaps you cannot forgive Mr. Chemist for writing a book that is contemptuous of management. But now that it is out, Mr. Chemist is doing

[2] Ibid., p. 37.

something that to him seems completely logical. He has to keep promoting it and subsidizing more printings.

Typically, an employee dissident, or a group of them, has more than one interest. Mr. Chemist, for instance, may be seeking not only a preferred status for professional employees as a class but security and advancement for himself. Or he may be after increased status and recognition from his colleagues, or perhaps from the chemistry profession. Possibly, intending to run for Congress again, he sees the book as a medium for keeping himself in the voters' eyes.

Instead of just letting these thoughts pass through your mind and possibly be forgotten, write them down when you have a moment to yourself later on. In so doing, you will remember them better and perhaps hit on some good ideas for dealing with them. If possible, rank them in order of their probable significance to the employee.

The most important thing is to get around to talking about your interests and the dissident's. Bring them to the surface and make them a vital part of the negotiation. Be candid about your own interests. "You see, Mr. Chemist, management is worried that a trade union will come in and organize the technical people. We don't want to get involved in the kind of bitter rivalry that Detroit suffers from." Or, if management's right to manage is a salient concern: "Frankly, Mr. Chemist, some of the executives around here think that if this goes on they won't be able to manage any more; they won't be able to keep high standards, get rid of nonproducers, that sort of thing. Personally, I'm not concerned so much about what your book has done as about what it might start some of the others to writing. . . ."

Be as specific as you can in outlining your interests. Details make your view more convincing. "Just last month, for instance, we asked one of your colleagues to help us interview candidates for the agricultural chemicals department, and he refused. He said that was below his level, an administrative job, not a professional's." Or, "Maybe you'll recall, Mr. Chemist, that we all got together at the beginning of the year and budgeted $800,000 for modifications of the equipment in Y-Lab. Well, they used up that amount in three months and went right on spending as if the budget didn't mean a thing, never bothering to tell us. Can you blame management for getting uptight? Everybody can't go flying off in his or her own direction."

When the dissident begins acknowledging his or her interests, show that you have listened and understood. It's the best way to encourage the employee to pay attention to your statements. "What I hear you saying, Mr. Chemist, is that you want credit for what you're doing, and you don't think the company has been fair with you. Am I right? Is there more to it than that?"

The point, as it was in the first step, is to get the focus off positions, away from a pointless debate over who's right. Once interests become the subject of attention, you and the dissident won't get trapped in recriminatory arguing, with you asserting, "Mr. Chemist, you can't treat us like that, don't forget who's in charge," and him crying, "The company wants to treat me like a blue-collar worker and I'm not going to let them!" Both you and the dissident can become sensitive to what concerns and desires are driving the other side.

As soon as possible, point to interests shared by you and the employee. "Mr. Chemist, the last thing we want is a decline in creativity in this company. If we're going to be first, new ideas have got to come out of the lab. We're in that boat together."

Note that this approach is not "being nice" or "taking it easy on the other side." In fact, it allows you to be just the opposite. As Fisher and Ury point out,

> You can be just as hard in talking about your interests as any negotiator can be in talking about his position. In fact, it is usually advisable to be hard. It may not be wise to commit yourself to your position, but it is wise to commit yourself to your interests. This is the place in a negotiation to spend your aggressive energies. The other side, being concerned with their own interests, will tend to have overly optimistic expectations of the range of possible agreements. Often the wisest solutions, those that produce the maximum gain for you at the minimum cost to the other side, are produced only by strongly advocating your interests. Two negotiators, each pushing hard for their interests, will often stimulate each other's creativity in thinking up mutually advantageous solutions.[3]

3.   *Think Up Creative Options that Will Enable Both of You to Come Out Ahead.*

After you've gotten the discussion away from "I'm right and reasonable and you're wrong and ridiculous" to "Now you know what I'm really interested in, and I think I know what you're really interested in," you can begin on the payoff stage: devising options and alternatives that will leave you both better off. For example, if personality conflicts are causing trouble, a transfer may help. If lack of communication seems to be a major difficulty, perhaps regular rap sessions will ease the problem. If a sense of helpless-

---

[3] Ibid., pp. 55–56.

ness seems to be part of the trouble, there may be ways to spread decision-making power a little more or in a different manner.

If the discussion starts to slip into position bargaining and recrimination, get it right back on the track. Don't defend yourself or blast the other side if all of a sudden the dissident attacks you or management again. Allow him or her to let off steam, show that you have paid attention, and rephrase the attack on you or your colleagues as an attack on the situation. "When you say we don't care about equipment problems," a manager at BART might have told the three dissident engineers, "I hear you saying you're worried about safety. I'm with you. None of us wants trains cracking up and riders injured."

Devising options calls for the same kind of process that many other types of problemsolving require. You begin with the nature of the problem or dissatisfaction. In the BART case, this would have been, for management, such problems as the anonymous memoranda criticizing decisions, rumors of leaks to the press concerning difficulty with switching equipment, or a hostile attitude toward managment on the part of some technical people. On the other side, Hjortsvang, Bruder, and Blankenzee might have complained of such problems as top management's unthinking commitment to the supplier company's ideas, apparent disregard of technical people's opinions, or obsession with meeting the construction timetable.

Next you begin sorting out the symptoms, defining the barriers and obstacles, noting causes. At BART, if you had been a manager dealing with the dissidents, you would have defined such causes as concern for safety, fear of being made the "goat" for operating failures, fear of retaliation for speaking up, worry about meeting public expectations of prompt opening of the new transit system, and so forth.

Next you turn to the *kinds* of solutions that might be possible—a major revision of the timetable accompanied by a public explanation, improved internal communications, changes in staffing, and so on. Finally, you translate these thoughts about approaches into specific ideas for action—rap sessions conducted by engineers with reports to management on the complaints and suggestions voiced (without naming the people), confidential consultation with the governor about the need for fresh planning, hiring a consulting firm to take a fresh look at the technical difficulties, and so on.

In choosing ideas for action, look for those that may satisfy both sides. At BART, anonymity in the rap sessions would have satisfied the engineers, and strict confidentiality about the results would have satisfied management; the hiring of a consulting team might have met the needs of both sides if the choice could have been made jointly; an approach to the governor might have met management's needs if management could be guaranteed in advance that its sincerity would not be challenged by the engineering staff.

Keep referring to the goals that you and the dissidents are interested in. "We want these trains to work . . . we don't want to disappoint the public . . . we want the best technical thinking we can get . . . we don't want any last-minute surprises . . . if the budget isn't right, we need to know enough in advance so we can get it revised . . . we don't want to scare away good people."

The important differences of interest and perception between you and the dissidents can be capitalized on at this stage. Don't expect naively that they will see it your way. At BART, the engineers thought of safety in a different way from management; they were less interested in meeting the timetable than management was; they attached less importance to budgets; and they were not so concerned about harmony through the ranks. Such differences were keys, not obstacles, to creative solutions.

For instance, if each side has a different notion about what safety is, they might agree to bring in outside experts who are knowledgeable about the kinds of standards that are acceptable to the California legislature and public. If each side has a different view about how long a time is permissible to get the construction completed, the engineers might agree to put aside their objections for nine months and go all-out on management's program if, at the end of the period, an impartial consulting team will come in to review progress and decide if a major change in approach is necessary. If the engineers pooh-pooh budget restrictions that management regards as very important, they might agree to respect a new budget for a period of six months, at the end of which time meetings will be called to consider changes in the amounts budgeted. If management wants harmony and unison in the ranks but the engineers feel more comfortable in an atmosphere of permissiveness over disagreement and encouragement of individual opinion, management's interest in the organization's "image" to the outside world might be preserved by a code of strict confidentiality; the engineers' interest might be served by regularly scheduled rap sessions. If the engineers are more interested in job security than management is, both sides' interests might be served by management's agreement to a policy of no layoffs except for reasons approved by an impartial panel of arbiters.

Throughout this stage, avoid trying to influence the dissidents by warnings. Focus instead on the beneficial consequences of adopting your proposal. The impartial panel to review proposed layoffs is not going to hurt capable people like Hjortsvang, Blankenzee, or Bruder but it will enable BART to deal with incompetents and misfits who are a pain in the neck to everybody. An agreement to go all-out on the present program for nine months won't affect the security or the reputaion of the engineering staff now, but an impartial technical review at the end of that period will identify major difficulties before anything serious happens, and the engineers can be given full credit then for any objections and reservations they may still have.

Try to keep in mind the "politics" of the other side's agreement with your proposed solution. In advance of the meeting, jot down how your proposal for a nine-month moratorium will be seen by the engineers' peers. Will it be criticized as a sellout? Would it be more agreeable if the technical review panel were named in advance? Suppose one of the three dissidents were to decide to seek a job elsewhere in the months ahead. How might your proposal affect the "track record" he can claim for his work at BART?

Fisher and Ury offer the following counsel:

A final test of an option is to write it out in the form of a "yesable proposition." Try to draft a proposal to which their responding with the single word "yes" would be sufficient, realistic, and operational. When you can do so, you have reduced the risk that your immediate self-interest has blinded you to the necessity of meeting concerns of the other side.

In a complex situation, creative inventing is an absolute necessity. In any negotiation it may open doors and produce a range of potential agreements satisfactory to each side. Therefore, generate many options before selecting among them. Invent first; decide later. Look for shared interests and differing interests to dovetail. And seek to make their decision easy.[4]

4. *Seek Results Based on Fair Standards and Criteria, Not Pressure and Willpower.*

In seeking a resolution of a dispute with employees, don't yield to pressure or let an outcome be based on the power of your will or the dissident's.

Suppose you are the manager confronting Greenwald in the North Miami Beach water supply case. He says, "Okay, I won't tell another soul about this water problem, but in exchange for that I want you to agree to turn the water off until the coliform count is reduced." If you see the illogic of his proposal, don't concede a thing. "Look," you might say, "the matter of the coliform count has nothing to do with whether you agree to keep the problem quiet." Or suppose you are one of the health board officials confronting Rittenhouse in the Painesville health department case. "Okay," says the health commissioner, "I'll agree to disguise the name of the city

---

[4] Ibid., pp. 82–83.

manager if you agree that I had authority to send the questionnaire out." Your response is incorrect if you agree to trade favors. A better reaction might be this: "Well, I'd like you to agree to disguise the name of the city manager, but you know that has nothing to do with the propriety of your sending the questionnaire out without consulting me in advance."

When you get down to the final stage of selecting a way to resolve the dispute, it may be tempting to throw up your hands and call off discussion if the dissident, unable to accept your proposal, becomes angry. "It's stupid to call an outsider in to arbitrate this matter," the dissident cries. "It's perfectly clear the equipment is unsafe, isn't it? Any featherhead can see that!" What manager is not tempted at this point to say, "All right, if that's the way you want it, goodbye." But the temptation must be avoided or you may find yourself heading down the nasty road that the employers of Greenwald and Rittenhouse took. Hold on to your temper, deflect the attack, return to the merits of the proposal, and even accept responsibility for the seeming ridiculousness of your idea. "Well, maybe there's another way to tackle it," you might say in a situation like the BART case. "Maybe it looks to you as if that proposal is unfair. Okay, we're both interested in safety. Right? But management also is interested in keeping operations going at a profit, and minimizing downtime, and in the long run that's in your interest, too. So what would be a fair way to decide on the proper safety level? If an arbiter from the Institute of Electrical and Electronics Engineers won't do, what about one from the Caltech faculty? Or what about a list of nominations from three or four of you engineers and a list from management, and then we make up a panel of people who are on both lists?"

Remember that in general you, as management's representative, have the advantage in these discussions. If it's the Greenwald case, you're the appointed official of the water department who is known by the mayor and administration, whereas Greenwald is an unknown recently hired. If it's the Rittenhouse case, you're the member of the health board, supported by several associates; you have the advantage of many years of service and recognition in the community, whereas Rittenhouse is relatively new and untested. If it's the Geary case, you're the vice-president of the steel company, with all the visibility and authority that your office confers, whereas Geary, though a veteran, is known only in the ranks of a certain group of salespeople. In other words, it is easier for you to avoid throwing in the towel than it is for the dissident to resist a reasonable offer or proposal. Your reasons for refusing to yield can be communicated to many more people—and faster—than the dissident's can.

"Look," you can say to the water-tester who thinks the coliform count is too high, "you want a public warned of a possible danger, and I want nothing said until we're sure there is a danger. Let's see if we can't work out some fair test of what the danger really is—somebody or some standard that both of us will respect." Or, to the health commissioner, "You think your thesis is fair and objective and won't hurt the reputation of our city government, but we think it is embarrassing for what it says and humiliating for the way it was done. Now, isn't there some fair way that we could work out a procedure that would help us both out of the jam? What about bringing in somebody from the conflict resolution center at the state university?"

An interesting variation of such an approach is suggested by Fisher and Ury. Ask the other side to put in writing the most reasonable proposal he or she can make; you do the same for your side. Then give the two most reasonable proposals to an arbitrator to choose between. The reasoning is that such a procedure puts pressure on both sides to make their proposals as fair as possible. In professional baseball and in states where the approach is compulsory in certain types of disputes in the public sector, it apparently has produced more settlements than have conventional types of arbitration.

If you and the subordinate agree on a criterion or procedure for resolving the dispute, ask the subordinate to synopsize the discussion and agreed-on solution and send you a memorandum. Write a memo on the talk for your own records, too, and, if there is much divergence between the two, get in touch again with the dissident.

Parting Observations

To sum up, try to avoid getting trapped into position bargaining when you confront a whistleblower or dissident who is challenging management. The more you expound on your position that a Greenwald or McIntire has acted irresponsibly, the more you defend your position stubbornly against attack; the more identified you become with the rightness of your position, the more hopeless it becomes to see a way out of a deadlock. What is more, all the time that you are defending the rightness of your position and attacking the wrongness of the dissident's, you are forcing him or her back against the wall.

"As more attention is paid to positions," observe Fisher and Ury, "less attention is devoted to meeting the underlying concerns of the parties. Agreement becomes less likely." Don't make the mistake of the position-bargainer who righteously announces that his or her position is a matter of principle and refuses even to consider the interests of the employee troublemaker. This is what happens so often when managerial prerogatives are threatened. The managers act as if they were about to be castrated. "Are you telling us how to run our job?" they shout at the employee. *"We're* responsible for managing the water supply in this town, and it's none of your business to intrude."

Constructive interest bargaining does not mean pulling your punches. It is no answer for those who hope to avoid the emotional costs of disputes by trying to see their adversaries as friends and applying the golden rule. These people make themselves vulnerable to the dissident who plays hardball, and also, of course, to hard-nosed second-guessers in management who say they should have followed a tough line.

What if the dissident never responds to your repeated efforts to get away from position bargaining to more constructive approaches? In other words, suppose the employee objector is more interested in being a gadfly and rabble-rouser than in being cooperative and helpful—and never improves? Then fire the person (or, in the chilly language of personnel administration, initiate termination proceedings). If anyone questions you, offer your notes on the discussions. If one or two others joined you at some stage, they can attest to your efforts. If company policy or government regulations require you to submit to a hearing procedure, your duly noted discussions should serve as documentation for your decision. To broaden your understanding of procedures at this stage, consult one of the good books available.[5]

CROSS-EXAMINING YOURSELF ABOUT THE ETHICS OF A SITUATION

One cannot examine the subject of whistleblowing and employee talk-back for long without bumping into questions of ethics: "Did I do the *right* thing?" "Can a Christian be a good executive?" "How can I handle these situations economically and feel good about it?" Students and management trainees, as well as managers, are keenly interested in the ethical aspects of management decisions.

In theory, there is a debate over whether a corporation or government agency can be ethical. A corporation, it is argued, is an artificial person; it does not have a conscience. Therefore how can it be ethical? In practice this theoretical reservation makes little sense. The actions of corporations and government agencies are taken after deliberation by flesh-and-blood people who, though perhaps not as immortal as the corporation, in every practical sense are its eyes, ears, mind, heart, and conscience. Indeed, some corpora-

[5] See, for example, Robert Coulson, *The Termination Handbook* (New York: Free Press, 1981) or *Employee Termination Handbook* (New York: Executive Enterprises, 1981).

tions and public agencies are as well known for acting ethically and responsibly as others are known for acting as if they were born crooked.

Although corporate codes may be extremely helpful guides to managers in ethically troublesome situations, they rarely solve a problem by themselves. Typically, managers have to wrestle with the ethics of an organization question as persistently and aggressively as they wrestle with the ethics of a vexing family problem or neighborhood zoning plan. There seems to be no substitute for managerial reflection, introspection, and soul-searching if one wishes to keep morality and ethics from being a charade. For the manager who feels secure enough to face this reality, seven questions are especially useful forms of self-examination. I borrow the ideas for these questions shamelessly, if not unethically, from a longer list by a colleague at the Harvard Business School, Laura L. Nash.[6]

1. *What Are Your Intentions in Making the Decision Under Consideration?*

Although many decisions to penalize or not penalize dissidents "blow up" and make managers rue the day they made the decisions, I would guess that most such decisions were made with at least one good intention. For instance, the decision to fire Marvin Murray probably was motivated by the desire to keep Dataform's reputation for delivering equipment on schedule. The decision to fire James Rittenhouse no doubt was motivated in part by the desire to protect a former colleague whose back was now turned. The decision to fire Michael Holodnak presumably sprang partly from a desire to protect the name and goodwill of an organization that hundreds of other employees were giving their working lives for. These were good intentions.

I wonder, however, if the decision-makers did not have other intentions as well, intentions that, although not revealed to outsiders, were perfectly clear at the time to the managers involved. For instance, one suspects that those who fired Murray said something like this to themselves: "He may be right, but let's hope he's not, and that means we've got to get rid of him." Those who fired Rittenhouse may have told each other, in effect, "This guy is making us look bad." And Holodnak's executioners probably intimated to one another something like, "Let's get rid of this pain in the neck."

Such intentions would have been more questionable. In ethical quality, at least, they would not have been as defensible as most decisions the managers generally made. Getting rid of someone for the sake of convenience is a notion that these managers, like most of us, presumably would have felt uncomfortable with if they had faced up to it.

---

[6] Laura L. Nash, "Ethics without the Sermon," *Harvard Business Review*, November–December 1981, p. 78.

Decisions to leave a dissident alone may be just as troublesome. The intention the decision-maker discloses to a superior may be something like, "She is a nice person and has worked here five years," or "Yes, he is a pain but I happen to know he is having family troubles." But another intention in the decision-maker's heart may be less justifiable. "He's argumentative and I hate to confront him," or "She'll break down in tears and I'll feel like a heel."

The point is simply this: Be very analytical and objective about your intentions; be sure you get them on your mental table so that you can look at them. The "purity" of your intentions is important. It is true that they do not control the future. What veteran manager is unaware of how fate can twist one's aims and plans around its finger? However, your motives have a chain reaction of effects. They are seen and adopted by other managers, becoming attitudes about "the way we do things here." Also, dissidents and whistleblowers have an uncanny sensitivity to motives. The employee objector who hears you say, though your words do not say so, "I want to be fair to us both," has to be hardhearted not to respond. By the same token, hearing between your words, "I'm going to destroy you," is a threat that starts the adrenaline flowing.

In my discussions with the employee objectors whose stories are told in this book, I sometimes got the feeling that they were motivated to strike back as if life itself were at stake. They read threatening intentions into their superiors' actions. In other organizations where the atmosphere was more friendly, however, the dissidents would have caused few problems. In the article cited, Nash writes,

> I argue that despite their complexity and elusiveness, a company's intentions *do* matter. . . . Sociologist Max Weber called this an "ethics of attitude" and contrasted it with an "ethics of absolute ends." An ethics of attitude sets a standard to ensure a certain action. A firm policy at headquarters of not cheating customers, for example, may also deter salespeople from succumbing to a tendency to lie by omission or purchasers from continuing to patronize a high-priced supplier when the costs are automatically passed on in the selling price.

2. *Whom Could Your Proposed Decision or Action Injure?*

If you are thinking about firing a Greenwald, let us say, who will suffer if he happens to be right—or partly right? Two or three residents of North Miami Beach or hundreds? And suppose he isn't right but the word gets around that he is. Who and how many will be hurt then? If you are the steel company vice-president who is angry at Geary, who and how many will be hurt if the casings are defective, as Geary claims? Though the casings may be satisfactory if used correctly, what might happen if users are a little negligent and subject the casings to too much stress or use them in improper ways?

Too often, such questions are left unasked in cases of manager-employee conflict. The superior is preoccupied instead with the question of prerogatives. "My judgment has been challenged! My authority has been questioned!" The reaction is normal, and naturally you may feel an impulse to express it, but it is hardly the right attitude to take to the meeting with the dissident. Defensiveness can be the blinder that keeps a troublesome ethical problem out of your view until too late.

3. *How Would You Define the Problem if You Were the Employee Objector or One of His or Her Friends?*

The purpose of asking this question is to help you break out of the habit of thinking exclusively in terms of your authority as a manager, your deadlines for getting a project done, the objectives given you for profit or cost reduction, budget compliance, and so on. These criteria are natural and necessary. They are part of your thinking as an administrator. Unfortunately, however, they tend to exclude ethical questions, to put issues of rightness and wrongness in left field. By trying to see a situation as the employee objector sees it, you may be able to anticipate the discomfort and embarrassment that you may later feel when that person, the union, a television station, or attorneys argue the other side in public.

Suppose, for example, that Berg's superiors had taken a moment to see the suspicious act in the warehouse as he saw it. Would it have been so easy then to assume, as they apparently did, that the unpleasant business would go away, melt into thin air? Would they have realized that Berg would have remained silent only if he had been an exceptionally compliant and enervated person? Or suppose the officials at HUD had taken a moment to look at Ripskis's "leak sheet" in the way he did. Would they then have been content to define the issue only in terms of loyalty and disloyalty? Might they have seen that, for many employees, a publication like *Impact* is a symbol of constitutional liberties, of a thinking person's interest in airing the errors of an institution so that its future performance could be improved?

As suggested, few managerial decisions are immoral or unethical from every point of view. Almost always there is at least one justification, usually economic or political, for them. By acting as your own gadfly, by becoming your own Socrates, you can often avoid the trap of seeing an issue too narrowly and missing implications that will offend and outrage others.

4. *Could You Tell Your Family, Your Golfing Partners, or Other Managers About the Action or Decision You Are Considering?*

The old axiom, "Would you want your decision to appear on the front page of the *New York Times?*" is a relevant one, Nash points out. Although executives may insist that a proposed action creates no problem, they may be reluctant to talk frankly about it. The result can be costly embarrassment. "Disclosure," says Nash, "is a way of sounding those submarine depths of conscience and of searching our loyalties."

In the Gellert case, the operating heads who tried to eject the rebellious pilot from Eastern's payroll presumably talked about their intentions to sympathetic colleagues. Would they have disclosed their intentions so readily to nephews in college, wives, or the editor friend next door? If they had, it might not have been long before they saw eyebrows raise or heads shake.

Once I was talking with a division manager about the problems of dissidence she had had to handle in her company. She described the situation of an assistant whose general manner had become irritating and whom she was tempted to get rid of. One day the assistant came in to blow the whistle on an expense account submitted by another member of the staff. Enraged, she decided that this was the last straw. For all his failings, the other member was a good friend, a talented person, and a veteran employee. Fortunately, she took no action that day. At supper, she began telling her husband about the situation but stopped midway through the story when, seeing the expression on his face, the truth dawned on her. The other person had been fudging his expense account for years and everybody knew it! If she dismissed the gadfly assistant for this act, the message sent out to the staff would be, "Don't criticize old Harry's expense accounts, that sort of thing is all right with the boss."

5. *To Whom and What Are Your Loyalties?*

One of the astounding things about whistleblower cases is how often administrators, in their hurry to protect their reputations for efficiency and authority, betray the stockholders (or, in the case of public agencies, the government and public). The harsh dispatch with which Geary was sent packing may have been pleasing to his superiors and improved their images as bosses who didn't brook nonsense. But it was costly to the owners of the company. It lost the company a good salesman, postponed the day of reckoning for a faulty product, and siphoned some earnings off into legal fees, unemployment insurance costs, and public relations expenses. In discussions of this case, management people may talk about loyalty to the corporation. It is interesting that they usually mention this argument as one against Geary. Is it not a better argument against Geary's superiors? After all, Geary was the one in this case who was working for the stockholders; those who fired him were not promoting the owners' interests.

In the Nelson case, the outraged state agency officials were loyal enough to themselves and their staffs when they fired the young critic of waste, but how loyal were they to the taxpayers of Georgia? In the Harless case, the top executives who sacked the employee objector were loyal enough to their cronies, but how loyal were they to the customers of the Fairmont bank? Murray's executioners were loyal to their deadlines but how faithful were they to future customers?

How do you probe your various loyalties in an emotional situation? You don't need a psychiatrist; an attentive friend will do. Role-play with him or her. "What would I do in this situation if I were the attorney for the stock-holders? What would I do if I represented customers and users? What position would I take if I were the chief executive? What would be my reaction if I were a priest, minister, or rabbi?" Then, though your administrative brain may not have questioned your loyalties, your common sense will have a chance to flash warning lights.

6. *How Will Your Proposed Action Look Several Years from Now?*

For the time being, it may be convenient to get rid of the dissidents, or perhaps to give in to them, to defuse them with a minimum of fuss. But how will this action look in a year or two or five? Will turning the other cheek encourage a rash of unthinking complaints from other employees? Will a summary firing tend to dampen employee spirit and discourage some potentially valuable critic from sounding off when you need it?

In reviewing the BART story, it is hard to escape the conclusion that management had a very short time horizon. It seemed to be looking only months ahead, hell-bent on completing the next stage in its timetable but paying little attention to the implications of its actions for two or three years down the track.

Senior executives hold an especially influential position. Naturally they must see to it that short-term goals are met. But if, in their talks and memoranda, they are concerned *only* with short-term goals, it is unlikely that subordinates will look far beyond the next deadline or milepost.

7. *How and Why Did This Situation Arise?*

Firing or negotiating a truce with the employee critic or objector may be only a temporary, makeshift solution. If an underlying problem caused this person to speak out, the problem is likely to induce others to sound off later. Ask yourself what caused this situation to occur in the first place. Is there a basic weakness or failing that should be confronted and dealt with?

If Berg's superiors had wanted to ask this question, they might have identified weaknesses in control and checking that tempted some employees to cooperate with crime rings. If Ripskis's superiors at HUD had asked the question, they might have detected a strong undercurrent of dissatisfaction and alienation that they needed to deal with. Murray's seniors, had they asked the question, might have learned about shortcuts being made in the engineering design department. Such knowledge could be invaluable in avoiding future dilemmas of an ethical nature.

One of the Last Joan of Arcs [7]

An interesting test of the guidelines described would have been the case of Dr. Carol Kennedy and the Food and Drug Administration. In its way the case is a classic. A crusader and missionary spirit, Kennedy was not the kind of employee objector you could negotiate with simply on the basis of goodwill. At the same time, the strength of her case might have led you, had you been her superior, into the trap of conflicting loyalties.

British playwright Tom Stoppard wrote a play called *Every Good Boy*. (The title is taken from the memory trick children use to remember the lines of the musical staff—EGBDF.) In the play two men occupy a cell in a Soviet mental hospital. They have the same name. But one is sane, the other insane. The sane one has been committed to the hospital for dissidence; he defended a writer who criticized the government. The hospital authorities try to get him to confess to insanity. If he'll cooperate, they'll let him go. But he won't cooperate. He won't give in to threats. The authorities bring a psychiatrist in to persuade him, but still he won't cooperate. "I have no symptoms," he tells the psychiatrist. "I have opinions." The psychiatrist answers, "Your opinions are your symptoms. Your disease is dissent."

The disease of dissent was of considerable concern to the Bureau of Drugs of the Food and Drug Administration when Kennedy joined it in March 1970. Kennedy was a psychiatrist. Two years earlier she had met her residency requirement in psychiatry; then she had served for a year as director of the Shelby County Mental Health Center for Children. At the FDA she became a medical reviewer in the Division of Neuropharmacological Drugs. One of her main jobs was to evaluate applications from companies wanting to put new drugs on the market.

[7] This account is based on the report, *Investigation of Allegations Relating to the Bureau of Drugs, Food and Drug Administration,* Norman Dorsen, Chairman (Washington, D.C.: Department of Health, Education, and Welfare, April 1977).

She often impressed associates as a crusader for children's safety. She had deep feelings about protecting children from risk in drug trials and about safe standards for medications. Even some of those who differed from her philosophically learned to have great respect and admiration for her. Dr. Eric Denhoff, one such colleague, told the Dorsen team investigating the FDA that it had become evident to him, as he got to know Kennedy, "that I was working with one of the last Joan of Arcs, and I say that with respect. She went into everything meticulously, into the records in great detail. . . . She's just the kind of person you need in Washington, obstreperous as she might have been."

By early 1972 she had been made responsible for the medical reviews of all applications for psychoactive drugs (drugs designed to stimulate the nervous system) for children. She worked hard. From the director of her division, Dr. Elmer Gardner, she received a performance evaluation rating of 4.55 on a 5-point scale, or "excellent." This was not the only high mark she would receive at the FDA. Late in 1973 the head of the Neurology Section, under whom she served briefly, wrote her that he had found her work "superior in quality and quantity. I have found you to be responsible, willing to accept assignment cheerfully and without complaint, and able to interact comfortably and effectively with the other members of the unit."

The series of events that were to change her life did not begin in a traumatic way. Abbott Laboratories believed that magnesium pemoline, which it marketed under the trade name of Cyclert, would be helpful in treating minimal brain dysfunction in children. In the usual lengthy application, the company sought the FDA's approval for marketing Cyclert. The application was assigned to Kennedy for review. As was customary, she did not make the technical review alone. She was joined by Walter Kletch, a chemist, and Frances Da Costa, a pharmacologist.

After studying the evidence submitted by Abbott Laboratories in favor of Cyclert, the three-member team decided against approving the drug. Their most important objection was that the company hadn't proved clearly enough that Cyclert would have no adverse effects on children, such as addiction, distortion of behavior, or cancer. Kennedy reported this conclusion to Gardner and to a medical officer at Abbott.

Judging from a note Gardner wrote at the bottom of one of her memoranda, he went along with her conclusion. However, something must have induced him to change his mind. One day Gardner met behind closed doors with the Abbott Laboratories people. Apparently he told them that the FDA *would* be able to approve the new drug. Curiously, Kennedy and her two associates were not invited to that meeting, so they were not witness to the conversation. However, two Abbott representatives at the meeting later told the Dorsen investigators that they had said good-bye to

Gardner believing that Cyclert would be approved. As for Gardner himself, he denied to the Dorsen group that he had conveyed such an impression.

At a hearing sometime later of a U.S. Senate subcommittee under the chairmanship of Senator Edward M. Kennedy, the young psychiatrist testified as follows about the closed-door session:

SENATOR KENNEDY: Were you present?

DR. KENNEDY: No; I was not present. I was not informed. I found out the following day. A Food and Drug officer informed me that the division director [i.e., Gardner] had told him that he had informed the drug firm that there were no serious problems with the drug, that it would be approvable subsequent to that. I will not bore you with all the details of phone conversations; but representatives of the drug firm did indeed confirm that they had received this information, that there were no serious problems with the drug.

In the meantime, Dr. Gerald Solomons, a medical consultant to the FDA, was reviewing the case. He wrote Kennedy that she had done "an excellent review." Dr. Roger Freeman, another medical consultant who reviewed the case, wrote her, "The report you did was excellent, and your points well taken. I could certainly not recommend approving Cyclert on the basis of the information provided."

Kennedy and her team members met with two doctors on the staff of Abbott Laboratories—Gardner did not join them—and discussed a letter of nonapproval that they wanted Gardner to send the company. The Abbott people demurred. They asked that the nonapproval letter be held back. When Kennedy refused to agree, Abbott executives appealed to high officials in the FDA. The official letter of nonapproval was delayed.

There followed a series of feverish meetings and telephone conversations between various FDA officials and executives of Abbott Laboratories. From some of the key meetings, Kennedy was excluded, but information leaked to her indicated that the company was pressing its cause with success.

The drug that Abbott sought to market as a partial cure of minimal brain dysfunction for children now began causing maximal brain dysfunction for adults. FDA officials scheduled an important review meeting with representatives of the company. Solomons, the medical consultant who sided with Kennedy, had been given to understand that he would chair that meeting. However, while he and the other medical consultant, Freeman, were working with Kennedy at her house the evening before the meeting, putting the finishing touches on their presentation, which included ninety slides, the telephone rang. It was Gardner. He announced that he, not Solomons, would chair the meeting scheduled for the next day. Solomons was furious. He threatened to boycott the meeting. Gardner backed down.

The meeting the next day was traumatic and, as the Dorsen report characterized it with deft understatement, "adversarial." The Abbott Laboratories people felt they were being treated like delinquents. The Kennedy side felt they were being treated like juveniles. Both sides became paranoid. When the reports of the meeting were reviewed by Dr. J. Richard Crout, deputy director of the Bureau of Drugs, he decided to send a letter of nonapproval to the company.

This decision was cause for joy among Kennedy and her associates. However, the remission was not to last long. Telephone calls and letters came to the FDA from Abbott officials. Kennedy and associates began sending memoranda to Crout, and he to them. Apparently Crout began shifting to Gardner's side. Kennedy says Gardner reminded her one day that "Abbott is a very powerful company." However, when the Dorsen group talked with Gardner later on, he could not recall making such a remark. However, he did say that Abbott "fought very hard about things—and they would bring everyone and everything. They were a nasty, not powerful, company."

Suddenly one winter day defeat came to the Kennedy side. Crout called her, Gardner, and another doctor to his office for a meeting. He announced his conclusion that the review made by the Kennedy team was incomplete. His prescription: appointment of a new review group to diagnose the evidence on Cyclert and decide its fate. He instructed her to make no contact with the new review group to be appointed or with Abbott Laboratories. She was directed to write no more memoranda for the files—this she testified in the hearings later conducted by Senator Kennedy.

To make her humiliation complete, she came to believe that an official decision really had been made in favor of Cyclert and that the second review panel was little more than a formality. Gardner and another FDA official appointed that panel, and then Gardner attended some of its meetings, which began in Chicago.

Late one evening in March, according to her testimony at the Senate hearings, her home telephone rang. It was another FDA official telling her that she had been transferred for 120 days (the maximum period permissible in such a situation) to another division, where her assignment would be to review soft contact lenses. A psychiatrist assigned to review contact lenses? Why? The official explained, "There's a backlog of applications in that division." She asked, "Do I have to go?" He answered, "Yes, you have to go." She asked if this unusual assignment had anything to do with her criticisms of Cylcert. Of course not, she was told.

She called Crout. As she described the conversation to the Dorsen group,

Crout laughed and admitted to her that, yes, the assignment must have seemed like "a bolt out of the blue." He added, "Give the job a whirl." The head of the new division to which she was transferred appeared equally casual. According to her testimony, he said he wanted her because she was known to be a good reviewer. "Someone smart" was needed, he said, even if the task was ludicrous for one with her talents and training.

If anyone in the bureau was naive enough to swallow the official explanation, the illusion would have been dispelled in a couple of months. Then the Neuropharmacology Division that had employed her advertised for a new medical officer specializing in psychiatry. The advertised position was substantially like the job she had been doing.

At the end of the 120 days, despite official efforts to persuade her to stay working on soft contact lenses, she insisted on going back to her old division, as she was entitled by official regulations to do. The minute she returned, however, she was quarantined again. This time she was assigned to the review of drugs used for nausea, vomiting, vertigo, and migraine headaches. (Did this area suggest itself to the panjandrums because of the dizziness and headaches she caused *them?*) It now was difficult for superiors to maintain the pretense of need, however, for in the new section there was no backlog of cases to justify her assignment there.

A psychiatrist can take a professional interest in Freudian slips, but for Kennedy it appeared to be a case of fraudian slips. After hunting for a new job for several months, she accepted an offer from the Social Security Administration.

In the meantime, things went better for Cyclert. Shortly after Kennedy left the FDA, an official letter of approval of the drug was sent to Abbott Laboratories.

When the Dorsen team made its study, it concluded that Kennedy (along with another whistleblowing medic on the staff) was transferred from her job in order to get her out of the way, and it called the transfer "mendacious." The investigators did not, however, find evidence of corruption in the decision to let Abbott Laboratories go ahead and market Cyclert. Kennedy's superiors had not been pathological; they were motivated by benign intentions for the FDA and its constituents. For me, this was an especially important point. "Good" organizations are the ones that can best use mechanisms to resolve disputes with dissidents fairly. Because they are "good," the mechanisms can work. It is only in "bad" organizations that little hope for internal due process exists.

The risk that high-handed, autocratic handling of an employee objector will, as in the Kennedy story, boomerang and hurt management is a real one, especially when the dissident is a professional or technical person. Don't let objections or protests that seem irrational or unrealistic turn you off against the person. As an individual with hopes and fears, a well-intentioned objector is worth courtesy, attention, and understanding. Once you have some appreciation and understanding of the person, look for the objector's interests and motives. What *prompts* the argument? What concerns lie *behind* that position that you may disagree with? When you have a feeling for these motives and concerns, begin the third step, suggesting solutions that will advance the objector's interests as well as your own. The objector may be able to help you create such solutions. If necessary, go on to the fourth step of negotiation; that is, devise ways of putting a proposed solution to the test and getting an objective evaluation.

In many conflicts between objectors and managers there are ethical dimensions to consider. Almost always, one or two or more of the seven questions described will help you see ethical problems in a better-rounded and more realistic manner than an uninquiring reaction will. Also, they will help you to discuss the situation in a fruitful manner if associates or superiors ask you about it.

If, because of your skill in dealing with employee objectors, you find yourself getting more than your share of such problems, remember that conflict and dissension are very old problems that have stirred the sages to wonder about them. "You have not converted a man," said Viscount John Morley, "because you have silenced him." According to an old Chinese proverb, "When you dig a grave for your enemy—dig two." That would seem to apply to a good many of the employee objector accounts we have considered! "I contradict myself," said Walt Whitman. "I am large, I contain multitudes." He would have seen quickly that today's employee objector is not just the person who takes a position in a debate but a person who also has ideals and aspirations, dual loyalties, and relatives and colleagues to please.

We must guard even our enemies against injustice.

THOMAS PAINE

8

THE OBLIGATIONS OF
AN EMPLOYEE OBJECTOR

$=$ Employee objectors often confuse their role with that of media reporters. An enormous gap lies between the two. Whereas the media reporter's loyalty is to a television station, radio station, or publication, whose commitments in turn are to stockholders and the viewer–listener public, the employee's loyalty is to the employer company or agency. Although both reporter and objector may have an interest in honesty, integrity, and efficiency, their diverging loyalties call for different standards of conduct. Some of the reporter's aims and motives are inappropriate for the employee; some of the criteria the employee should observe would fetter the reporter.

The triumphs of employee critics in recent years have made them favorites with much of the public. In this more benign climate it is tempting to overlook the possible dangers of talk-back. Not all employee objectors have solid motives. Not all criticisms are based on fact; not all are reasonable. Not all cries of "foul!" do more good than harm. "There comes a level of internal prying and mutual suspicion," states Sissela Bok, "at which no institution can function. And it is a fact that the disappointed, the incompetent, the malicious, and the paranoid all too often leap to accusations in public. Worst of all, ideological persecution throughout the world traditionally relies on insiders willing to inform on their colleagues or even on their family members, often through staged public denunciations or press campaigns." [1]

Unlike the media reporter or the missionary legislator, the employee objector has an implied duty of loyalty to the employer organization. He or she may even have taken an oath of fidelity. Muckraking, sensationalism, ridicule, and publicity feats usually do not fit in with this basic obligation. They are distracting, they tend to pit one employee against another, and they throw shadows of suspicion in every management corner. I have seen organizations virtually paralyzed as a result of accusations and counteraccusations in the ranks; it might almost have been better for employees to remain closemouthed and crooked than for operations to grind to a near standstill, with workplaces becoming shouting matches that accomplish nothing.

In short, the employee objector, the whistleblower, the internal dissenter all have obligations, just as their superiors have obligations. Let us turn to the rules and guidelines that comprise an employee objector's "code of conduct."

THE SUBJECT MUST BE APPROPRIATE

Employee critics and objectors should concern themselves with specific improprieties and tangible dangers. If it is waste they speak out against, there should be specific acts and evidence of waste; if it is a danger to the public created by a product or service, the danger should be present and real; if it is an illegality, the act should be committed, or in progress, or concretely and definitely planned.

Generally speaking, the requirement of specificity rules out a number of subjects. For instance, as indicated earlier, disagreements with management over policy are inappropriate subjects, except in informal discussions where management invites criticism and exchanges of views. Management's philosophy of direction (e.g., speed of growth, variety of product line, use of debt in financing) also is an inappropriate topic for whistleblowing or protest, and the reasonableness of executive decisions normally is not a suitable topic of complaint or talk-back, especially if the decisions are ones ordinarily made by managers in the course of operations.

"In dissent concerning policy differences rather than specific improprieties," say Robert J. Baum and Albert Flores, "whistleblowing, with its accusatory element, is an inappropriate and dangerous form of warning. It

<hr />

[1] Sissela Bok, "Whistleblowing and Professional Responsibilities," in *Ethics in Teaching Higher Education*, ed. Daniel Callahan and Sissela Bok (New York: Plenum Press, 1980), pp. 279–280.

threatens the public interest, in that it so easily derails into ideological persecution. Many other forms of dissent exist when there is reason to voice policy disagreement or ideological differences." [2]

Personal vendettas are inappropriate topics for protest talk-back and complaint. So, as a general rule, are the personal lives, foibles, and idiosyncracies of seniors. The boss's gambling, the chief executive's income tax troubles, and the marketing vice-president's Parisian mistress, though great subjects for gossip and also prized tidbits for a media reporter, are inappropriate issues for dissidence.

Out of bounds, too, is a *reasonable* difference in judgment on a question of user safety, hazardous working conditions, infringement of the law, or related problem. For instance, let us suppose that three scientists in a chemical company recommend against a certain material or product because of a conviction that it is a potential hazard to the environment. Their superiors review the recommendations, appoint a team of impartial scientists to study the material, are told by that team that the material is safe, and instruct the three scientists to proceed with the project. Are the latter justified in going over the heads of their superiors to the chief executive, or in attacking management on a television show, or in protesting the decision in a letter to a federal agency? No. Only if they can show that the conclusions of the impartial panel were rigged or clearly defective are they justified in rocking the boat—at least while they're on the payroll. The same goes for an employee who, having charged his or her superior with unfairness or discrimination, receives a fair hearing by appointed officials and fails to convince them that wrong was done.

An especially appropriate subject for complaint or protest is the disclosure required by law—for example, falsification of a government agency's budgetary reports, spurious data in an engineering report on a product being designed for the military, false data in an application for a license to construct or operate a nuclear facility for the Nuclear Regulatory Commission, or violation of a safety standard in coal mining. In some cases of this sort, in fact, the federal criminal law makes it a felony punishable by imprisonment for an employee or other person to hold back evidence that a breach of the law is being committed.

The Importance of Being Ernest in Earnest

Some interesting issues concerning the appropriateness of a whstleblower's subject are raised in the A. Ernest Fitzgerald case. Although it is perhaps the

[2] Robert J. Baum and Albert Flores, ed., *Ethical Problems of Engineering* (Troy, N.Y.: Rensselaer Polytechnic Institute, 1978), p. 186.

best-known case of whistleblowing by a federal employee, the facts have been poorly understood by the public. The story has gained fresh relevance as a result of reported flaws in military weapons recently produced. In 1981, for instance, as reliable a journal as *Science* reported that the new radar systems on the Navy's most advanced ships were working only 60% of the time because of random failures among some 40,000 parts in each tracking and firing system. Also, according to *Science,* the Army's tank-killing helicopter, the Cobra, was using a targeting and firing system that broke down repeatedly, causing missiles to veer in the wrong direction. In a military establishment relying on high technology, dissenters can play a valuable role if they respect the obligations of dissent—and an obstructive role if they do not.

A. Ernest Fitzgerald reported to work at the Pentagon in the fall of 1965 as deputy for management systems in the Air Force, succeeding J. Ronald Fox, who returned to teach at Harvard Business School. Born in Birmingham, Alabama, Fitzgerald had received a B.S. degree in industrial engineering from the University of Alabama, married, and become the father of three children. Though some people felt he was "hard to get to know," he was affable, jaunty, and a hard worker. Prior to 1965 he had been president of a small but successful industrial engineering firm that had done cost-control work for the Air Force. This work had led to his appointment.

Although no one realized it then, Fitzgerald was doomed almost from the start. The agency was committed to a system of alliances and mutual support with industry that was alien to a cost-conscious country boy, as Fitzgerald called himself. Air Force leaders had found natural allies in the corporations that manufactured planes and equipment. These powerful contractors gave the agency needed political reinforcement in Congress, and in return the Air Force tried to keep the contractors happy with profitable contracts. One of the Air Force's strongest and most influential allies was Lockheed Aircraft Corporation.

The fact that a company like Lockheed knowingly made unrealistically low cost estimates for contracts it sought with the Air Force apparently bothered neither its own top executives nor the top brass at the Pentagon. If the estimates were not very low, management believed, Congress would not authorize production, thus jeopardizing national security. However, inside the "club" no one was deceived; only congressmen, journalists, and parts of the executive branch were misled.

When Lockheed's head, capable Dan Haughton, wrote to Deputy Secretary of Defense David Packard in 1970 and demanded an additional $500 million for the C-5A air cargo transport that Lockheed was manufacturing, neither Haughton nor Packard saw anything wrong with the request. If

Lockheed was in difficulty with cost overruns, they would have reasoned, that was the fault of an outmoded political system. Since it was in the nation's interest to bail out the company, Packard gave Haughton a prompt and reassuring reply.

Nevertheless, the plane seemed doomed for disaster. The original cost estimates submitted to Congress had been so unrealistically low that the outer limits for overruns were crowded early on. Lockheed had begun to take shortcuts, and the shortcuts were leading to operating failures. Setbacks like the following were becoming predictable: In June 1970, a wheel fell off as the great plane landed before a collection of dignitaries at Charleston Air Force Base in South Carolina. In September 1971, a C-5A engine ripped loose from the wing and took off by itself, rising into the air and crashing down on the runway. The wing of the C-5A was supposed to have a flying expectancy of 120,000 hours, but experts reported that fatigue cracks began showing up at 2,000 hours.

For its dismal record, the plane would come to be known to many as "Fat Albert."

Unknown to Fitzgerald, as early as January 1969 Defense Secretary Harold Brown and Air Force Secretary Robert Seamans, Jr., were, according to some sources, talking about getting rid of him. Because of information Fitzgerald had given the press about the plane project, Brown is supposed to have suggested that the young deputy no longer was valuable to the Air Force. Of course, Brown and Seamans saw support of the C-5A as an employee duty. Though the plane might run into bumpy test weather, its problems could be worked out, they believed. The plane was needed, its concept was sound, and top management was committed to it.

In the fall of 1969, Fitzgerald, who had long been trying to separate fact from fiction on C-5A costs, received a letter from Senator William Proxmire of Wisconsin requesting him to testify before the senator's committee, which was investigating cost overruns and other matters of defense contracting. Although Proxmire's letter was addressed to him personally, Fitzgerald found that it had been opened before he got it. As he was wondering about this, he got a telephone call from the comptroller of the Department of Defense. The comptroller asked if Fitzgerald had received an invitation from Proxmire to testify. (Fitzgerald did not have to think long on the question of how the comptroller had learned so soon!) When Fitzgerald answered that he had indeed received such an invitation, he was asked if he would bow out and let the comptroller handle the matter. After talking with his boss, Fitzgerald decided not to default. He accepted the senator's invitation.

From that point on, Fitzgerald was a target waiting to be shot down. It did not matter that a year before he had been cited by the Air Force for "exceptional initiative . . . remarkable insight . . . and outstanding leadership on improving cost analysis capability." [3]

The day before the hearings on Capitol Hill, Fitzgerald says, he had a talk with Assistant Secretary of Defense Robert H. Charles. The two of them discussed the questions Proxmire would ask. Fitzgerald thought the C-5A would be brought up. He reports that the assistant secretary warned him, "Stay away from the C-5A."

The next day at the hearings, Proxmire asked Fitzgerald, "Is it true that the costs of that contract will be approximately $2 billion more than was originally estimated and agreed on?" Fitzgerald zigged and zagged a little in his answer, out of loyalty to his superiors, but he finally acknowledged that the senator had found the range. "Your figure could be approximately right," Fitzgerald said.

Reporters descended on him after the hearing, and his allegation of a $2 billion cost overrun—later called "The Great Plane Robbery"—was emblazoned in the newspapers. To many people, the figure seemed too outrageous to be true. However, congressmen and others would come to realize, despite the furious verbal counterattacks of the Pentagon, that Fitzgerald had not exaggerated.

Life on the wing was short for Fitzgerald. On November 4, 1969, the bureaucratic missile hit. He was notified that his position was being eliminated, hence there was no more need for his services. (Doubtless the Pentagon would have preferred to eject Fitzgerald directly and immediately, but summary discharge, except for gross incompetence, was not permissible under civil service regulations, which applied to Fitzgerald's position.)

Three days later, sixty members of the House of Representatives signed and sent to President Richard M. Nixon a letter of protest against the firing. The congressmen pointed out that the Air Force's alleged reason for the move, "economy," was an incredible irony.

Senator Proxmire held a committee hearing to investigate the reasons for Fitzgerald's firing. Secretary Seamans had the unenviable task of taking flak aimed at the Pentagon. As Fitzgerald reports,

> Each time one of the subcommittee members referred to my firing, Dr. Seamans would object that I had not been fired at all, but instead my job had been eliminated. When the large audience laughed loudly and disrespectfully at Seamans' stubborn, bureaucratic semantics, the Secretary would turn deep red from his collar to the roots of his white hair.[4]

[3] Wall Street Journal, December 1, 1970.
[4] A. Ernest Fitzgerald, The High Priests of Waste (New York: Norton, 1972), p. 274.

Fitzgerald went job-hunting. He soon learned that he had been blackballed. In fact, he says that the Pentagon had a dossier on him indicating he was simultaneously a womanizer and a homosexual.

Reportedly, two aides to President Nixon wanted to direct the Air Force to reinstate Fitzgerald. Alexander P. Butterfield, a senior member of the White House staff, replied "We should let him bleed, for a while, at least." When he explained these words, written in a memorandum to Robert Haldeman, to Fitzgerald's lawyers, Butterfield said the phrase was "a very poor choice of words . . . I meant let him cry, let him suffer, for at least a while." Although Butterfield rated Fitzgerald a top-notch cost analyst, he felt he should be penalized for his disloyalty and refusal to fly in formation with his bosses.[5]

Felix Morley once said that big shots are little shots who keep shooting. By this definition, Fitzgerald was a big shot. He fought one legal battle after another. The American Civil Liberties Union helped, contributing about $300,000 worth of volunteer legal time. To pay the enormous legal fees he was running up—$400,000, he estimated in 1973—he lectured and wrote the book cited earlier. Finally he got his job back and collected some damages, but in 1976 the U.S. Court of Appeals ruled that, though the law requires a wrongfully dismissed federal employee to be made "whole again," it does not permit the government to pay the dissident's legal bills.

From beginning to end, one of Fitzgerald's powerful allies was Senator Proxmire. Because of his closeness to both sides in the conflict, Proxmire was able to observe details of the Pentagon's interception tactics. In a press release dated April 8, 1974, the senator from Wisconsin summarized as follows:

> Following his testimony he [Fitzgerald] was subjected to a campaign of abuse and harassment that boggles the mind. A submission he made to the Committee was doctored without his knowledge. He was given the most menial tasks to perform. He was falsely accused of leaking confidential documents to the Congress. He was the subject of a rigged security investigation. And finally the ultimate sanction was applied. He was fired.

> I urged the Justice Department to proceed to prosecute the guilty (Pentagon officials) under the criminal code. Specifically I referred to 18 U.S.C. 1505, which makes it a crime to threaten or injure a Congressional witness. The response on the part of the Justice Department was an act of foot dragging that makes the unfolding of the Watergate story seem a model of speed.

[5] *New York Times Magazine,* June 29, 1975.

The Commission's decision (Civil Service Commission decision late in 1973 to reinstate Fitzgerald, after hearings) . . . demonstrated that General Joseph Cappucci, former Director of the Air Force Office of Special Investigations, had initiated a security investigation of Fitzgerald on the basis of unfounded charges and had then proceeded to destroy information arising from the investigation that was favorable to Fitzgerald. The derogatory charges were kept in the file while proof that these charges were false was destroyed.

In 1980 Richard Nixon agreed to pay Fitzgerald $142,000 to avoid a suit for damages; reportedly Fitzgerald's attorneys had a White House tape documenting Nixon's order to "get rid of that son of a bitch." In 1982 Fitzgerald settled with the Air Force for a promotion and $200,000 for his legal costs.

As for Pentagon officials, my impression is that many of them are as unforgiving now as they were years ago of actions like Fitzgerald's (though they may truly regret the harassment inflicted on him). They feel that it is deplorable for a person in his position to speak out critically against a program to which top management is committed, after diligent analysis and hard effort. Naturally, Fitzgerald sees things differently. It is never too late to speak out against a mistake in national defense, he argues, and it is always worthwhile to protest a waste of taxpayers' money.

Though people may disagree on the loyalty question, most concur that the subject of Fitzgerald's whistleblowing was appropriate. The subject was specific and impersonal—cost overruns, a cover-up. The dangers were tangible—hazards in the plane resulting from shortcuts to control costs. Moreover, something could be done to correct the problem; the dangers were not irreversible, and it was not too late to take action.

THE OBJECTOR'S MOTIVES MUST BE LEGITIMATE

To be entitled to a fair hearing, employee objectors should be motivated by the good of the organization, stockholders, the public, or customers, or by standards of decency and integrity. They are not entitled to take the time of superiors or to upset other employees in order to justify the correctness of their judgments, gain publicity, grind an ideological axe, or advance their personal interests in other such ways. To be realistic, I know of no case in which the objector or critic appeared to be acting *solely* for the good of the organization or society; sooner or later, ego becomes involved. But in my opinion the objector has no standing and, to borrow the legal phrase, should be thrown out of court unless he or she can demonstrate clearly that broader interests will benefit if the objections produce a constructive response. Bok says it all:

> The motives may be partly self-serving, the method questionable, and still we may judge that the act was in the public interest. In cases where the motives for sounding the alarm are highly suspect, for example, but where clear proof of wrongdoing and avoidable risk is adduced, the public must be grateful that the alarm was sounded, no matter how low its opinion of the whistleblower himself.[6]

What about the motives for whistle-*swallowing?* Similar criteria apply. Inappropriate motives for swallowing the whistle at the expense of societal or economic interests include the hope of pleasing a superior with a view to personal advancement, a saccharine conviction that something that looks wrong is all right because management says so, and the rainy-day cynic's feeling that "it won't do any good."

PROMISES AND UNDERSTANDINGS SHOULD BE HONORED (UP TO A POINT)

Sometimes employees make express commitments to keep a technical process, contract, or happening secret. Sometimes they become committed to such secrecies implicitly, as when a subordinate is taken into confidence or trusted in ways that oblige him or her to be tight-lipped. Such commitments should be scrupulously observed unless heavily outweighed by some greater good. For example, suppose a saleswoman accidentally learns that her sales manager is authorizing salespeople to tempt prospects to sign with kickbacks or call girls. The knowledge comes to her at a staff meeting that the manager opened with the admonition that everything said was to be treated confidentially. How free should she feel to blow the whistle? The answer depends in part on the gravity of the offenses and the existence of a company policy prohibiting chicanery.

In an article addressed to technical people, scientists, and other professionals, attorney Peter Raven-Hansen elaborates as follows on constraints to be observed by employee objectors:

> Just as there is information that a professional must disclose, there is information that must *not* be disclosed. Private-sector professionals

---

[6] Bok, op. cit., p. 288.

are frequently constrained by sweeping promises of confidentiality that were signed at the time of employment and then promptly forgotten. Such contractual obligations typically cover "trade secrets" as well as other proprietary data that might be helpful to competitors. Even if such obligations are not enforceable in court, breaking them may furnish a justification for firing.

Much information given to regulatory agencies is also subject to a statutory pledge of confidentiality and is, for example, exempt from disclosure under the Freedom of Information Act. Some federal statutes actually make it a misdemeanor for officials to disclose certain information for purposes other than those specified.

The unauthorized disclosure of classified security materials is clearly ill-advised and often unlawful. Yet much government information is inappropriately overclassified, sometimes for the very purpose of improperly keeping it from the public. Classified information sometimes even includes data such as procurement costs, budget overruns, and construction plans.

An even larger grab bag of information is informally "classified" as "official use only," "confidential," "eyes only," "draft," "preliminary," or some other imaginative phrase conceived to restrict circulation and disclosure. Such informal classifications have no statutory significance—disobeying them is not illegal—yet they can determine the outcome of a whistleblower's case. Disclosure of informally classified information can be branded as an act of "disloyalty" sufficient to justify a firing, or at least a black mark on a personnel record.

In a closed congressional session, for example, a public employee who disclosed military cost overruns was accused by his superiors of leaking "confidential documents." There was a clear implication of security violations. Only after the employee's dismissal did the agency admit that no security breach had occurred and that the released information was at most "confidential with a small 'c.' " [7]

THE FACTS OF WRONGDOING OR DANGER SHOULD BE INVESTIGATED CAREFULLY AND COMPETENTLY

"Be very analytic and careful in assessing the facts on which your protest would be based," Alan Westin urges would-be employee critics and

[7] Peter Raven-Hansen, "Dos and Don'ts for Whistleblowers: Planning for Trouble," *Technology Review*, May 1980, pp. 36–37.

objectors. "Can you document company wrongdoing in a way that would persuade a skeptical reporter or a dispassionate judge that the actions and motives of management are what you say they are? If you were to put yourself into the position of the chairman of the board of that company acting ethically to advance the firm's well-being and the public interest, would you follow the course of conduct that your protest as an employee calls for?" [8]

For some employees, the gaining of good factual evidence is more difficult than for others. For instance, it may be crystal clear to a computer programmer that a program has been fudged or altered for some ulterior motive; it may be indisputably clear to a salesperson that the "real" price for which a product or service is sold is the written price minus a kickback. But for an engineer it may not be so easy to demonstrate that the reliability of an engine part is not great enough, and for an environmental biologist it may not be so easy to prove that the toxicity of a new fertilizer is too great. So there is no pat formula for ascertaining when a would-be objector should hold back or set forth. The answer depends on the kind and quality of information obtainable, the potential danger, and other such circumstances.

In any case, rumors that cannot be substantiated are insufficient grounds for making a fuss. Fragments of evidence usually are insufficient—for instance, one or two test failures in a hundred, when failure may be due to extraneous variables. And of course, hearsay is out. Raven-Hansen counsels the potential objector as follows:

Hearsay is something heard from another. Since it is secondhand, it is not . . . reliable as evidence and may be given less weight or even totally excluded by a court. Although there are exceptions to this rule, the whistleblower should not expect simply to recite what others have told her, no matter how damaging it may be; she needs others to testify themselves. Time and again, professionals without legal training fail to understand this rule, and what they thought was a powerful and convincing case is reduced to the weakest circumstantial evidence or thrown out of court altogether.

Opinion testimony is limited to that which is based on the witness's perception or personal knowledge and which is helpful to a clear understanding of his testimony or determination of the fact at issue. "Opinion" concerning someone else's state of mind is practically never admitted. Unless the witness can read minds, he does not know

---

[8] Alan F. Westin, *Whistle Blowing!* (New York: McGraw-Hill, 1980), p. 161.

what others are thinking or what motivates them, and he is not permitted to speculate.[9]

What about accidentally overheard telephone conversations, surreptitiously recorded talks, "leaks" from employees in the know, and similarly obtained evidence? Aside from the fact that it may be inadmissible in court, such information may so offend the susceptibilities of reasonable people that no employee objector should use it to justify a militant complaint or protest.

In short, the burden of proof is on the objector. Bok mentions the case of a newly hired assistant director of admissions in a university who begins to wonder about the transcripts of some applicants with football-playing ability. Next the new official hears rumors that sometimes surrogates take the admissions tests for a football star for a fee, signing the name of the star. Bringing the question up in a conversation with the director of admissions, the assistant is told that the rumors are unfounded. "And please forget it," the director adds. "I'd appreciate it if you don't bother yourself further with the question." What should the concerned assistant director do? Clearly, it is premature to blow the whistle. Depending on his or her convictions about the seriousness of such wrongdoing, however, the assistant might want to look further into the base of the rumors.

One of the most spectacular cases of whistleblowing is Robert F. Sullivan's run-in with the Boston division of the General Services Administration. For those who have studied the story, one of many interesting issues is the manner in which Sullivan first got wind of wrongdoing and later confirmed it.

Bluebeard (GSA-Style) Was Alive and Well and Living in Boston [10]

Robert F. Sullian didn't realize he was poking into a place in the organization where poking was forbidden. Since he was well liked and admired, and a veteran of more than twelve years of service in the New England branch of the General Services Adminstration, it is probable that others wanted to warn him to stay away. Small voices and worried looks must have been telling him things like "Don't investigate there!" "Stay away!" "Turn away, Bob—before it's too late!" But if he heard these warnings he didn't pay much attention to them.

"Don't pry around in that area! *Look what happened to Tucker!*" Even that warning Sullivan didn't heed. Only a few months earlier Robert F. Tucker,

---

[9] Raven-Hansen, op. cit., p. 43.

[10] This account is drawn from articles in the *Boston Globe,* government reports, and notes supplied by Robert F. Sullivan.

an electrical engineer in the GSA, had looked into the forbidden files and been dispatched as a result. It was obvious that this area was for top management's eyes only.

Before Tucker, some observers believe, others had made the terrible mistake. The identities and circumstances of these earlier victims have long since been lost from the record.

It was like the old folktale of Bluebeard. "You may look into all the chambers but one," Bluebeard told each new wife. Unable to resist looking, each became a fresh victim.

Sullivan knew the latest GSA victim. In fact, it was while interviewing Tucker in Boston that he had realized something was wrong. Tucker had gotten fired in 1975 because he had become convinced that the Construction Management Division of the GSA was awarding contracts improperly. Top officials were bypassing the competitive bidding procedures required by law and negotiating contracts in secrecy with favored private firms. Tucker had raised questions about all this inside the agency, but Albert Gammal, Jr., a former Republican state legislator who had become New England regional administrator of the organization, told him he was mistaken. "You can't see the difference between legitimate practices and corrupt ones," Gammal had told Tucker.

However, for Tucker there was no mistaking the odor of foul play. He had thought of going to U.S. Attorney James Gabriel, who headed the Boston office of the U.S. Justice Department. But he had decided against that because of his knowledge that Gabriel was a close friend of Gammal; both men were appointees of the Nixon administration. So Tucker had brought his information to the government's Organized Crime Strike Force Unit based in Boston. Naturally he had assumed his visit would be confidential. But his name was turned over to Gabriel, and Gabriel, having directed his own investigation proving that the charges were unfounded, had lost little time in helping Gammal get rid of Tucker.

Because Sullivan was the GSA's criminal investigator in Boston, it was his turn next. Could he resist looking into the forbidden activities? Even before talking with Tucker, his professional curiosity had gotten the best of him. As background for the interview, he had studied various reports produced by FBI investigators. They and other documents showed evidence of favoritism, false justifications, inflated prices, and other irregularities suggesting conspiracy and collusion. Yet, strangely, the FBI had concluded that there was no evidence of wrongdoing. The forty-one-year-old Sullivan couldn't understand that. After talking with Tucker, his suspicions had grown.

In the GSA's Office of Audits Joseph Leland had completed an audit of the Construction Management Division. Sullivan met with him. Had

Tucker been chasing a phantom? Not at all, Leland answered. Tucker had been chasing a monster.

It became increasingly apparent to Sullivan that more than half of the $9 million in GSA contracts under review was tainted. In order to get the contracts awarded to the contractors it favored, officials had been claiming "emergency situations." This procedural farce had allowed them to take shortcuts and negotiate privately with favored firms to do the work.

Though the GSA's own auditors had produced the incriminating evidence, neither Sullivan's boss, the chief criminal investigator for the GSA in Boston, nor the director of the GSA Investigative Division in Washington seemed concerned. Knowing that the auditors' findings existed, they had nevertheless found it unnecessary to study the incriminating reports or take any action other than to direct routine processing, filing, and forgetting.

Sullivan pondered what to do. A graduate of Weymouth (Massachusetts) High School and a veteran of the Marine Corps and the Army, he had, with only a few college credits, worked his way up into an enviable job paying, in 1975 dollars, more than $23,000. Since he had close to twenty years in government service, he also had a substantial pension to keep an eye on. A tall, soft-spoken, methodical, and hardworking man, he liked his job and enjoyed the respect that his colleagues accorded him. He was grateful for stability and friends; his wife had died two years previously, leaving him with two young children to raise.

On the other hand, he was something of a idealist. The agency he worked for was powerful and prestigious. It employed 36,000 people, managed an $8 billion national stockpile of commodities, purchased $3.5 billion in supplies and services annually for other federal agencies, and spent $4.5 billion yearly on construction, maintenance, and repair projects. Wasn't an organization like this supposed to set a good example?

For six months Sullivan pondered what to do. Discuss the evidence of corruption with his superiors? The superiors already knew of the wrongdoing. Go to the FBI? That would probably snare him as Tucker had been snared. Get the ear of a prominent politician—Senator Edward Brooke, for instance? But it was Brooke who had sponsored Gammal for the regional GSA head post. Go to the U.S. Attorney's office in Boston? That route, too, seemed to be closed because of links with GSA officials.

He consulted the Code of Ethics for Government Service. According to the first rule of the code, a government employee should "put loyalty to the highest moral principles and to country above loyalty to persons, party, or Government department." The ninth rule of the code stated that any government employee should "expose corruption wherever discovered."

He talked with his priest, the Reverend Gregory F. Wyse of Saint Anthony's Shrine in Boston. The priest encouraged him to listen to his conscience.

The more Sullivan thought about possible solutions, the more the press seemed to be the answer. He remembered that Tucker had considered this route, too, but had abandoned it. However, Tucker's approach to the press had been impractical. He had talked with the *Boston Globe*'s Spotlight team about his incriminating evidence and got the reporters interested, but then he had told them that he couldn't give them more data without a written agreement that he be allowed to approve any newspaper stories they produced, an unacceptable restriction.

The *Globe* had won a reputation for entering the forbidden rooms of some of Boston's most powerful political figures and for reporting in detail the skeletons it had found inside. The *Globe*, Sullivan saw ever more clearly, was the place to go.

In December 1975, Sullivan, without a word to anyone, went into the forbidden files and selected nine incriminating documents—six FBI reports on alleged irregularities, the recently completed audit by GSA auditors, and two audits made in 1974. He hurried with the documents to his car and drove tight-lipped to the *Globe* offices on Morrissey Boulevard. *Globe* reporter Stephen A. Kurkjian photocopied the documents and thanked him. Sullivan drove back and, later in the day, buried the originals in the files again.

The *Globe* Spotlight team spent several weeks studying the documents and questioning some key figures, including Gammal. On January 18, 1976, it burst its front-page story:

US Audit Uncovers Contract Abuses by the Boston GSA Office

The Boston office of the General Services Administration (GSA) has violated Federal purchasing regulations in awarding millions of dollars in government contracts to favored construction firms, according to an internal GSA audit examined by the *Globe* Spotlight team.

The auditors, who examined $9.5 million worth of construction and architectural engineering contracts, found that the Boston GSA office had used spurious arguments to justify circumventing the formal advertised bid procedure used to award contracts. . . .

The detailed revelation nowhere mentioned Sullivan's name, though Tucker's termination was mentioned. However, the report did pull Gammal out into the open. The regional chief denied to the *Globe* that political influence or favoritism played a part in the awarding of contracts, though in all modesty he conceded that his organization, and the Construction Management Division in particular, probably weren't perfect. Gammal showed a little less cool when responding to questions, prompted by the reporter's interviews with architects and builders, that contractors were put under pressure to make political contributions to Gammal's friend Senator Brooke.

"That's ludicrous. It's inconceivable, incomprehensible and unconscionable," said Gammal. "And, as for me, I wouldn't know a contractor if I tripped over one."

Five days later it was Sullivan's turn to be interviewed—by Gammal's own investigators. Was he the one, they asked, who had given copies of the reports to the *Globe*? He said yes.

The next month he got his job performance and "promotion potential" ratings from management. After a dozen years of uninterruptedly good marks, the ratings had suddenly and ominously dropped. When Sullivan asked his boss, John J. Rooney, Jr., about this, Rooney answered, in effect, "Well, you know, Bob, you didn't handle a couple of cases in the best possible manner. Also, there's that matter of the documents you gave the *Globe*."

Angry and worried that his own boss, with whom he had once shared some confidences about the shenanigans, had turned on him (he had expected others to retaliate, of course, but not Rooney), Sullivan wrote Rooney a letter. It was Rooney himself, he reminded him, who had once suggested that they anonymously contact the *Globe* about what was going on. Rooney had lost his courage to take such a move, however, because of Gammal's political ties; he had feared that a revelation might backfire on the GSA dissidents.

When word about this letter got to the *Globe* Spotlight team, it questioned Rooney. He tried to laugh it off. "Listen, guys, my statement had no real meaning. In fact, it was made in jest."

In the ensuing weeks, Sullivan continued to argue that the drops in his ratings should be annulled. He had limited success. Management did agree to invalidate some of the low marks, but it took its time letting him know. In fact, it didn't tell him about the corrections until a month and a half after proceedings to fire him had been begun.

The proceedings got under way one hot August day with a letter cheerily entitled, "Notice of Proposed Removal" and beginning, "This is a notice that I propose to remove you from your position." Signed by William Clinkscales, Jr., director of the GSA's investigations division in Washington, the letter accused Sullivan of failing to bring the incriminating information to the attention of his superiors before releasing it (in other words,

"Tell Bluebeard first"). Clinkscales also scolded Sullivan for violating the agency's rule against removing and disseminating government documents without approval ("If you do blunder into Bluebeard's room, don't tell anybody"). Conveniently, Clinkscales said nothing about the ethics of the situation, the Code of Ethics for Government Service, or the correctness or incorrectness of the dissident's allegations. In Clinkscales's view, indeed, it was an open and shut case. Weighing the case on the GSA's own scales of justice, in fact, Clinkscales concluded that Sullivan's removal would "promote the efficiency of the service." In fact, Clinkscales added, perhaps shuddering involuntarily at the thought, Sullivan's actions had "seriously affected the integrity and credibility of GSA's office of investigations, and, if condoned, would not only adversely affect the morale and efficiency of all GSA employees but *would result in administrative chaos*" (italics added).

With this letter clinking behind him, Sullivan went to Washington in October to defend himself at a formal hearing. There he referred to his duties under the Code of Ethics, the demands of his conscience, the sincerity of his motives, the importance of high standards of conduct at all levels, and the fact that there seemed to him to be no reasonable alternative to whistleblowing. All these arguments and others went for nought. On the federal scales, Clinkscales's condemnations outweighed Sullivan's defenses, and on November 12 Sullivan was officially removed by a letter from Robert E. Reeb, director of investigations, which echoed the "administrative chaos" and other lines of the Clinkscales letter in August.

In the meantime, Sullivan had gotten in touch with the American Civil Liberties Union. It had recommended that he ask Henry P. Sorett, a bright and energetic attorney with offices in Cambridge, to represent him. "He knew a lot about the civil service legal field," Sullivan says, "and I had a lot of experience as a criminal investigator. Between us we thought we could manage to build a decent case."

Armed with their case, which bristled with cogent combinations of legal, ethical, and practical arguments (see the final commentary in this section), Sullivan and Sorett appealed to the Civil Service Commission's judgmental arm, the Federal Employment Appeals Authority. The FEAA examiner listened to both sides of the case. The outcome of his ruminations was a fascinating ratiocination.

The provisions of the official Code of Ethics, a congressional resolution, and the calls of conscience were pretty weak stuff, the examiner reasoned, because they were not law. The only regulation that really counted was the GSA's prohibition of going public with official information—the "Bluebeard's room rules." The examiner was as appalled as Clinkscales had been at Sullivan's action. He wrote in his opinion, dated April 28, 1977, "For an employee to assume authority on his own initiative to make his own private decision as to what he will elect to remove from agency records and to turn over to an outside party when he is not the custodian of the records, and when the turnover is a personal, unofficial act, *smacks of anarchy regardless of motive"* (italics added). Shades of "administrative chaos"!

In a review of the case a year later, U.S. Senator Abraham Ribicoff's Committee on Governmental Affairs later would comment tersely on this reasoning of the examiner. "The demands of an agency for cohesion, order and public image," noted the Ribicoff study satirically, "far outweigh the need for federal employees to be able to follow the dictates of their conscience or the Code of Ethics." [11]

There followed the worst days of what Sullivan calls "the toughest battle of my life, which was not in the Marine Corps or Army but right in my own backyard—Boston." He no longer drew a monthly paycheck. Because he had been fired for cause, he was ineligible for unemployment benefits. Most of his rights to pension benefits, accumulated during twenty years of government service, had been forfeited. He received a few anonymous warnings. Apparently his car brakes were tampered with. He was a near victim of a hit-and-run "accident."

His son who was in high school dropped out; the son wanted to find a job to help pay the family bills. As a result, the boy's education got fouled up. "Obviously," says Sullivan, "it was hard for my children to comprehend why I was fired by the government for exposing dishonesty when society teaches them honesty is one of man's greatest values." He didn't know where the next meal was coming from. The priest helped, giving Sullivan a "To Whom It May Concern" letter commending him for his honesty, dedication, and loyalty and noting that, with the "rubber consciences" of Watergate fresh on people's minds, it didn't make sense to punish an employee for "following his conscience in the service of his country."

Then he got two good breaks. The first, a stopgap aid, was landing a job with a Massachusetts state agency. Although the pay was about half of what he had been getting at GSA, this money made it possible to pay the food and heat bills. Second, the American Civil Liberties Union helped interest the Washington, D.C., law firm of Shaw, Pittman, Potts, and Trobridge in taking his case to court. This step was to prove of great long-run value.

Two attorneys in the firm, William Bradford Reynolds and George D. Crowley, Jr., prepared a strong case to take to a federal court. In addition, they worked hard to muster some political support for Sullivan. U.S. Senator Patrick Leahy of Vermont and his aide, David Julyan, came forward and

[11] *The Whistleblowers, Committee on Governmental Affairs, U.S. Senate* (Washington, D.C.: U.S. Government Printing Office, 1978), p. 280.

helped enormously. The attorneys also contacted the new GSA chief administrator, Jay Solomon, and found to their pleasure that, despite his newness on the job, he was willing to take a gutsy approach to the case.

In 1977, Senator Charles Percy, ranking member of the Senate Government Operations Committee and its permanent subcommittee on investigations, reviewed the same evidence as the *Globe* Spotlight team. Senator Percy determined that there were "serious violations of applicable federal procurement regulations" by the Boston GSA, including (but not limited to) frequent use of negotiated contracts without reasonable justification, routine acceptance of contractor prices for awards and change orders without adequate and proper independent estimation by the GSA, and encouragement of favored customer status among a few contractors. Senator Percy requested investigation because of his concern that the conditions widely permeated the GSA.

In 1978, Sullivan testified before the Senate Committee on Governmental Affairs and was commended for his public service in calling attention to abuse. Sullivan told the senators, "If federal employees fear to report wrongdoing in government, we could eventually become a nation of apathetic sheep, fleeced of our ethics and constitutional rights. Loyalty to moral principles and country truly must take priority over loyalty to persons, party, or government department."

The case was never tried. In 1978, federal district court judge Harold Green brought the Sullivan and government attorneys together in his chambers in Washington for a pretrial hearing. He listened to the contentions of both sides. Turning to the government attorneys, he remarked, I am told, "You don't seem to have much of a case."

With the judicial handwriting on the wall, the government settled in Sullivan's favor. The GSA agreed to restore Sullivan to a noninvestigative job. Tucker also was reinstated. Sullivan was given $15,000 in cash as restitution and his choice of a region to work in, in case he feared retaliation in Boston.

For this happy ending Sullivan credits the prayers of the Franciscan Fathers as well as his Cambridge and Washington attorneys, the American Civil Liberties Union, several senators, new GSA head Solomon, and others. "Much to my surprise," he says, "I am the first federal employee in history to be voluntarily reinstated by a government agency!"

In May 1978, Solomon appointed an experienced prosecutor, Vincent Alto, to fling open the doors and windows of the forbidden rooms in Boston and other cities to make an accurate assessment. Alto reported "the biggest money scandal in the history of the federal government." Even so, he may not have realized the extent of the shenanigans. So deeply imbedded in GSA operations had subterfuge and dissembling become that a year later, in the fall of 1979, Senator Max Baucus of Montana would charge that the agency still hadn't put its house in order. In a sad revelation, Clinkscales testified, under questioning before Senator Baucus, that prior to 1978 "GSA management did not want GSA investigators to investigate anything of consequence."

Did Sullivan's whistleblowing pass the test of careful and competent investigation? He was familiar with the subject and knew the ins and outs very well. Although hearsay started him on the trail, he ended up with factual data. But did he collect the data in a defensible way? Obviously his superiors thought not; his actions were tantamount to disloyalty, in their opinion. Sullivan himself agonized over "stealing" from the files. However, there was no other way. The *Boston Globe* investigators could not take his word for it; they had to have proof. The incriminating documents were not highly classified material, and revelation of their contents did not endanger the public or the aims of the GSA.

What about the earlier tests described in this chapter? Sullivan was under no commitment to confidentiality, other than the respect any employee is obligated to give company property, so no problem of privileged information was present. What about his motives? Clearly he was not acting for selfish benefit but for the good of others. Moreover, the Code of Ethics would seem to command him to do what he did. Was the subject appropriate? It was specific and tangible, and although Sullivan may not have thought highly of certain agency heads, certainly his motive was not to satisfy a personal vendetta.

IF POSSIBLE, THE PROTEST SHOULD BE CONFINED TO ORGANIZATIONAL CHANNELS

In order to meet their obligations to their employer organizations, employee critics and objectors should do everything possible to keep their protests inside the corporation or agency. They are not justified in going to outsiders with their complaints unless there is no point in going to senior managers, ombudspeople, or impartial investigators (as when, for instance, top management itself is the perpetrator), or until they have exhausted possible internal remedies. As Bok points out, "it is a waste of time for the public, as well as harmful to the institution, to sound the loudest alarm first." Whistleblowing in public "has to remain a last alternative because of its destructive side effects; it must be chosen only when other alternatives have been considered and rejected." [12]

The objector should follow this approach not only out of loyalty to the employer but also because it strengthens his or her hand in case of a legal hearing. Attorneys with whom I have consulted agree that the use and outcome of a hearing procedure in the organization is relevant evidence in a law case. If the dissident doesn't use such a procedure, if available, the court may well wonder why not.

Also, the objector should make sure that he or she is the appropriate person to be challenging a superior or a management decision. Should someone else be raising the question, because of position or expertness? Would the challenge be more credible coming from another person? An attack on the legality of a company's pricing system would be more convincing coming from someone in the corporate legal department rather than from an employee without legal training.

A leading example of an employee's efforts to confine a challenge to the executive suite occurred some years ago in a leading milk cooperative. The story that follows is based on an interview, newspaper articles, and a detailed personal account published in the *Civil Liberties Review*.

The Rose Who Couldn't Be Cowed

Joseph Rose had just turned thirty-five in April 1973 when he went to work in San Antonio for Associated Milk Producers, Inc. AMPI was the nation's largest dairy cooperative. Its annual sales exceeded $1.4 billion. Its headquarters were in San Antonio.

He had lunch the first day with an Oklahoma City attorney who for many years had served as outside counsel to AMPI. According to Rose's sworn testimony later before the U.S. Senate's Watergate Committee, the attorney told Rose about an antitrust suit that was pending against AMPI. The attorney mentioned a troublesome witness and suggested offering him a job at AMPI in order to get him to "clarify" his testimony.

Rose was horrified at the suggestion. A few weeks later, talking with AMPI's general counsel and general manager, George Mehren, he referred to the attorney and asked, "Why is a man like that even on AMPI's payroll?"

"Well, you see," Mehren answered, "it's like this." Mehren explained, according to Rose's later testimony, that the preceding general manager had run a corrupt operation. Among other things, that executive had made po-

[12] Bok, op. cit., p. 286.

litical contributions out of AMPI funds. One scheme, according to the charges that Watergate prosecutors made later, was to overpay an outside attorney; the attorney would return the excess payment to AMPI officials, who would then give the pasteurized sum to politicos. Mehren explained that he had halted the illegal contributions when he had become general manager. However, according to Rose's subsequent testimony, Mehren said that the Oklahoma City attorney must be kept on the payroll "because he knows where all the dead bodies are." The attorney had received $66,000 after Mehren took over, Rose says he discovered; apparently the purpose of that sum was to enable him to pay income taxes on the bloated fees received.

Rose began questioning and probing. He suggested to AMPI people that the illegal donations should be returned to the cooperative. It was the members' money, wasn't it? Although he didn't know it, he was becoming a marked man.

One of the ironies in the situation was that Rose, the only executive at AMPI, apparently, who sought to correct the wrongdoing, had a great deal to lose—probably more than anyone else did. He had begun his legal career as a civilian lawyer for the Department of the Air Force at Kelly Air Force Base in San Antonio. His job there had been to police the work of civilians who were doing business with the Air Force. After four and one-half productive years in that job, he had gone to work as a labor-relations attorney for Gates Rubber Company in Denver. He had admired many of the executives he worked with there and had considered himself "extremely pro-management." Next he had taken a position with Montgomery Ward, where again he had liked and respected his co-workers. Montgomery Ward, like the previous employers, had given him "good marks," reports Rich Jaroslovsky in a carefully detailed write-up of Rose's case in the *Wall Street Journal*.[13] Rose's boss at Montgomery Ward recalled him as "a straightforward guy and a very satisfactory employee."

By the time he had gone to work as regional labor counsel for Montgomery Ward, Rose had had five children. When his wife suffered a heart attack, he had cut back on his heavy travel schedule. When she suffered a second heart attack, he had decided to stay closer to home still. Contacting his old law school, the St. Mary's University School of Law in San Antonio, he had been put in touch with people at AMPI. At the same time, his father, who also lived in San Antonio, had become quite ill. All of this gave him the strongest possible reason *not* to get himself into trouble. But whistle-blowers are not rational people—at least, by the standards of the world.

Actually, Rose did not think he was taking a major risk when he began

---

13 *Wall Street Journal,* November 9, 1977.

trying to persuade AMPI executives to return the illegal payoffs to the dairy farmers whom they represented. As in-house counsel, one of his jobs was to approve the payments made to outside attorneys. He objected to approving what he believed to be dubious payments not only on the grounds of principle but also for fear that he himself might get into trouble with the law. Jaroslovsky reports that Rose mentioned these objections to John Butterbrodt, president of the cooperative and a Wisconsin dairy farmer. When Rose said he didn't want to be involved in possible criminal acts, Butterbrodt looked at him and laughed and said, "How do you know you are not already implicated? You don't know what you have signed!" (Butterbrodt later denied to Jaroslovsky that he and Rose had such a conversation.)

Really worried now, Rose decided to go to the forty-four-member board of directors. He approached those directors he could reach in Minneapolis at their annual meeting in 1973. "Something has to be done," he insisted. He was told that the illegal payments would be investigated by a lawyer to be retained by AMPI. But, Rose asked, why hire an outsider to investigate what they themselves already knew? The idea made no sense to him. He suspected some kind of ruse. His suspicions may have been correct, for later he was told by members of a large law firm in San Antonio that the board's purpose in later hiring an outside law firm was "to investigate the investigators," that is, Rose himself and the firm first hired to "investigate."

Rose tried in vain to get the directors to understand that it was the farmers' money he was talking about. "There are things that I still vividly recall about those disastrous days when I was trying to reach the board," he says now. "I recall at one point calling my wife long distance from Minneapolis to assure her that at least I had seven members of the board of directors who had come to my room to listen to what I had to say."

Unfortunately for him, his seniors did not see things so simply. They lost no time in deciding to try to cow him.

Returning to his office, Rose found a guard posted at the door. The lock on the door also had been changed. The next day he was put out to pasture for "failure to perform your assigned duties."

He began looking for another job. One day when he was out, Butterbrodt telephoned him. First putting another attorney on the line, so that the conversation could be corroborated, Rose returned the call. When Butterbrodt asked why Rose had "tried to go around me," Rose went into the facts in detail, stating that the situation was known to the president, that management had simply refused to act, and so on. Butterbrodt asked if Rose would meet only with the executive members of the board; Rose answered that he would be glad to meet with the full board, but not with a handpicked number. His request to meet with the full board was never granted.

It was the time of the Watergate revelations. The Select Committee on Watergate of the U.S. Senate asked Rose to testify. Before doing so, he told the AMPI lawyers and even sent a telegram giving the exact date and time of his scheduled testimony. Meeting with the committee, however, he first raised the question of what the law calls attorney–client privilege, that is, whether it was proper for him to divulge facts about his former employer. The committee ruled that he should testify and ordered him to do so under subpoena. He testified. Later he was compelled to appear before Archibald Cox's grand jury. Refusing at first to testify here, he was overruled by Judge Sirica. One of the counsel to the Senate Watergate Committee told Jaroslovsky, "Rose was a very courageous guy. He knew he was taking a big risk in coming forward."

Rose emphasizes that he was acting in the most ethical way he knew how. "In my battle against the dishonesty of AMPI, I never went outside of the corporation with any accusation or statement until served with subpoena by Congress and the Watergate task forces."

Rose also testified against AMPI (with its consent) in a federal antitrust suit. The hearing was held in Kansas City. AMPI issued a press release calling his deposition "a shocking sequence of gross lies."

Day after day and month after month Rose tried to find another job. Inquiring about his brief five-month stay at AMPI, prospective employers turned into milksops. Jaroslovsky reports that Rose's friend, San Antonio lawyer James Gillespie, tried to land him a job with the county government in San Antonio. The county official whom Gillespie was trying to convince "looked at me and shook his head and said, 'Right now, Joe is hotter'n a pistol.'"

For six months Rose looked in vain for another employer. He moved his family from a nice home to a cramped two-room apartment. Finally he got two offers, one from a leading company in the Southeast and one from a small firm in west Texas. Although the latter offered a low salary, Rose took the job because his father was dying, and Rose wanted to be near him. "That choice proved to be a disastrous one," Rose says. Soon the firm dissolved, and he was back on the streets again.

He advertised for another job. An attorney answered and agreed to take him on. Soon the attorney fired him for the same reason that AMPI had— "failure to perform your assigned duties." In a careful account of his adventures in the *Civil Liberties Review*,[14] Rose contends that this job was set up with AMPI's collusion specifically to shatter his credibility prior to further grand jury appearances scheduled. The attorney denies this ruse but Rose points to the man's connections with the dairy industry and AMPI specifically.

[14] *Civil Liberties Review*, September–October 1978, p. 27.

Despite her health problems and a large family to take care of, Rose's wife was able to return to a job at Datapoint Corporation in San Antonio for $6,000 a year. The seven-person family scraped by on that income and food stamps. They lived on salads, corn bread, and pinto beans.

He wrote to President Gerald R. Ford. To his delight and astonishment, a reply came, and he was granted an interview with the government's Wage and Hour Division. "At first, I was ecstatic, believing that someone did care and that indeed some degree of justice could be obtained," Rose says. But after the interview, he learned that the official who interviewed him had been in the Department of Agriculture and had friends in the dairy industry. No job offer came.

"I remember praying daily for the help of the Lord," Rose says. More interviews. More turndowns. "I can recall vividly finally praying and saying that this time I had been confronted with a mountain that I could not overcome by myself."

There were anonymous threats and telephone calls. Some of these calls were taken by his father, who was then in the final throes of emphysema. His father died in September 1974 believing that Rose's career was irreparably ruined. "If I'm bitter about anything," the son says today, "I'm bitter about that."

Then, miraculously, help came from a small federal union in Washington, D.C., the National Treasury Employers Union. Accepting a job there, Rose began to rebuild his reputation and recoup financially. With the new connections he made, he was able to find paths around the pitfalls of his experiences at AMPI and with the dairy attorney.

Later he went back to San Antonio to take a job with a small law firm and teach part-time at the University of Texas. He earned more good references. He began representing insurance companies as well as other corporations and business interests. He was able to move his family to a new house in a pleasant suburb. Impossible as it once seemed, he began leading a tolerable life again.

=====

Did Rose's actions meet the test of appropriate channels and procedure? Although he ended up going public, he did so only after he had exhausted the means of bringing the illegalities to the attention of top management. He went right to the board itself—in person, face to face. Was he the appropriate person to be challenging top management? He protested a practice in his special area of concern and he was knowledgeable about the legal issues. What about the criterion of careful investigation? He talked frankly and fully with AMPI's outside counsel, who personally knew about the payoffs; he probed further before going to the president and the board. Were his motives legitimate? They were to keep the organization on the safe side of the law. Was the subject matter appropriate? The payoffs were of specific amounts to specific people; they were illegal.

OBJECTIONS AND PROTESTS SHOULD BE CONCENTRATED ON SUBSTANCE, NOT PERPETRATORS

Sometimes employee objectors with good cases beat themselves. One of the most unfortunate mistakes made is to let a charge with substance deteriorate into a personal accusation. Even if the critic believes that certain culprits are to blame, he or she should not allow the criticism to become a charge against individuals. It will unless the critic sticks rigorously and stubbornly to the facts of the *situation*. Let others follow the clues leading to the culprits, if they want to, but don't let them say to themselves, "Ah, it's Joe Jones whom he's trying to frame," or "What she's really doing is carrying on a personal vendetta against Betsy Brown."

In one case I know of, an employee filed what was apparently a legitimate complaint over working conditions with the Occupational Safety and Health Administration. Subsequently, the employee felt he was being penalized by his superiors, who presumably learned about the complaint from the OSHA investigators. Instead of sticking to the facts of the hazardous condition and perceived retaliation from management, the employee began blaming two superiors who, he alleged, "were out to get him." When he did that, he began losing credibility fast. Other supervisors drew together in self-defense with the accused; even associates of the employee began to lose sympathy with him, suspecting that personal animosity had more to do with the problem than the hazard itself.

Again, consider two whistleblowing cases earlier described. Suppose Joseph Rose's protest of payoffs had degenerated into an accusation of one or two executives in particular. Or suppose Robert Sullivan's case against illegal contracts had been framed in terms of willful wrongdoing by one or two top officials in GSA. How would the dissidents have fared then? Probably Rose's case would have seemed less convincing—more spectacular, perhaps, but less solid. And in all probability Sullivan would not have been able to elicit the attentive response that the press and legislators gave him, for the word would have been passed around by top management that a personal feud was going on.

Raven-Hansen points out that there is still another reason that objectors and critics should avoid getting into personalities when they speak out:

Accusations of fraud, deliberate concealment, reckless behavior, lying, negligence, and even mismanagement are serious—indeed, so

serious that society has assigned them to a special class of professionals: prosecutors. Moreover, a precious body of law has developed
around these terms, and unless the whistleblower is familiar with that
law, it is likely that what she considers bribery, perjury, or even negligence does not coincide with the courts' definition of these terms. By
personalizing her disclosure, therefore, she may unwittingly expose
herself to a libel or slander suit or other legal entanglements.

Furthermore, even if legal problems do not result, antagonisms from
personal accusations may effectively destroy a career. In government
employment, for example, the Supreme Court has suggested that a
subordinate's public criticism of his superior, however accurate, can
justify the subordinate's termination because of its effect on working
relationships.[15]

THE EMPLOYEE OBJECTOR SHOULD BE OPEN AND VISIBLE

"In fairness to those criticized," says Bok, "openly accepted responsibility for blowing the whistle should be preferred to the denunciation or the
leaked rumor. What is openly stated can more easily be checked, its
source's motives challenged, and the underlying information examined.
Those under attack may otherwise be hard put to defend themselves
against nameless adversaries." [16]
    In some situations, of course, anonymity is virtually dictated. For in-
stance, had Sullivan gone directly to his superiors—and he might have had
to do that repeatedly to get anywhere—he would have been an easy target,
and after being discredited, he might have had a harder time convincing the
Globe team that his case was solid. In cases of this sort, the objector can offer
ways for others to verify his information. Thus, Sullivan offered the incriminating documents. In *Impact*, Ripskis, while carefully protecting his
sources, generally gives readers plenty of factual leads to check out the
truth of his stories. And in the BART case, the three engineers offered
numbers, engineering facts, and other hard data to those who wanted to
listen to them.
    Mary P. Rowe, an ombudsperson who has mediated hundreds of per-
sonal-conflict cases for different universities and corporations, believes that
the complainant should shoulder the responsibility for protest in a rational

---

[15] Raven-Hansen, op. cit., p. 39.
[16] Bok, op. cit., p. 286.

and responsible way because it helps the person to focus his or her anger on the external situation instead of becoming sick and depressed from introspection. Openness and visibility have further advantages, Rowe points out. If the egregious decision or practice was started unthinkingly, the perpetrator is given a chance to make amends quietly and internally, before being subjected to the embarrassment of gossip, a hearing procedure, or a public outcry, and before possibly subjecting the organization to embarrassment. Also, open and responsible action by the objector often produces more evidence of the offense, as when others come forward with facts or the culprits incriminate themselves further. Perhaps most important, says Rowe, such action gives "the offended and offender a chance, usually for the first time, to see things the same way. Since neither person may have any understanding of how the other sees the problem, discussion may help. Entry of a third party at this stage usually further polarizes the views of the opposing persons." [17]

NORMALLY, THE CRITICISM OR DISCLOSURE SHOULD BE PUT IN WRITING

In most situations, employee objectors should put their information and views in writing. They might do this at the time they go to superiors or ombudspeople; they might choose to wait until after the first conversations, using the memorandum as a follow-up on the talks. In any case, they are wise to state their views in an appropriate manner, avoiding any suggestion of arrogance, contempt, or a holier-than-thou attitude. Phrases such as "it seems to me," "my own feeling is," and "it would appear" are preferable to dogmatic assertions. And critics should always bear in mind the writer-reader relationship. Who are they to be reporting these criticisms? What are their credentials? How did they obtain their evidence? What is the likely attitude of the reader? Needs like these, which can have an astonishing impact on the effectiveness of a memorandum or letter, are discussed in detail in my book, *Writing for Results*.[18]

Raven-Hansen offers other rules that may be helpful to the employee objector:

A clear, *short*, summary of the information—describing what it means, why it is significant, and what should be done about it—is very impor-

[17] Mary P. Rowe, "Dealing with Sexual Harassment," *Harvard Business Review*, May–June 1981, p. 42.
[18] David W. Ewing, *Writing for Results* (New York: Wiley, 1978).

tant. Many professionals, particularly those trained in the sciences, believe that numbers speak for themselves and so are content to disclose raw data, lab reports, or statistics without comment, analysis, or summary. Such professionals often assume both that the recipient will read the information and that she is qualified to understand it. Neither assumption is valid. When the disclosure is made outside the normal chain of command, as is often the case, the recipient may not be technically qualified and the disclosure will be totally ineffective unless phrased in plain English. And even if the reader is qualified, she may not be willing to go through voluminous material or may feign ignorance. A clear one- or two-page summary, stripped of euphemisms and jargon, not only makes the disclosure more understandable but also more difficult to ignore.

It is also helpful to specify how the information was obtained and to provide supporting materials. Describing the exact source of the information makes it more credible, as well as more difficult for superiors to claim that they could not have known about it.

Verification of the information by outside sources or other professionals can obviously be helpful, and confirmation by a professional society lends an aura of objectivity that may help protect the whistleblower from retaliation. However, most professional societies have been inexcusably slow to rally around their members or even offer their services in a review or verification role. So instead the whistleblower most often turns to individual colleagues for verification. Unfortunately, there are many problems with this. The more people involved with the information, the greater the chance of a leak; verification may be only "fair weather"; and the colleagues may get into trouble.

The disclosure's format should force management to go on record about the information. This might be achieved by specifying a reply date, providing an acknowledgement box, or sending copies to other recipients who might expect a response.[19]

SUPERIORS PRESUMED TO BE AT FAULT SHOULD BE GIVEN SOME BENEFIT OF A DOUBT

Often dissidents annoy others because of their perfectionism. They score their supervisors for the most human failings; they are impatient at

---

[19] Raven-Hansen, op. cit., p. 38.

the slightest management delay; they expect zero defects in administration. As anyone who has lived for a while in a pressurized management world knows, such expectations are unrealistic. With the best of intentions, good managers make mistakes, and even when they don't slip up, events sometimes have a way of making them look foolish. Just as a wise manager often gives a subordinate the benefit of the doubt, so should subordinates give supervisors the benefit of the doubt—at least until the senior person has clearly demonstrated a persistently egregious motive. The principles of negotiation discussed in Chapter 7 are helpful because they lead both parties to look behind an apparent conflict and seek opportunities for shifts in position. The "bad guys" are given the opportunity to become more rational.

In numerous situations, another person in the organization may be able to help the objector clarify the problem. Of course, the ideal is an ombudsperson or employee assistance office; if they are not present, there may be a senior manager known for his or her helpfulness in sticky situations, or perhaps an attorney in the legal department. Employee critics should try to seek out such people, tell them the story, and request their help so that the problem can be solved as peacefully and promptly as possible.

An extraordinary case of an objector who tried to keep a problem from exploding is that of a woman whose promotions, ironically, got her into an increasingly ticklish relationship with her boss. The story follows.

No, No, a Dozen Times No [20]

It looked at first as if Mary K. Heelan chose just the right time to take a job at Johns-Manville Corporation. The company was moving its world headquarters from New York to Denver, and Mr. X, who was in charge of planning the new headquarters, needed help. Heelan began working for him in August 1971 in Denver as a senior secretary, starting at $6,650 per year. She was instructed to get in touch with different department officials in New York, find out how much space they would need in the new headquarters, and relay this information to the designers in New York.

Now twenty-six years old, Heelan had been born in New York, raised in Iowa, and graduated from Heelan High School (the school name was unrelated to her future husband's family). She had married young, had three

---

[20] The facts of the manager–subordinate relationship narrated here are drawn from the lengthy court record in the case of *Mary K. Heelan v. Johns-Manville Corporation,* 16 Employment Practices Decisions 8330, pp. 5737–5748 (U.S. District Court, Colorado, April 3, 1978). In fairness, it should be pointed out that Judge Finesilver's findings came from often-conflicting testimony. The verdict was not appealed, however. Some of the background information about Heelan is drawn from a personal interview. Only the name of Mr. X is omitted from this account.

children, worked in several clerical jobs, and divorced her first husband before moving from Iowa to Colorado. She had fallen in love with Glenn Heelan and married him. They and her children lived in Colorado Springs, a fifty-five mile commute from Denver.

Mr. X also had been a New Yorker. Before the corporate move to Denver, he had been in charge of building services in New York. Now he found himself promoted to the position of director of facilities planning, and the good life was in reach. He enjoyed or would soon enjoy a variety of new fringe benefits, including a company car, which was a Cadillac El Dorado, and membership in a country club. He, too, had just moved to Colorado. He and his wife lived in Denver.

Mr. X lost no time in appreciating Heelan's energy and ability. About six months after she had been on the job, he wrote a memorandum about her to the executive vice-president. Already, he noted, she was doing a great deal more than routine checking and secretarial work. She was making surveys for space, furniture, and equipment requirements. She was preparing work orders and following through on the performance of the work. "She is functioning as a planning and construction coordinator," he wrote. He rated her excellent in each of the five categories for employee performance ratings—ability, application, job performance, cooperativeness, and capacity for growth. He recommended what the company called a two-step raise for her instead of the usual one-step raise. This recommendation was accepted, and in July 1972 her salary rose to $7,500.

In the meantime, however, the story was developing a new twist. It appeared that Mr. X saw more in Heelan than ability. In the spring, when he was recommending her for the two-step raise, he told her that her expanded duties would involve travel, especially to New York and Boston, and family sacrifices. Was she willing? Of course, she answered. All her children were now in school, and her husband, who was starting a new business, was at or near home most of the time. "During the conversation," according to the district court, Mr. X "put his arm around plaintiff [Heelan] and said that she really did not yet understand the job requirements but that she would in time."

In September she went to lunch with him, as they did from time to time to discuss company business. This time, however, she found herself being driven not to a restaurant but to the Cherry Creek Reservoir, southeast of Denver. There he parked the car. Did she like him, he asked—personally as well as professionally? Well, yes. According to the U.S. district court findings, he "again placed his arm around [her] and told her he was concerned about growing older and needed to know if she was 'grateful' for all he had done for her."

"The sea hath bounds," wrote Shakespeare, "but deep desire hath none." A couple of months later, Mr. X made his first big move. The two of them had flown to New York—it was to be but one of many trips they made to the East because of needs to meet with top company executives, members of the Architects Collaborative, officials of Turner Construction Company, and officials of Space Design Group, which had been chosen to do the interiors of the new buildings in Denver. They took rooms in the same hotel, he in the Johns-Manville suite, she in a single room on a different floor. He asked her to drop by for a drink; she accepted. While she was sitting on a sofa in the parlor of the suite, according to the court record, he asked her to go to bed with him. She told him she was happily married, put her drink down, and left the suite.

Meanwhile, back at the daily job, the industrious Heelan was doing better than ever. The company asked Mr. X to tell the board of directors about the design for the new world headquarters. He asked Heelan to make one of the presentations for his department. This was an honor because, until then, no woman had addressed the board of the international corporation. She did well. In fact, the executive vice-president recalled later that her presentation had been "very good." Her performance made Mr. X look good, too, especially in view of the fact that Johns-Manville was not known for bringing women along in management. With only occasional exceptions, men completely dominated the ranks above secretarial, clerical, and routine administration.

At the end of the year, she got another raise, a new title as well. She was promoted to the position of associate facilities planner at $10,000 a year. The fact that she did not have the formal qualifications for the position, which called for a person with a college degree or its equivalent in architectural design and courses in business management, attests to the high regard in which she was held by many people in the company.

In January of the new year, 1973, according to the judicial record, Mr. X had lunch with an executive of Space Design Group. After they had discussed business matters for some time, Mr. X surprised the New York designer by beginning to talk about his affection for Heelan. Although he liked her very much, he said, he wasn't sure he could have an affair with her because he was married. Wisely, the designer did not volunteer opinions or suggestions. His judiciousness was soon to be tested again.

On January 23, according to the court, the designer was approached by Heelan herself, who had now been working with him for a year. She confided that she worried about her relations with Mr. X. "He had offered her an apartment if she would leave her husband and consent to an affair." Once again, the designer offered little or nothing in the way of a response, and (until called to testify in court) he apparently told no one about either this unusual talk or the conversation with Mr. X.

The next month Mr. X went into action again. He told Heelan there was an outside meeting they should go to. On the appointed day, he drove. Instead of taking her to a business meeting, however, he told her he wanted to show her some land he owned about 20 miles outside of the town of Fairplay. The court record states that he drove her to a barren area, parked the car, and again asked her to make love. Apparently not considering *this* fair play, despite the name of the area, she refused.

A month or two later she had to say no again—this time in New York, where they had flown to attend a management meeting.

Back at the job, Heelan continued to perform well. On May 23 she received an outstanding annual evaluation for her work, and another pay raise recommendation from Mr. X. In addition, he recommended her for a Johns-Manville "A" award. Such an award was given to an employee demonstrating, according to the corporate literature, "initiative, ability and wholehearted interest in the company . . . with unusual merit and . . . a high degree of managerial judgment." Heelan received the "A" award with a letter from the company president and a check for $1,000. In July her salary was raised again.

Whether because of or in spite of these successes, the cycle of evaporation and recondensation of desire in Mr. X seemed to accelerate, judging from the testimony. In August, when he and Heelan again found themselves in New York on business, and staying this time at the Doral Hotel, he called her room and offered a fresh proposition. He told her, according to the district court record, "that he no longer wanted a permanent affair, but would be satisfied if they made love just one time." Heelan's answer: No.

Now, how were these covetous gestures affecting Heelan? Inwardly, of course, she was distressed. Outwardly, however, she appeared about the same as ever. Aside from the moments when Mr. X was propositioning her, she liked the job, enjoyed the traveling, and didn't want her husband to start worrying about her when she was away. "So I didn't ever mention to him," she says, "that I was getting these big hassles at the office and in New York."

Nor did she feel like confiding in other women on the Johns-Manville staff—at least, not yet. For one thing, she worried that they might be feeling a little resentful toward her because of her success. For another, the "culture" of the company discouraged her from talking out loud about her worries. This constraint bothered her then and still does. She says, "I didn't feel close enough to other women to really sit down and tell them my troubles. I think women in business generally don't have enough support for one another, and I think that's probably one of the biggest problems they face. Each of us is alone in the business world, and we shouldn't have to be. Men take each other aside and talk to each other, but women don't—I don't know why. Too much jealousy between them, I think."

Mr. X, it would appear, sensed this weakness in her armor. From time to time in their talks he would mention a rumored affair that was going on at a higher level in management. He suggested, she recalls, that the other affair was a wonderful example of how well their own relationship could work if only she would let it.

But still she wouldn't buy his schemes. An affair wouldn't work, she kept insisting. In September Mr. X struck again. They were dining at a New York restaurant while in the city for several meetings with company executives, contractors, and architects, when he sought to convince her that she was unable to handle both her marriage and her job. She should choose between them, he urged. According to the district court, he also advised her to reconsider having the affair he yearned for. "He offered plaintiff [Heelan] an apartment in Denver if she would leave her husband."

She walked out of the restaurant.

The unquenchable Mr. X approached her again back at the Doral Hotel, where they had rooms. He got another straight-arrow answer.

Later in the fall she talked with her boss about her pay and title. She was doing the same type of work for him as Eric Dienstbach was, she argued—Dienstbach had been hired by Mr. X several months earlier to work as a project manager—but she was getting less pay and she had a lower title. It appeared to her like a case of illegal sex discrimination.

Troubled, he talked with his boss, the executive vice-president, Francis May, Jr. It turned out that, despite Heelan's superb record, there were reservations about her at the summit. Some top executives felt she was abrasive, and they questioned her ability to handle the job of project manager (even though she was already doing it). Nevertheless, after several meetings with top executives, Mr. X recommended her promotion to project manager. Early the next year this recommendation was approved.

It is difficult to tell from the judicial record how serious or legitimate the reservations were. The critics are unnamed. Perhaps they reflected only the male tradition at Johns-Manville, where senior executives were unused to seeing women questing for positions in upper middle management. It is undisputed, however, that there was also strong support for Heelan. In court four years later, the executive of Space Design with whom Heelan had worked stated that in his entire employment with his firm he had never served with a better project coordinator than Heelan. Eric Dienstbach, the other project manager, rated Heelan's record as good as his own. Henry McElyea, another member of the department, who became vice-president for architectural planning in 1973, testified that, though he had had little hope for Heelan at the beginning of her assignment because of her lack of construction experience, she did an amazing job.

As the autumn weather turned the leaves to flame, Mr. X apparently felt, in the words of the old song, that he couldn't go on with the waiting game.

One morning in late November of early December, stated the district court, he telephoned her at the office at the Greenwood Plaza in Denver. Would she bring certain files to him at the Regency Hotel in North Denver? She found the files, drove to the Regency, and went up to the assigned room. There, according to the court, she found Mr. X "dressed in a bathrobe, standing next to breakfast setups for two." He made the now-familiar request; she made the now-familiar answer.

There seemed to be no bottom to his persistence. Later in December, according to the judicial findings, he told her that they were both expected to attend a meeting at the Hampshire House Hotel in downtown Denver. They went to a suite maintained by the company for visiting members of the construction team. Was there really a meeting scheduled? No, it turned out, this was just a ruse for more amorous advances. Once more Heelan repulsed.

Now, it may appear to the reader at this point that Heelan was well in command of the situation. Not only had she remained impregnable to her boss's repeated blandishments and lures, but she was finding it possible at the same time to work her way up in management. In reality, however, she was getting worried. Power doesn't bring the boss love, they say, but it puts him in good field position, and Heelan may have begun wondering how long her luck would last against his advantages.

At any rate, later in December or early in January 1974 she called Isabelle Dienstbach for an appointment to talk. Isabelle Dienstbach, the mother of Eric, was an assistant vice-president in the company and assistant to the president. The highest-ranking woman at Johns-Manville, she also was a personal friend of Mr. X and his wife. For some time she had served as a sounding board for many women employees who had problems. In fact, she was in charge of the company's affirmative action program and, as Heelan said, she was trying very hard to get women promoted.

With the office door closed, Heelan broke her long silence and told Isabelle Dienstbach about Mr. X's advances. "I felt like she was the only one I could talk to about the subject without being laughed out of the room," Heelan says. She knew, too, that the older woman had the ear of the company president. Heelan confided that Mr. X was accosting her almost weekly and that she didn't know how to cool him. The older woman listened but had no immediate solution to offer. Heelan recalls her saying that Mr. X probably had "male menopause."

Isabelle Dienstbach heard about the problem again from her son. In February or March, according to the record, Eric told his mother that Mr. X was pursuing Heelan. She then asked Mr. X if this were true; he denied it, and she let the matter drop. For Heelan, it was back to the one-on-one game. She might be a project manager and earning many thousands more than she had at first, but the company was leaving her on her own to fend off her superior's advances.

On February 1, the date of her official promotion to project manager, she agreed to meet him at the Littleton Bank building in Denver. A Johns-Manville executive used an office there that needed redecorating. What Mr. X really had on his mind, though, was a more personal question, and in a lot near the bank building (he chose that spot, he testified later, because he felt she got too emotional when discussing her job with him in their offices) he told her, Heelan says, that if she could not show more gratitude, she would have to leave the company.

Heelan's anguish rose. Glancing around at other possible opportunities in Denver, she saw an unattractive picture. Unemployment was between 10% and 15%, and for women in particular, jobs above the secretarial and clerical levels were hard to get. So Mr. X had chosen a good time to give her his ultimatum. "It just bugged the hell out of me," she says, that he seemed "able to do whatever he wanted, no matter how wrong."

Nearly once a week after that, according to the later testimony in court, Mr. X continued to proposition her, and as often she answered no. On April 23, according to the judicial record, he called her into the office and gave her his final ultimatum: Make love with him or be fired. Her final answer: Absolutely no.

She was given notice that May 31 would be her last day on the job. Desperate, she went again to Isabelle Dienstbach for counsel. The mentor told her to get an appointment to talk with the executive vice-president, May. At their meeting, held at the end of the month, Heelan explained to May that her discharge was due not to poor work performance but to her refusal to sleep with Mr. X. May suggested she talk it over with the personnel manager. But you're the personnel manager's boss, she argued, and he's not going to do anything unless you give the sign. May agreed but declined to give the personnel manager an order. Instead, he got Mr. X on the phone and asked him if the charges were true. He'd done nothing wrong, the man protested. May decided to drop the whole thing.

So Heelan was on the streets when June 1 arrived. After about half a year of job-hunting (during which time she drew unemployment insurance) she zeroed in on a nice opening with a digital equipment company. The first interview at the computer firm went well, but during the second interview the time came to reveal to the recruiting manager why she had left Johns-Manville. She told him the truth. His response: Thank you, and good-bye.

She began thinking about suing Johns-Manville. First, however, she went over the whole story with her husband and discussed with him the possibility of legal action. "He was the one who was going to have to put up with it as much as I," she says. "Also, he was the one who would have to listen to comments from his friends." Taking all that into account, they nevertheless decided to sue.

After making a lengthy tape recording of her recollections of her problems with Mr. X, she telephoned the legal referral service in Denver. She was given the name of a young attorney, Lynn D. Feiger, a member of the small firm of Feiger and Lawson. Heelan got in touch with Feiger, found she and her associates had trial experience, and asked if she would be interested in taking the case. Feiger agreed to represent Heelan on a contingency fee basis.

If Feiger, her partner Leslie Lawson, and their trial lawyer, Richard Shaffer, worked hard on the case, so did Heelan. She went to each pretrial conference in the courtroom, even though her presence was not required and the meetings consisted of legal feints and maneuvers between the opposing counsel. "I wanted the judge to know I was interested and involved all the time," Heelan says. "Also, I wanted him to know what I looked like, and most of all I wanted to feel comfortable there because I knew I was going to have to spend some time there."

As the date of the trial neared, Heelan explained for the first time to her three children what had happened at Johns-Manville and what was going to happen next. Because they lived in Colorado Springs, a rather cliquish and independent community, the family was spared much of the gossip and attention it would have been exposed to had it lived in Denver. In fact, few of Heelans' friends even read the Denver papers except on Sunday. Nevertheless, shortly before the trial began, every paper around carried some item about the event. One Colorado Springs journal carried the headline: "Chastity Costs Local Woman Her Job."

Her attorneys coached her on appearances. When you're sitting at the table, they instructed, look the judge in the eye. Keep your chin up at all times. Don't cry. Don't make faces. Don't laugh. Don't slouch. Look interested. Body language is very important. She determined to follow this counsel exactly. Later on, at one point in the proceedings, she would feel a moment of quiet superiority when, happening to glance at Mr. X, she saw him slumped down in his chair, chin buried in his hand, as if he were at death's door.

Her husband said he would appear in the courtroom every day. He also was instructed by her attorneys. He must remember that the judge would know who he was. Like his wife, he must look dignified, interested, confident. No sharp comments. No wry faces.

When the trial opened, she described ten specific incidents of Mr. X's propositioning. Although she was very nervous and found the courtroom intimidating ("courtrooms are meant to be intimidating, and so is the whole legal justice system—the lady with the scales, and all that"), she gave the descriptions without notes. She had memorized the incidents by using a mnemonic trick: taking a key letter from the description of each incident to form a couple of words. As she spelled the words out in her mind, each letter triggered a new incident to describe.

After her case was presented, the Johns-Manville attorneys got up and argued that she was fired, not for sexual uncooperativeness, but for poor performance. Mr. X introduced as evidence eleven typewritten comments he had allegedly made reflecting his own concerns and concerns of other Johns-Manville employees. She had become, according to these comments, defiant, disobedient, and disloyal. He testified that these comments were transcribed by his secretary from handwritten notes. One damaging fact was that no other witness claimed to have seen them. Another was that they contained factual inaccuracies here and there. Possibly most damaging of all, his notes were made after February 1, 1974, when, according to Heelan's evidence, his persistence was getting him nowhere, and his actions were being brought to the attention of others in the corporation.

She felt crushed when Isabelle Dienstbach testified. The senior woman in the corporation denied categorically that Heelan had told her, early in 1974, about Mr. X's passionate overtures. All she could remember, stated the senior, was Heelan telling her about all this *after* receiving notice of discharge. Legally, the point was damaging to Heelan's case. She could scarcely control her indignation. This woman who was mentor and coach to her and other aspiring women in the corporation had the gall to stand up there under oath and say, in effect, that Heelan was lying!

On April 3, 1978, Judge Finesilver awarded his decision to Heelan. She was, he concluded, entitled to damages in the form of back pay and lost employment benefits.

At first the piqued Johns-Manville lawyers told Heelan's group they would appeal. As she thought of the additional years of waiting and emotional turmoil this would mean, she grew quite worried. When the company's lawyers suggested a settlement, she and her attorneys agreed. Terms were worked out, and the company decided not to appeal.

Heelan began free-lancing in the interior design field. She found herself working with other women, and she enjoyed being able to set her own hours. After about a year, she took a leave of absence so she could help her husband more in his business. They do a lot of traveling, and from time to time she appears on television and before other audiences to speak about problems and opportunities for women in business.

===========

The Heelan story raises some interesting questions for potential employee objectors and personnel officers. For instance, how does an objector's loyalty to the corporation (or government agency) compare with his or her loyalty to superiors? Does one call for a different amount or quality of tolerance than the other does? In the case, did Heelan go too far—or perhaps not far enough—in giving her superior the benefit of the doubt?

The Dienstbach role also raises a question. Some employee cynics will say, "I told you, it does no good to call on someone else in management for help. You might as well save your breath and not bother. They'll just do you in if they can." Yet I feel confident that Heelan, if she could do it over, would not skip her April meeting with Dienstbach. First of all, it gave her confidence that she was meeting her obligations to management and the corporation. She could go to the trial knowing she had done everything she could to avoid a suit. Second, she was able to testify to the meeting with sureness and conviction—and surely this would have helped the judge conclude that she, not the senior woman, was telling the truth.

Finally, Heelan's approach to the trial is worth careful attention. Future employee objectors could do worse than study the advice given by her counsel; so, too, could the corporate and government agency officials who testify in court in defense of their organizations. As every trial attorney knows, cases are not always won or lost on the cold facts; the manner, attitude, and dignity of the parties may have a significant bearing on the way the judge or jury hears the facts.

IF THE OBJECTOR MUST GO PUBLIC WITH CRITICISM, THE ATTACK SHOULD BE TIMED APPROPRIATELY

As we have seen in the Sullivan and Ripskis stories, employee objectors may be well within their rights to blow the whistle while still on the employer's payroll. The rationale is that it is not they but their superiors who are negligent or disloyal. Even so, as earlier emphasized, objectors have a duty to try all other means first in order to avoid public embarrassment and ill will toward the employer.

What is more, in many cases objectors should delay public criticism until they have left the organization. The most obvious case is one in which the objectors differ with management on an issue of judgment—for instance, the three General Electric engineers mentioned earlier who believed that the nuclear reactors GE was producing in the 1970s were a danger to society. Delay is also advisable when speaking out as an employee would invite retaliation from superiors and jeopardize the critic's career, make it impossible for the critic to continue working productively with others, or command public attention less effectively than speaking out after resignation.

Often such needs are far from clear. In the majority of whistleblower accounts given in this book, the timing of the disclosure is one of the issues that generally provokes discussion. For instance, reasonable people may disagree on whether Louis McIntire was obligated to resign from Du Pont before publishing his book, on the timing of James Rittenhouse's questionnaire sent to public employees in Painesville, and on the timing of the whistleblowers at BART. As stressed earlier, a responsible employee objector is as thoughtful and judicious as possible, choosing wise counsel, if such can be found, to gain an independent viewpoint on the problem.

If the objector decides that it is necessary to go public with the attack, either as an employee or ex-employee, what sources of help should be approached? Although Sullivan's approach to the *Boston Globe* was successful, media people are by no means an obvious answer. They may distort the information, violate pledges of confidentiality, or drop the subject if it fails to have news value. Public interest groups also are not an obvious answer; like the bureaucracies they oppose, they may act arrogantly and unsympathetically. Federal and state legislators are not always a help, either. Though Michael Nelson's appeal to the Georgia legislature, discussed earlier, was successful, other whistleblowers have fared less well when appealing to legislators.

The Federal Bureau of Investigation may be a good ally to seek out, if the case is of potential interest to the FBI. Sullivan wisely avoided the FBI in his case, for reasons described, but his situation in that respect was unusual. Raven-Hansen believes that regulatory agencies are usually a valuable ally. He points out,

> Disclosures to many federal regulatory authorities are now protected by statutes that prohibit retaliatory actions against employees who report possible regulatory violations. In addition, the Civil Service Reform Act of 1978 protects federal employees who make disclosures of waste, fraud, or substantial health or safety hazards to the Merit Systems Protection Board or agency inspector general. Also, disclosure to civil authorities may be the most effective since they usually have the duty and resources to follow up.[21]

What makes the question of timing so difficult is that often it is tied up with the would-be critic's personal security. One's conscience may urge, "Blow the whistle *now.*" But family considerations may cry, "Don't!" Such an agonizing conflict arose in a well-known whistleblower case that broke late in the 1960s.

[21] Raven-Hansen, op. cit., p. 41.

How They Played Chinese Baseball in Troy [22]

Kermit Vandivier came to work at the B. F. Goodrich Company plant in Troy, Ohio, in 1963. He started as an instrumentation engineer and later became a data analyst and technical writer. With a wife and seven children at home, he was delighted to have a job that he felt he could settle down in. There would be no more Sunday mornings wasted on the "Help Wanted" ads, no more hassles moving the kids to different schools, no more "House for Sale" signs on the front lawn.

As happy baseball players say, he liked the team, the park, and the city. The Goodrich plant at Troy, Ohio, was a one-story building that employed about 600 people—not an imposing-looking plant, by any means, but one of the leading manufacturers of aircraft brakes and wheels. Troy, a small city in the grassy fields of western Ohio, is about fifteen miles north of Dayton, birthplace of the airplane, and within easy driving range of other flat, comfortable towns with grandiloquent names like Russia, Palestine, and Versailles. He drew a good paycheck. He got along with the people in the plant. He could relax in the pleasant, stable, well-ordered community.

On April 11, 1968, after five years on the Goodrich team, Vandivier was looking over the data from the latest test of a new brake that the plant was preparing to manufacture for LTV Aerospace Corporation. LTV, in turn, planned to install the brake in a new light-attack aircraft called the A-7D. One of Vandivier's duties was to analyze the reams of technical data from the testing laboratories, massage them, and transcribe them into a more usable form for the plant's engineering department.

Something was wrong, Vandivier noticed as he pored over the data. Here are his words:

> One particular notation on the test logs caught my eye. For some of the stops [simulations of the brake and wheel in landing] the instrument that recorded the brake pressure had been deliberately miscalculated so that, while the brake pressure used during the stops was recorded as 1,000 psi [pounds per square inch]—the maximum pressure that would be available on the A-7D aircraft—the pressure had actually been 1,100 psi.

Vandivier discussed the irregularities with his boss, Ralph Gretzinger, the test lab supervisor. Gretzinger was prepared for the question. He explained

---

[22] This account is extracted from Kermit Vandivier's detailed story, "Why Should My Conscience Bother Me?" in *In the Name of Profit*, ed. Robert L. Heilbroner (New York: Doubleday, 1972), pp. 3–31, and rounded out with information supplied in personal correspondence with Vandivier.

that a brilliant young engineer named Searle Lawson had told the lab technician to miscalibrate the instruments. Why did Lawson do that? Because Lawson had been told to do so by his boss, "a short, chubby, bald man" named Robert Sink.

Lawson had known for some time that the brake was doomed to fail. However, his warnings got him nowhere, like a batter arguing with the umpire over a called third strike. The brake had been designed by John Warren, a senior engineer, and Warren was the one who had the last word.

His curiosity provoked, Vandivier went to Lawson. Lawson recounted his frustrations with trying to persuade his boss Warren and Warren's boss Sink that the brake was too small to do the job. Warren had miscalculated, the young engineer had told them. The brake simply didn't have enough surface area to stop the plane without generating excessive heat and causing the linings to burn out. But Warren would hear nothing of it. The need could be met with different metal materials, he claimed. Besides, the deadline for producing and delivering the first brakes for real-plane testing was just a few months away.

Vandivier was astounded. What sense did it make to pretend? Before the brake could be used in a test flight, there had to be documentary proofs for the contractor and the Air Force that it was safe for flying. This documentary proof was called a qualification report. Vandivier would be involved in writing the qualification report for the new brake. The report couldn't be produced, Vandivier reminded Lawson, unless it passed the tests.

Lawson shook his head. No, he had been told the qualification report would be issued no matter what. He had been told this in so many words in a meeting with Sink and Sink's boss, a man named Russell Van Horn. The latter managed the design engineering department.

Whistling softly, Vandivier went back to his boss and told him what he had just learned. Gretzinger reacted quickly. "If they want a qualification report, we'll write them one, but we'll tell it just like it is," he said. "No false data or false reports are going to come out of this lab." He didn't realize how soon his reaction would qualify for the book of "Famous Last Words."

About a month later Lawson asked Vandivier to start massaging the data on the brake tests. Vandivier refused. Gretzinger, when he heard about the request, was so furious that he marched right off to the office of Russell Line, a senior executive in charge of technical services.

In an hour Gretzinger returned, looking as meek as a batter who had struck out on three pitches. They hadn't told him at Northrup Institute of Technology, where he had gotten his engineering degree, that business would be like this. He was flabbergasted.

According to Vandivier, Gretzinger sat quietly for a few minutes and said hoarsely, "Well, it looks as if we're licked. The way it stands now, we're to go ahead and prepare the data and other things for the graphic presentation in the report, and when we're finished, someone will actually write the report." He began rationalizing to make himself feel better. He had two children to put through school (an argument that must have amused Vandivier, who had seven). He was new to the business world. Besides, they would just be drawing some curves, and what happened to the curves after they "went upstairs" was someone else's concern.

Vandivier's reaction was "This can't be!" Undaunted, he decided to go to see Line. It didn't occur to him that he might become the second victim of a double play.

Well liked and respected, Line was tall, powerfully built, and tanned. He listened sympathetically as Vandivier told him all he knew. Vandivier also ventured the opinion that the higher-ups wouldn't tolerate the cover-up if they were aware of it.

Line asked what Vandivier wanted him to do about it. Vandivier suggested going to the chief engineer at the plant, Bud Sunderman. Line laughed and said, sure, he could do that but he wasn't going to. Vandivier asked why not.

"Because it's none of my business," Line answered, "and it's none of yours. I learned a long time ago not to worry about things over which I had no control. I have no control over this." When Vandivier asked him if his conscience wouldn't bother him if the brakes failed in a test landing and the pilot were killed, Line became exasperated. "Look," he said, "I just told you I have no control over this. Why should my conscience bother me?" Line advised Vandivier to follow his example and just do what he was told. In other words, as Milwaukeee outfielder Jim Wohlford once put it, "Ninety percent of this game is half mental."

Trudging home that night, Vandivier knew that the only question left for him to decide was whether to become a party to the cover-up. If he refused, he would be fired, but he would have the satisfaction of leaving with clean hands and an honest batting average. However, honesty didn't enable him to hold the house, keep the children in school, and pay the bills. Unable to face those losses, he decided to play with dirty hands.

For nearly a month he and Lawson worked on the qualifying data for the defective new brake. They put together nearly 200 pages of facts, figures, and charts. If a temperature recorded in the laboratory test was too high to pass, they lowered it a few hundred degrees. If a temperature was too low, they raised it. They were like hitters umpiring their own balls and strikes.

In his personal account written later, Vandivier recalled, "Occasionally, we would find that some test either hadn't been performed at all or had been conducted improperly. On these occasions, we 'conducted' the test—

successfully, of course—on paper." He kept reminding himself that not he but someone else, thank goodness, would be preparing the signed written report that would go to the contractor and the Air Force.

In the meantime he began blowing the whistle lightly—too lightly, as it turned out. He told me:

> After I realized that complaining to my supervisors at Goodrich was not going to accomplish anything, I made several anonymous phone calls to the Air Force's civilian engineer in charge of that end of the A-7D contract. The problem was, I could not be too specific in giving him information without revealing my identity—or at least my position. The information I did supply him allowed him to sniff in the right direction, but it did not point him to the right hole.

He delivered the bundle of data to Gretzinger and returned to his office with a sigh of relief. Now he could become an honest man again. His relief was short-lived. In a few minutes Gretzinger, who had hurried off with the data to the chief engineer's office, returned with a white and angry face. The chief engineer had told him he and Vandivier must write the qualification report because no one in his department had time. Gretzinger had refused and left.

Vandivier was stunned. So the game was Chinese baseball, was it? Chinese baseball is like American baseball in most respects. The number of players is the same, the field is the same, the bats and balls are the same, and so on. But there is one crucial difference: After the pitcher goes into his motion and the ball leaves his hand, any player can move any of the bases anywhere until the ball hits the ground or is caught.

It was Chinese basball they were playing, only Vandivier, Gretzinger, and Lawson hadn't known it. After they had completed the data and sent it to the chief engineer, the bases had been moved and they were now caught off base.

As Vandivier and Gretzinger sat there, Line burst into the office. He was in a rage because he had heard Gretzinger wouldn't write the report.

"I've told you before," Gretzinger said to Line, "that we weren't going to write the report. I made my position clear on that a long time ago."

Line waved at Gretzinger to be quiet, turned to Vandivier, and yelled, "I'm getting sick and tired of hearing about this damned report. Now, write the goddam thing and shut up about it!" He slammed the door and left.

Staring at each other, Vandivier and Gretzinger knew they had been had. What they should have done, they saw now, was quit months earlier. Now the only thing to do was keep playing.

After he finished the written portion of the qualification report, Vandivier refused to sign it. So did Lawson. Even Lawson's boss Warren and Warren's boss Sink refused to sign it. Sink's neat rationalization was, "On something of this nature, I don't think a signature is really needed." Chinese baseball again.

In a few weeks Lawson flew to California as the plant representative at the flight tests at Edwards Air Force Base. After the tests had been completed he reported the grim news to the people in Troy: The brake had failed disastrously, causing several near crashes during landings. It had failed exactly as the tests had indicated it would.

That night Vandivier called his attorney and told him the story. The attorney arranged an appointment the following week at the Dayton, Ohio, office of the FBI. There the agent told Vandivier to keep quiet for the time being. The agent wanted to report the story first to the FBI chiefs in Washington. Next Lawson saw Vandivier's attorney and followed up with a visit to the FBI.

In the meantime, Goodrich officials were running around the field in a panic. One hot Saturday morning in late July an emergency meeting was called. Sink chaired the meeting. Sink said he thought they should tell the whole truth to the contractor, LTV. "We're going to level with them and let them handle the ball from there," he announced.

"Isn't it going to be pretty hard for us to admit to them that we've lied?" Vandivier asked.

To Sink, that question was a foul ball. He answered, "Now, wait a minute. Let's not go off half-cocked on this thing. It's not a matter of lying. We've just interpreted the information the way we felt it should be."

Sink got angry at Vandivier in the session. After lunch he took Vandivier aside and apologized. But he insisted that they had not been guilty of lying. "We were just exercising engineering license," he said.

As the summer wore on, tempers everywhere grew short. The Air Force demanded to see the raw test data. It was like an angry baseball commissioner who, learning that a game had been rigged, demands to see a television replay of the action. What it saw made no one feel easier.

In the fall, Lawson resigned. Soon afterward Vandivier resigned. In his letter of resignation, which he addressed to Line, he mentioned the fraud, deceit, and distrust of the testing period.

He was summoned to the office of the chief engineer, Sunderman. Like a wily veteran pitcher, Sunderman threw a variety of pitches at Vandivier. First he acknowledged the resignation letter and said that he was shocked—not at what the team had done but at Vandivier's irresponsible charges (screwball). Then he demanded an explanation (fastball). Before Vandivier could say much, he cut him off and lectured him on his ignorance and disloyalty (curveball). Next he threw a knuckleball. He said that it would be best for all concerned if Vandivier were to leave the plant immediately rather than stick around for ten days, as requested in the letter. In twenty minutes Vandivier had cleaned out his desk and left.

Two days later Goodrich recalled the qualification report and announced it would replace the defective brake with a new design, at no cost to LTV and the Air Force.

About ten months later Vandivier was the chief government witness at a hearing arranged by the Senate's Economy in Government Subcommittee, under the chairmanship of Senator William Proxmire. Following Vandivier's testimony, Lawson offered confirming testimony.

Representing Goodrich at the hearings were Sink and a top executive from the headquarters in Akron. These two gentlemen pooh-poohed the testimony of Vandivier and Lawson. Vandivier, they said, had no technical training, and Lawson was young and inexperienced. Neither was a big leaguer; both were bush leaguers. What had really happened, Sink explained to the solons, throwing his best sinker pitch, was that there were inconsistencies in the data because they came from several sources. Therefore it had been necessary to rationalize the figures in order to get a true story.

The subcommittee came to no conclusions about who had been guilty and guilty of what, but the Department of Defense did not take long to act. The next day it decreed sweeping changes in its procedures for inspecting, testing, and reporting on the work of contractor and subcontractor companies.

Taking a $25 per week pay cut, Vandivier went to work as a reporter for the *Troy Daily News,* where he remains today. "Believe me," he says, "this cut hurt." On the other hand, he feels that the experience "helped me to achieve a good measure of community respect and has resulted in many pleasing experiences that I feel I would otherwise not have had."

_____

Did Vandivier's actions meet the test of appropriate timing? From his standpoint, yes; because of his family, he thought it necessary to delay as long as possible. From the employer's standpoint, yes; he waited until after his resignation and departure. From the public's standpoint, however, it would have been desirable for him to speak out earlier. That might have saved the Pentagon some money, and it might have avoided a near accident at Edwards Air Force Base. If the events had happened a decade or so later, when there were more precedents for whistleblowing, Vandivier might not have waited so long.

EMPLOYEE OBJECTORS SHOULD TRY TO AVOID BECOMING PART OF THE PROBLEM

As attorneys, ombudspeople, personnel officers, and others know all too well, employee objectors may become part of the problem. This is understandable, for often they are humiliated, discredited, embarrassed, harassed, tested beyond a normal person's endurance. Nevertheless, they then become not assets to their organizations and to society but liabilities. If this happens, one cannot blame their superiors for trying to get them out of the way. Naturally, a responsible organization, recognizing its role in producing trauma, will try to relocate the objector in a job where is less stress and less danger of upsetting other employees. In time the person may be able to resume the prior responsibilities. But for the time being, some kind of removal from the line of duty is necessary or hardship and economic deficiencies will be caused.

Not long ago I was describing to a colleague some of my accounts of whistleblowers. After listening thoughtfully, my friend, who had had considerable experience as an executive, referred me to a front-page story in the *Wall Street Journal*. "Read that story," he advised. "It comes very close to describing several well-known whistleblowers I came to know. Talented as they were, they were almost unbearable to work with."

The story he referred me to ran in the October 23, 1980, issue of the *Wall Street Journal*. It pointed to the obsessions that employee objectors sometimes develop. "They so often have the same behavior pattern," a lawyer is quoted as saying. " 'I have five cartons of files I want you to look through. I'm up against big people.' " Turned off by such reactions, many lawyers become hardened and unsympathetic. The would-be client is more trouble than he or she can be worth.

The article goes on to describe Richard Fuller, an employee objector who, after three years of fighting, won a $25,000 breach-of-contract suit against ten former business associates. During the process, he suffered three years of unemployment, lost most of his friends, and spent $75,000 to get vindicated in court. According to the *Wall Street Journal*'s writer,

Fuller paces the floor of his house, talking of a recent murder in this poor and unsafe neighborhood on the west side of Chicago, He is short and stocky, with untrusting eyes and constantly moving arms. Jan, his wife of 10 years, stands nearby, tall and thin, her infrequent smile appearing to hurt.

They talk of the intervening years with a passion. The suit, they say, has been all they've talked about, all they've thought about. "It has consumed all our concentration," Mr. Fuller says. He remembers the old expensive restaurants, the friends they visited, the movies they saw, and their hobby of collecting and restoring old furniture. Now, he says, "we don't go on vacations or read books. We don't talk about anything else. We're boring, so we have no friends. Just three dogs."

After mentioning how the Fullers, during the three-year litigation, had to sell their car, house, and other possessions, the *Journal's* writer notes:

> Still, the biggest costs haven't been financial. Those who know the Fullers say they have become prisoners of their own obsession. Thomas Fuller, Richard's older brother and president of Thomas Industries Inc., a lighting-fixture maker in Louisville, remembers when Richard would call up and ask about the family. In recent years, he says, "I would call him up with family information that I thought he would or should be interested in, but the case was all he wanted to talk about. I admire his guts. I just worry that he has become so obsessed that he will continue with another effort."

> Mr. Fuller admits he is still consumed by the case. He suspects that the judge, defense attorneys, defendants and his own attorneys all joined in a plot against him. He continues to write the Securities and Exchange Commission, the Justice Department and others, pushing the fraud charges.

What can objectors do to avoid becoming obsessed to the point that they aggravate the problem rather than help to solve it? Perhaps the key is perspective. They can keep in mind that a rewarding life consists of playing not one role, or even two, but many roles. Whistleblowers never should be whistleblowers for more than part of the time. They should also be members of community organizations, lovers, sports nuts, artists, hikers, political workers, secretaries of clubs, poker players. Like Zorba and the narrator in *Zorba the Greek,* they should be able to turn away from an economic disaster, throw off their business hats, and dance on the beach.

What can organizations do to help employee objectors from developing tunnel vision? Many opportunities are available—and they cost little. A prompt and fair hearing procedure, perhaps the best way, may defuse the combatants before the conflict becomes irreconcilable. An employee assistance department may relocate the critic somewhere else in the organization, so that anguish and retaliation are minimized. Ombudspeople, counselors, and others may be able to help the objector keep the problem in perspective. Generally speaking, the best way to prevent obsession is to deal with the problem promptly. Several organizations that make strong efforts of such a nature are described in the next chapter.

SUMMARY

If you are an employee objector, you should observe eleven tests:

1. The subject of your protest, conflict, or whistleblowing should be appropriate; that is, it should be specific, tangible, and (if your doubts are borne out) clearly a wrong rather than a reasonable difference of opinion.
2. Your motives should be legitimate. For example, they should not be self-serving. (Similarly, your motives for not blowing the whistle, if that comes to pass, should be more than self-serving.)
3. Your actions should not violate express promises or commitments you have made to your superiors unless the danger is urgent and overwhelming.
4. You should check the facts and have reasonably solid evidence. For example, hearsay is insufficient grounds for protesting to your superiors or leaking a story to outsiders. On the other hand, you aren't required to have an airtight case, for that would impose an impossible burden of proof.
5. If possible, confine your protest to channels inside the organization. Go public only as a last resort.
6. Focus your protest on the substance of a danger or wrongdoing, not on culprits and perpetrators.
7. Don't hide behind a screen unless there are compelling reasons to do so. Let the people who must be informed know who you are and, if possible, let them question you.
8. Put your criticism or protest in writing, if possible, before or after speaking to the superiors or authorities who should be informed.
9. Give management some benefit of the doubt. Don't hold executives to some unrealistic ideal or standard of perfection; don't fault them at every opportunity.
10. If you must go public, do so at an appropriate time. Should you wait until some crisis or particularly acute transitional period is passed, for the sake of other employees or customers? Should you resign from the organization first?
11. Try to avoid becoming part of the problem. Sometimes the bizarre

and unsettling behavior of employee objectors is worse than the alleged wrongdoing.

If you are the manager to whom employee objectors come, remind them that they, like yourself, have obligations to the organization. If it is questionable that one or more of the foregoing criteria are met, point out that fact (and make a note of it in your memorandum on the conversation). This is part of your job as a trainer and standard-setter.

The First Amendment to the Constitution
presupposes that right conclusions are more likely
to be gathered out of a multitude of tongues than
through any kind of authoritative selection. To
many this is, and always will be, folly; but we have
staked upon it our all.

LEARNED HAND

9

HOW "GOOD" ORGANIZATIONS NOURISH HUMAN DIGNITY

As we saw earlier, the nature of the "good" organization is forever changing. Once upon a time an organization was "good" if it gave a person a job and paid him or her as promised. Then, as affluence began to grow, employees and society came to expect more, and management was able to provide more. Working conditions and hours became a factor. Today the nature of the good corporation or public agency is far more complex. In addition to meeting physical and environmental needs, it meets a range of psychological needs. It seeks to meet the same kinds of expectations during working hours that employees have as citizens during nonworking hours. In short, human dignity and employee dignity, once two quite different things, are becoming basically the same.

Does this trend threaten managerial prerogatives? In one sense, yes; in another, no. It diminishes prerogatives in the sense that no longer is a manager entitled to expect subordinates to work like robots. The good soldier approach is out. But in another sense, managerial prerogatives are stronger. In the new thinking person's environment, the manager can expect and demand more of subordinates. As we saw in the previous chapter, employees assume new obligations in order to make their civil liberties practicable. But that is not all. The manager is entitled to get more alertness, a keener sense of self-responsibility, more intellectual input. No longer is it *enough* for a subordinate to be a good soldier.

Now let us turn to ways employed by good corporations and public agencies to establish and sustain human dignity in the workplace. It will become apparent that such an ideal is not impractical or visionary. Every element of it has been tried and found workable by at least a few companies. In fact, I believe that there is probably a higher quality of planning participation, due process, conscientious objection, and privacy in some leading corporations today than there is in numerous communities around the country. We now know it is possible and practical for corporations and public agencies to lead in developing a higher quality of life just as they traditionally have led in producing economic goods and services.

REASONABLE WORKING CONDITIONS

First, the good organization meets employee expectations for satisfactory working conditions. This need can be stated briefly because it has been discussed for many years and long since has become familiar to Americans. Here are the *kinds* of expectations that management concerns itself with:

Air Movement, Temperature: Offices and factory work areas should be well ventilated. The air should move. If there is no air conditioning and the temperature goes up to 100°F, the windows do not remain closed.

Cleanliness, Sanitation: The air, walls, floors, steps, and rest rooms are kept clean.

Maintenance and Repair: Just as the company or agency keeps its large machines and expensive processes in good repair, so it keeps the air conditioning, water heaters, lighting systems, elevators, and other such equipment in good working condition.

Security: The corridors, stairways, and parking lots are kept safe for employees to walk in.

Rest and Recreation: Places are provided where employees can rest and relax after lunch or during a break. If there is a vacant area next to the building, it is converted into some sort of recreation yard rather than left to grow weeds.

Robert Schrank, expert on employee sociology, believes that workplace amenities are a good deal more important than many executives realize.

They "may be the stuff of which high levels of job satisfaction are made," he says. He thinks wise managements get a great deal of mileage simply from such steps as improving the lunchroom, reducing noise level, and improving the materials supply system so that employees don't have to chase around in frustration looking for machine parts, solvents, markers, graph paper, and so on.[1]

Of the estimated 80,000 organizations in the United States that employ 100 or more people, probably a clear majority meet employee expectations regarding satisfactory working conditions. Actually, some of the finest exemplars are firms employing only a few dozen people, for in such organizations no "we-they" line is easily drawn between managers and non-managers.

PARTICIPATION IN WORK PLANNING

Although worker democracies appear to be impractical for most companies and agencies, a large and fast-growing number of organizations make sure that employees have an influential hand in planning and controlling their jobs. Since the boss is still responsible for output, he or she must have the final say; but workers have a strong voice in the process of decision and usually can offer alternatives for the senior person to choose from. Significantly, these approaches almost always lead at least into the outer areas of civil liberties protection. The dividing line between what we call participative management and such rights as employee due process and freedom of inquiry becomes very fuzzy.

The first corporate chief executive to *systematize* participative decision-making was James F. Lincoln of Lincoln Electric Company in Cleveland. (Employee participation had been practiced long before Lincoln came on the scene, but it had been a reflection more of leadership style or happenstance than of a planned corporate system.) In 1913, Lincoln was catapulted into the top job of Lincoln Electric when his older brother, who had been head, became sick. He knew little about manufacturing, since he had concentrated on sales in the past, but manufacturing was the key to the company's survival. Everyone in the plant knew about his ignorance. It was clear to him that he had to draw heavily on the knowledge of rank-and-file workers, that he had to develop a type of cooperation and joint problem-solving that no plant had had before.

So he talked with the department heads. They decided that each department head should pick one man to work with Lincoln on a management

[1]. For a detailed exposition of this viewpoint, see Robert Schrank, *Ten Thousand Working Days* (Cambridge: M.I.T. Press, 1978).

committee that would meet every other Monday to discuss company problems and opportunities. That committee began meeting in 1914, and it has met with Lincoln and his successors to this day.

He realized, however, that the management committee was not enough. In his innocence of industrial relations, and in his need for cooperation, Lincoln saw the importance of quality of work life. And so he and his lieutenants created what they called the *Advisory Board*. This group, which also met with Lincoln every other week, consisted of employees elected from each department. Its job, as explained in the *Employees' Handbook*, was to "bring up and discuss the grievances and complaints" of employees in the departments represented, as well as to make suggestions to Lincoln for improving working conditions and safety.

The Advisory Board, too, has been meeting regularly since 1914. Departments elect members each month in rotation so that the board changes gradually. Representatives must have had two or more years of service in the company, and no representative can serve more than two consecutive terms. Sometime later, the Advisory Board was enlarged to include two elected representatives of foremen. Two superintendents and the personnel director also attend meetings. Lincoln presided in shirt-sleeves over the meetings, which generally included more than two dozen members.[2]

For many years Lincoln Electric, which prospered, was a kind of employee-relations freak, an oddball organization that few industrialists could understand; it utterly baffled scholars. However, during World War II many companies set up so-called labor-management committees that performed functions similar to those of Lincoln's Advisory Board, and after World War II other firms began taking steps toward participative work planning and control.

A quite different approach has been pioneered by Donnelly Mirrors, a family-owned concern in Holland, Michigan. The man responsible for developing the approach, John F. Donnelly, retired from the presidency in 1979 after nearly four decades as company head. At about the time he left, the company began suffering economically because its principal customers were U.S. automobile manufacturers. Nevertheless, since the company's fine economic performance for many years was beyond question, and since Donnelly's approach to the work force clearly had something to do with that excellent record, it stands as a reassuring case for participative management.

Donnelly was trained as an engineer at Notre Dame University in the late 1920s. After graduation he entered a seminary to prepare for the priest-

---

[2] See John Glover and Ralph Hower, *The Administrator* (Homewood, Ill.: Irwin, 1957), pp. 554–555.

hood. When his father died in 1932, he left the seminary to return to Holland and run the company. He did this not through choice but out of a sense of obligation to the family, which depended on the business. After a short time as president, Donnelly went back to the priesthood, leaving a new president, an outsider, to take over. But the outsider did not work out, and, at the request of the family, Donnelly returned to the presidency. Donnelly Mirrors had not always been famed for worker governance and participative management. For close to half a century, before Donnelly took over, it had been as authoritarian as most other companies. Founded in 1905, it began by manufacturing mirrors for the thriving western Michigan furniture industry as well as glass for auto replacement parts and for church art. The company was able to capitalize on the honesty, diligence, and loyalty of residents of a rural town started in the mid-nineteenth century by Dutch Calvinists and strongly influenced to this day by people of Dutch descent.

When the Great Depression hit, the company was selling about $350,000 worth of products annually. It barely survived the 1930s. "I would make my own decisions and then convince others," Donnelly told a case-writer. "We didn't even have engineers or sales people. I had to do it all myself." [3] But when the United States entered World War II, the company managed to get war contracts for optical glass components for tanks and aircraft, and it began to mechanize and diversify. By 1950 annual sales volume was $1 million and the work force had grown from a couple of dozen people to sixty. In the 1950s, sales and the work force doubled, and by 1976, when I (with Pamela Banks) interviewed Donnelly and other employees for a *Harvard Business Review* article,[4] sales exceeded $18 million, and more than 500 employees were on the payroll. There were four plants in the town of Holland and a fifth plant in Ireland; the company had gained 70% of the domestic automobile market in mirrors and had become a major manufacturer of other glass products.

A handsome, soft-spoken, graying man, Donnelly worked in a small, unpretentious office in one corner of a plant. He spent considerable time on the plant floor, where employees seemed to feel little hesitation in speaking to him and consulting with him about a problem. This plant and two others were loud with the noise of machinery, cluttered, busy. Here and there a meeting room could be found where the machinery noise was muted and an employee decision-making group would meet. When Donnelly joined

[3] "Donnelly Mirrors, Inc.," Harvard Business School case, 1973; Case Clearing House No. 2-473-088.
[4] "Participative Management at Work," An interview with John F. Donnelly, *Harvard Business Review*, January–February 1977, p. 117.

these groups, he did so at their meeting places, not in some executive meeting room or in his office.

For all this, he was an exacting chief executive who, quiet and gentle manners notwithstanding, was a stickler for method. As one manager in the company told the Harvard Business School case-writer; "He projects a very tough and demanding attitude in one-to-one situations. On technical issues he insists on detail and all the supporting data. Often, say around a major capital expenditure request, he gets highly involved in all the nitty-gritty of methods and procedures. And he always follows up. Meetings usually start with John pulling out a file full of detailed comments from the last meeting."

At the same time, Donnelly is a voracious reader and a restless student of philosophy. "He is intent on reaching the ideal organizational system here," said another company executive. This person added, with whimiscal understatement, "There is a certain amount of frustration when something happens to obstruct this development." Donnelly is especially concerned about protecting and encouraging individual dignity in an industrial setting. Both the systems and leadership attitudes of the typical corporation have, he believes, worked to put down the employee and dampen normal human drives for growth and responsibility.

The company's personnel policies are set by an elected group. Donnelly contrasted this side of operations with production management in the following way:

"We have what some people call two systems—an *executive* system and a *representative* system. The executive team does the work of the company. The representative system deals with the frictions that normally develop in the course of work. The executive system consists of the work committees linked together. The representative system is the Donnelly Committee, which represents all levels of the company. This committee deals with grievances; establishes pay policies; takes up questions of holidays, fringe benefits, and pay; considers exceptions from policy on promotion; and handles other matters of that kind." A question involving confidentiality of personnel information or some other aspect of privacy, if it came up, normally would be dealt with by this committee. So would a question involving the right of an employee to speak up without fear of retaliation, or the right to object to a possibly unethical order, or an allegedly unfair discharge or demotion. Also, the mechanisms of due process in the company can be considered and revised by this group.

The Donnelly Committee meets on a scheduled day once a month. Meetings may last up to three hours, depending on the number and complexity of questions brought by the elected representatives.

What is the relationship between a representative and his or her constituents? Donnelly explained to us:

"For every thirty-five or so employees, there is one representative on the committee. The representative is elected for a two-year term, and the terms are staggered, so that every six months some elections are held. However, a representative can be recalled by his or her constituents if they don't like what he or she is doing. The representatives are not paid extra for this work, even though it is time-consuming.

"They may be reelected, of course, and some have been, but because the job takes time, they are not likely to serve on and on.

"There is actually quite a bit of turnover. One representative, Paul Lubbers, who is now finishing his second term, says that none of the faces he used to see in meetings when he started are there now. This means that there is a good opportunity for quite a few people to serve on the committee over a period of years."

The Donnelly Committee does not lack for power. It does not take its cues from the president; in fact, for long he had no vote, though he attended the meetings. And when a representative presents a case of employee conflict with a supervisor or other manager, the committee does not hesitate to rule in favor of the subordinate if it thinks the latter is right.

The voting system is unusual. Donnelly explained:

"Every vote is equal, regardless of whom the member represents—whether maintenance teams, grinders, management, or someone else. Unanimous agreement is required for passing a recommendation. If a representative votes no on any issue, it doesn't pass. So a representative cannot pass the buck when he or she goes back to the teams represented and they ask how come such and such was voted. If the committee passed it, the representative must either have voted in favor or not voted at all."

In general, a representative's constituents are a functional group, or some part of one. We asked Jo Ann Czerkies, an employee in the molded products department who had served on the committee for two terms, how she represented the employees who elected her. She answered;

"I'll go around and inform my people about the issues that are on the agenda for a meeting. Sometimes I'll take a vote so I know exactly how they stand. But at the meeting, I may hear some new facts we didn't know about beforehand. So I'll have to decide with that information how to vote. What I vote is not always agreeable to the people I represent, so I'll have to go back to them and explain the reasons why I voted as I did. I've been on the Donnelly Committee for four years—I just got off—and for me it's the heart of the company. That's where a lot of very big decisions are made and where we've got management people, production people, office people—everyone—represented. The company is everybody, you know."

What checks does top management have on how well the committee is doing its job, especially how effectively employees think their complaints are handled? Regular surveys on employee attitudes are conducted. In addition, there was a fairly widespread feeling that most people had no trouble in getting Donnelly's ear if they wanted it. A tool-and-die maker told us that the president came by often and could be counted on to sit down any time and talk, if there was a problem. His attitude appears to be representative.

Donnelly is frank about certain problems that never seem to go away. One is the employee who simply can't feel comfortable in a self-governing atmosphere. Entertaining no illusions that the corporate philosophy meets everyone's need, he explained:

"Some people—managers especially—find it threatening. Some of these men and women adjust after a while, but others never become comfortable in our system and leave. They are used to the 'I'll tell you what to do' approach, and in turn they want to be told what to do by their own bosses. In other words, they have a high need for authority. There are psychological tests that help to identify such a need in an applicant, and we have used them either to choose less authoritative people or to help people relate more effectively with others. At present, though, we rely on interviews for hiring."

Donnelly also believes that the job of explaining the system and its values is never done. The job must go on and on—and it must never be taken for granted that all employees understand the principles of sharing power, information, and responsibility for action. He told us:

"After one industrial engineer had been in the company for about a month, I happened to see him, and he said, 'This is absolutely unbelievable.' I said, 'What do you mean?' He said, 'Well, I go around to talk to people about problems that I see, and they're willing to let me have the information without any fuss about it.' 'Do you know why that is?' I asked. 'Well, I suppose it has something to do with the system,' he said. 'They expect that you're not going to abuse the information and that if you want to do something with it, you'll talk it over with them and that if there are problems because of it, you'll work it out together.'

"That's true—we do give out information that's not usually given out, and we trust employees to use it properly. So people can see a difference here. They may think it's a magic formula and that you don't have to keep working at it."

For production management, the company relies heavily on a system of work teams, with at least one member of every team belonging to a team on a related task, thus linking the two. The team members are both managers and nonmanagers. One manager gave the following description to the casewriter:

"The work team sets goals and develops plans to determine how best to carry out their work, solve their own problems, and make their own decisions whenever possible. Very often a team will call in outside resources from engineering, maintenance, or purchasing to help them carry out suggestions or to make feasibility studies. Recently, in our chrome processing area, engineering was asked to look at a troublesome piece of equipment and find a replacement for it. Together, they ended up justifying new equipment and process changes which cost over $40,000. The engineer, one of the supervisors, and an operator chosen by the production team flew to California and processed several boxes of glass on the new equipment before the decision to buy. All of this resulted in total savings approaching $50,000 annually.

"The teams often set their own rates and standards, and we sometimes find they overcommit themselves and set unrealistic goals, but in situations like this we say 'go ahead and see if you can do it.' If we find they can meet their commitment, we then establish it as a standard."

The work teams may get into questions of plantwide personnel management; they do not confine themselves to nuts-and-bolts matters. Thus in 1970 a work team got to discussing time clocks and concluded that they should be discarded, and that everyone should draw a salary. It produced a formal proposal that was offered to the other work teams for consideration and debate. After this step, the proposal was put up to a vote of all employees, and voted in. Since then, each employee's salary has been agreed on at an annual team meeting, with new people generally placed in the lower portion of the salary range, adequate performers near the middle, and outstanding performers in the top portion.

The company tries to keep employees thinking about better methods and processes. Banks and I asked a material control supervisor to describe the suggestion system. He replied as follows:

"Generally, the quickest route is for the person to go to his supervisor. But if he doesn't choose to do that, he can get a suggestion form—they're all over the place. He writes up his suggestion and turns it in to the Suggestion Processing Committee. Its function is to make darn sure the suggestion gets assigned to someone who can do something constructive about it. Now, if the idea is totally unworkable, this committee wants to make sure the suggesting person understands why it's unfeasible—what the reasons are. We don't want to just throw the idea into File 13 or some place like that."

Once Donnelly was discussing the alleged evils of the factory assembly line with the case-writer. He said:

"It's not the production line that's the evil, it's the thinking behind it. If the line makes it more convenient for someone to do his work, then it's not necessarily bad. But it's how he is treated that's important. If he wants to change the job—is there a way to do it? Or if he wants to do different work—can he? Every man should be master of his own destiny. I know that if I had to do a production job, I would sooner do a monotonous job in a place where I was respected than do a varied job where I was not respected. We've tried to provide a context for respect here."

Is there a danger, the case-writer asked, of paternalistic attitudes influencing management's style? Donnelly answered:

"Paternalism is not a description of what a good father should do—that is, to help his children become independent from him. The way the term is commonly used suggests you make people become dependent *on* you. That's what we're trying to get away from."

Most skepticism about Donnelly's approach comes, he thinks, from managers and supervisors who are afraid of losing needed authority. Why, we asked him, do so many people feel that authority works better? He replied:

"Because that's the way it's been done, and that's the way organizations are structured. They're mostly modeled after the military, and it's difficult for people to conceive of any other system working. I would be the last one to say that we don't use authority in this company. We do. But, to the extent that you have to rely on the authority of your position, you're a questionable manager. If you are not in the position to get people to accept ideas because they're sound and if you are not willing to accept an idea because it's sound, then you're really not a good manager.

"So it's not a matter of throwing positions of authority out but of playing them down. That's difficult for people to do. It's an unknown world. The first time you really stick your neck out to make it work, you see that it's a risk. You can look awfully silly if you stick your neck out and people don't respond. The first few times you stick your neck out, people may not respond. They may say, 'What kind of stuff is this?' So until people have models that they can see are successful, it's going to be quite hard."

Donnelly likes "achievers" in his company. What he dislikes are people who ride over someone else in order to ge their way. He told us:

"If you can get people focused on an achievement rather than on defeating somebody, it's just a much healthier atmosphere.

"So many businesspeople talk about wanting an 'aggressive' person. *Aggression* connotes destroying the other. What you really want is a person who can *achieve*, who wants to get things done. You want energy, you want a self-starter, you want initiative, responsibility. You can get the same thing done with much more positive motivation than is normally thought.

"These are almost childish sorts of distinctions, but there seems to be a need to reiterate them. When you build an organization on destructive characteristics, it's going to have problems. You're always going to be fighting those destructive tendencies. You can't rule out human nature, and you're going to have problems under the best of circumstances, but I think if you foster constructive traits in people and play down the destructive, you're going to have fewer problems."

For still another kind of approach, consider the Eaton Corporation, mentioned in Chapter 1. Beginning in 1968 and continuing through the 1970s, it began establishing new approaches to operations at thirteen plants manufacturing steel parts, truck transmissions, axles, hardware, and other types of equipment. Donald N. Scobel, a veteran employee-relations executive at Eaton, describes some aspects of the "responsive workplace" that the company now maintains:

Almost a third of the work force diagnoses its own job methods and scopes. At one plant, a janitor persuaded his boss that he, rather than the purchasing department, could order local cleaning supplies because he would give it higher priority than they would. He was allowed to do so, while other janitors wanted no part of the telephoning and paper work. At another plant the lathe operators insisted they be allowed to join a meeting of equipment engineers to learn why their lathes were malfunctioning. Many times poeple came forth with combinations of jobs or changes in sequences that can improve output. Some improvements require that the job and pay structure be changed, but many can be accommodated by the existing system. . . .

If a plant is on a two-shift, five-day operation, and business expands, the different departments will discuss different work-schedule options, such as weekend work, extended daily hours, or a third shift that could be used to handle the increase. Often management will express its thoughts and invite reactions; more often, the options are put to a vote. In either case, employee inputs are specifically invited before any decision is made.

At one plant several employees suggested the company try a four-day week. The suggestion was put to a vote—and passed; in another plant, it failed. Elsewhere, management asked the employees in one departmental unit to restructure their own job contents and assignments when the current system was obviously inequitable. At a few locations, employees have nominated and selected candidates for supervisory positions, and in one situation, the employees said another supervisor was not necessary! . . .

The plant manager chairs a periodic roundtable with representatives from all office and factory departments who are selected in whatever way the department decides. The participants prepare the agenda of concerns and the minutes, as well as post follow-up action notices on central and departmental bulletin boards. . . .

At some locations, factory and lower-level office people are editors of the plant's newssheets. Often the recreational, social, and community affairs activities are independently managed, including direction of the fiscal aspects, by joint committees of factory and office people. Special committees (little ad hocracies) are formed from time to time to handle contingencies. . . .

Even in layoff circumstances, decision participation is invited. Although people do not like to vote on only negative alternatives, such as a reduction of the work force versus a reduction in working hours, if the company submits its preferred course to employee consideration, it will often find the attitudinal "pulse" and more often than not receive ideas for policy redirection. During one temporary layoff, plantwide discussion brought forth more layoff volunteers than were needed! In almost all cases, when the employees participate in decisions, they cooperate to the full with the final decision. As one manager put it, "I can no longer conceive of making a decision of major impact on any segment of that work force without first inviting meaningful dialogue." [5]

Another innovation in participative management is the so-called jobholder meeting, a phrase coined by Pitney Bowes. In 1980 the company held nineteen such meetings in its Stamford, Connecticut, headquarters and more than a hundred across the country. At these meetings, employees offer suggestions, ask questions, and air complaints. They do so directly and through employee representatives, depending on their desire for anonymity.

The issues raised may be embarrassing. The chairman's salary, for example, may be challenged. Usually, however, questions pertain to such matters as after-hours supervisory training, a new data-processing system that some employees feel may threaten their jobs, and security. Managers try to solve problems raised at the level closest to the problem, but if that is not possible, the question is escalated to the next level—right up to the president, Fred T. Allen.

In addition, Pitney Bowes has established a council of employee and management representatives that meets each month to discuss questions

[5] Donald N. Scobel, "Doing Away with the Factory Blues," *Harvard Business Review*, November–December 1975, pp. 137–138.

concerning employees. Reportedly, the sessions produce valuable ideas and suggestions. For instance, during a cost-cutting campaign, employee suggestions enabled production crews, when raw materials arrived late, to make up readily for lost time.

Participative planning and control of work lead naturally into the kinds of employee rights and privileges that will be discussed in the following sections. For instance, at Lincoln, Donnelly, Eaton, and Pitney Bowes—or, for that matter, in almost all organizations encouraging participative approaches—a limited freedom of speech is encouraged. It has to be. The employee has what the organization considers a right to speak out against poor air quality, inconsistent directives, or an awkward inventory-control system. It is a relatively small step to go from a right to this kind of inquiry and argument to rights of conscientious objection. Sooner or later it may be natural for managers and subordinates to think about procedures for institutionalizing equity, such as fair hearing procedures and other forms of due process. Employee privacy becomes still another right that freedom of discussion seems to lead to sooner or later.

In the workplace, human dignity implies a voice in decision-making, especially decisions of important and immediate concern to different employees. In this respect, some corporations seem to be well ahead of many cities and towns in the country, where municipal government is a closed club and residents exercise only indirect control at election time.

DUE PROCESS AND FREEDOM OF INQUIRY

Fair hearing procedures, which are the corporate equivalent of due process, have four practical values:

1.   They correct many injustices. The employee unfairly fired can get reinstated; the supervisor who harasses a subordinate is required to mend his or her ways.

2.   They are the means of protecting such rights as freedom of inquiry, conscientious objection, and privacy. It does little good to set such rights forth in a corporate code, an employee manual, or speeches by the top executive unless there are measures for implementing them fairly *in the eyes of employees.*

3.   They are helpful to management—despite the momentary sting they may produce. Writes John W. Gardner:

I would lay it down as a basic principle of human organization that the individuals who hold the reins of power in any enterprise cannot trust themselves to be adequately self-critical. For those in power the danger of self-deception is very great, the danger of failing to see the problems or refusing to see them is ever-present. And the only protection is to create an atmosphere in which anyone can speak up.[6]

4. They make life more interesting in the office, factory, and warehouse. As Ronald Berenbeim points out,

> The conflict generated by the grievance procedure is more interesting than the monotony and boredom of the work and provides a very important distraction. Making the assumption that it is almost impossible for people to be creative, autonomous, or participative in a repetitive manufacturing or processing job, I perceive the griping, complaining, arguing with the foreman, and filing of grievances as social activities that alleviate the boredom.[7]

If Machiavelli were alive today, I suspect he would be willing to revise his famous statement in *The Discourses* to read this way: "Nothing renders a corporation or agency more firm and stable than to organize it in such a way that the excitement of the ill humors that agitate employees may have a way prescribed by law for venting itself." (In the orginal, not knowing of modern organizations, Machiavelli referred to "a republic" instead of a corporation or agency, and to "a state" instead of employees.)

Cumulatively and synergistically, these four values are a vital part of the meaning of human dignity in the workplace. Is such an achievement practical and possible in corporations and government agencies? The experience of a few leading organizations suggests that the answer is a resounding yes. The procedures are relatively inexpensive. They do not require a particular size of organization or type of operation. Although they are imperfect (as indeed due process in the community is) and sometimes talked down by employees, the record shows that they work and are beneficial in many ways.[8] My conclusion is that the only real obstacles to them are lack of experience with open decision-making and an absence of management will to establish them. The first can be gained in a few years with participative management, as explained earlier. The second has to come from the hearts and minds of top executives themselves or, less desirable, from legislative pressure and administrative regulation.

---

[6] Quoted in Fred Foulkes, *Personnel Policies in Large Nonunion Companies* (Englewood Cliffs, N.J.: Prentice-Hall, 1980), p. 303.

[7] Ronald E. Berenbeim, *Nonunion Complaint Systems: A Corporate Appraisal* (New York: Conference Board, 1980), p. 4.

[8] Foulkes, op. cit., pp. 303–304.

Let us turn now to the efforts of the Bank of America to maintain forms of due process and related rights. Although the Bank of America is by no means the only leader in this respect, it probably has had more experience with the approach than any other organization, public or private. Thanks to the bank's due process procedures, I believe that an employee there who has been wronged has a better chance of obtaining justice fairly and promptly than do citizens in numerous communities in America. Following the description of the bank's experience, we can look at the work of several other organizations in instituting due process.

Due Process at the Bank of America

The world's largest bank, with nearly 1,100 branches and a net portfolio of $48 billion in 1980, the year I (with Pamela Banks) studied the organization,[9] the Bank of America has conducted some of its employee-rights programs for many years. Others are more recent. All of them keep evolving as employee expectations change and the organization gains fresh experience with the programs. Five programs in particular are noteworthy:

1. *Employee Assistance.*   Employees who have problems, questions, or complaints are urged to talk first to their operations officers and supervisors, and next (if necessary) with their managers, department heads, or district administrators. If the problem is still not resolved, the employee can contact an employee assistance officer. All of these contacts are kept confidential. If the employee gives permission, the employee assistance officer will go to the supervisor and attempt to resolve the problem equitably. Thus an employee assistance officer often performs the role sometimes known as that of an ombudsperson.

2. *Let's Talk It Over.*   This is the bank's formal problemsolving process, giving employees the right to discuss their concerns with several officers in their unit and to obtain a review by impartial third parties. Six steps are available: (*a*) discussion of the concern with the immediate supervisor, (*b*) discussion with the district administrator or department head, (*c*) discussion with an employee assistance officer, (*d*) written appeal, with an employee assistance officer's help, if desired, to the district administrator or department head, (*e*) written appeal to the regional senior vice-president or statewide department head, and (*f*) review of the written request by a committee consisting of the head of the personnel department, the head of the legal department, and the executive officer of the employee's division.

[9] "Listening and Responding to Employees' Concerns," An Interview with A. W. Clausen, *Harvard Business Review*, January–February 1980, p. 1.

3. *Open Line.*   Using printed forms widely distributed, employees can address questions to the office of the Open Line coordinator. Upon receipt of the form the writer's name is detached and given a number and subject code. Then the question or concern is typed on a plain sheet of paper and forwarded to the appropriate bank officer for response within ten working days. Usually responses are mailed to the writer's home, but if the writer prefers, a personal interview can be held with a bank officer to discuss the answer.

The painstaking attention given to creating and protecting employee trust in Open Line has awed some observers. For example, *Modern Business Reports* writes,

> To preserve confidentiality, Open Line employs an elaborate security program. First, the Coordinator opens all the incoming mail behind closed doors. He assigns a number to the name stub at the bottom of the form and puts a corresponding number at the top. He then separates the two and places the name stub in a locked box to which he has the only key. The stub remains in the locked box until it is time to mail a reply. Meanwhile, the Open Line writer is known only by number.

> To be certain that no one can identify the writer's handwriting, the letter (now with the identifying number) is retyped on white paper before being circulated for a response. Included on the form are codes which indicate whether the letter was signed, whether or not the publication of the letter is restricted, and whether the employee wants an interview.

> After the letter has been retyped, the Coordinator reads it and decides where to send it for an answer. Sometimes the question has been answered in an earlier Open Line. If this is so, the coordinator or his assistant will check with the person who answered the first question to make certain the answer is still current.

> What happens when the writer names specific offices, officers, or statistics that are important but would probably reveal the identity of the employee? The employee is telephoned and asked whether his or her name may be revealed. If the employer objects, the name is not revealed and the Coordinator gets the question answered as best he can, but possibly less satisfactorily.

> After the response is returned to the Coordinator's office (normal turnaround time is 10 working days, although answers involving several departments may take longer), the Coordinator reviews it from

the employee's point of view. Will it be perceived as candid? Does it really answer the question? In cases where management policy does not permit comment, the Coordinator makes certain that the letter explains why the information can't be disclosed.[10]

4. *BankAmerican.* To broaden understanding of answers to employees' questions, this magazine for the Bank of America's employees prints (with the writers' express permission) many questions, concerns, and complaints of general interest, along with responses from bank officers.

If analogies are made between employee freedoms and the freedoms guaranteed in the Bill of Rights, *BankAmerican* is the vehicle for freedom of the press at the Bank of America. We asked George Skoglund, executive vice-president for personnel administration, about censorship of submissions. He answered; "Well, we don't publish every submission. For example, if there's an answer right in the manual of the corporate code, we don't usually publish the submission. And if an employee wrote an editorial damning the bank, we wouldn't run it. But if it's something we can answer, or want to try to answer, we'll run it."

Suppose an employee writes in, as did a Dow Chemical Company employee in Dow's company magazine in 1978, and criticizes a raise in salary of the chief executive or some other top executive. Would *BankAmerican* print a tempestuous antimanagement question like that? Skoglund said it would. But someone in the bank would defend the salary raise in a postcript to the letter. It would be pointed out that the change was made in a rational manner—to be competitive with salaries in other banks, or because of earnings changes, or for other reasons stipulated in the executive salary scheme. In short, he emphasized, a question wouldn't be censored because it dealt with a touchy subject, raised an unpopular issue, or excoriated management for some practice or policy.

5. *Privacy.* Internal access to personnel files is extremely limited at the bank, and particular attention is paid to the proper use of information in the files. Every employee has the right to review his or her files, to request changes in records he or she regards as unjust, and to know what grade level he or she has attained at the company (there are more than a dozen grade levels).

How much use is made of the bank's programs? One learns to worry that a nice-sounding program of a company or public agency may be more for show than for everyday use. Happily, this seems not to be the case at the Bank of America. Just the opposite. In 1978, about 7,000 employees used Let's Talk It Over—about one employee in every ten. In meetings and individual sessions that year, employee assistance officers talked with more

---

[10] *Modern Business Reports,* March 1978, p. 7.

than 17,000 employees—sometimes there was a series of talks with one of those individuals. As for Open Line, the bank's biannual surveys showed that more than 97% of employees gave it a positive rating for credibility. Moreover, almost all employees were signing their written communications to Open Line, evidence they trusted its policy of confidentiality. In 1978, more than 900 letters to Open Line were received; the number of letters received since the program's beginning in 1973 was in excess of 11,000. It should be emphasized here that many of these letters were not "nice" letters but letters of the "I think such-and-such a project is terrible and you guys ought to have your head examined" nature.

Although I believe that a conflict or grievance is handled more fairly and more promptly at the Bank of America than an alleged injustice would be handled in many towns, cities, and states, and with less possibility or discrimination because of race, color, creed, or the way a person "parts his or her hair," I have no illusions that injustice is eliminated. I am sure that employee assistance officers can make mistakes. A subordinate can be so terrified of a superior that no complaint is ever made. Something can go awry in Open Line. But this is the underside of the rock of any human system of justice. Juries and judges too, are not free from error and prejudice.

Let us look at three examples of how the bank's programs work.

A Conflict Over Leave.   A clerical worker and her husband decided to adopt a child. She told her supervisor that it would take a long time, and she told him about the different things the adoption agency wanted her and her husband to do, such as attend five classes late in the afternoon. He gave her permission to leave work early to attend the classes.

Everything went along fine at first, and she received a letter from the adoption agency saying all the paperwork was done, that the only thing she had to do was wait for the child and arrange to take six months off from work to be with it. She went to the Employee Assistance Office to see if she was entitled to maternity leave. She was told no, because was she not disabled; she was advised she would have to get permission from her supervisor for a so-called personal leave of absence. But when she went to her supervisor and made this request, he said the Employee Assistance Office was wrong. "Let me call the man you talked to," he said.

Here we need to halt the story temporarily to explain that the clerical worker had not enjoyed a good relationship with her supervisor. Let her tell it in her own words:

"He had a very bad habit of cursing and swearing. I had asked him not to talk to me that way and to call me by my name or not say anything to me. Then I had gone to Employee Assistance, and they wanted to call him and talk to him and have me transferred, but I said, 'No, I'll give him another chance.' My husband told me to apologize to him and call a truce, which I did. But the next day he wrote me up for something wrong in my work—it's called a counseling form. It was the only way he could get back at me. I had stayed fifteen minutes late because my work was not complete, and instead of just warning me, as he did the others who stayed late, he said he'd fire me if I did that again."

With this background in mind, the next incidents in the clerical worker's case may not seem surprising. Several days after the superior vowed to call Employee Assistance and set them straight about the procedure for her getting time off for the adopted baby, as required by the adoption agency, she went in and asked him if he had made the call. Her report of what happened follows:

"He yelled at me, 'This takes time, you know. I can't do everything overnight.' He had always treated me with very little respect. But the adoption agency needed an answer, so the next morning I went to him again and told him they had to know one way or the other. He started yelling at me again and told me about all the phone calls he had to make. I told him I would not accept that. I wanted the same courtesy and respect that his wife would get. And he told me to get out of the office—'Get out!' I went to the Employee Assistance Office again—I was hysterical—and they calmed me down.

"I went back to my office and asked my supervisor if he had talked to Employee Assistance, and he said yes. I asked, 'Who did you speak with?' He said, well, he had only talked with the receptionist. I was very upset.

"He said, I know how you feel, but that's all I can do. I said, 'You don't know how I feel,' and he answered, 'The trouble with you is, you just don't think anybody knows you.' So I went back to Employee Assistance again and explained this to them. They set up a meeting with my department head.

"My department head said [at the meeting] they could not give me time off because I would not be disabled, and what would they say to the next person who wanted time off? When he told me this, I said, 'You can't compare the two. And why couldn't you have told me this last year when I first started looking into it?' All he could offer was my two weeks vacation as leave. I told him, 'Please don't insult me.' I went back to Employee Assistance, and Employee Assistance went to him again. He finally agreed to give me two months off."

But for the employee assistance officers, this clerical worker would almost surely have been fired. In fact, she probably would have been fired long before the adoption incident, when she first began challenging her boss's scabrous manners. The supervisor, not the subordinate, was the one who needed help—and discipline—in this case. I think this is one of the morals of the story. No institution tries harder than the Bank of America does to develop competent, effective supervisors and managers. But 100% quality control in this respect is impossible. It is impossible for any organization, whether it be a bank, manufacturer, government agency, philanthropic agency, military unit, or church. The value of an agency like Employee Assistance is not only that it rectifies injustices but that it polices supervisors and managers who tend to be arbitrary and unfair from time to time or with certain types of employees.

A Dispute Over An Evaluation.   Now let us turn to a second case. It involves a very capable young employee who works in one of the branches of the Bank of America. The problem here is one of the most nettlesome and insidious ones that employees complain about and fear. That is the problem of being blackballed or bad-mouthed in one of the files, thus blocking or impeding chances of promotion, opportunities for transfer, and prospects for salary increases.

Here is the story as told by the employee (and confirmed by others in the bank):

"My supervisor gave me my performance report, and I was reading it. It said what a great employee I was and what a fantastic job I was doing and all that kind of stuff, but at the very end I came to a comment that I was moody and uncooperative. So I asked her why this was put in, and she said she'd had nothing to do with it, that if I wanted to know anything about it I'd have to speak to the operations officer at my branch.

"So I went to him and I told him I wanted to know why the comment was put in and who had said it. All he would tell me was that it came from one side of my department.

"I didn't like that answer, because it was so vague, so I called the Employee Assistance Office and asked them where I stood as an employee and how to get this removed because all my performance reports had always been really good. The employee assistance officer wasn't in, but one thing I liked was that he did call me back right away.

"He was very nice to talk to. He didn't say, 'You're right and he's wrong,' or 'You're wrong and he's right.' He just said, 'This is where you stand.'

"He said that, first of all, they're not supposed to put anything in your performance report that's bad if they haven't discussed it with you first. If you don't correct the situation, then they can knock you down for it. Nothing had ever been said to me about it in all ten years I'd been at the bank. Second of all, he said I had the right to know who had said it and why they felt I was uncooperative.

"So, then I went back to my operations officer, and I told him all this and that I wanted the derogatory comment removed because I didn't think it was fair." It turned out, the employee told us, that the criticism had come from a manager several rungs up the ladder. The employee reported:

"What it boiled down to was that I was working at a very busy desk, and this manager liked to talk with me. When he'd come over, I was always busy doing my job and usually not eager to talk for long. When I went back to the operations officer, we talked it over and figured out what the real problem was. Then they just took the comment off, and he wrote the new report up, and then I signed it, and there was no problem."

Problem of "Illegal" Dismissal.   The third case comes from a senior officer of a branch bank. This case is interesting not so much for the substance of the conflict and grievance as for the Bank of America's insistence on *procedure*. Though a personnel decision against an employee may be defensible on the merits of the case, it is not right, in the bank's view, if the employee is not properly notified and counseled along the way. The bank's approach reminds one of the traditional approach of the courts, which refuse to let a decision go against a person unless well-known rules of evidence and procedure are followed meticulously.

Here is the story as told by the senior officer:

"One day here, one day there, an individual we'd recently hired would call in sick. After only ten weeks of employment, there'd been seven days of absence. Now I can live with an individual out for two weeks with some kind of illness more than I can with an individual out a day every week. Well, this pattern became unbearable for the people supervising, so they told me that they thought they were going to fire the person.

"My reaction to that was, if everything's in order, go ahead. So they did. They let the person go.

"When we dismiss someone like that, we know we have to have a good reason. We don't just all of a sudden say, 'Hey, we can't use you anymore.' We write the reason down, and then we have a conversation with the person—'We're dismissing you for this or that reason. If you don't agree with the reason, you can talk to our manager, or to me, or to the regional office. That's what our Let's Talk It Over program is all about. That's your right to due process.' And that's what we told this person.

"Then the employee signs the statement, and the officer that releases the employee signs it.

"In this case, the person didn't agree and got hold of the employee assistance officer for this region. The employee assistance officer knows I don't just fire people for the heck of it, but he said, 'I'm not sure that this person was given due process. Before being fired, the person was only verbally told that his absence had been too high.' "

The point, as the senior officer emphasized, was that the employee had not been warned *in writing*, as required by the bank's rules. The senior officer explained:

"Employees have to know where they stand. This should have been written down a month before on what we call the Employee Discussion Record: 'If this absence continues, then we're going to have to dismiss you because we can't live with this.' And then the officer should've called the person in and said, 'I've written this about you. I want you to read it, and if you disagree with what it says, you don't have to sign it, but at least there'll be some understanding about what's expected.' "

So the employee was brought back. Managers listened to his story again. They began to feel that some of his absences had been legitimate—not all of them, but a portion of them. Let the senior officer finish:

"So I said to this employee, 'If those problems come up again, and you know you absolutely cannot come to work, call me and tell me why beforehand. If it doesn't happen constantly, I'll understand. We are reinstating you with the understanding that if your excessive absences continue, your job will be terminated permanently.'

"I signed the statement; the employee signed it; and absence has not been a problem since."

We asked the senior officer if he worried about the repercussions on the supervisor whose dismissal action had been reversed. The senior officer answered.

"That is always a concern, and I talked with him about it. 'You had every right to fire such an employee,' I said, 'but there was nothing in the file showing that you had gone through the bank's review process. Now you may feel hard toward me for taking your authority away in this case, but in my judgment we haven't gone as far as we should've. We've got to give this person a second chance.' "

Managing Due Process.   Now let us turn to some more general questions about employee rights at the Bank of America. What does management do—and avoid doing—to make the different programs a reality rather than an illusion?

One important "secret" of management success is organizational: In 1980 George Skoglund, personnel head, was an executive vice-president. He sat on the powerful management committee, reported directly to the chief executive officer, and talked with him often. A. W. Clausen, CEO in 1980 (in 1981 he resigned to become head of the World Bank), told us, "I tell George that he's got to be an advocate. Somebody has got to be spending forty hours a day ten days a week thinking about the needs of the people who work here. In big organizations with massive, complex geographies, there's a tendency to think in terms of labels. Those people over there are tellers, those are managers, these are officers. These are grade 20s, those are grade 15s, those are grade 30s, and so on. The names are forgotten along with the sensitivities, anxieties, frustrations. Dehumanization. That's why we need people advocacy."

By *people advocacy* Clausen meant going to bat for the employee who worries, "How am I going to get any identity around here? Who's going to know I'm around? Who cares?" Clausen elaborated: "An employee gets captured in a profit center—in the note department, say, or in a branch bank, or in a division or group somewhere. He or she gets locked into that place, lost. There's no way to go to escape. And he's got a bad boss. He doesn't know what to do. Complain to the boss? 'There goes my career,' he says. 'There goes not only my next raise but my hope to advance.'

"So we've got to provide escape routes, which is what we do with Open Line, Let's Talk It Over, and discussion with an employee assistance officer."

The cause of the whistleblower, in particular, is aided by another policy: speaking out about wrongdoing is seen not only as a right but as an obligation. For instance, one provision of the company's Code of Conduct states, "Any employee having information or knowledge of any unrecorded fund or asset or any prohibited act shall promptly report such activity to the controller." Clausen explained to us:

"Let's say I'm working around the church, and I see somebody dipping into the collection plates as they are carried back. If I don't say anything, am I not a kind of silent partner in the crime? It's the same if I'm a teller and I notice some money going into your pocket on occasional days when you come up $50 short. If I stand by and let you rip off the bank, I'm a kind of silent partner in the crime.

"In the banking business, one of the essential ingredients is public trust. If we permit any deviation from the square corner, we're letting the system erode. The word gets out that the bank doesn't square its corners, permits skimming and dipping, that if you go to a certain window you'll get special treatment, or whatever. Standing by and letting a reputation like that develop would be disloyalty."

An especially important technique is the employee survey. Skoglund described it: "Regularly every six months a fourth of the employees are polled—what do they think of the bank? Are men and women treated the same? Are minority-group employees treated differently from the majority? And so on. And we have built with that information a kind of morale and supervision index that indicates where morale is strong or weak, and where supervision is rated high or low. You get feelings about trends from the index, and about where correction is needed."

Clausen said this: "We ask the same questions perhaps 95% of the time so that we can feel the directions of opinion. We compare the results we got in April with the results we got last October to see if the trend is up or down. Then we try to react, to address the trend."

How do the surveys preserve confidentiality, yet point to trouble spots? Clausen answered, "They are mailed not to just a cross section of all employees but to employees at a cross section of the branches. So when reports of bad supervision come in, we're not left knowing only that the trouble is somewhere in, say, northern California. We know just what branch it's at. We can deal with it. If the trouble's at a department or profit center *within* a larger branch, we can sort that out, too. The demagogue isn't identified, but if everyone in a certain place is crabbing, the confidentiality of the answers doesn't keep us from locating the trouble."

What kind of question might produce a red flag? The chief executive answered, "We ask if the employee would be reluctant to go to his or her boss with certain kinds of problems. That's one example. If the confidence level is falling at a profit center, we know that the supervisor has changed his or her spots, or is having trouble at home, or maybe that there's a new supervisor who's not working out."

What are some of the problems and practical difficulties of making the rights programs work?

First, there is the ever-present possibility that employees will hesitate to speak up for fear that supervisors will get back at them. Explains Jenifer Renzel, vice-president in charge of the Employee Assistance Section: "You always have the problem—and I don't think there's any way around it—of employees being concerned that there's going to be some form of reprisal. It shouldn't happen, and if we find out it ever does, we deal with it. Employees need to feel comfortable, that they are somewhat protected if they're going to use this system."

Second, there is the danger that the rights programs will be seen as unfairly favoring supervisors *or* subordinates. Renzel said, "We try to maintain our objectivity. We don't view ourselves as being necessarily an advocacy group when an employee comes to us. We want to hear the employee's side, we want to hear the supervisor's side, and we want to make a judgment. Our job is to help the managements of the units as well as the employees under them."

Third, the rights programs must discriminate between people whose perceived grievances should be dealt with for the sake of the organization and equity, and people who are chronic malcontents, misanthropes, organization-haters who "constantly throw gravel in the gearbox." Happily, efforts to discourage and reject the latter usually bring hurrahs from fellow employees as well as from harassed supervisors.

Fourth, not all managers greet employee-rights programs and decisions with enthusiasm. We asked Skoglund how management tries to deal with the supervisor who drags his or her heels. He answered, "The boss talks to that supervisor. 'Part of your job,' the boss says, 'is to understand what our policies are. You may not agree with all the policies, but one of your jobs is to implement them. Now, here's the policy statement in our Corporate Code of Conduct. Your job is to carry it out and help to sell it, and if you don't like it, you'd be better off going to a corporation whose policies you do like.' "

Worker Sounds at Puget Sound Plywood

Puget Sound Plywood, a worker-owned company in Tacoma, Washington, had about 400 employees and annual sales of about $30 million when Pamela Banks and I studied it in 1978.[11] Although it is an unusual company in American industry, with policy decisions made by employee vote, top executives elected by employees, and equal pay for all employees, its system of due process is based on principles that are workable in a great many organizations. To be sure, the ultimate tribunal at Puget Sound is the board of trustees, and that body is so differently constituted in most other organizations that it could not act, as at Puget Sound, as a "supreme court" for employee conflicts. However, a specially formed tribunal would work as well. For instance, at Polaroid Corporation in Boston employee disputes are heard (if appealed) by an employee-elected committee.

For elaboration of the company's approach to due process, we went to a shift foreman with thirty-one years experience in the mill, Bill Kittinger. Our question-and-answer dialogue with him follows:

Q. *We're interested in the system of discipline. Could you tell us about it?*

A. If someone breaks a rule—we have a booklet of rules which maybe you've seen—we write out what we call a warning slip. In the case of the first offense, usually we just give the slip to the person. There'll be no penalty. Then the second time, the person may get laid off for three days. Maybe the third time the penalty will be a week of layoff, and then after that, we would send the offender to the board. The board of directors would give out some penalty or reprimand, or it's possible that it would fire the person.

Q. *Could you give us an example of how the system works?*

---

[11] See "When Employees Run the Company," An Interview with Leamon J. Bennett, *Harvard Business Review*, January–February 1979, p. 88.

A. I had a fellow who worked on the saw, and he had a drinking problem. This problem was a strange one in the sense that he didn't drink every day. He wouldn't drink at all for four or five months, and then he would start drinking, and maybe he would drink for three weeks. He would be gone from work for maybe two or three weeks.

We didn't really recognize what the problem was for a while, but when we did, we brought it to his attention, and we laid him off. Then he came back to work. Things went along pretty good for a few months; then, right over again, he did the same thing, so we laid him off again. And then it happened a third time. That time we sent him to the board with a recommendation that he not be allowed to come back to work until he got involved in some kind of a program and was cured. So he had to go to the hospital to take a cure.

Now, the cure has been very successful, and he has completely reversed himself. He says that he's a new man, and it's the happiest thing he ever did in his life, and he gets along better with his family and his wife and everybody.

Q. *When the offender appears before the board, who talks to him or her?*

A. Any one of the nine trustees. The chairman, of course, generally does, but there is usually a period when people who wish to can talk to him and put in their views.

Q. *Before the person comes, does the board get briefed on the problem?*

A. Oh, yes. We send a form all filled out—what the problem is and so on.

Q. *And you would be the one to write up the slip?*

A. Right—always one of the foremen or the superintendent, not a fellow worker. Another worker may recommend action to the foreman or the superintendent, for we don't see all the problems. Someone may come and tell us that a fellow has some kind of problem that might bear watching.

The fact is, I have one such case today. My attention has been brought to someone who supposedly has not been doing his work, and I have been watching him pretty closely.

It can happen to all of us—something happens, so we're not quite as alert as we should be, or we're not thinking as well as we should, or we daydream. Some of the work is quite montonous, and it's pretty easy to begin to think about something else.

Q. *Is going before the board like having a trial? Does someone argue for the offender and someone else argue against him?*

A. No, it's more like an assembly in the sense that they're trying to accomplish a result, trying to get this person, or persons, whoever they might be, to realize and accept the fact that they've had a certain problem and that they need to cure the problem. Usually it's quite successful.

It seems like the higher up the person is who disciplines the offender, the more success there is. Now, the department head might get after a person about some particular problem and not get much of a result. Then it goes up to me, the foreman, and I get after him, and maybe the result is a little bit better. Then maybe the superintendent gets after him next, and he gets more concerned. When the board gets after him, he takes it very seriously, and he usually accepts its judgment.

Q. *Suppose a person goes to the board and says, "Kittinger gave me a bum deal; he's all wrong." Would they thrash it out?*

A. Oh, yes. If the superintendent or I discipline a person, he has the right within forty-eight hours to apply in writing to the board to change the ruling. Recently one of the other foremen disciplined a fellow—sent him home for a week. He petitioned to the board that the foreman was wrong and asked that he be paid for back time. The board held a hearing. Several witnesses appeared for both sides. The board rejected his claim. But it saw there had been some kind of personality conflict between the worker and the foreman, and so it sent the man to another shift to ease the problem.

A Hospital's Grievance Procedure

A short distance north of Puget Sound Plywood, in Seattle, Washington, is Providence Medical Center, an organization that has a five-step grievance procedure for employees. According to George W. Mauer, assistant administrator for personnel services, the procedure was instituted in 1974 after management realized that its open-door policy was insubstantial, providing not enough form or substance for employee due process. The Grievance Procedure Policy Statement is as follows:

All employees, inclusive of management, shall have the right to utilize the following procedure in reconciliation or resolution of complaints. The Personnel Department will function as an advocate of employees.

Step 1: Discuss the complaint with the immediate supervisor. If the complaint is about that supervisor or if the employee is not satisfied with her/his decision, the employee may take the matter to the next level of supervision or to a representative of the Personnel Department. If the matter is taken to Personnel, the supervisor should arrange for a convenient time to meet within three working days of the complaint.

Step 2: A Personnel Representative will meet with the employee within three working days of the complaint. If she or he is unable to solve the problem, a written grievance will be filed at the employee's request. The Personnel Representative will assist the employee in its preparation.

Step 3: The Personnel Representative will forward the grievance to the Administrative Head responsible for the employee's department (or, if absent, his or her designee) within three working days. The Administrative Head, the employee, or the Personnel Representative may request a meeting of all parties before a recommendation is made. If the recommendation of the Administrative Head is unsatisfactory to the employee, the Personnel Representative will so document the reasons and forward the grievance to a joint Management–E.A.C. (Employee Advisory Committee) Grievance Committee within three working days of receipt of the grievance by the Administrative Head.

If the review process, Steps 1 through 3, cannot be followed due to organizational structure, the Assistant Administrator for Personnel Services or the Administrator shall designate a comparable review process.

Step 4: The joint Management–E.A.C. Grievance Committee shall be composed of two non-interested members of the Department Management and two non-interested members of the E.A.C. The two members from the E.A.C. shall be selected by the Assistant Administrator for Personnel Services from a list of six provided by the chairperson of the E.A.C. He/she shall also select the two representatives of Department Management, basing both decisions on the directive that all should be non-interested members.

This joint Grievance Committee and the Assistant Administrator for Personnel Services shall meet to review the grievance and recommend a decision in the matter to the administrator within three working days of receipt. Majority and minority recommendations are allowable. In the case of management grievances, the Committee shall be composed of two non-interested members of the Department Management staff and two non-interested members of the Administrative Council and the Assistant Administrator for Personnel Services. The latter shall function only as an advisor.

Step 5: The Administrator, or in his/her absence his/her designee, shall render a decision within twenty-four hours of receipt. The decision shall be in writing with supporting rationale.

Employee Fission at the Nuclear Regulatory Commission

In 1980, after lengthy investigation and study, the U.S. Nuclear Regulatory Commission set up a system of due process for its staff. In order to avoid repeating previous sections, I shall excerpt only a few portions of the description of the system in the employee manual. (The complete description runs under the imposing title, "Chapter 4125: Differing Professional Opinions," Volume 4,000 Personnel.)

It is the policy of the Nuclear Regulatory Commission, and the responsibility of all NRC supervisory and managerial personnel, to maintain a working environment that encourages employees to make known their best professional judgments even though they may differ from a prevailing staff view, disagree with a management decision or policy position, or take issue with proposed or established agency practices. Each differing professional opinion of an NRC employee will be evaluated on its own merit. Further, each differing professional opinion will be pursued to resolution and the employee's statement of differing professional opinion, together with the agency's final response, will be made available to the public to ensure the openness of NRC decisions that may affect the public.

It is not only the right but the duty of all NRC employees to make known their best professional judgments on any matter relating to the mission of the agency. Moreover, both the general public and the Nuclear Regulatory Commission benefit when the agency seriously considers NRC employees' differing professional opinions that concern matters related to the agency's mission. This policy assures all employees the opportunity to express differing professional opinions in good faith, to have these opinions heard and considered by NRC management, and to be protected against retaliation in any form. . . .

To assist originators in preparing adequate written statements of differing professional opinion, NRC management will allow a reasonable amount of (1) the originator's work time, (2) time of other NRC professional personnel in a consulting capacity, and (3) administrative support. The originator's immediate supervisor, in consultation with his or her manager, will determine the nature and level of resources provided in response to the originator's request for assistance.

The purpose of this assistance is to ensure that the pertinent issues are clearly and accurately presented, that related matters are considered, and that relevant documentation is included. In determining the level of resources to be made available to the employee, consideration will be given to (1) the potential significance of the proposed differing professional opinion and (2) the urgency of resolving the differing professional opinion in comparison with that of other mission-related activities.

As an alternative, employees may prepare a statement of differing professional opinion on their own time and in that statement describe what work, including proposed commitments of their own time, would be needed to resolve the concerns or issues. . . .

Once a signed differing professional opinion has been submitted, a written record must be maintained to provide accountability for all subsequent actions taken to resolve that differing professional opinion on its merits. This record will consist of signed notations of all supervisory and managerial determinations and actions based upon the differing professional opinion. Changes in the original documentation that are requested by the originator will also be made a part of this written record. All pertinent documentation will be retained for a minimum of 10 years. . . .

When submitting a differing professional opinion, the originator may request that it be presented to an impartial peer review group for review, evaluation, and comment. If such request is not made by the originator, and if the responsible office director determines that such review is justified by the complexity or the potential significance of the issues raised, he shall convene an impartial peer review group to address the substance of the issues raised in the differing professional opinion. In either case, the responsible office director will assure that members of the peer review groups convened for this purpose are specifically selected for their impartiality and professional competence concerning matters discussed in each differing professional opinion. The responsible office director will carefully consider peer review group recommendations in the resolution of applicable differing professional opinions and will provide the originator with a copy of the peer review group's report. . . .

Any NRC employee who retaliates against another employee for submitting or supporting a differing professional opinion is subject to disciplinary action in accordance with Chapter NRC-4171 (Separations and Adverse Actions). . . .

Retaliation consists of injurious actions taken against the originator of a differing professional opinion in which a motivating factor for such actions derived from the submission of a differing professional opinion by the originator. Retaliation may involve transfer; detail; ostracism; loss of staff assistance, space, or equipment; physical isolation; the absence of assignments involving substantive work; or the denial of promotion, attendance at professional society meetings, or justified training.

Employees who allege that retaliatory actions have been taken because of their submission or support of a differing professional opinion may seek redress through the negotiated grievance procedure or through the grievance procedure described in Chapter NRC-4157 (Employee Grievances).

The Special Review Panel described . . . will annually review all differing professional opinions submitted during the prior year to identify employees whose differing professional opinions made significant contributions to the agency or to public safety but who had not been recognized by his or her supervisor for this contribution. It is anticipated that employees who provide significant contributions to the agency or to public health and safety will be recommended for appropriate awards by their immediate supervisors.

Due Process under Collective Bargaining

For more than one-fifth of the American labor force, due process is not new. It has been established by collective bargaining agreements for decades. In the opinion of Clyde W. Summers, Fordham Professor of Law at the University of Pennsylvania and a teacher and practitioner of labor arbitration for about thirty years, the procedures developed to protect union members from unjust discharge or suspension have worked so well that they should be applied to all employees. Summers believes that laws should be enacted establishing for all employees a right to be disciplined or dismissed only for just cause, with an accompanying right to appeal a superior's decision to arbitration in the same manner that union members have been doing.

In enforcing the provisions of collective bargaining agreements, arbitrators have established standards for what constitutes just cause for discipline. They have also developed effective procedures for determining the guilt or innocence of accused employees, reviewed the appropriateness of penalties, and devised effective remedies of reinstatement and awards for back pay. Summers describes four characteristics of the body of law created by arbitration:

> First, it has been built without elaborate or detailed definitions. Collective agreement language is typically terse, simply prohibiting discipline "without cause" or "without just cause." Even where these words are missing, an arbitrator will read them into the contract as implied by seniority clauses or grievance and arbitration provisions. As one arbitrator has said, "It is the part of the 'common law' of industrial relations—one of the tacit assumptions underlying all collective agreements—that an employer shall not arbitrarily exercise his power to discipline workers."

> Second, arbitrators have built a comprehensive, integrated, and stable body of both substantive and procedural principles. The thousands of reported cases are not merely a mass of random decisions. Although what constitutes just cause inevitably depends on the industrial setting and the circumstances, arbitrators have achieved substantial consensus about underlying principles and many rules.

> Although arbitrators do not consider other cases as binding precedents, they do feel bound by the general principles that have gained acceptability in the last five decades. Arbitration of discipline cases now consists largely of applying established principles to new problems and special-fact situations. The results are quite predictable, perhaps more predictable than most cases in the courts.

> Third, protection against unjust discipline through arbitration has demonstrated its acceptability and workability in the eyes of management and employees. Collective agreements barring discipline except for just cause cover nearly 25 million workers from professional engineers to bank clerks to truck drivers. More telling, in negotiating new agreements the parties retain the "just cause" language with few or no elaborations or limitations; the parties continue to rely on arbitrators to develop general principles and apply them to particular cases.

Fourth, arbitration of discipline cases does provide needed security. A study by the American Arbitration Association shows that in more than half the discharge cases the employee was reinstated, either with or without back pay. Where the penalty was less than discharge, it was reversed or modified in 44% of the cases.[12]

FREEDOM OF THE PRESS

Although corporations and public agencies print and distribute billions of pages of written materials to employees every year, perhaps only several hundred pages of employee questions and challenges of management are published by organizations. However small the latter number is today, however, it is more than it was a few years ago.

In the early 1970s a few underground employee newspapers existed to print employee complaints about such matters as alleged discrimination, layoff policies, and inequities. The papers operated surreptitiously because their editors and writers feared reprisals. In the September 13, 1971, issue of the *Nation*, for example, Timothy H. Ingram reported on the suspicions that greeted a person thought to be associated with an underground publication. Nevertheless, such publications existed—*Met Lifer*, printed off and on at Metropolitan Life Insurance Company, *Stranded Oiler*, printed at Standard Oil Company of California, and *AT&T Express*, printed at Pacific Telephone and Telegraph Company, among others. In addition, as we have seen, Al Ripskis began a successful employee publication at the Department of Housing and Urban Development in Washington.

Today, however, there is evidence that published employee-to-management communication is coming out in the open. Earlier in this chapter the Bank of America's house organ was mentioned. Some other organizations have made similar efforts. One of the best-known is Dow Chemical's *Brinewell*, published every other month. For instance, one issue carried a two-page spread featuring seven employee questions accompanied by answers from named managers. Here are two of them:

Q. *We Dow retirees are really grateful to be able to use the employees' store. It really helps our budgets and enables us to use those wonderful Dow products.*

But why must we retirees purchase a minimum of $10.00 in merchandise from the Dow Store? Many of us do not have the purchasing power we had formerly, and unless we can afford to give away much of what we buy (which

[12] Clyde W. Summers, "Protecting *All* Employees Against Unjust Dismissal," *Harvard Business Review*, January–February 1980, p. 136.

some of us cannot afford to do) we find our pantry shelves greatly overstocked with certain items.

Could you give us a break and allow the minimum purchase for retirees to be $5.00 instead of $10.00?

A. We try to satisfy our customers. Our complaints, registered at the Employee Sales, amount to only one or two per week out of 500 to 600 customers.

We believe our policy is liberal, but if retirees feel that this puts an undue hardship on their budgets, we will allow a $5.00 minimum.

We will still maintain the $10.00 minimum for all other customers. Thanks for your input.

W.R. Liston
*Senior Cost
Accounting
Leader*

Q. *The new group insurance coverage change (effective July 1) has cost my family a great deal of money. In the past, I have always considered the Dow group insurance plan to be tops in its field, better than everyone else's; now I am considering additional health insurance policies.*

My question is, why has Dow decided to lower its coverage? I feel cheated out of a very important benefit. I would have gladly paid higher premiums just to retain the old benefits. Why weren't we given a choice?

A. The changes in our Group Insurance Program were for the purpose of cost containment and are needed to protect our medical benefits long term.

We continue to have an excellent medical care program even though a few changes took something away in terms of coverage. An example of a change in a benefit would be the payment for hospital confinement that is not medically necessary. This would include most oral surgery cases. (Our program will continue paying confinement for extractions and impacted teeth when a person is under treatment for a severe medical problem such as a heart condition or hemophilia.)

During the review stage for possible changes in our Group Insurance Program, consideration was given to increasing the employees' contribution rather than increasing the deductible, but it was evident the increase would have to be substantial in order to cover the increase in medical cost care. Because approximately 25 percent of our employees do not use the plan in any one year, it was decided to increase the deductible and leave the employees' premium the same. This will require users of the program to pay the extra. Our deductible had not increased since 1968 and because of inflation, had lost the impact of cost containment.

Duane Dosson, Speak-Out Coordinator, said that your problem arose because of oral surgery and hospital confinement which is unfortunate. When medical treatment is anticipated, employees are urged to contact our office regarding their insurance coverage. If you have questions that have not been answered, give the Group Insurance Department a call.

KATHLEEN JACOBS
Supervisor,
Group Insurance

In past issues of *Brinewell* management has been taken to task for a wide variety of other matters, including, in one issue, the fact that the chief executive had received a pay increase when many other employees had not.

PRIVACY AND INDIVIDUAL INTEGRITY

Although corporations get good marks from the public on many subjects, such as the ability of leaders and efforts to strike a fair balance between profits and public interests, reports Alan F. Westin, they don't get high ratings for protection of individual privacy. "Of the five social institutions that the public believes are worst in collecting or using more personal information about people than is really necessary, four are businesses: finance companies, credit bureaus, insurance companies, and credit card agencies. The only government agency that makes this top five villains list is the Internal Revenue Service. Not even the FBI, the CIA, local police, or the Social Security Administration were seen as equaling the top four business activities in intrusiveness." [13]

In response to increasing public sensitivity about privacy, a growing number of companies are adopting privacy policies. Typically, such a policy contains both authorizations and prohibitions. For instance, it may authorize an employee to inspect the information in his or her personnel file and dispute any items found there that are untrue, misleading, or irrelevant. It may prohibit supervisors from surreptitiously monitoring employees' telephone conversations or spying on employees. It may also prohibit the company from disclosing to outsiders more than nominal information about an employee without the latter's permission. In the fall of 1981, *Pri-*

[13] Alan F. Westin, "Good Marks but Some Areas of Doubt," *Business Week*, May 14, 1979, pp. 14–16.

vacy Times, a newsletter published in Washington, D.C., estimated that more than 450 companies had adopted or were preparing employee privacy policies; this figure was nine times greater than the comparable figure for 1979, according to the publication.

So far as I know, no company with a strong privacy code has found the employee inspection privilege onerous. At AT&T, much fewer than 1% of employees ask to see their files, the company reports. Detroit Edison reports getting only about fifty such requests per year (often from disciplined employees); at Levi Strauss, only about five employees per week want to examine their files. Yet privacy policies apparently are desired by a large percentage of employees and, where established, are found to be reassuring.

Eight states require companies to give employees access to certain sections of their records. As for federal government agencies, the Federal Privacy Act of 1974 requires a variety of fair information practices, including employee access to records. In 1977 the U.S. Privacy Protection Study Commission called on all private employers to adopt various privacy protection policies. The Business Roundtable, the U.S. Chamber of Commerce, and the National Association of Manufacturers have urged corporate managements to adopt the privacy measures urged by the commission.

The corporation that pioneered in the development of employee privacy codes is IBM. For a number of years now, individual privacy at IBM has been better protected, in my opinion, than in any political society in the world. Not only is IBM's code rigorous but it is applied strictly and impartially. You can get into much deeper trouble, as an IBM employee, by violating the privacy code than by committing a faux pas in, for example, purchasing or forecasting.

Several years ago, Wanda Lankenner and I talked with Frank T. Cary, then chief executive officer of IBM, about its privacy policies and management's motives in developing them.[14] "Organizations have invaded people's privacy with steel file cabinets and small manila folders for years," he noted. "But computer systems with remote access have intensified both the problem and public concern. Thomas Watson, Sr. and Jr., both had very strong beliefs in the dignity of the individual, but privacy in particular didn't begin to get special attention until the middle 1960s. That was when an IBM employee asked one day to see his personnel folder. The question ended up in the office of Thomas J. Watson, Jr. After he reviewed it thoroughly, his answer to the employee was yes. He then wrote to all IBM

---

[14] "IBM's Guidelines to Employee Privacy," An Interview with Frank T. Cary, *Harvard Business Review,* September–October 1976, p. 82.

managers, saying that employees throughout the company ought to be able to see their personnel folders. The subject has been growing with us ever since."

When management looked at employee privacy in IBM from the top down, things appeared to be pretty good. The company seemed to be handling personal data in a sensitive and careful way. "But then we organized a corporate task force to look at the subject from the bottom up," Cary told us. "At different IBM sites, local task forces were organized to find out what actually was being done. We found that in some cases information about employees was being handled in a way that we didn't like, that seemed to violate our principles."

For example, managers would keep in informal files information that shouldn't have been kept—a piece of hearsay, a private criticism from another employee, a derogatory quotation. What was more, other than routine facts would be communicated to outsiders from time to time.

There was no demand from employees en masse that such practices be stopped. On the other hand, there was no doubt that some IBM employees worried about what might be in their files as well as about what might be conveyed without their permission to banks, landlords, credit agencies, and other outsiders.

What concerned IBM's top management was a new set of dangers. In the 1950s business had buzzed with arguments over dress codes, loyalty and security programs, and other primitive restrictions. But with the rise of the computer in the 1960s and 1970s a whole new array of questions arose with the collection of sensitive information, data that could be more dangerous and more compromising than any of the restraints of the 1950s had been. This new information was gathered and computerized in the course of administering health plans, pensions, the occupational safety and health law, equal opportunity laws, and other tasks. It was a potential danger not just to hourly employees or middle-management people. It was a potential danger to nearly everyone at every level in an organization. So management went to work on a whole new approach.

What are the rules in IBM's privacy code?

First, only the most essential information is collected from a job applicant. The applicant is asked to divulge only the bare bones of what management considers necessary to making the decision to hire or not hire—name, address, previous employer, education, and a few other basic facts. Explained Cary, "We don't even ask for date of birth at this time, although if the person is hired we will need to get his or her age. We don't ask about the employment of the applicant's spouse, about relatives employed by IBM, or for previous addresses. We don't ask about any prior treatment for nervous disorder or mental illness. We don't ask about arrest records or pending criminal charges or criminal indictments. We do ask about convictions—but only convictions during the previous five years."

In making this rule in the early 1970s, IBM deliberately chose to omit some data often collected from applicants in prior years. Cary said, "We were getting a lot of data we really didn't need. It was cluttering up the files. Worse than that, it was tagging along after people. Particularly in the case of unfavorable information about an employee, there's a tendency for the material to follow the person around forever and to influence management decisions that it shouldn't. It's better not to have the data in the files in the first place."

Knowing how reluctant many executives are to leave any stone unturned, in the fear that facts may lie underneath that may become relevant later, we asked Cary if interviewers could be sure in advance what they would need. He answered, "No. But you know what you need at the time, for just this decision. Later you can collect more data as needed. This is part of the problem, you see. There's a common attitude that 'It doesn't hurt to have all this information, it can't do any harm, so why not get it?' That's what we're working against. When we looked into this problem a few years ago, we found that it could indeed do harm to have information that wasn't of current relevance. For example, information about how young or how old a person is, or about an arrest a couple of years ago—it shouldn't influence the hiring decision, but it might do so if it were on hand. So we decided the best thing to do was simply not to collect it."

Second, the company has stopped using certain kinds of tests for applicants, especially tests that probe personal information or that reveal information the applicant doesn't know he or she is revealing. Cary put it this way: "We have stopped excursions into applicants' emotional and private lives through the use of personality tests. We don't use polygraphs in hiring or at any other time—we never have. But we use aptitude tests and consider them useful. Some tests have credibility, for instance, in forecasting a person's aptitude for programming, or typing, or certain other types of occupation. Also, this sort of information isn't so personal or sensitive. It's more job-related than personality tests are."

Third, the company continually purges the personnel files of dated information. Cary explained, "We keep purging data that no longer seem relevant. Performance appraisals usually are kept for three years only—in unusual cases, for five years. All grades and appraisals from IBM course instructors are kept for three years only. A record of a conviction is thrown out after three years. Then there's all that information many managers keep on an employee's attendance, performance, vacation schedules, and so on. We tell managers to keep this material for a limited time only."

How much of the onus is on operating managers, rather than on the personnel department, to keep the files stripped down to the essentials? Cary answered, "Since there are some files operating managers never examine, obviously the personnel department has to purge them of old data. But we hold individual managers responsible for seeing that job-related information, which they do see, is kept to a minimum. Now, the personnel department is responsible for developing guidelines, and it may check up on the manager to see that the purging is done, but he or she can't pass the buck. We say, in effect, 'This is your job, and you know what the rules are—they're not terribly complex. It is up to you to see that the rules are followed.' "

Fourth, IBM line managers can see only information about an employee that bears on their decisions about promotion, transfer, special assignments, work loads, and so forth. Cary considered this restriction quite important to the privacy issue: "An employee's performance appraisals, performance plans, letters of commendation, records of awards, sales records, production assignments, and so on—all such job-related information is kept available for the line manager to see. The manager needs to see it to make decisions. The only other people who can inspect this material are those with a need to know, such as a manager considering the employee for a new position," Cary said.

What, then, *can't* a supervisor or line manager see? "Every large company has to have quite a bit of personal information on an employee that has little or nothing to do with work performance," said Cary. "So this information is out of bounds for the line manager. This file is open only to the personnel and financial departments. It includes medical benefits data, records of personal finances such as wage garnishments, payroll deductions, life insurance, beneficiaries, payments for educational programs, house valuations, and so on. These items are required to administer benefit plans, to meet the company's legal obligations, and to carry out other aspects of personnel administration, but the operations manager does not need to know them."

As access to personal information is limited for insiders, so is it limited for outsiders. According to Cary, "If an outsider wants to verify that a person works for us, we will release the most recent job title the person has, the most recent place of work, and the date of employment at IBM. We'll do this much without contacting the employee. But if the outsider wants to know the person's salary, or wants a five-year job chronology, we don't give out that information without written approval from the employee.

"As for creditors, attorneys, private agencies, and others desiring non-job-related information, we give out none of it without the employee's consent, unless the law requires disclosure by us.

"We honor legitimate requests for information from government agencies, though we require the investigators to furnish proper identification, prove their legal authority, and demonstrate that they need the information sought. If a district attorney's office is making a criminal investigation, we cooperate within limits. It's hard to make rules to cover all situations that may arise, but we have specialists in the legal and personnel departments who use their judgment in an unusual situation, and they handle these problems pretty well."

Fifth, for both insiders and outsiders there are limitations on the reporting and use of social security numbers. Cary explained: "In 1973 we looked into the use of social security numbers and agreed that thereafter we would release them only to satisfy government and legal requirements—at least, until some national consensus was arrived at on the use of universal identifiers, or until new legislation was passed. So we don't give outside private organizations an employee's social security number without the person's consent; we don't even supply the number to the organization that administers our company scholarship program."

But isn't it true that social security numbers often are considered useful for personal identification? The chief executive answered: "Some organizations seem to think so, but we won't put social security numbers on company badges or identification cards. Also, we have taken them off all IBM medical cards; insurance companies get an IBM employee identification number when they process a medical or a dental claim."

Sixth, employees can see most (but not all) job-related and non-job-related information in their files. Here is Cary's explanation of this important point: "With just a few exceptions, employees can see what's in their personnel folders—job-related information as well as non-job-related. We want them to know what's there—no surprises. If they find something to quarrel with, they can ask for a correction. The key document, of course, is the performance appraisal. But there's less curiosity about this than you would think, and the reason is that the manager has already told the employee how he or she was rated. That was done when the appraisal session was held. In fact, the manager's appraisal that contains the ratings is reviewed by the employee, at which time he or she can add comments."

What are the exceptions? There aren't many, but they are important to management. One exception is notes made on complaints and conflicts that employees report to the chief executive's office in the hope of obtaining corrective action: "Employees can't see notes on 'Open Door' investigations of complaints they made. At IBM, the 'Open Door' is a system for allowing employees to take a grievance over their supervisors' heads to a higher management level. The employee identifies himself or herself (in this respect, the 'Open Door' system is different from 'Speak Up!') so the case goes into a special file, which, by the way, has very stringent access and retention standards. As chief executive, I'm the court of last resort, so to speak, and many cases come to me. I assign an executive to investigate each situation, and I personally review the findings. During the investigations, these senior managers talk to many people and get honest, frank answers to many tough questions. They couldn't get such candid answers if they didn't talk off the record, in strict confidence. So we don't allow an employee to see the notes made on a case he or she was concerned with. If we did, the 'Open Door' system wouldn't work."

Cary emphasized, however, that the employee is not left in the dark about the results of an Open Door investigation. The investigator sits down with the complainant and discusses the findings with him or her (but without quoting the people interviewed).

Another kind of information withheld from the employee is salary plan data. Said Cary, "Our managers make salary forecasts for their employees as a matter of course in business planning. In effect, a manager says, 'I expect to increase so-and-so's salary by this much on such-and-such a date.' We don't consider this personal information. It's business planning information and subject to change. Once the increase is acted on, the data become personal information, but until then the figures are not available to the employee concerned.

"In fact, such figures are not kept in the employee's file but in some place like the desk drawer of the manager."

Also withheld is information about an employee's promotion prospects: "It's just good planning technique to know who is ready to take over the management jobs at certain levels," Cary said. "We prepare replacement tables with the names of, say, the top three candidates for every one of those jobs. Now, there are surely people who would love to see those tables and know who will be moved up if a certain individual gets hit by a streetcar the next day. But this, too, is business planning, not personal information, and so it's not available for employees to see. Besides, it would be misleading and misunderstood. We do not always do what is written in the replacement planning tables. Nor do we always give the amount of salary increase that is forecast."

Seventh, IBM prohibits surreptitious recordings of employee conversations. Said Cary, "There's absolutely no taping of a person's conversations on the telephone without express permission, or at business meetings without prior announcement. I consider this a simple matter of respect for the individual."

This rule, too, apparently reverses a practice that had taken place from time to time in the past (and is a continuing subject of complaint in other organizations). The chief executive extended it to outside business contacts:

"Some time ago, an employee had a hidden tape recorder he used for recording some sales calls he made on customers. He did it innocently, I think—for his own use to analyze what transpired. I think you just do not record conversations with customers or prospects or anyone else without telling them first. People act differently depending on the kind of talk they think they're having—recorded or not recorded, on the record or off, for a newspaper or for TV. As the saying goes, the medium is the message. I think it's the same principle that has influenced the courts to keep television out of the courtroom."

Eighth, since 1968 (before Cary became chief executive) IBM has directed managers not to be concerned about away-from-the-job behavior of subordinates except when it impairs ability to perform regular job assignments or tarnishes the company's reputation in some major way. This would rule out the kind of spying that employees in other companies and public agencies have complained about, such as checking up to see if the employee actually went on a business trip, or is home sick as alleged and not playing golf, or is having an amorous adventure, or is meeting with a government agent.

Ninth, desk searches in the employee's absence are limited to obtaining facts necessary to running the business while the person is away. Suppose, we asked Cary, an engineer goes on vacation and forgetfully leaves some confidential new product specifications in his desk drawer. Is his privacy being invaded if his manager goes into the drawer to get the specifications when needed?

"In one sense, there's no violation, because desks and files are IBM property. But the manager must have a very good reason for looking. No one should be fooling around in someone else's papers. Of course, it's important to try to avoid this sort of situation. When a person leaves on vacation or a trip, he or she should leave any business documents that might be needed in the hands of someone else who will carry on."

Tenth, IBM does not try to control an employee's outside activities except where there may be a conflict of interest, or where the employee is capitalizing on his or her ties with the company. Cary explained, "We ask employees who want to become involved in public problems and want to take a position on them to do so as private individuals, not on behalf of IBM. They should make that clear to the press. But only if there is a potential conflict of interest do we ask employees to excuse themselves from the discussion and any decision to vote on it. This might be the case if, say, the employee sat on a board of education and the board were going to vote on an IBM proposal."

Turning now from the substance of the code to its enforcement, how does management see to it that managers and supervisors down the line observe the guidelines? Several approaches are followed. One is the opinion survey, which asks whether employees *feel* subjected to unnecessary intrusions. If they do, management knows that policy isn't working. Second are the company's procedures for investigating complaints; an employee who thinks his or her privacy is invaded can get prompt help from the top. Third, the company is tough on managers who violate the privacy guidelines. We asked Cary to elaborate on each.

"We use opinion surveys a lot in our business to find out how employees feel about certain things," Cary said. "Periodically we include a question about whether the employee feels that his or her manager and the IBM company in general treat personal information in a confidential enough way, or appropriately—something like that. The great majority (close to 85%) feel that personal information is handled with sensitivity by IBM, and this feeling grows over time."

Regarding the investigative procedure, Cary said, "We do get some feedback on privacy questions through our 'Speak Up!' program. 'Speak Up!' is a system of communicating problems and questions to higher levels of management when they're not handled to an employee's satisfaction by his or her manager. The employee remains anonymous—no one knows the employee's name except the coordinator in the 'Speak Up!' office. 'Speak Up!' complaints about privacy have been minimal, but they indicate a widespread awareness of the issue."

As for IBM's expectations of individual managers, Cary expressed them without equivocation: "We try to make it very, very clear to managers what's expected of them. The rules for handling personal information are incorporated in our management training programs. We describe the principles we want followed, and we walk them through the specific dos and don'ts of practicing the rules. We try to produce uniform understanding on this. Within thirty days of becoming a manager, every first-line manager begins to receive basic training.

"In addition, we ask all IBMers to help by bringing to management's attention infringements of personal privacy in their areas of the business. And we ask every employee to refrain from any practice that would unnecessarily invade the privacy of others."

What happens to a manager or other employee who violates a guideline? Cary answered, "Depending on the violation, the manager may be subject to dismissal. It's very clear-cut what we're trying to do, and I think everyone understands that we mean it. If there's confusion for some legitimate reason—and there may be, because it's hard to anticipate all situations—we make allowances for errors. But there have been cases when the manager has gotten into trouble."

Is it fair to say that people are penalized more severely for infractions of ethical standards at IBM than for, say, lapses in performance? Replied Cary, "I think that failures in ethics and integrity here are less excusable than errors in performance. People can perform their jobs on a range from satisfactory to outstanding, but there's only one standard of ethics and integrity that we recognize. So, yes, there are two levels of assessment."

ENCOURAGING THE "EARLY WHISTLEBLOWER"

During the past decade we have heard a lot about employees who, to the chagrin of management, blow the whistle on some fault or wrongful action. Whistleblowing has come to be associated with Davids challenging Goliaths, often losing, to be sure, but frequently inflicting distress. However, there is another type of whistleblowing that has received little publicity. That is management-*encouraged* criticism of a new product or process. In fact, it may not only be encouraged but at considerable expense institutionalized in formal procedures and systems.

A leading practitioner of such an approach is Monsanto, which operates in an industry where faulty products and troublesome processes can be very expensive if the shortcomings are not heralded before commercialization. (One event that fortified the company's determination to establish a good early-warning system was its recyclable plastic beverage bottle, Cycle-Safe, banned in 1976 by the FDA after Monsanto had spent over $100 million in developing it.) In an effort to eliminate surprises, management asks for assessments of the possible hazards of a new material or process at every major stage of development. It wants employees and consultants to take a kind of devil's advocate stance, at least for a time, examining the known or expected impurities of a new product, its expected toxicity, foreseeable dangers in disposal, the ability of customers to use the material properly and safely, the ability of employees to handle the material safely, and so on.

First, there are early tests. If the new product passes these and goes into development, so-called technology-risk reviews are held. This means bringing together the most knowledgeable people the company can find inside or outside—doctors, industrial hygienists, chemists, biologists, safety experts, epidemiologists, animal toxicologists, and others. How, where, and when might the material or process cause trouble to any people or become a hazard to the environment? What might go wrong? What exposure levels might cause what risks? Sometimes the outside consultants come from leading universities and research institutions; a few have even come from foreign countries.

If the experts spot potential hazards, management poses the question:

Can these hazards be managed? If it is found, for instance, that a change in production methods will recycle the hazardous dust successfully, or that a user risk can be eliminated by installing a special valve, then the change is made and development continues. But if no such answer can be worked out, the project is stopped.

For example, when Monsanto's well-known herbicide, Roundup, was developed, it was first formulated as a dimethylamine salt. But this salt is a secondary amine and in certain circumstances can form a nitroso compound. So experts blew the whistle. They pointed out that later on the company might have a hard time defending the use of that product because of the chance, admittedly remote, that nitrosodimethylamine, a known carcinogen in animal tests, might form in the environment. So the development team went back to the labs and developed a new formulation using isopropylamine, a primary amine that cannot form a nitroso compound. With that formulation, the new product sailed through all its tests and has now become a well-known herbicide in agriculture. Had a substitute chemical not been found, however, the project would have been shelved.[15]

Dexter Sharp, a research director in the company's agricultural products division, elaborates as follows on the organization's approach:

> Suppose you use water in the manufacture of a new product, and you pump that water into the Mississippi. After the discovery and product development work—a dozen or so stages going from the research idea through synthesis, biological evaluation, research field tests, environmental chemistry, residue studies, and others—we ask if that water is so free of chemicals that there's no problem in simply returning it to the river. If the studies show chemicals, then we ask how the water might be cleaned up, and treatments will be developed to remove the chemicals. And we may find that we can even put the water back into the Mississippi cleaner than when we took it out.
>
> Or suppose we find that a chemical gets into the air when a pesticide is made. We measure the quantities in the air, then talk to the people involved in production: "You've got to tighten up your system. You can't have an open vat there; put a lid on it." So Manufacturing devises controls or modified equipment to eliminate that air emission.[16]

What is the impact of such an approach on individualism? By authorizing and systematically encouraging employee inquiry, management bestows

[15] For a detailed exposition of the Monsanto system, see "Monsanto's 'Early Warning' System," An Interview with John W. Hanley Conducted by David W. Ewing and Millicent R. Kindle, *Harvard Business Review*, November–December 1981, p. 107.
[16] Ibid, p. 119.

more dignity on employees than top executives could do in thousands of speeches. I suspect that the approach would have this impact on almost any group of employees, but its potency may be especially great for professionals and technically trained people who, as a result of training, cannot visualize obtaining self-fulfillment in any way *except* by thinking individualistically.

In the course of our study of the company, we talked with Roger Folk, director of the Environmental Health Laboratories. He pointed out to us how important it is to the men and women in his labs to be able to go as far as their minds will take them, without regard to whether they have satisfied conventional norms and government regulations:

> We could never keep the scientists here motivated if we saw our job as just checking out new products according to standard protocols. That would be mesmerizing; it would be like putting hubcaps on the assembly line in Detroit. If we said, "We've got to weigh all those test animals and do it just like this, at the expense of other observations," we'd be trapped.[17]

Folk's laboratory is staffed by such people as toxicologists, pathologists, clinical chemists, histologists, pharmacologists, geneticists, and computer programmers. He says they enjoy the feeling of having more data on the company's materials and products than anyone else has, and they want to be number one in understanding what those data mean. He told us,

> Let's say we see something in the data that is a little bit different from what we expected. We don't pass it off and say, "We don't have to worry about that." We're interested because we're scientists and our training makes us interested in apparently minor discrepancies. The discrepancies may turn out to be the most important thing about a whole study.
>
> Also, we're interested because such an approach will produce better risk analyses for the company. Finally, we're interested because we're professionals. I can attract better people to the labs if we foster a spirit of inquiry here. There's always a big piece of every scientist that has to hold onto the inquisitive attitude learned in school, and I want to encourage that innovative and entrepreneurial spirit.

[17] Ibid, p. 120.

IN SUM

The nature of "goodness" in an organization is related to mechanisms, programs, and attitudes. It means having such mechanisms as hearing procedures or employee representatives to permit an employee's complaints to be aired promptly and resolved justly. It means instituting programs and continuing efforts to include as many employees as possible in decisions that affect their jobs and working conditions. It also means establishing programs and codes to prevent unfair use of a person's personnel file by insiders or outsiders, and to uphold the right of an employee to challenge unfairly prejudicial information in that file. It means instilling in top management willingness to give a subordinate a "day in court" when requested, to acknowledge that he or she may be right in a conflict with a superior. As A.W. Clausen put it aptly, "No employee complaint is considered frivolous."

For the sake of clarification, what is *not* included in the new concept of "goodness"? The concept does *not* mean (a) that middle managers and supervisors must manage without firm, vigorous support from top management; (b) that managers must automatically "be nice to people"; (c) that every employee should be free to "do his or her own thing"; and (d) that a subordinate has a right to harangue a superior or argue with the superior over the good judgment of a decision concerning budgets, products, services, or other operational matters.

The real question facing the American business community today is not whether it can "afford" stronger ethical standards, but how much longer it can go without them.

WILLIAM E. SIMON

10

SHOULD AN
ORGANIZATION
HAVE RIGHTS?

In the United States we talk frequently about the rights of individuals. At least one group of experts has discussed the question of whether nature, too, should have rights. Other authorities have presented the case for rights for animals.

What about organizations? In law, corporations have the right to sue and be sued. Also, the federal and state governments can sue and be sued. Organizations can own property. They can act as agents for individuals and other organizations. But these are quite limited rights, created for legal convenience and hardly comparable to the rights possessed by human beings or the rights advocated for flora and fauna. Is a corporation or public agency by nature entitled to rights, perhaps even a bill of rights, as lovers of mankind advocate for people? Should this bill includes rights against employee objectors as well as against managers?

PRELIMINARY QUESTIONS

If something has rights, others usually have to give up a piece of their freedom. If you have a right to free speech, for example, I may have to swallow my desire to hit you over the head because what you say irritates me; if an animal is to have rights, I may have to give up my desire to kill it for sport. Similarly, if organizations are to have rights, many people will have to give up something. The first question that arises, therefore, is whether organizations are important enough to have rights. Do we have enough at stake in our organizations to justify some curbs on our rights and desires as individuals?

This question is answered readily. Organizations are essential to our survival. They are essential not just to economic affluence and material progress but to the continuation of civilized life. For instance, when answers are found to the energy crises, organizations will find them. The new inventions may be devised by individual inventors, but no individual or even series of individuals will be able to complete the inventions, produce them, and market them; only organizations will be able to do that. Again, when answers are found to some of the pollution problems that threaten the chain of life, organizations will find them, because the tasks are far beyond the reach of individuals and groups. Also, only organizations can continue to meet people's needs for food, shelter, clothing, health care, and communications.

A second question has to do with the appropriateness of organizations as rights-holders. Are corporations, government agencies, research institutes, health management societies, and so on of such a nature that they deserve rights? After all, corporations are creations of the law, and government agencies are created by statute. They are legal fictions, artificial persons, whereas we think of rights-holders as visceral, organic, breathing things.

It is true that organizations are not visceral in the way that flora, fauna, and human beings are. On the other hand, they are collections of human beings. In fact, an organization is a kind of superbeing, a collective organism, if you will, whose relationship to the individual employee is somewhat analogous to the body's relationship to the limbs and organs that make it up, an organ's relationship to the veins and muscles that make it up, and a vein's relationship to its individual cells. Mirroring their collectivity of people, organizations have personalities, aspirations, attitudes, moods, and talents. The Herman Miller company in Zeeland, Michigan, has a collective designing talent and a marketing personality that are as different from the design and marketing functions of most other companies as any one individual at Herman Miller is different from other individuals. Dayton-Hudson in Minneapolis has a set of collective talents and attitudes that distinguish it markedly from other retail organizations. In Japan, Toyota's "personality," so different from that of U.S. auto manufacturers during the 1970s, was one of the keys to its astounding success; this Japanese superbeing wanted to be number one with the same kind of zeal and single-mindedness that a Muhammad Ali or Jack Nicklaus wanted to be number one in their sports fields. Harvard University has a "personality" that is distinctly different from that of many other universities.

One well-known text makes this observation about organizations:

> Organizations are assemblages of interacting human beings and they are the largest assemblages in our society that have anything resembling a central coordinative system. Let us grant that these coordinative systems are not developed nearly to the extent of the central nervous system in higher biological organisms—that organizations are more earthworm than ape. Nevertheless, the high specificity of structure and coordination within organizations—as contrasted with the diffuse and variable relations *among* organizations and among unorganized individuals—marks off the individual organization as a sociological unit comparable in significance to the individual organism in biology.[1]

Organizations often interact with individuals as potently as individuals interact with one another. Countless employees have been influenced deeply by the "culture," as it is often called, of their employer organizations. It may be true, as Sir Adrian Cadbury of Cadbury-Schweppes says, that his company tends to have a work force qualitatively different from the staffs of other companies in the industry because of its tendencies to attract and select certain types of employees. But it is also true that the corporate culture of Sir Adrian's organization exerts an enormous influence on its employees, affecting them in ways that other companies would and could not.

Employees may describe their companies or agencies in such terms as *youthful, mature, growing, moral, prudent,* or *bold.* Facetiously they may point out that some corporations "marry" and "go to bed with one another," as when they merge, and even perhaps "reproduce," as when a larger company spins off a division that becomes a separate company operating on its own. In so doing they recognize the anthropomorphic characteristics of organizations. Companies and agencies are extensions of human beings, three-dimensional and unique.

More than a century and a half ago, U.S. Supreme Court Chief Justice John Marshall made this famous pronouncement: "A corporation is an artificial being, invisible, intangible, and existing only in the contemplation of

[1] James G. March and Herbert A. Simon, *Organization* (New York: Wiley, 1958), p. 4.

the law." For his purpose and that time, Marshall was right. The complex, tightly controlled, precisely coordinated corporations we know today, however, are as real as people. In its in-house booklet *The Conoco Conscience*, printed in 1976, Continental Oil Company noted,

> Although it may be true that Conoco remains an inanimate being for legalistic purposes, the company has a very personal existence for its shareholders, employees, officers, and directors. The success or failure of Conoco affects most of them during their working lives, and may affect them during their retirement. And to the employees, officers, and directors, Conoco's reputation concerns their reputations as well. . . .
>
> Perhaps it is then appropriate in today's context to think of Conoco as a living corporation; a sentient being whose conduct and personality are the collective effort and responsibility of its employees, officers, directors, and shareholders.

A third question has to do with the practical value and utility of rights for corporations and agencies. Would the possession of rights enhance organizations, improve their well-being, nurture their creativity? To make the comparison again with people, flora, and fauna, the writers of the Declaration of Independence believed in the practical value of rights; they saw that people are frustrated in the pursuit of happiness if they do not possess liberties and a government capable of protecting individual freedoms. Also, advocates of rights for plants and animals believe that these subjects cannot fulfill their natural and necessary functions on earth unless they possess protected rights.

The answer to the third question depends, of course, on the specific rights we might want to give organizations. On the other hand, it perhaps dictates the kinds of rights we *should* consider bestowing on organizations. Let us postulate, therefore, that no right qualifies for serious consideration unless it clearly advances the practical value, productivity, and vitality of organizations.

One other question must be disposed of before we consider specific recommendations. Is the question of organizational rights relevant to this book? What difference does it make to the issues of managerial prerogatives and employee rights analyzed in previous chapters?

If organizations should not possess rights other than the few legal rights mentioned, then a manager's authority must come from stockholders or elected officials, and the quality of the manager–subordinate relationship must b⟨...⟩ of that authority, qualified by such co⟨...⟩nd the countervailing rights of unions. ⟨...⟩ are seen to possess inalienable rights sir⟨...⟩en a manager's authority may spring fro⟨...⟩ce (as well as from stockholders or elected⟨...⟩-subordinate relationship may evolve in different ⟨...⟩rms than it could otherwise.

From the standpoint of management as well as the public, it would be advantageous to find that organizations do have rights. For a management group's authority to be derived only from the stockholders is a very shaky proposition these days. The majority of American stockholders have little interest in the affairs of their companies, only in share prices and dividends, and the control exercised by stockholders at most annual meetings is something of a joke. The whole proposition is denigrating to management. On the other hand, if organizations are seen as possessors of inalienable rights, then a management team that is legally in power, having been duly appointed or elected, is also morally in power as long as it manages well and represents the organization's interests effectively. All requirements are satisfied if, as the "mind" of the organization, management enables the corporation or agency to function as a good, law-abiding economic and social citizen. The organization does not have to be popular or powerful to survive. Its right to the pursuit of economic happiness springs, as with a person, from its existence, and its existence is considered precious.

What rights, then, should organizations possess? For the sake of simplicity and convenience, I shall refer to corporate rights in the following discussion. With often minor variations, however, the proposals apply equally to government agencies, educational organizations, community service organizations, research institutions, and other types of organizations.

A PROPOSED BILL OF RIGHTS

To begin, a preamble might briefly recite the rationale for a bill of rights. The preamble could be a statement as simple as the following:

Whereas corporations are formed, staffed, and directed by people, and mirror the collective will and aspirations of their employees, and whereas in modern society corporations are essential and indispensable to the production and distribution of the necessities of human life, including food, pharmaceuticals, shelter, clothing, transportation, communication, and personal services, we the people resolve to bestow the following rights on all duly incorporated and chartered corporations engaged in lawful pursuits.

Small companies, especially those employing fewer than, let us say, forty full-time people, might be exempted from the bill. The following rights would be included:

1. *The right to be managed efficiently.*

Although conscientious managers take this right for granted, not all members of the public do. So the first item in our hypothetical bill should state the necessity for authority, planning and control systems, rewards, and disciplinary procedures without which a food producer, chemical manufacturer, construction firm, insurance company, or other corporation cannot hope to be a capable economic citizen. The visions of many students and idealists notwithstanding, we simply do not know of any way to make a corporation run effectively except with management authority, unpleasant as this notion may be to some iconoclasts.

Since the norms of management are variable and evolutionary, no attempt should be made to define the form or pattern of management that a company should have. The intent here is only to guarantee every corporation the right to an executive group that is free to plan, control, deputize, and administer effectively in ways normally employed by viable organizations and customarily taught in schools of management.

2. *Employee loyalty.*

A corporation is entitled to managers and employees who are loyal to its legitimate interests and purposes. Disloyal members are equivalent to a cancer in an organism; sooner or later they interfere with the operation of the whole. Judges, arbitrators, academics, and managers have *in effect* recognized this right for many years. Here are some examples of the everyday implications of this right:

> An executive worked evenings and weekends for another organization with competing interests. For this conflict of interest he was liable to dismissal.
>
> An employee told a number of people, including fellow workers and people with whom his company was negotiating for government contracts, that the staff was misusing government funds by employing un-

qualified inspectors and in other ways defrauding the government. In the grievance hearing it was determined that the statements were made maliciously and without any factual basis. Because he was violating a basic right of his organization, management was entitled to dismiss the employee.

An employee of an energy producer testified in public hearings that in her opinion the whole industry was dangerous and should be shut down. Although she had a right to her opinion, she did not have that right as an employee in that business, for its purpose was lawful, it operated in compliance with safety codes, and it met all other legal requirements. Its "right to life" was violated by her testimony.

========

How essential is the right to loyalty? Could a corporation get along reasonably well without it? If the executive moonlights for another company with competing interests, his employer may go bankrupt. Even if it doesn't, the executive's example may be contagious, and if many managers moonlight the employer company is in obvious trouble. As for the government contractor, if it is bad-mouthed enough, it is going to lose important contracts and suffer damage to employee morale. As for the energy company, it might be put out of business by anti-industry legislation and public boycotts; although that end is appropriate for outsiders to work for, it is not appropriate for an insider.

3. *Obedience.*

This right, which is related to loyalty, means that a corporation is entitled to managers and employees who faithfully serve its codes, clearly established policies, and charter. Just as a body cannot function efficiently if its arms and legs do not respond to the routines and habits learned over the years, so an organization cannot function well if managers and employees pay no attention to its rules.

Obedience, in this context, relates primarily to a manager's or employee's on-the-job behavior—in particular, respect for agreed-on policies and rules. Thus it is more specialized than loyalty, which relates to a person's state of mind and priorities whether on or off the job.

Here are some practical implications of an organization's right to obedience. Except for the last, it will be seen that this concept, too, is generally familiar in managerial and legal thought.

If a salesperson signs a code of conduct forbidding secret monitoring of conversations with customers, and then proceeds to violate the code, he or she violates the organization's right as egregiously as the privacy right of the customer is violated. As long as that code is on the books and generally complied with, the salesperson is not privileged to take the law in his or her hands, no matter how justified the violation may appear to be in terms of developing sales. In essence, this is the position that IBM and some other companies take, and I understand that in at least one case IBM has applied the rule to a star salesman, dismissing the person despite the immediate cost to the sales department.

Several top executives in a construction firm overlook shortcuts and deficiencies in the work of subcontractors, even though the practices violate the building codes and may eventually return to haunt the firm when the buildings are put into use. In return for their "oversights," the executives are paid off by the subcontractors in the form of free remodeling of their homes, free landscaping services for their homes, and complimentary supplies. Since compliance with construction codes is implied in the construction company's charter (even if compliance is not mentioned in an in-company code of conduct), the executives violate the employer organization's rights.

A supervisor goes outside the company to hire an assistant, without investigating whether the post could be filled by an employee who wants it. The company's clearly established policy is to promote from within. Although aware of this, the supervisor hires the outsider because of a personal conviction that the outsider is better qualified. The supervisor is liable to discipline for violating the company's rights.

In each of the three instances described, let us further suppose that a subordinate protests the violation by the superior and is demoted or fired. In each case, the act of penalizing the objector is a second violation of the company's rights, for these rights cannot be upheld if voices raised in their support are muffled.

―――――――

Is the right to compliance essential to an organization's productive functioning and well-being? It is no less essential than obedience of law is for individuals. Even though sometimes individual violators can prove that their acts are more intelligent or useful than the law is, society cannot function if individuals feel free to interpret the law in their own ways. Neither can an organization. What is more, management cannot manage unless employees comply with policies and codes.

4. *Commitment.*

An organization is entitled to a sense of commitment on the part of each manager and employee; that is, it is entitled to have each person work diligently and earnestly on the job. In the sense employed here, commitment, though related to loyalty and obedience, differs from them in that it emphasizes intensity and thoroughness of service. Thus:

> An information-desk employee, though utterly loyal to his employer company and completely obedient to its policies in answering outsiders' questions, often gets in late, leaves early, stays home when feeling just a little off, and takes extremely generous coffee breaks and lunch hours. Even if not warned by a supervisor, or even if doing what some others do, the employee violates the organization's rights.

The following case is reported by *Employee Relations in Action:* [2]

> While driving a bus through busy city traffic, Ralph Judson struck and injured a pedestrian. No charges were brought against Judson by the police, but the accident victim brought a lawsuit for heavy damages against Judson's employer, the Hafferton Bus Line.

> The case against the bus company languished in the courts for almost two years. Then, just before the case came to trial, the pedestrian's attorney served papers on the Hafferton Bus Line's attorneys, which contained a wide range of questions pertaining to the accident.

> For the Hafferton Bus Line to answer the questions properly, it was essential to obtain Ralph Judson's help. At the time, Judson was at home nursing an injury he had sustained in a mishap unrelated to the lawsuit. The Hafferton attorneys contacted Judson at home to arrange a mutually convenient appointment during which he could answer the questions.

> Judson failed to keep any of the appointments. When he was pressed to cooperate, he angrily retorted that he would not answer any questions at all. Bus line officials were so exasperated by this response that they fired the driver.

Management's action was correct; it was upholding the company's rights to a sense of commitment among employees. When the case went to arbitration, the arbitrator correctly ruled in favor of management.

The following case was reported by *White Collar Management:* [3]

> Supervisor Gerald Pierson's dander rose when he spotted Arthur Brickfield moving away from his work station and engaging another employee in an animated political discussion. A few minutes later, his

[2] June 1981, pp. 1–2.
[3] November 15, 1981, p. 2.

ire rose still further when he spied Brickfield handing another employee a political leaflet, which was accompanied by a short speech.

Pierson decided that he'd seen enough; he dashed over to Brickfield and suspended him, pending an investigation. Brickfield stormed out of the building, only to return the following noon to resume his politicking.

Accompanied by three confederates, Brickfield brushed past a security guard and invaded the cafeteria, where he delivered a political harangue to the astonished lunchers. Company officials soon came running and not only expelled Brickfield from the premises but also fired him forthwith.

In this case, too, management's action was correct, for Brickfield was showing less commitment to the company than to his personal political convictions. Although he had a constitutionally assured right to air the latter on his own time, he could not assert that right to the detriment of company productivity and employee morale during working hours. When this case went to arbitration, the arbitrator affirmed the firing decision.

Is the right to commitment significant? Can a corporation get along without it? The violations described, though not severely injurious by themselves, could contribute to a fatal malady if allowed to spread. Two industrial psychologists, Richard M. Steers and Daniel G. Spencer, point out that the opposite of commitment is boredom; the insidious ravages of boredom in an organization need no documentation here. To have a sense of commitment and to identify with the employer organization, say Steers and Spencer, the employee needs to have (a) a strong belief in and acceptance of the goals and values of the organization; (b) a willingness to work hard for it; and (c) a strong desire to be a member of it.[4]

5. *Competence.*

An organization is entitled to the competence and skill that its employees can contribute to their tasks. If its people are unreasonably frustrated or harassed, it cannot function well. This right has such implications as the following:

In the Carol Kennedy story (Chapter 7), the psychiatrist was maliciously

[4] Richard M. Steers and Daniel G. Spencer, "Dimensions of Employee Commitment," *Journal of Applied Psychology*, No. 2, 1978.

transferred to a position in which she could not hope to contribute her skills to the work of the agency. This action violated the organizational rights of the Food and Drug Administration; a similar action in a company would violate the rights of the company. Whether the FDA management was right or wrong in wishing to get rid of Kennedy is beside the point; it was obligated to use her talents as fully as possible *as long as she was on the staff.*

When a new marketing head took over in a company manufacturing school supplies, he clashed with the sales manager. Instead of asking the sales manager to resign on the basis that they could not cooperate, the marketing head sought to get rid of the subordinate by hounding him. After a while the tactic succeeded—the sales manager became so upset that, despite a fine prior record, he began making disastrous mistakes and resigned in disgrace. In the period prior to departure, however, the organization suffered needlessly from his oversights and errors.

To vent their displeasure with the night shift in a plant, members of the day shift created a series of inconveniences for night-shift workers. For instance, they tampered with the lighting, put supplies out of sight, and left the machines with misadjustments. The result was that the night shift spent many unnecessary hours putting things back in order before it could be productive. Although the day shift had a perfect right to air its grievances, it interfered with the organization's rights by lashing out in this manner.

Who is the enemy of the corporation? The conventional management wisdom answers that it is the whistleblower, the internal critic, the employee objector. Sometimes this may be so. But is not the *worst* enemy always the incompetent employee? In *Our Mutual Friend*, Charles Dickens said, "The incompetent servant, by whomsoever employed, is always against his employer." Corporate and agency leaders who do not distinguish employee objectors from incompetents risk getting the worst of both worlds, for society, in a misdirected attempt to protect critics and dissenters, could enact legislation making it difficult to fire anyone except for the most egregious causes. If that happens, managers will be saddled for life with both whistleblowers *and* incompetents—and then the corporation indeed will be in trouble.

6. Freedom from unnecessary intrusion and oppressive regulation.

Even with capable management and with loyalty, obedience, and commitment among all managers and employees, an organization may be unable to survive, prosper, and fulfill its potential unless it has a reasonable amount of freedom of movement. If government places unreasonable demands on it for paperwork and reporting, or if special-interest groups force it to comply with this whim or that, or if the media pry into its affairs and slander it, its rights are violated no less than are the rights of the individual whose privacy is violated by meddlers and predators.

The intention of this right is not to frustrate regulatory agencies seeking to make sure that companies comply with the law, or to curb the rights of critics in unions, the media, and special-interest groups, or to restrict the efforts of legislators to change laws. The intention is only to block the hostility that seeks to destroy or cripple an organization, or make it comply with minority-group notions that are not expressed in the law. Is it sensible and consistent to protect the liberties of 1, 50, or 50,000 employees as individuals but not when they are joined in a common enterprise? In the 1960s and 1970s, countless corporations in effect were persecuted by regulatory officials and special-interest groups under the theory that a corporation somehow was bad and, even if it wasn't, could tolerate much harassment. Yet we do not make that assumption about the employees of a corporation as individuals. We now know that the corporate chain of life, like that of individuals and nature, is vulnerable; it has become abundantly clear to more and more people that when corporations fail, many personal aspirations fail and society is the loser.

7. Means of Protecting Rights.

To assert and protect its rights, a corporation should have a variety of remedies. Stockholders should be able to bring suit against perpetrators, whether insiders or outsiders. Consumer interest and public interest groups should be able to go to court to protect corporate rights. Government agencies should protect such rights no less vigorously than those of individuals.

The fact that corporations as rights-holders cannot appear in court to defend themselves, as you and I can, is no obstacle. Many persons and organizations regularly prosecute others and defend themselves in legal proceedings even though they cannot personally appear. Who ever saw a church enter a courtroom? Who ever saw a labor union sit in the witness chair?

Above all, managers and employees should be able to speak up with impunity for the rights of their employer organizations. If, seeing such rights infringed, they feel they must be silent for fear of losing their jobs because of a superior's whim, organizations lose what may be the most valuable form of support that is possible and practical. What this means in practice is that every sizable corporation needs an effective hearing procedure or means of due process; if its internal mechanisms are inadequate, as they sometimes are despite the best of management intentions, the objector should be authorized to appeal to an outside arbitrator.

Zechariah Chafee, Jr., has argued the case for due process as well as anyone:

> Now, if into this delicate process (open discussion up and down the line) be injected threats of penalties for the expression of views which are unacceptable to superiors, the powerful emotion of fear impedes the process at every point. The multitudinous sources of impressions upon the minds of members of the enterprise begin to dry up. Ideas no longer come to them. Or if they do, their entrance into minds is impeded by the barriers of anxiety. Everybody down the line ceases to ask the vital questions, "Do I believe this as a fact?" "Is this course of action good or bad for the enterprise?" Instead, everybody asks, "Is this illegal or disloyal or liable to hurt me in some way which perhaps I can't precisely foresee?" The prevalent attitude becomes, "We must be neither good nor bad—we must be careful." [5]

Limits and Qualifications

It may be argued that organization rights subordinate the individual and subvert the concepts of the Bill of Rights in the Constitution. However, organization rights in no way limit a person's freedom to speak out, to object, to enjoy privacy. In fact, as indicated, they extend such rights by protecting and nourishing them during working hours. On the other hand, certainly organization rights conflict with a manager's or subordinate's freedom to be malicious, lazy, or disloyal; certainly, too, they conflict with an outsider's freedom to "regulate the organization to death" or cripple it by slander or tortious interference.

It may help to put this matter in perspective if we look at what the proposed bill of rights does *not* authorize organizations to do. The proposed bill does not authorize or enable a corporation or agency to—

Remain in existence longer than its stockholders, its charterers, or the government wish it to.

Resist normal, necessary, and reasonable amounts of government regulation.

Violate the constitutional rights of individuals.

[5] Zechariah Chafee, Jr., "Freedom of Speech inside an Enterprise" (Address given at Radcliffe College, June 11, 1955).

Gain immunity from criminal or civil prosecution.

Restrain an employee from leaving it.

Subdue criticism from the media, public interest groups, and others.

In the real world the proposed rights of an organization are not always obvious, even if there is agreement in principle on what they should be. The accounts that follow raise interesting questions concerning both the rights that organizations might possess and the rights that employees and outsiders should be able to exercise against them.

The Case of the Wayward Whistleblowers [6]

One hot day in the spring of 1974, a young secretary in one of Southwestern Bell Telephone Company's offices in San Antonio had a talk behind closed doors with her supervisor. He was a security official; his task involved controlling the endless types of abuse that an enormous company in the Bell System must guard against constantly. The secretary told her boss about firsthand reports she had received concerning promiscuity and financial cheating in the commercial department. This information no doubt rang a bell in the supervisor's mind, for there had been gossip of such things. He listened carefully and passed a report on to his boss. Eventually the information got to the head of the company's scurity department, G. A. Larkin. In turn, Larkin passed it on to Southwestern Bell's vice-president of operation, L. C. Bailey.

At first Bailey did nothing. However, when the alarm bells of wrongdoing kept ringing, he got in touch with Larkin and asked him to investigate. "Be discreet, of course," Bailey instructed. So Larkin got on the phone with Edwin McKaskell, who was the company's security chief in Kansas City. "Make some inquiries and keep it as quiet as you can," Larkin said. He suggested starting with the secretary in the San Antonio office.

McKaskell had a long interview with the woman. She had a lot to say. Many women employees had had affairs with James H. Ashley, commercial manager in the San Antonio district, she reported. But it was not just that they had gone to bed with him—that, after all, might not have been anybody else's business. What mattered was that cooperative women got promoted afterward.

And that's not all, the secretary said, dropping her voice. She herself had been involved. Not only with Ashley, whom she rebuffed, but also with

---

[6] This account is drawn from judicial records and articles in the *New York Times* and the *Wall Street Journal.*

Ashley's friend and boss, one T. O. Gravitt, vice-president and head of operations in Texas. The personable fifty-one-year-old Gravitt had taken her to an apartment rented by the head of a printing firm, Quik Print, with whom he was friendly. Gravitt had a financial interest in the firm and in violation of company policy he gave it a generous amount of the telephone company's printing business. At the apartment, which they visited alone, Gravitt asked her about her future in the company. She was interested in getting ahead, wasn't she? There should be a future there for a young woman of her talents. What happened next is tersely summarized by Judge Robert R. Murray of the Court of Civil Appeals, in a decision rendered several years later. Gravitt then "took her into the bedroom and asked her to 'try the bed.' When she declined his advances, he attempted to fondle her bosom." [7]

This young lady obviously didn't know how to get ahead in Gravitt's operation. It was no wonder, McKaskell may have mused as he listened to her story, that she was bitter about the promotions reportedly given to women who had been more cooperative with Gravitt and Ashley.

McKaskell thanked her and left. He followed up on some of the leads she had given him, other women employees who had been solicited by Gravitt or Ashley or both. What the discreet investigator heard must have deafened him. Although many details were not revealed until later, during a sensational trial, McKaskell's ears rang with the sounds of stories like these (all from later testimony in court):

One attractive thirty-two-year-old woman, then married, said she had had sexual relations several times with Ashley because she feared for her job. Ashley had hired her in 1971. On several occasions he talked confidentially with her, raising the possibility he might have to dismiss her. "The whole course of his conversation was, 'You know who's responsible for your job,' " she said. "He made me feel very obligated. 'You owe me' was the context of his conversation." She told about a three-day party at a motel in San Antonio in September 1974. Ashley ordered her to attend. When she got there, she joined two men, two women, and Ashley. The women were Bell employees, the men were described as "insurance men from Dallas." (In court several years later, it was revealed that they were a city councilman from Denison, a community near Dallas, and the company's district manager there.) The men and women paired off, she said, and she went to bed with one of the "insurance men." For all this she did not go unrewarded. She drew a $22,000

---

[7] *Southwestern Bell v. Dixon and Ashley*, 575 SW 2d 596 (1978).

salary, after Ashley ordered her transfer from Dallas to San Antonio, and received a promotion (the order for the promotion went to the San Antonio division manager).

Another woman said she had had sex with both Ashley and Gravitt at their private offices in San Antonio.

A winsome sales manager who rebuffed Ashley's advances was humiliated. In front of other employees, Ashley derided her work.

Several women who had accommodated Ashley and/or Gravitt apparently received hidden promotions, though the company's regular procedure was to announce all promotions publicly.

After the results of this preliminary probe were passed up the line, Bailey talked with other top executives and decided on a course of action. First, a more comprehensive investigation would be launched. It would be carried out as discreetly as possible, it would be limited to talks with company employees, and all interviews would be held in confidence. Second, he told C. L. Todd, Ashley's boss, to suspend Ashley for the duration of the probe, with the implicit understanding that the suspension would become permanent if the early findings were confirmed. On June 9 Todd suspended Ashley.

Bailey was in a ticklish situation and he knew it. The danger went beyond the possibilities of bad publicity, the perennially feared specter in any Bell System company because of the corporation's dependence on good public relations. The danger also went beyond the grim prospects of personal embarrassment for individuals, with all that might portend for marriages, friendships, and self-esteem. The danger even extended beyond the unpleasant possibility that Southwestern Bell's attack would be seen as an unfair attack, an arbitrary singling out of two executives who were not alone in their ways, and therefore as bad for morale. Bailey knew, as many others knew, that rumors of sexual tradeoffs had been heard off and on in a variety of dark corners of Southwestern Bell. (No less an authority than Zane Barnes, president of Southwestern Bell, would concede this in court in 1977.) Was it arbitrary and inequitable to single out Ashley and Gravitt for investigation?

Worst of all, the danger extended to the ominous possibility that Southwestern Bell's probe would be seen not as an attack but as a counterattack, not as an act of managerial whistleblowing but an attempt to retaliate against two employee whistleblowers. Both Ashley and Gravitt were known to have sounded off about company policies they didn't like. Although they hadn't done more than make a little noise here and there, their scratchy notes had been heard by others. For instance, they had accused the company of rate-fixing, abuses of voucher procedures, kickbacks to government officials, and improper attempts to influence officials by political contributions.

In short, Bailey had to consider that even a low whistle by management probers would touch off a shrieking counterattack. This was exactly what happened, despite the investigator's best efforts. Only the result was even worse than Bailey had feared. After Ashley pleaded for his job, or for a consulting job as a substitute, and failed, he began beating warning drums and blowing battle horns against Southwestern Bell, rocking the political and legal countryside. And after Gravitt heard about the investigation and flew to Barnes's office in St. Louis to protest his innocence, he decided to take his life.

Here we must backtrack a little. What kind of men were Gravitt and Ashley, and how did they relate to one another?

Gravitt was regarded as an executive with a bright future. Already in charge of Texas operations for Southwestern Bell (the company served five states—Texas, Missouri, Kansas, Arkansas, and Oklahoma), he had proved himself an able manager. He had negotiated with great success with political officials, raised a family, learned to fly a private plane, and in general impressed people with his good looks and talent. After Gravitt took over the Texas operation in April 1974, John deButts, chief executive of AT&T, had written him a commendatory letter. "I am sure that under your leadership Texas will always lead the parade," deButts had written. He was referring to the fact that Ma Bell's operations in Texas had been highly profitable for years. In the forty-eight-state Bell System, Texas had ranked first for ten of the past nineteen years.

So Gravitt was doing fine, and there seemed to be plenty of room to go further. If anything, he may have been too much of an achiever—that is, overly anxious to prove himself by executive accomplishments. Although no one thought of him as a suicidal personality, as a Baylor University psychiatrist would later find, he apparently could not stand the thought of a serious defeat in his business life.

To most observers, Ashley must have seemed like the same sort of person—if anything, even more achievement-oriented. As a boy in Texas and Louisiana, Ashley had moved from town to town and had known the ups and downs of fortune. "Sometimes we were well off, sometimes not," he told a reporter. "It made me very conscious of job security. When I got married and had a family, economic well-being was the most important thing to me." In 1951 he had joined Southwestern Bell as an executive trainee. He worked hard, and like Gravitt he had great ability as a manager and negotiator. He served in St. Louis and in various towns and cities in Texas. By 1974, at the age of forty-five, he was general commercial manager in San Antonio, reporting to Gravitt, heading an organization of about 1,500 employees (1,200 of whom were women), and drawing a salary of $55,000 (plus $15,000 more in direct benefits, according to the *Wall Street Journal*). His performance rating on the Bell System appraisal charts was 110%, the highest possible score. He and his wife had four children, including two sons attending the University of Texas.

Soon after top management's quiet investigation got under way, word got to Gravitt and Ashley that employees of the company were being asked if the two men had taken kickbacks from suppliers, falsified expense accounts, stolen money, solicited gifts from subordinates, and engaged in promiscuity. The two executives huddled. In the spring of 1974, Gravitt told Ashley that Ashley's phone was being tapped, and on several occasions later he repeated the warning. There was nothing that the ex-intelligence agents of the security department would stop at in order to achieve their ends, the senior man warned, and he told Ashley that they must devise a system of talking to one another by code and by safe telephone lines.

After Ashley's suspension, the two kept in close contact. During the week of the Oklahoma–Texas football game, Ashley remembers, Gravitt called him in an angry mood. "Jim, I told you to use safe telephones," Gravitt said, "and you didn't." Ashley answered, "What do you mean, I didn't?" Gravitt said, "What does the name 'Ralph Nader' mean to you?" Ashley thought a moment and remembered that in a recent telephone conversation with another friend he had jokingly referred to himself as a possible Ralph Nader of the telephone company. Well, Gravitt informed him, that conversation had been reported to Bailey, and Bailey had spoken to Gravitt about it. As Ashley recalls the talk with his friend, Gravitt said that Bailey had repeated the exact line to him. Bailey had gone on to say: "Ashley is like a puppet dangling on a string, and we know more about him than he knows himself." Bailey had laughed but Gravitt's sense of humor was not so delicate. When Gravitt had protested to Bailey and demanded that the monitoring stop, Bailey had retorted, "Stay out of it, Gravitt, it is not your affair." Gravitt was sure that his own phone, too, was bugged, he told Ashley.

So Gravitt and Ashley worked out a system for avoiding surveillance. Gravitt, who was based in Dallas then, would call Ashley and give him a phone number to call back. Purposely the fourth and seventh digits would be reversed; if, say, Gravitt said to call him back at 475-8213, Ashley knew he was to go to a phone other than his own and call 475-3218 instead.

Ashley also began telephoning Gravitt and others from the home of the Duvals, his next-door neighbors. Once a day or more often he would visit them for that purpose; he told them the reason—his fear that his home phone was bugged. Whether his home telephone actually was tapped is disputable, at least in the opinion of the Court of Civic Appeals. However, the woman who bought the Ashley house in late 1974 found, one day the next spring, something that looked like a battery in the flower bed. It was about six inches tall and four inches across, lying by an air-conditioning unit. She was told by a Bell telephone serviceman that it could have been equipment used for wiretapping, and when she talked to Ashley about it, and he came over to look at it, he was sure it was a wiretapping device. On the other hand, he never made a note or took a photograph to substantiate his beliefs, and the court apparently felt he was paranoid. If indeed he was paranoid, it is no wonder, for on another occasion in the fall of 1974 Ashley asked a telephone expert to come over and examine some strange wiring in the wall behind his kitchen phone. The expert said that there could be no explanation other than a "bug." [8] (Because of evidence like this, the jury believed Ashley even though the judges of the appellate court didn't.)

Whatever the truth about the accusations of wiretapping, Ma Bell was learning a lot about her two problem children. In addition to Gravitt's unethical relationship with the Quik Print printing firm, and the sexual liaisons of both Gravitt and Ashley, company investigators found that the vice-president had cheated on his expense accounts. He had made a trip to Washington, D.C., in 1974 as an official of the San Antonio Chamber of Commerce. Not content with having the Chamber of Commerce reimburse him for a $1,204 hotel bill for five days in Washington, he had also billed Southwestern Bell for that charge. In addition he had spent $220,000 in company funds to redecorate his Dallas office, including such luxuries as onyx drawer pulls, teak wall paneling, remote-control lights, stereo equipment, and gold-plated bathroom fixtures. Not having authority to authorize such expensive work, he broke the project down into three contracts of $75,000 each, which enabled him to pass the expenses through the controller's office. George Swank, the architect who testified to this sleight of hand in court in 1977, was also told to take care of a private contractor's bill for $5,000 of work on Gravitt's house, meaning that he paid the bill himself, then got reimbursed from Southwestern Bell.

Company investigators also heard some sour notes concerning Ashley's dealings. He too, they decided, had improperly funneled company business to the printing concern; one manager alleged she had been instructed by Ashley to give company work to the concern without letting other employees know, and even though the quality of the concern's printing was "very poor." Moreover, the investigators found evidence that Ashley had doctored and destroyed company records, and filed false expense vouchers. ("I

[8] See *Southwestern Bell Telephone Co.* v. *Ashley*, No. 5105, Court of Civil Appeals, 11th Supreme Judicial District, February 16, 1978, pp. 7, 8, and 10.

guess I liked my $55,000-a-year salary more than I should have," he would admit in court several years later.)

Another company manager said that he had been ordered by Ashley to show pornographic videotapes to certain employees. The tapes were played on television monitors in the conference room on company time.

During the course of the interviews, employees kept harping on sexual improprieties. Some women revealed they had been harassed in the office and at social functions by Ashley. Others said that they had been propositioned by him; still others mentioned dinners, trips, and other encounters with Gravitt. Again and again the refrain was that sexual cooperation was the obligato to the music of promotion (though, as some of these people would testify later, they possessed all the normal requirements for advancement). According to the *Wall Street Journal*, most of the harassed women were managers in the $16,000–$25,000 pay bracket.

One other off-key note about Gravitt and Ashley was heard from time to time during the probe: Both executives were critical of the company. They had made noises about such matters as manipulation of state government officials and misrepresentations of costs. Of all the discordant sounds heard by the probers and reported up the line to management, these may have been the most jarring. The highly profitable, fast-growing Southwestern Bell was being described by two of its own top people as "inadequate, incorrect, duplicitous, deceitful, and grossly unfair to the public."

In sum, the Bell System's response to the reports about Gravitt and Ashley was strong and swift. It was virtually a model of what management can do if it wants to hold the initiative in a free-for-all whistleblowing contest. It will be said that this vigorous effort didn't keep the case from blowing open in Ma Bell's face, and that is true. But in retrospect it appears clear that, one way or another, Ma Bell was going to "get it," and to management's credit it wasn't caught dozing when the explosion happened. Had it waited, it might never have succeeded in obtaining some crucial evidence that later proved very useful. Worse, it might have been able to produce no good defense at all when public opinion was aroused. For all of the bad publicity, Bell at least was able to say: "As soon as the alarms sounded, we went to work."

Returning now to the fall of 1974, to Gravitt and Ashley it must have seemed clear that the company was out to get them for their outspokenness as well as for their waywardness.

Shortly before the middle of October, Gravitt flew to St. Louis to talk with Southwestern Bell's top man, Barnes. Gravitt pleaded to have the investigation stopped. He insisted on his innocence. Barnes could promise him nothing.

Gravitt couldn't take it. One morning he went to the Dallas airport and flew off in his private plane. He flew for hours. Feeling weak, he leaned back at the controls, closed his eyes, and climbed by automatic pilot. Around midafternoon, he was wakened by the engine dying. He was at 21,000 feet over the Gulf of Mexico. In his daze he thought he was over a big lake. But he got the engine going again and called on his radio; an answer came from Alice, Texas. With his head "splitting open," as he noted in a memorandum, he flew back to land, refueled at Victoria, and returned to the Dallas airport.

On October 17 he wrote his suicide note:

Ever since last Thursday, I have not been able to keep my head from spinning. It hurts and I feel bad. I am afraid of brain damage. My right arm has started to go to sleep.

This coupled with the fact the Bell system has permitted some of our people to question over 150 people and in so doing, has caused me irreparable damage to my reputation. Questions like:

1. Have you bought him gifts at his request?
2. Have you fixed him up with women?
3. Have you gone to bed with him?
4. Has he made a pass at you?

This is unfair for a company to do without letting me be present. They have accused me of being partners with contractors. This is totally untrue.

I did try to get reimbursed for using my airplane. It was used on company business and to haul politicians.

They have accused me of having financial arrangements with [name of a company is illegible]. This is totally untrue. I have known Bill [last name illegible] for 10 years. We have been in each other's homes. . . .

I think records should be subpoenaed according to attached memo.

Also a memo showing a few things others have done.

There is bound to be much more. Watergate is a gnat compared to the Bell System.

He signed the note "T. O. Gravitt" and left it in the house.

He went into the garage, closed the garage doors, started the car motor, and began breathing carbon monoxide.

After his body was discovered and the police had been called, company investigators also arrived. Gravitt's son, Micutze, saw one of these executives go through his father's briefcase. He didn't object until one of the men tried to take the suicide note. "I thought there might be something important there and I took the note away from him and asked him what he was doing going through my father's briefcase," the son told a reporter. "He said he was looking for a notebook to write on."

Eight days after the suicide, Ashley was fired outright. He claims it was the first time the company had fired someone at such a high level of management.

For Southwestern Bell, what ensued was a nightmare. Ashley's strident accusations were played up in all the media. In November Ashley and Gravitt's wife Oleta sued Southwestern Bell for $29.2 million for slander. Ashley and his wife also sued the telephone company for wiretapping and eavesdropping.

Ashley's contentions hurt the company where it could be hurt most, that is, its coveted reputation for propriety and honesty in relationships with legislators and the public. He claimed that he and Gravitt were victims of a corporate power struggle because they had fought wasteful spending and unfairly high telephone rates. Their fault, he said, was that "they dared to resist the corporate rapacities. He claimed that executives at the department head and vice-presidential levels in Missouri were given pay raises that included $1,000 a year to cover political contributions, which was illegal in that state (only bona fide individual contributions were lawful). When he himself had been in the St. Louis district, he claimed, he was one of the forty Bell executives whom the company had ordered to contribute $50 a month to designated political candidates. Also, he asserted that Southwestern Bell routinely asked employees to make out false expense vouchers so that illegal payments could be made.

Ashley charged that telephone company agents tapped the telephones of municipal and state officials who would rule on a rate proposal, thus acquiring information that could be invaluable in company lobbying efforts for the increase. He himself, Ashley alleged, had been directed by Ma Bell to listen to thousands of private telephone conversations. Worried, the Texas legislature appointed a subcommittee to look into the charges. After a seven-month investigation, the subcommittee concluded there had indeed been wiretapping and other forms of illegal electronic surveillance. The subcommittee report even cited instances of Southwestern Bell employees who "entertained themselves by listening to the private conversations of telephone users." It also found evidence of improper wheeling and dealing—for instance, a city mayor who sold more than $70,000 of supplies to a telephone company after presiding over rate hearings and voting for an increase, and a city councilman who did more than $140,000 of business with a Bell affiliate.

Ashley's wiretapping case was tried first. The jury in San Antonio was convinced by his charges and in December 1976 it ordered Southwestern Bell to pay $1 million in damages to him and his wife for invading their privacy. (They had asked $4 million.) The company appealed.

The next year the Ashley–Gravitt suit for slander was tried. This case attracted widespread attention, not only for the testimony about sexual affairs but also for Ashley's claims that the whole company was corrupt, that he and Gravitt had known it and criticized it, and that for this they had been persecuted.

Gravitt's widow (now Oleta Dixon) claimed that the company's slander of her husband had driven him to his death. At the trial, Gary G. Byrd of Baylor University, a psychiatrist with 200 "psychological autopsies" to his credit, testified that corporate retaliation was indeed the "proximate cause" of the suicide.

Ashley testified vividly about Southwestern Bell's efforts to control rate-making officials and legislators. The city councils lacked the staff and skills to question the company's petitions for rate increases, he said. "The councilmen for the most part went on blind faith. It was easy to befuddle them." A big part of his job had been to cozy up to them.

When he had become a district manager in one Texas city, he said in court, "the first thing I did was go to the local bank that handled our multimillion-dollar account, whose president was mayor of the town. He told me how close he was to Bell, and gave me advice on what organizations I ought to belong to. He said I ought to take on the United Fund campaign and he saw I was appointed to run it. Well, I put it over. Used a lot of Bell manpower. In a short time, I was one of the top guys in that town. They knew that when it came to asking for a rate increase, I could be trusted."

What was done to avoid giving the public the impression that the city councils were in Bell's hip pocket? "We'd talk to the mayor and tell him that we have to have a $1.3 million increase, and that we'll file for $1.9 million so he can cut us by $600,000. This way, he'll look good and we get what we want." He testified that he gave business to city council members wherever possible. For example, if a council member had an auto agency, Ashley would buy extra cars from that agency for the phone company, and fewer from other dealers.

Clearly, some Southwestern Bell managers were exploiting the fact that in Texas regulation was accomplished by hundred of municipalities (rather than a state commission), tempting hundreds of company executives to wheel and deal with local politicians. Bell executives could rationalize that

SHOULD AN ORGANIZATION HAVE RIGHTS?

they were doing the best thing for their employer if they found ways to influence municipal and state officials.

Since the trial was well publicized—media people reveled in reporting the alleged wrongdoing of a giant telephone company—there was no way Bell could win. All it could hope to do was minimize its losses. To accomplish this, it produced evidence of Ashley's and Gravitt's sexual liaisons, cheating, and improper dealings, all of which were designed to show that its investigations were necessary and proper. Witness after witness for the company paraded through court testifying to one kind of wrongdoing or another on the part of the two whistleblowers. Even the conservative *Wall Street Journal* couldn't resist reporting such titillating allegations as that a company executive took one female employee aloft in his plane, put it on automatic pilot, and attempted to seduce her.[9]

To the company's charges of sexual misconduct, Ashley and Gravitt's widow could only defend that it was going on in other places, too. In fact, Ashley testified, he had been told by his friend Gravitt that the vice-president personally had been forced to serve as a pimp for company executives from the New York headquarters who had come to Texas to wine and dine. To the charges of Gravitt's extravagance, the defense could only be that other executives, too, had connived to acquire such elegance. Only in the case of Bell's accusations about expense account cheating could Ashley offer direct factual rebuttals, and even these struck some observers as being incomplete.

In September 1977 the jury of the state district court decided in favor of Gravitt and Ashley. It directed Southwestern Bell to pay each of the plaintiffs $1.5 million in damages for slander. Embracing his tearful wife, Ashley said he was proud of his role as "Ralph Nader of the telephone industry." Immediately the company appealed.

For the phone company, 1978 turned out to be a much more harmonious year. Now it was the company's turn to sing hymns of exultation, and Ashley's and the Gravitt estate's turn to listen to dirges. Early in the year the Court of Civic Appeals of Texas overturned the wiretapping verdict. "We have concluded," wrote Associate Justice Esco Walter, "the evidence creates nothing more than a mere surmise or suspicion on the Ashleys' allegations of eavesdropping and wiretapping." In November, another Court of Civic Appeals overturned the verdicts for slander. "We believe that the information received as a result of the investigation would reasonably indicate to appellant (i.e., Southwestern Bell) that Ashley and Gravitt had been promiscuous with subordinate employees, that there was an apparent conflict of interest involving Quik Print, and that Ashley and Gravitt

[9] *Wall Street Journal*, January 17, 1977, p. 1.

submitted false claims for reimbursements for purportedly business-related expenditures," intoned Associate Justice Robert R. Murray. He noted that the company "made inquiries only after it had received reports which related to serious wrongdoings. Any reasonable employer would investigate such reports in order to preserve its own effectiveness."

As for the allegations of retaliation, the court felt that Ashley and Gravitt's estate did not prove that Southwestern Bell had started the probe in order to silence the two men for their criticisms of the company.

Because its probes had been timely, the company was able to convince a great many employees to speak out in its defense. Ashley himself paid eloquent tribute to management's power in this respect. He said that he was warned by one executive that if he filed suit "Bell employees (there are 900,000 of them in the AT&T system) would hound me to the ends of the earth." And because uncensored copies of the trial transcripts were distributed to many company offices, numerous employees were kept fully informed of both accusations and defenses.

Politically and economically, however, Southwestern Bell paid heavily. For instance, early in 1975 in Missouri it settled for a $32.5 million rate increase as against $52.3 million requested, a compromise that many observers felt was a reflection of the company's weak bargaining position. In Texas a new central commission was created with power to veto the rate increases authorized by city councils; Texas also cut in half the proportion of current replacement costs that Southwestern Bell could use as a basis for rate increase requests. Some state commission members friendly to Southwestern Bell resigned because of the cacophony. One of them, William R. Clark, a ten-year veteran of the Missouri Public Service Commission, bowed out when the media disclosed that he had been a guest of the company on a three-day hunting trip some years before.

Following the results of the probe of Ashley and Gravitt, AT&T lost no time investigating other parts of the Bell System. In 1975 in North Carolina, for instance, it found evidence of kickbacks and expense account padding, and took corrective action.

For those of its employees who risked their personal reputations at the trials by testifying to Ashley's and Gravitt's promiscuousness, the company did what it could to make things easier. One such case was the woman who worked in the company security department and who, after being propositioned by the two executives, reported the incidents and started the chain reaction of company counteraction. (Ashley contended she was a spy who had set him up.) She transferred from San Antonio to an AT&T subsidiary in New Mexico.

What has happened to Ashley? At last report, he was working as a real estate agent in a town near Austin, Texas. "He no longer has the big salary, five-week vacations, and free telephone calls of his former job," reported the *Wall Street Journal*, "but he says he doesn't miss the corporate life a bit."

"Not What I Said, but Whether I Could Say Anything at All" [10]

John M. Shea was sitting over an eight-ounce steak at the Trade Mart in downtown Dallas, where President John F. Kennedy was due to speak shortly, when the news of the assassination came. The people around Shea's table were stunned. Someone said, "I hope the killer didn't come from Dallas."

Numbed, Shea went to a telephone booth to cancel an appointment with a friend. The telephone operator was sobbing; he comforted her. She said, "That wonderful man—why did it have to happen in Dallas?" At his friend's office, the secretary who answered the phone said, "Oh, Mr. Shea, I'm brokenhearted. It *must* have been somebody from out of town; nobody in Dallas would do such a thing." His friend came to the phone and said, "Well, they finally got what they wanted." Shea, who knew "they" meant the Kennedy-haters, answered, "Yes, but suppose it turns out to be a communist or a Black Muslin?" In typical loyal-to-Dallas fashion the friend responded, "Well, I sure as hell hope that whoever he is, he's from out of town."

During the ensuing days, Shea heard and read such reactions over and over again. Certain words and phrases became engraved on his mind. Proud and staunch Dallasites did not want to believe that their city was guilty. Thinking back over the six years he had lived in Dallas, Shea reflected on the city's strong and weak points. On the one hand, there were the shining buildings, the hard-won wealth, the commitment to honest government, and the dedication to useful work and independence. On the other, there was the hubris, the phobias about Kennedy and "liberals," the hysterical "Impeach Earl Warren" bumper stickers, the affectations like alligator cowboy boots and mink chaps, the trivia on TV and, untalked about, behind the shiny buildings, awful slums and violence.

Dallas was trying to hide from itself, Shea thought. It was important for itself and the world that it stop hiding and face realities. In his mind a message began to form, and the more it grew the more certain he became that before long, like the character in an Ernest Hemingway story who "got rid of many things by writing them," he would have to commit his thoughts to paper.

---

[10] This account is based on an interview with John Shea and data in "The Individual and the Corporation," Intercollegiate Clearing House (Harvard Business School) No. 1-368-018.

Born in Santa Barbara, California, in 1922, he had gone to high school at St. Joseph's Academy, started college at St. Mary's, and graduated from the University of Washington in 1943 after majoring in international trade. In a U.S. Navy officer's uniform he had seen action in the Southwest Pacific and the Philippine Islands, been wounded, and received the Bronze Star.

After V-J Day, Shea had returned to the Philippines and, working mostly out of Manila and Hong Kong, started an import-export business. He married; his business prospered. Early in the 1950s, his business having grown to an annual volume of $12 million in sales, he and his family had gone back to California. Using part of the proceeds of his business in the Orient, he had organized a firm to finance home builders, and the Shea Oil Company, an independent distributor for a major oil corporation.

The entrepreneurial life had suited him fine. His oil firm had doubled the supplier corporation's volume. In addition, he had introduced a line of tires, batteries, and auto accessories that he sold from "rolling stores"—old school buses that he had bought and renovated for retailing. In three years his rolling-stores business alone had climbed to $150,000 a year.

His work had attracted the interest of the head of American Petroleum, a Belgian oil company that sought to get a foothold in the United States by purchasing and consolidating small integrated oil companies. After several talks with the Petrofina president, in 1957 Shea had joined the corporation as marketing manager. He had moved his family to Dallas.

There, too, he had prospered. In addition to establishing good working relationships with independent jobbers and retailers, he had demonstrated an unusual flair for merchandising and promotion. In a busy industrial section of Dallas he had built a station consisting of separate islands, each a thirty-foot concrete tower with a mushroom-like design, offering gasoline, service, and customer facilities.

Another coup had been the development of mobile self-powered service stations that offered "Petrofina a la carte." Still another coup had been an advertising campaign that spoofed the additives fad to which competitors seemed to be addicted. The stations and ad campaigns both had received lots of publicity and awards, Shea had found himself in demand as a speaker before business groups, and he had been praised as one of the main reasons for Petrofina's rapid growth in the Southwest. He had been promoted to the corporation's top marketing position, senior vice-president in charge of marketing, refining, distribution, and transportation. In addition, he was appointed to the board of directors.

Brooding in late 1963 over the Kennedy assassination, Shea drafted a letter proposing that, as a means of confronting its shame and guilt, Dallas erect a memorial to the late president. He sent the letter to one of the two leading newspapers but it was not printed. The reason for its rejection, he realized, was that the Dallas media chose to print only praise of the city; the Oswald and Ruby slayings were seen as isolated events quite unrelated to the prevailing atmosphere of the city.

He mentioned these thoughts at a dinner meeting with George Harris of *Look* magazine. The dinner had been set up by Shea's good friend Howard Gossage, who headed the firm that handled Petrofina's advertising. Harris had been sent to Dallas to examine the city's mood following the assassination. He read the copy of Shea's unpublished letter, found it provocative, and discussed the possibility of Shea's writing an article for *Look*. The odds were against publication, Harris stressed, but from time to time the magazine did run articles by nonprofessional writers, so there was at least a chance of success.

Shea thought the idea over carefully. He knew that the *Dallas Morning News,* among other powers, would be outraged. If the article were publicly acclaimed, that would make no difference to the editors; the *Morning News* simply wouldn't publish any of the favorable reactions. (Ironically, the *Morning News* was the newspaper that had run some admiring accounts in the past of Shea's marketing and advertising feats.) He knew also that any article he published in *Look* would irritate some of the top officers of Petrofina, and perhaps some of its customers, too.

At the same time, he knew he could accept some risks. For one thing, Petrofina would think twice about jettisoning its number-one marketing man. For another, he had set aside some capital from his days as an entrepreneur in California and the Orient; he was not completely dependent on his salary and stock options. Besides, he had got used to working for himself in the years before joining Petrofina. "I had not," he tells me, "many years of conditioning by superiors and peers on the ultimate righteousness of any corporate policy imposed on a young man trying to work his way up the corporate ladder."

In fact, at the time of the dinner with Harris, he and Gossage had been working on some copy for a newspaper advertisement in which Shea would express his feelings about Kennedy's death, his own failure to act as a responsible member of the community (he had not spoken out about the things in Dallas he hadn't liked), and his conviction that the city should erect a memorial to the late president. Shea had planned to pay the full cost of the ad. Would an article for *Look* get him in any more trouble than the ad would?

But the decisive factor was his grief and self-remorse. He had been a supporter of Kennedy. He believed he had not stood up often enough for Kennedy during the presidential campaign and White House years. He recalls, "I had not responded often enough and strongly enough to the vituperativeness and venom which almost all the political, corporate, and social leaders in Dallas had displayed toward Kennedy. Too often I had let it go by, with little or no comment. So I had regrets—it was really self-disgust—as well as grief, and George Harris had seen my grief."

For two weeks Shea worked on a manuscript for *Look*. He spent part of his writing time in a Dallas hotel, and when he had drafts ready, he dictated them to his secretary or a recording machine. He told no one about his project except his wife, Gossage, and Harris, who gave him day-to-day encouragement. He considered it a personal venture and the expression of a personal viewpoint. Neither in the text of the article nor in the by-line did he identify himself as an executive of Petrofina. While he was writing, he stayed in charge of his usual managerial tasks at the company, and both he and his secretary were very careful not to let the manuscript impinge on their regular company duties.

He wrote and he rewrote. Finally, he sent a manuscript to Harris at *Look*. Some time went by before *Look* responded. The editors liked the manuscript but wanted some revisions. Eagerly Shea went to work on the alterations requested. The magazine was pleased with most of his revisions but came back with still more questions. He revised again. "No tears in the writer, no tears in the reader," Robert Frost once said. With everyone finally satisfied, the article was scheduled for publication.

When an advance copy of the article was sent to him, Shea told the president of Petrofina about it. Shea also assured him that he had written the piece on his own time, that all the while he had done his company job as thoroughly as he knew how. The president, a political conservative, was dismayed by the text but said little.

The article appeared in the March 24, 1964, issue of *Look* under the title "Memo from a Dallas Citizen." (The issue appeared a couple of weeks before the date on the cover.) Shea's by-line was printed, but nothing in the issue connected him with Petrofina. In the article, Shea made the following statements, among many others:

We are rich, proud Dallas, "Big D" to Texas, and we have never learned a lesson in humility from any man. Not even from a murdered President of the United States. We have lived for three months with national tragedy, and I won't be popular for bringing this subject up now. But somebody must. To say nothing, more important, to do nothing, only says to the rest of the world that, as they have read, we shrugged the whole thing off.

If we are to learn the lessons that President Kennedy came to teach, we must build a living, searching memorial. We could, for instance, buy the Texas School Book Depository, from which the fatal shots were fired, and rebuild it for a better purpose. It would become a civic research center, under Southern Methodist University, dedicated to study of the urban evils that lead to violence and hatred.

None of us can claim to be blameless. For six years, I have been helping build an oil business, a successful one, but at church, civic functions and parties, I have sat on the sidelines like a foreign observer at a tribal rite.

In one sense, those who say, "It could have happened anywhere," are quite right. But somehow Big D doesn't derive much comfort from that, nor is it possible. For I'm afraid the record shows all too clearly that in addition to having the world's ills, Dallas has managed to develop a few special complications.

After the March 24 issue of *Look* hit the newsstands and caught public attention, Shea was asked to speak to a Democratic women's group. He gave his speech to a raptly attentive audience and handled numerous questions from the audience afterward. Although many did not agree with him, he was acclaimed. Was he going to succeed again? Was his gamble with the powers of Dallas going to pay off after all?

The first note of pending disaster came after the speech. Word came to Shea, through an intermediary official in Petrofina, that thereafter he must clear all speeches and articles with the president of Petrofina. This was an unpleasant surprise in two ways. First, it was odd that the order came through an intermediary rather than from the president himself, for until the writing of the article, Shea had been in continuous personal touch with the president, talking with him almost daily. Second, the order was a putdown. Never before had Shea been asked to clear his remarks with top management, even though he had made numerous speeches on all sorts of subjects, business and otherwise.

"The issue was not *what* I said," he wrote later in the year, describing the incident in *Look*'s August 11 issue, "but whether I could say anything at all." Shea was unintimidated by the sudden demand. He reminded the intermediary that he hadn't had to obtain clearance for his speeches in the past. He told the intermediary he was unwilling to clear future talks and articles, especially ones reflecting his personal viewpoints, with the president's office. However, he did assure the man that, as with the *Look* article, the company's name would not appear in connection with any speaking or writing of a personal nature that he did.

In the meantime, reactions to the article were running mixed and strong. The owners of some of the companies Petrofina had purchased were indignant and called Shea's article an act of treachery. They wrote to the president as well as to Shea. Critical mail from other sources, too, came to the company. The *Morning News*, as predicted, printed dozens of hostile letters in its Letters to the Editor column (no favorable letters were produced). About a dozen credit cards were returned from customers.

Outside Dallas, too, there were angry words. The March 13, 1964, issue of the Borger, Texas, *News Herald*, for instance, interpreted the article as meaning that Shea "would have been a lot happier had the President, John F. Kennedy, been assassinated by someone among us who had dared to exercise the privilege as an American citizen, to disagree with the establishment, the communist-serving bureaucracy in Washington, D.C., instead of being killed, as he was, by an admitted communist."

On the plus side, several employees told Shea that they liked the article. The *Houston Post* published a lead editorial under the title, "Come to Houston, Mr. Shea." (Parenthetically, Shea notes that the editorial didn't sit very well with most of his critics in Dallas.) Several other small newspapers in Texas also noted the article with approval. Shea received more than 800 letters and phone calls, about 90% of which praised his position. After the dozen or so credit card returns, no others were received. The remaining card holders—several million of them—were silent, presumably continuing to patronize Petrofina stations.

Early in April Shea was asked to meet with the president and several directors. "At all times during this conversation," Shea remembers, "the attitude was cool and reserved. It was apparent to me that the legalities were being considered, and the only demand was that I not give any more interviews on the subject. The rumor had been circulating that I would be interviewed by CBS and by NBC's 'Today' show." But the coolness of the president and directors did not conceal their anger. They suggested to Shea that if he would resign from the board, he would be paid full salary through the end of 1964. Shea, who could clearly see the handwriting now on the wall, made no comment except to note that the extra months' pay they were offering was not as generous as what they had given an incompetent vice-president they had fired a little earlier. The incompetent had received a full year's pay instead of eight months' worth.

Although he had been asked only to resign from the board, Shea was not fooled. What they really wanted was his resignation—*out!* He decided to agree with them on this one issue. When a statement of resignation was presented to him shortly thereafter, he signed it.

A formal board meeting was scheduled for mid-April in the East. For some time, since he was a director, Shea had had plane and hotel reservations for the trip. Physically and emotionally tired, he decided not to cancel his reservations but to go "just to see what would happen." Besides, he thought, maybe the trip would help him to unwind. Yet when he flew East, he did not attend the board sessions. No one from Petrofina got in touch with him.

On April 14, the *Dallas Morning News* reported that Shea had resigned; the company, not Shea, was given as its source. The next day the *Morning News* reported a speech made by a member of Dallas's powerful Citizens Council, a band of more than 200 prominent businessmen, all company presidents or board chairmen, who were extremely influential in deciding what directions and goals the city should strive for. "If Mr. Shea would learn to know Dallas better," the executive was reported as asserting, "he would probably like it better. So much for the gratuitous defectors and journalistic buzzards that are still circling our town. Don't waste your breath lashing back."

However, Shea was not to suffer alone. The April 17 issue of *Advertising Age*, the best-known publication of the advertising industry, reported that his good friend Gossage had decided to scratch the Petrofina account. Gossage must have swallowed hard before making this decision, for he was enjoying more than $750,000 a year of commissionable advertising from American Petrofina—it was his firm's largest account. But he felt his loyalty to Shea more keenly than the economic loss. "One of the few privileges you have in the agency field," said Gossage wryly to an *Advertising Age* reporter, "is deciding whose money you want to accept. We just decided that we didn't want Petrofina's any longer."

After his resignation became public, Shea was asked to a going-away party at the company. It was attended by about a hundred employees of departments he had managed, who presented him with several thoughtful gifts. Still, the tone of the party was an index of the current sensitivity. Such a touchy issue was Shea's past criticisms of Dallas that, though they were the reason for his departure and the party, they were not referred to in any of the speeches.

Several business leaders in other regions, including Norton Simon and J. Irwin Miller, offered Shea good positions in their organizations. In between his talks with them, he took on well-paid consulting assignments for a large farmers' cooperative and another foreign oil company.

Six months after his resignation he was still debating what to do. He would have enjoyed returning to the corporate scene but he worried about causing future embarrassments of the sort he had caused Petrofina. Engraved on his mind was one conversation he had had with a company president who, after making an attractive offer, had asked how he could be sure that Shea wouldn't repeat his "foolishness." The question of the proper balance between loyalty to top management and loyalty to one's principles bothered him then as it does to this day. "How much one owes the company store," he tells me, "is a question I guess I still haven't resolved fully."

In the end, life as an entrepreneur, such as he had enjoyed before joining Petrofina, attracted him most. He moved his family back to California and began working to build his own business again. He was successful. For some years now he has been in charge of Beacon Bay Enterprises, Inc., which builds, owns, and operates a chain of automatic, full-service car washes in California. It is the largest such chain in the state. Beacon Bay Enterprises also operates a number of fast-food outlets, some small industrial parks, and some office buildings. As the president and majority stockholder, Shea has the fun of making the major business deals; for building and running the operations on a day-to-day basis he has a staff that enjoys his full confidence. He tells me:

> Annual sales of $20 million and an organization of several hundred employees are quite a comedown, I guess, from the corporate life [at Petrofina] involving billions of dollars and many thousands of employees. But no longer do I have to look over my shoulder. Also, much of my time is free to spend as I choose. I spend almost as much time as president of the board of trustees of the Newport Harbor Art Museum in Newport Beach, California, as I do at my company. A dozen years ago I began collecting modern American art. This museum activity has become as absorbing and challenging for me as any I've undertaken.

How were Petrofina's organization rights served by the dismissal of Shea? Of the seven rights in the proposed bill, the ones most affected were the right to commitment and the right to employee competence. Those who side with the board's action argue that Petrofina was not getting the needed commitment from Shea because he let his personal convictions interfere with his dedication to the company. On the other hand, those who side with Shea point out that he did not interrupt his corporate work to write the article. Those who side with the board argue that the hostile letters and credit card returns show that Shea sacrificed corporate commitment to personal conviction. Those who side with Shea point out that the total number of returned credit cards was small (fourteen) and the hostile letters were emotional outbursts. As for the competence requirement, those who defend the board's action maintain that Shea became dispensable when he provoked the wrath of the Dallas community. However, those who take Shea's side argue that the board cut off Petrofina's nose to spite its face when it dismissed this very talented marketing leader.

Stopping the Inequity at Equity Funding [11]

The Bible says that the lion and the lamb shall lie down together. Woody Allen adds an important qualification: "The lion and the lamb shall lie down together but the lamb won't get much sleep." Ronald H. Secrist seemed to be proving the truth of the qualification. He took a prestigious and comfortable job working under Stanley Goldblum, the lionized head of Equity Funding Corporation of America, but what this lamb saw going on around him made him lie awake at night.

Secrist was thirty-four years old, slim and balding, a graduate of the University of Washington (his degree was in business administration and he had majored in insurance), and an enthusiast about the insurance industry. He intended to make his career in insurance. After working in several companies he had moved to Equity Funding, beginning in its Los Angeles offices. But operations there didn't smell right to him, and he became unhappy. His tension and worry began affecting his marriage and he knew he had to get a change of scene. With enthusiasm and relief he seized a chance to move to New Jersey and become vice-president for administration of a subsidiary company, Bankers National Life Insurance Company. He thought the New Jersey office would free him from the contamination of the Los Angeles office, but he was wrong. The scent of crime was everywhere.

For one thing, there were telltale signs that the company was writing phony industrial bonds and U.S. Treasury bills. For another, a friend of his was under relentless pressure to help make fraudulent transfers of the subsidiary's assets to the parent company. The purpose of this deception was to make the assets of the parent look larger than they really were, and the purpose of that ruse, in turn, was to keep Equity Funding a favorite of investors. Its track record of growth had astonished Wall Street and awed the whole insurance industry. The fact that the company was suffering from negative cash flow did not worry the bulls on Wall Street.

Still, Secrist wasn't blowing the whistle. He wanted very much to blow it, and he intended to later, but there were all sorts of reasons for delaying. For one thing, Equity Funding was his fourth employer in a dozen years. If he left soon he might become known as a job-hopper. He didn't want that sort

---

[11] This account is based on an interview with Ronald Secrist, newspaper and magazine articles, and Raymond L. Dirks and Leonard Gross, *The Great Wall Street Scandal* (New York: McGraw-Hill, 1974).

of reputation. For another thing, he had worried off and on about his personal implication in the crime. On the West Coast he had once worked on a bogus file and signed his name to a confirmation slip. Technically, at least, he had been a participant in the crime, though not a willing or fully aware one. Finally, the enormity of the fraud going on seemed beyond belief. It permeated the whole company—a prestigious, celebrated company adored by thousands of security analysts! Was his imagination playing tricks on him? At times he may have felt like Mark Twain commenting wryly on Wagner's music: "It *can't* be as bad as it sounds."

But if the fraud seemed incredible, it also was real. Secrist had no doubt about it when he woke up in the deep hours of the night. In fact, he had little doubt that senior managers knew without a doubt. "Almost every employee knew generally what it was all about, including most clerks," he recalls. "Some top executives might not have known [a few sales executives, for instance] but the feeling of most of us was that others who professed ignorance were either stupid or crooks. For instance, Jim Smith and I discussed the fraud on various occasions, along with all the other life company officers."

At the same time, Secrist felt he was regarded as loyal by senior managers. There seemed to be no fear in the upper echelons that he might blow the whistle. If there had been, the story that follows might not have happened, for there is a good chance, Secrist thinks, that top management wouldn't have considered sacrificing him if it had perceived him as a potential noisemaker. He knows of other managers who were kept on in order to reduce the risk that they would sound off.

Late in 1972, unbeknowst to Secrist, top management decided to pare expenses, including the size of the managerial staff. He was still unaware of this decision when, on February 12, 1973, he flew to Los Angeles. In his mind it was just a routine trip to the home office to go over some operating matters. Blissfully ignorant that he was being stalked, he checked into a Holiday Inn and found a message to call James Smith, an Equity Funding executive. He called and agreed to go to Smith's office the first thing the next morning.

What Smith had to tell him came as a shock. As part of a big economy move, the senior explained, the company was pruning some 20% of its personnel. "You're going to have to go," Smith announced.

Several months earlier Secrist had met his old friend Pat Hopper for dinner in Pasadena. While they ate, Secrist had told Hopper that he was going to break the story of Equity Funding's wrongdoing to the outside world. Hopper had suggested contacting Raymond L. Dirks, a brilliant and unorthodox stock market analyst who had been written up in the *Wall Street Journal*. Secrist had agreed Dirks was a good prospect. He had also decided—though he didn't tell his friend this—to call the New York State Department of Insurance, which he believed to possess the greatest integrity of the state agencies regulating insurance companies.

Following the traumatic meeting with Smith, Secrist made up his mind. He returned to New Jersey, interviewed for a job in an Atlanta company, received a firm offer, and called both Dirks and the state agency to make appointments to tell them what he knew. He met with them separately on March 7 and told his story.

The culprit of Secrist's story was Goldblum, the head of Equity Funding. But Goldblum did not look or act like a villain. In fact, people thought of him as just the opposite. Goldblum "was a big man, heavily muscled, broad of chest and shoulder, six feet two inches tall," recalls Dirks.[12] His office was "the choicest corner of the highest floor of the handsomest building in the country's most sumptuous financial complex." He wore expensive suits, enormous cufflinks, monogrammed shirts, "and a touch too much cologne." He loved to drive his new Ferrari, his Rolls-Royce, and his Honda motorcycle. He rejoiced in sailing his racing yacht. But most of all, remembers Dirks, Goldblum enjoyed working out in his $100,000 weight-lifter's gym, which adjoined his house in Beverly Hills. He was determined to find out whether a man of forty-five could develop himself physically to resemble a twenty-year-old. He liked goals; he thought he could do it. "You can be anything you want to be," Stanley Goldblum said.

He was chairman of the business conduct committee of the Los Angeles branch of the National Association of Securities Dealers. Some people thought that he inspired confidence in others. He loved fine paintings—he had bought Picasso and Chagall lithographs to decorate his home. Dirks thought he had a sense of humor. He was easy to contact; often he answered the phone himself, and he returned calls promptly. He was generous with relatives. He was impatient with subordinates who tried to cut corners or cheat in ways other than those required by his master scheme.

Secrist didn't know Goldblum well. The two had talked several times but Secrist remembers their relationship as an impersonal one. "He was neither friendly nor outgoing with me—tough, stern, and all business. I never knew anyone in the company who spoke of 'liking' Stanley. There may have been two or three on his immediate staff who considered him a friend, but he was generally feared or disliked." One time when Goldblum was needed for a meeting and didn't turn up, a company officer called his home and was informed he was still asleep. It was noon. Spitefully the officer told Secrist, "He sleeps till noon and screws the world."

How was Goldblum able to preserve his jungle of fraud for so long?

---

[12] Dirks and Gross, op. cit., p. 1.

Secrist and others feel that the complexity of the business was what made the crime possible. "Virtually none of the auditors, even, understood it," Secrist says. "It wasn't planned that way. It just evolved that way, as did the fraud."

Goldblum, Gordon G. McCormick, and a third partner had raised the capital necessary to form Equity Funding in 1960. The three contributed equally to an initial $10,000 investment. In a matter of months, Goldblum had got impatient and dissatisfied with McCormick, so he and three other employees bought him out. By paying extremely high commissions, the owner–managers were able to create a highly talented sales force and a very high-pressure marketing program. They parlayed the original investment anthill into a $500 million mountain. Not all of this was built up from scratch; substantial chunks came from a program of acquiring other companies. Richard M. Hodgetts writes,

> Many people were puzzled by the exorbitant prices Equity paid for some of these concerns. What no one realized was that in most cases, the parent company was draining off the assets of its subsidiaries in order to inflate its own earnings. One such transaction, which has been documented by the California State Insurance Department, showed that in one year Equity Funding Life Insurance Corporation had earned a net profit of $3,056,724 and had paid $3,535,000 in dividends to the Equity Funding Corporation. No one could recall a case in which a life insurance subsidiary had paid its parent company more in dividends than it had earned. It was also later revealed that the parent company had repeatedly tried to get assets illegally transferred from Equity Life's New Jersey-based insurance subsidiary, Bankers National Life, to its own accounts.[13]

Late in the 1960s Equity Funding Life, the part of the conglomerate in which Secrist had been involved originally, devised a new "special class" insurance. Shortly after this was done, someone in the organization hit on the idea of creating phony life insurance policies to sell to companies that reinsured Equity Funding Life. The phony policies came to be known as the "Y" business. Because they required the cooperation of many people, a considerable amount of planning, organization, and stealth was necessary. On certain evenings a pack of executives would steal to a certain conference room. They would have the accomplice clerks pull a real file and copy certain sheets. Then some of that information would be altered slightly to create fictional policyholders. The latter would be given new policy num-

[13] See Richard M. Hodgetts, *The Business Enterprise* (Philadelphia: Saunders, 1977), pp. 85–86.

bers but the substance of their policies might be different only in detail from the real policyholders. Names might be spelled differently (e.g., Bennett might become Bennet, Anderson might become Andressen), birth dates might be changed a little, and the types and amounts of insurance sold the individual might be altered. Then these fictional policies would be fed into the computer as new business.

By the time Secrist was chased out in February 1973, the company had created more than 64,000 fictitious insurance policies with a face value of more than $2 billion; most of this amount was reinsured with other insurance companies.[14] If Equity Funding was a jungle of fraud, it was one of the lushest jungles that had ever grown.

Why couldn't the auditors who regularly came from government agencies to check the validity and honesty of operations see what was going on? The key to the deception was the so-called Department 99. This was a code number on the EDP records to identify the "Y" business. Records in this department were mixed with real business during the year. When billing was done, Department 99 was not billed. It was a jungle camouflage hiding the phony business among the real business, doing the task so well that auditors would look right at it and not see it.

One time in 1973 some employees in Equity Funding Life tipped off the insurance examiners about Department 99. Moving swiftly and efficiently, Goldblum's lieutenants manipulated the records while the audit was being done. For instance, thousands of false insurance policies were swept out of Department 99—into "Department 92."

After Secrist disclosed his intimate knowledge to Dirks at the New York State Department of Insurance, Goldblum's lieutenants fought a game but losing battle. Last-ditch efforts like that described were made. The most adroit attempts were made to discredit Secrist, throw Dirks off the scent, and baffle the examiners. Step by step, like hunters snaking through a morass of vines and undergrowth, the investigators got to the heart of the problem, however, and the scheme was revealed. At first institutional investors and financial analysts couldn't believe it. Only gradually did the light dawn on them.

After he blew the whistle, says Secrist, his wife was apprehensive. She got a phone call with a death threat from the wife of one Equity Funding manager. Threats were made that the company's Mafia connections would take care of one or both of them. (Secrist thinks that in fact there were no such connections with the underworld.) His wife worried day and night, and so, for several months, did he. Other lambs who had tried vainly to blow the whistle also received threats.

For Dirks, too, the hunting down of Goldblum was full of complications.

[14] Ibid., p. 91.

Until Secrist met with him and laid forth the facts, he had been living the good life in New York City. He enjoyed a $100,000-a-year job as an insurance analyst for the Wall Street firm of Delafield Childs. A maverick who delighted in shaking up corporate loyalists and stuffed-shirt types, Dirks was chubby, energetic, and precocious. He had a flair for publicity, and later in the decade a business associate would say of him, "Ray's motto is, early to bed, early to rise, work like hell and advertise."

Listening to Secrist's story, Dirks had been barely able to believe it. Like everyone else, he had had the reaction, "How could so many good analysts and auditors be wrong?" But he had known just enough about the pratfalls of analysts and the pitfalls of insurance regulation to realize that Secrist *could* be right. So though he hadn't believed the revelation right away, neither had he dismissed it.

Beginning with the names of knowledgeable insiders that Secrist gave him, Dirks began investigating. Soon it became apparent to him that the fraud was indeed real, perhaps even more enormous than Secrist had suspected. He tipped off some of his most prominent clients and investigated some more. Despite disguises and deceptions in his way, he tracked doggedly. When he had the necessary facts, he informed the press and went to the Securities and Exchange Commission with his findings. Trading in Equity Funding's stock was halted on March 27.

One might have thought Dirks would be acclaimed a hero. His unraveling of the mysteries at Equity Funding in a month's time was a prodigious feat. But reaction to him in Wall Street and Washington circles was anything but warm and adulatory.

Wall Street howled because he had violated a trade rule by tipping off some clients before making his disclosures. All the time that he was sleuthing in California, some investors, such as Loew's Corporation, not knowing of the wrongdoing, were buying Equity Funding stock. The New York Stock Exchange was angry because he did not let its officials in on the secret at the start. The Securities and Exchange Commission protested because he had gone public before revealing all to its staff. It preferred to do the prosecuting—"One lion to a hill." (However, says Secrist, at least three people had tipped it off before he and Dirks blew the whistle.)

Dirks defended himself. "Time was the element," he says. "I felt my job was to check out the information given to me and expose the fraud. I had to act quickly, and the only way to do it was to make it public." He says that if the predatory cats of Equity Funding had gotten wind of an impending Securities and Exchange Commission investigation, or an impending New York Stock Exchange inquiry, "they would have made off with millions. Had I gone to the SEC first, it would have taken months, even years, to get it exposed."

In a sense, Dirks was a whistleblower against leaders in his financial community. First, he was blowing the whistle on Wall Street, on numerous financial analysts and brokerage houses. "Few men in the Street dig deeply," he claims. "Superficiality is the name of the game." He accused them of playing follow the leader too often. "The easiest way for an analyst to do his job is to copy another analyst's work. Part of an analyst's function is to read what the competition is saying; but when an analyst uses another analyst's work to produce his own, a line of integrity has been crossed. This line is repeatedly crossed on Wall Street." It was because of these tendencies, Dirks believes, that Equity Funding was a popular recommendation in the financial community right up to the time of its exposure.

In another sense, Dirks also was blowing the whistle on regulatory agencies. They were bureaucratic dinosaurs where tigers were needed.

On April Fools' Day in 1973, realizing he was hopelessly trapped, Goldblum resigned as president of Equity Funding. Eleven days later, the New York Stock Exchange formally accused Dirks of violating its rules as well as transgressing provisions of the Securities and Exchange Act. Dirks had spread rumors, exceeded the bounds of propriety, and failed to follow "good business practice," the exchange accused. For these offenses he could be expelled for life from trading on the exchange.

The Securities and Exchange Commission also leaped on him. He had profited from inside information, it accused. It began planning a ten-month-long administrative hearing on his role in the Equity Funding affairs. The commissioners and many others in the securities industry were enraged by his assertions that he had only done what other analysts often did. The industry's dander wasn't soothed when he alleged, "The exchange is trying to hang me to save some of the big boys."

Thus, for tracking down Goldblum, Dirks himself was tracked down by senior officials in his profession. As the old saying goes, "The shrike hunting the locust is unaware of the hawk hunting him."

Dirks's relations with his employer firm, Delafield Childs, became strained. Some financial institutions who ordinarily dealt with him refused to deal with him any longer. The reason, he assumed, was they feared to offend the regulatory agencies. With his clients disappearing, he decided to resign from the firm.

For most of the next year he was unemployed. He lost weight, grew a beard, and spent long hours in his cluttered apartment in Greenwich Village.

To pay the fast-mounting legal fees for defending himself against his official pursuers, Dirks got together with Leonard Gross, a well-known professional journalist, to write a book about the Equity Funding scandal.[15]

---

[15] Dirks and Gross, op. cit.

McGraw-Hill, which agreed to publish the book, gave the two men an advance of $45,000. (The book would sell more than 25,000 copies.) The advance and royalties on the book, however, did not come close to paying the lawyers. By early 1978 Dirks had paid more than $150,000 for his defense.

Late in 1973 a grand jury indicted Goldblum and twenty-one others on 105 criminal counts. Equity Funding went into bankruptcy. Although not sucked dry, it was found to be short some $120 million in assets. In addition to the life insurance policies it fabricated, it had counterfeited bonds and forged death certificates. It had set an example of organized fraud that would be hard to match for many years to come.

Still, the exposure came in time to allow the trustees in bankruptcy to save the 35,000 policyholders from loss. Their policies were transferred to a healthy company in Seattle, which, ironically, had been a subsidiary of the doomed parent corporation. This happy result, Secrist believes, was made possible by "very adept, very fast footwork" by the California Insurance Commission. "Normally," he says, "the policyholders would have lost all cash value in their policies."

After the dust settled, what happened to the principals? Given an eight-year prison term in California, Goldblum was jailed in Terminal Island federal prison. Number-two man Fred Levin got the same sentence. Samuel Lowell, executive vice-president of the company, was sentenced to five years in jail for his cunning. Other employees as well as some independent auditors were convicted of securities fraud and of filing falsified financial statements with the Securities and Exchange Commission.

Some observers believe that Goldblum and his fellow conspirators hoped gradually to restore financial integrity to company operations. Realizing that the phony reinsurance schemes could not be written indefinitely, they hoped—or professed to have hoped—that they could phase out the spurious reinsurance business altogether, reducing the bogus business gradually until operations were clean. Such action would cause earnings to sag, but the heads were said to believe that they could keep analysts and investors from losing faith by judicious explanations. However, Secrist believes that their hopes of eliminating the "Y" business were a dream, a fantasy. "It was impossible," he says. "They were trapped. The phony 'Y' business had to be increased exponentially each year to keep the scheme going."

As for Dirks, the Securities and Exchange Commission investigations made it impermissible for him to supervise fellow employees of a member firm of the New York Stock Exchange. Therefore he had to switch to another career path. In 1976 he joined the firm of John Muir and Company on Wall Street, set up a division called Ray Dirks Research, and soon became the firm's prime mover. Although enormously successful for several years, Muir filed for bankruptcy in a New York federal court late in 1981.

What about Secrist, the lamb with a lion's heart? For him fate was more capricious. At first he appeared to emerge unscathed from the fray. After joining American Agency Financial Corporation in Atlanta, he was promoted to vice-president. But again he began seeing—could he believe his eyes?—improper dealings taking place. After being approached by a company director, he reported what he knew; next the Georgia Insurance Commission investigated, found evidence of violations, and sent the firm a cease and desist order.

Secrist decided he had had enough of the insurance business. Moving to Olympia, Washington, he invested all his savings in a light-fixture store, Capital Lighting. Today, he says, he is making several times his best earnings while in life insurance. He has started a second business, served as chairman of several business groups, and played an active role in a local church.

He likes to go salmon fishing in Puget Sound. Ironically, for a few years Goldblum was in prison on one of the islands in the sound, McNeil Island. A reporter asked Secrist if, while sitting in his boat with the island in view, he ever pondered Goldblum's fate. "No," he replied, "I think about the fish."

========

What is the significance of this tumultuous and discordant case for the organization rights of Equity Funding Corporation? The right most directly affected would seem to be loyalty. In promoting their illegal operation, Goldblum and his associates were undermining the long-run health of the company. Equity Funding's right to obedience also was affected. From the standpoint of his superiors engaged in the subterfuge, Secrist was disobedient, but from the standpoint of the organization charter it was Goldblum and crew who were disobedient. What about the right to freedom from unnecessary intrusion and regulation? Only the accomplices in crime might argue that this right was infringed; the agency investigations were made solely to ensure the company's compliance with the law and public interest. The right to a means of protecting employees and others who sought to uphold the company's interests? Equity Funding had no such mechanism. If it had, the mechanism would have had to be a very strong one, for, of course, the chief executive himself would have sought to frustrate its operation.

The rights of Dirks' employer, Delafield Childs, were affected more subtly. For instance, what about the firm's right to obedience? Dirks violated the firm's policy—clearly implied if not written—of complying with the letter and spirit of the rules of the Stock Exchange and the Securities and Exchange Commission. In rebuttal, he argued cogently that in no way could he serve the long-run interests of his employer and the investment community by observing the rules literally.

A THREE-LEGGED STOOL

The combination of managerial prerogatives, employee rights, and organization rights discussed might be viewed as a three-legged stool. If any of the legs is weakened, the stool may collapse. No matter how strong any two of the legs may be, that will not keep the stool upright. If the stool collapses, society is the big loser, because society, so to speak, sits on the stool.

In the Southwestern Bell case, for instance, management's prerogatives to investigate, suspend, and fire for just cause were important because management had to be able to manage or its will to manage would suffer. On the other hand, Ashley's and Gravitt's rights to blow the whistle for good cause were important because that had to do with working in dignity as a concerned, inquiring human being. And the organization's rights to good management, loyalty, commitment, and competence were important if it was to stay competitive. As for society—in particular, the five-state region served by Southwestern Bell—it stood to be the loser if these three sets of rights were not kept in a strong and creative balance, for if management couldn't manage or if employee morale suffered or if the organization was slowed down, an enormous communications network with all its projects in planning and capital invested would begin to deteriorate, with all that would mean for people's lives and affairs.

In the Petrofina and Equitable Funding cases, a similar situation obtained. If managerial prerogatives held sway at the expense of employee rights, or vice versa, or if either or both dominated at the expense of the organization, the stool suffered a leg injury. And in each case a sizable region of society sat on the stool.

In the Southwestern Bell case, hundreds of thousands—perhaps millions—of words were written and spoken about the equities in the situation. So far as I know, all of the attention was focused on who was right—Ashley and/or Gravitt or the top executives who went after them. It seemed to be commonly assumed that, whoever prevailed and in whatever manner, the company would go merrily on its way. Not so. If we did not know it before the late 1970s and early 1980s, we know it now: A corporation, no matter how large and strong, is vulnerable. It is as vulnerable as the Furbish lousewort, the leatherneck turtle, or anything else on the endangered species list that conservationists so worry about. Although usually not as vulnerable as a single human being, it is as vulnerable as a large family of people. The roster of corporate witnesses to this obvious but often unappreciated proposition is becoming impressive: W. T. Grant, Underwood, Pan American, Chrysler, and more.

Looking down the road, it might be highly desirable for Americans to recognize that organizational rights should be added to the rights-at-work picture. In the meantime, managers do not need to wait for a public consensus to develop and be translated into some sort of appropriate legal action. By acting *as if* their corporate or agency employers have rights—which is, of course, what many capable administrators have been doing for some time—managers can secure for their organizations a major part of the gains that are needed.

The reasonable man adapts himself to the world.
The unreasonable one persists in trying to adapt the
world to himself. Therefore, all progress depends
on the unreasonable man.

GEORGE BERNARD SHAW

11

MAKING MANAGEMENT
LEGITIMATE

≡ Corporations and other organizations are accomplished in producing significant technological changes. However, they are not so accomplished in foreseeing and responding to the social changes created by technological change. When the social-change chickens come home to roost and organization leaders are caught woefully unprepared, someone else, usually government, has to move in and fix things up.

For example, late in the nineteenth century great changes occurred in the food and drug industries. Until the late 1890s, food had been produced and sold near the farm, mainly in bulk, and drugs (except for those sold by itinerant "snake oil peddlers") were recognizable. But then companies began to package and can food products and to bottle or can drugs. For the first time, retailers could not see the contents of the packages they sold to consumers, and consumers could not see the contents until they ate the food or consumed the drugs. Naturally, consumers began demanding that food and drugs be clean and accurately labeled. However, not all businesses complied with this understandable wish; food and drug acts had to be passed to regulate all producers. Yet business fought these laws.

Again, corporations pioneered in developing mass-production techniques early in the twentieth century. Although these techniques brought enormous benefits to the public, they changed the lives of workers. Artisans and craftsmen were assigned to simple, monotonous, repetitive tasks that were but steps in the production of a finished product. When business was

333

unprepared to respond to the fears and dissatisfactions of employees, unions stepped in and took over, and legislators changed the laws to accommodate union organizers. Business fought these changes, too.

In the 1920s, as corporations grew, they solicited funds for growth from the public; millions of securities were sold, and the stock markets became a symbol of capitalism. Naturally, stock buyers wanted to rely on the statements and promises made about securities; they were helpless to check the assertions of dealers and issuers. When buyers were cheated by some firms, they demanded controls. Unprepared to cope with such demands, companies found themselves regulated by new laws concerning securities and by the Securities and Exchange Commission. Again business resisted.

In these and many other instances, Robert W. Austin points out, "business has refused to consider itself responsible to society for alleviating the social impact which business itself causes." By its refusal it virtually invites government to step in and devise ways and means to adjust to the changes.[1]

Today, corporations and other organizations are engaged in bringing about a new round of changes that affect the lives of employees and their families. As we saw earlier, they are demanding and training enormous numbers of technicians, professionals, specialists, and knowledge workers. These people are assigned to complex tasks and sophisticated equipment. Often they are asked to move repeatedly from one region and assignment to another, to adjust (with their families) to one great change after another. Many of them find themselves working with equipment that must be carefully designed and maintained or it will be dangerous, and the processes, materials, products, and services they produce may contain hidden hazards for users.

With all this increasing size, complexity, knowledge, mobility, and potential risk, there is no way that employees can remain comfortable with the authoritarian systems of the past. They want to be able to speak out, to object, to participate. Trained to do these things in school and college, they want to be free to do them in the workplace.

Once again, therefore, social change is resulting from the technological, structural, and procedural changes created by organizations. Will management take some responsibility for this development and devise ways to help employees and their families adjust and cope? Or will it repeat its old habit of letting outsiders step in and assume that responsibility?

There is a difference with the past, however. This time the stakes may be a little higher, for the questions are becoming more internal to manage-

---

[1] Robert W. Austin, "Responsibility for Social Change," *Harvard Business Review*, July–August 1965, p. 51.

ment. They are coming closer to the heart of management. Who runs the organization and how? Who shares power with whom? How should decision-making power be distributed? Questions like these are being asked. The issues they affect are terribly sensitive.

Looking ahead, one can imagine alternative scenarios as alike as life and death. In one scenario, corporations and other organizations become more open. Though working diligently to carry out the policies set by management, employees still feel free to speak out against wrongdoing and dangers when they see them, to call for more privacy rights and due process when they feel existing procedures are lacking, and to suggest new approaches to their work. Because their words and actions attract public attention to problems in their organizations, executives appear more often in the media, just as mayors, governors, and legislators do. The executives find themselves being praised, criticized, second-guessed, lionized, and maligned, just as their counterparts in public life are. Tempers sometimes run high in controversies over the acts of this power producer or that bank or that airline, but temperatures never reach the boiling point because the conflicts get out in the open as soon as discussion becomes serious.

In the other scenario, the situation is reversed. Here corporate and other organizational leaders are shadows in the background, hard to reach, hard to identify. They leave public contact to underlings and, increasingly, to computers that both write letters and simulate the human voice over the telephone. The sound of the whistle is rarely heard for there is unquestioning obedience to authority. If someone deviates or steps out of line, the pack turns against him or her. The atmosphere is quiet with totalitarian efficiency, and it is dark.

The second scenario leads to repressed public anger and impatience. Although this anger is ubiquitous, it is a waiting anger. It waits not for the opportunity to destroy physically (though it may erupt and do that from time to time), for that is deemed stupid, but for the opportunity to destroy politically. Finally the awaited time comes. A man on a white horse arrives on the national scene. In his campaign he appeals to all the repressed hates. Close down the dangerous plants—we can get along without them. Nationalize the profit-greedy giants. Break up the conglomerates that violate norms of human dignity. Flush the corpocrats out of their secret offices and put them on trial!

It's a Bonnie and Clyde style of economics that he preaches, and deep down it doesn't make much sense to Americans, for they know that no system of invention, production, and distribution has ever matched the efficiency of private enterprise. But nobody wants to question the demagogue's motives closely. People just want to get rid of the corporation as they know it, to show its leaders what they think of it. It has no chance against the rising tide of disenchantment, despite all its achievements. And so the demagogue wins at the polls, not in a close contest, but by a landslide.

THE PENTAGON OF LEGITIMACY

If management as we know it is to survive and prosper, it must be *legitimate*. The notion of legitimacy has received much less attention than it should. Until the mid-twentieth century there was little need to think much about legitimacy because it was conferred, in capitalist systems, by ownership and compliance with the law. Since World War II, however, the requirements of legitimacy have been changing. For all organizations, and especially for the corporation, it no longer is the simple proprietary and legal proposition that it used to be.

What is legitimacy? Generally speaking, it is a term used to denote the acceptability and "rightness" of leaders in the minds of followers and the public. It has to do with whether the leaders' power and manner of exercising power is seen as appropriate, desirable, justifiable, and defensible. Legitimacy, though not so precise as legality, and though its effects—or, rather, the effects of its absence—are not swift and clear, is a powerful quality. Many kings who were overthrown held power legally but their rule was illegitimate, in the minds of the people, because it was perceived as cruel or inequitable. President Richard M. Nixon was forced to resign because in the public mind he had used his office illegitimately in covering up the Watergate affair. Later in the 1970s several top executives in industry were forced out of office on the grounds of illegitimate governance; they had been negligent in stopping payoffs, bribery, and other unacceptable practices.

The power of legitimacy is evident in another way. Leaders who acquire power by questionable means may make enormous efforts to justify their usurpation by legitimizing their rule. When Henry IV of England usurped the crown from Richard II, he and his son Prince Henry (who succeeded him as King Henry V) anguished over the illegitimacy of their administrations and sought to justify their accession by ruling more successfully and satisfactorily than Richard II had ruled. By the same token, dictators may try to provide the appearances of legitimacy by publishing detailed constitutions guaranteeing rights, checks, and balances, and by going through the motions of holding elections.

Now, just as the requirements of legitimacy are always changing for political office—a century ago few dictators would have felt constrained to publish constitutions—so do they change for corporate office and agency leadership. The requirements used to be met if the chief executive of a corporation was duly elected by the board, if the head of an agency was duly appointed by the president or the governor or the mayor, if the dean of a college was approved by the trustees. But the rightness of one's governance has become a more complex thing today. From its original shelter of simple legality, legitimacy has expanded into a pentagonal structure. Its five facets are as follows:

1. *The Organization's Leaders Must Be Visible and Accountable.* This long-familiar test in democratic government is finding its way into the corporate and public agency world. The public wants to know, or to be able to find out, who makes the decisions for your chemical company, bank, regulatory agency, or other organization; it wants those decision-makers to feel accountable to the people whose lives and well-being are affected by its actions.

For instance, in the Shea case, the directors apparently felt accountable to the people of Dallas when they dismissed their marketing star (or so it has been argued). Again, when Exxon in 1981 decided to get out of Libya, it did so in part because of popular indignation over the Gaddafi government; this was a way of demonstrating accountability to public opinion. Despite his high nasal voice, Frank Perdue personally advertises his chickens in radio commercials, making his leadership visible and, by his messages, showing how responsible he feels to the public about quality.

2. *Top Management Must Share Some of Its Decision-Making Power.* Wherever they work, most employees want a piece of the action. They want a hand in what goes on. Though gladly leaving the rarefied air of financial policy, market strategy, and so on to top management, at ground level they want to influence the way their jobs are done. It doesn't matter how efficient the system is; if they don't have a share in controlling it, they are dissatisfied with management. Making employees feel powerless is one of the surest roads to illegitimacy.

At a practical level, this requirement means that as a manager you inform your subordinates about conditions, problems, and plans that will affect their work and working relationships. It means that if your company is developing a new material that will affect quality, you tell your quality-control inspector about it in advance. It means that you give the people assigned to a work area some control over the materials, money, and other resources they need to do their jobs. Also, you must let them influence the plans and programs for their work. And it means that you give them some discretion to innovate, so that when something different needs to be done, they don't always have to chase up and down the hierarchy for approval carrying requisition forms in triplicate, wearying so much that finally they decide it is better to do nothing at all. Some employees will have modest "slush funds" to draw from; others will have discretion to order supplies and equipment up to a certain amount; some will have authority to plan their own trips, within limits; others will have the power to make and sign contracts of certain types; and so on. Many varied ways of power-sharing have been documented in numerous articles, books, and training programs.

The day of the programmed human being is fading as robots take over the programmable jobs. "Slaves are the most inefficient form of labor ever devised by man," notes David C. McClelland. "If a leader wants to have far-reaching influence, he must make his followers feel powerful and able to accomplish things on their own." [2]

3. *The Organization Must Act by and Large in a Rational Manner.* Your store is not entitled to close on Tuesday at the whim of management; your airline is not entitled to call off its flights to Knoxville without notice because management suddenly gets sick of that route; a state commission is not entitled on the spur of the moment and for no good reason to cancel summer vacations for employees; as a department head you are not entitled to depart from a policy of promotion from within because you have taken a shine to an outsider you happened to meet.

Rationality is related to power-sharing because it affords subordinates a means of anticipating decisions and planning their work around them. Also, as a discipline it tends to increase accountability.

4. *Management Must Act in an Ethical Manner.* Your law-enforcement agency is not entitled to violate standards of common decency or privacy in its zeal to get evidence on law violators; the heads of your company are not free to allow supervisors down the line to defame an employee they happen not to like; your oil company is not free to bribe environmentalists to keep quiet about the pollution from offshore drilling rigs; a manufacturer has no license to fudge data on test results of a new product.

In prior chapters of this book, some of the accounts of employee discharge and discipline strike most people as unethical and egregious. In generations past, too, such accounts might have struck Americans as unethical, but many people then would have sighed with resignation and said "Well, that's our lot." Today they bristle more. They ask, "What's wrong with that management?" They think about inviting union organizers in, or telling the story to the press, or organizing a boycott, or writing their senator, or sending a delegation to protest to the chief executive. In one way or another they will get back at the manager or management that has not lived up to their ideas of rightness.

---

[2] David C. McClelland, *Power: The Inner Experience* (New York: Irvington, 1975), p. 263.

5. *Management Must Act in an Equitable Manner Toward Employees, Suppliers, and Customers.* You are not entitled to fire an assistant without just cause (whatever the law may say about your prerogatives to hire and fire). You are not free to favor redheads at the expense of blondes, or pay different amounts for identical materials to suppliers because of personal friendship, or refuse to answer customers' questions or deal with their protests, or charge unconscionable fees and interest rates when the traffic will bear them. Perhaps most important, this test means that in conflicts over the fairness of some action you have taken that affects an employee's well-being, the employee is able to defend himself or herself in a prompt and fair hearing. In other words—and this is the main point—your people may judge the fairness of your management as much by the existence and effectiveness of mechanisms that you support for resolving conflicts as by the quality of the decisions you make and the policies you pursue.

What is the relationship between the concept of organization rights, as proposed in the preceding chapter, and legitimacy, as described in this section? The relationship could be as simple as this: Intuitively Americans have come to accept the superbeing quality of corporations and agencies. In their reactions, if not in their ideology, a great many people treat the power company, the steel company, the auto manufacturer as if it were an animated, independent force different from the individuals who compose it. In consequence, they have found it natural to place obligations on organizations. Like individuals who, using their power and position to affect other people, must behave responsibly in so doing, organizations must meet certain norms and expectations when they alter people's lives.

NEVER UNDERESTIMATE THE POWER OF A FOLLOWER

Years ago the *Ladies' Home Journal* used to advertise with the slogan, "Never underestimate the power of a woman." It became the subject of many jokes in men's magazines and locker-room talk, for the "power of a woman" at that time was subtle and indirect. During the past two decades, however, the joke has worn thin as female power has asserted itself politically and economically.

If there is a test of the difference between wise and not-so-wise managers today, it might be reactions to the line, "Never underestimate the power of a follower." Some administrators dismiss the idea; others take it seriously. The future belongs to the second group. This is the group that understands the importance of legitimacy.

Granted, if your corporation or agency exercises its power illegitimately, you are unlikely to pay a swift penalty. Your employees and the public may not vent their anger for some time. You may be able to delude yourself into thinking, therefore, that you can suspend the five tests of legitimacy without suffering retribution. This is where you are wrong. Only for a while can you and your successors avoid paying the price.

For instance, thousands of executives are troubled and incensed over the low ratings business gets in public opinion polls. If you study a report prepared by an organization like Gallup, Opinion Research, or Yankelovich–Skelly–White, however, you can soon detect at least one of the reasons for the dismal reactions. Too many respondents don't feel that business is meeting the criteria of accountability and ethics.

Again, many leaders of agencies and companies are greatly disturbed over the apparent apathy and indifference of employees. "The work ethic has disappeared," they say. But if you review the employee-opinion surveys conducted for organizations by knowledgeable consultants, you will soon detect a major cause of the disenchantment: In almost every case, the employees feel they are treated like pawns, and they are bitter that they are not brought in on decisions they think they know something about. In other words, the organization flunks the criterion of power-sharing.

In Michigan, where a "just discharge" statute has been passed, and in other states where legislators are seriously considering such a statute, company officials decry this newest legislative intrusion on their prerogatives. But you will not have to study the history of the legislative debates long to learn that the public has become impatient and incensed over cases of abusive discharge reported in the media. In other words, the fifth criterion of legitimacy has been failed.

In short, many organizations have been getting poor marks on their legitimacy tests, and public reaction is beginning to hurt. Although public reaction was slow in forming, its strength and impact are becoming quite visible.

Still another reason for not underestimating the power of followers is the work of professional associations such as the Institute of Electrical and Electronics Engineers, the American Chemical Society, the American Association for the Advancement of Science, and others. All over the country, local chapters and headquarters offices have been discussing and writing codes of conduct for those of their members who are employees of agencies and companies; they are pressing organizations to recognize certain ethical obligations; they are supporting members who get into trouble with employers because of disputed concerns for the public interest (the BART case, for instance). In a polite exercise of countervailing power, these organizations are bidding for professional loyalties in order to establish new standards of legitimacy.

But perhaps the most devastating example of all is public reaction to the agencies of big government. To be sure, the backlash that became visible in the late 1970s and in the election of 1980 was due in substantial part to high taxes. But do not discount the effect of illegitimacy, or, more accurately, what was perceived as illegitimacy. After many years of watching state and federal administrators disregard the tests of accountability, participation, ethics, and equity, the public struck back in anger. It was sick of agencies that seemed to spend more time administering themselves than serving a public need. It was disillusioned by reports of wasteful spending. It was turned off by too many second-rate Robert Moses types in state and federal administration, officials who, without the compensating brilliance of New York's famous urban planner, imitated his arrogant ways and disdain of voters and legislators.[3]

In much of the public mind, a different notion of what is a good organizational atmosphere has been developing. At the risk of stereotyping, it seems fair to say that the management community lags behind the public in accepting this notion (presumably because managers find the idea threatening and inconvenient). This is the notion that discord in the workplace, as in rock music and pop, can be a good thing. As Joe Kelly pointed out over a decade ago,[4] most Americans no longer see conflict as an evil produced by troublemakers, boat-rockers, and dissidents; they see it as a function of individualism, economic problems, and the environment. No longer do they see conflict as avoidable; they regard it as inevitable, and a minimal level of it as natural and useful. As Kelly argued,

The modern organizational revolution has been characterized by an acceleration of healthy subversive tendencies which gathered force and speed in the 1960s in protest against the brittle iron law of corporate oligarchy; a protest against the presumption that, in organizations, policies and instructions flow down the hierarchy and reports flow up.

It is a protest against the cozy paternalistic world of classical management theory where top management carries total responsibility. It is a protest exemplified by the success of *The Peter Principle* which was on the best seller lists for many months. It is increasingly a middle-class

---

[3] See Robert A. Caro, *The Power Broker* (New York: Random House, 1978).
[4] Joe Kelly, "Make Conflict Work for You," *Harvard Business Review*, July–August 1970, p. 103.

protest by executives and professionals, and decreasingly a protest from a diminishing shop floor.[5]

Kelly went on to discuss evidence that "an environment devoid of novelty can be unbearable to human subjects" and that some uncertainty and some anxiety are not only acceptable to most people but desired:

> Ethologists like Konrad Lorenz are bringing forward persuasive evidence that controlled aggression has survival value; that although dominance ultimately depends on force, it leads to law and order. Lorenz has argued that aggression is a function of normal selection and produces an increased expectation of survival; further aggression brings about a dispersal of individuals. Lorenz, who has observed animals in their natural habitats, believes that fighting may generate a stable "pecking order." Much the same discussion can be repeated about our own society, which is learning to allow dissent but not unlimited dissent.
>
> Aggression, apparently an essential characteristic of executives, makes many managers miserable with guilt. Adopting an "attack ethos" usually stands an executive in good stead, but it is aggression moderated by a need to maintain social acceptability.
>
> Conflict management recognizes that executives have aggressions to expend, can withstand a fair amount of anxiety, and welcome uncertainty as an opportunity to restructure their environment. Hence the way conflict is *managed*—rather than suppressed, ignored, or avoided—contributes significantly to a company's effectiveness.[6]

The way conflict is managed also contributes to the perception of legitimacy held by employees, customers, and the public. When there is conflict between your company or agency and an employee or public need, do you come out in the open and argue the merits of your side of the case? Do you encourage people in your organization to help in the making of as many decisions as is reasonable, despite the likelihood of conflict? Do you and your subordinates endeavor to meet the tasks of rationality, ethics, and fairness in administration, so that conflict can be discussed openly and without prejudice to those who disagree with you?

Your actions translate first into impressions and opinions among those concerned. For a while, nothing visible may happen. But this is only the

[5] Ibid., p. 104.
[6] Ibid.

illusion of delay. Subjectivity becomes objectivity. The impressions and opinions become translated into actions of support, neutrality, or hostility. The "subjective meaning-complex of action," as sociologist Max Weber called it, sooner or later emerges into a tangible, visible fact or part of an event that is as real as your initial action.

WHAT CAN YOUR ORGANIZATION DO FOR AMERICA?

The Founding Fathers were concerned less with governmental forms and economic theories than with human nature; they sought a believable alternative to the grim choice that despots had given humankind. The dream of the Constitutional Convention was a dream of change—more than that, a dream of continuing change. *Revolution* was a word to be spoken with pride. *Dissent* was a word deserving dignity and respect. Freedom was not something to be stored in pine chests or in glass cases in museums, but a concept to be used and experimented with and batted around. *No* authority—no state or federal government, no church, no political party, no leader—had the right to define freedom for anyone else. The courts and lawmakers could define it temporarily, but only temporarily; they were to be forever subject to challenge and revision.

It was no accident that the intensely religious people who adopted the Constitution and the Bill of Rights saw man as a communicator. "In the beginning was the word" opens the Gospel according to John. God's first act was to rid the world of silence. Silence isolates. Speech, even dissenting or contradictory speech, preserves contact. The heart of darkness is non-speech, the unspoken feeling, the uncommunicated observation. "First the Nazis came for the communists and I didn't speak up because I wasn't a communist," pastor Martin Niemoller is supposed to have said. "Then they came for the Jews and I didn't speak up because I wasn't a Jew. When they came for the trade unionists, I didn't speak up because I wasn't a trade unionist. And when they came for the Catholics I didn't speak up because I was a Protestant. Then they came for me. And by that time there was no one left to speak up for anyone."

But a funny thing happened on the way to freedom. Whereas federal and state government officials were the only major oppressors of civil liberties when the republic was founded in 1789, in the nineteenth and twentieth centuries they became just *one* group of potential oppressors. Alongside them came to stand new legions of officials with the power to destroy a person's freedoms. These were the officials of corporations and other corporate-like organizations that proliferated as the economy expanded.

So the nation that was divided by slavery and reunited by Lincoln came to be divided against itself once again as corporations came into their own. Inside the plants and offices of these corporations the kinds of rights specified in the Bill of Rights were carefully omitted. The corporations were private property; they were their owners' castles. Accordingly, no right was created for employees to speak out, write about wrongdoing or irresponsibility, object to an immoral or unethical order from a superior, engage in outside activities of their own choosing, enjoy privacy, or have a prompt and fair hearing when wronged.

In short, the executives of corporate governments, as they evolved in the twentieth century, had the right to be autocratic and dictatorial. For a long time almost all executives of federal and state agencies enjoyed a similar prerogative. Fortunately for many employees, not all corporate and agency executives exercised their prerogatives. Like benign rulers of old, some of them voluntarily instituted codes and procedures to protect the dignity of all their workers.

Gradually inroads were made on the prerogatives of organization leaders. America began to perceive an important difference between a person's prerogative to run his or her home and the prerogative to run an organization in which a multitude of unrelated people might spend their working lives. In the federal government, civil service was instituted to protect agency employees. In the 1920s and 1930s, labor unions came of age in the corporation. In the 1960s and 1970s, laws protecting minority-group employees and female employees were enacted.

But for many thoughtful organization leaders these statutes did not go far enough. Though recognizing that the Bill of Rights could not be extended literally to corporate and agency employees, they realized that the *kinds* of rights expressed in the Bill of Rights are applicable to the workplace and needed by employees. They began innovating in four ways.

First, a human being does not become a worker—like a robot or computer—once working hours start. The human being stays human. To repeat the manager's remark in Max Frisch's play, quoted in the beginning of this book, "We hired workers and human beings came instead." If it is important to treat a person with dignity as a political and social citizen, it is important to treat him or her with dignity as an economic citizen. If dignity means rights to speech, privacy, conscience, and due process in the community, it means that also in the plant and office building.

And so companies like Lincoln Electric, Bank of America, Donnelly Mirrors, Pitney Bowes, Puget Sound Plywood, Polaroid, and IBM began experimenting with organizational equivalents of the rights guaranteed in the Constitution. In so doing, they went far beyond the measures set forth in the Civil Rights Act of 1964 and the equal employment opportunity statutes of the 1970s. Sometimes, in fact, they went beyond any applications of the Bill of Rights to political and social life.

Second, some organization leaders felt that it was managerially advantageous to establish employee rights and limit superiors' prerogatives. Although most bosses might be fair and well intentioned, not all are, and those who are not can make a person miserable, even ruin a career. Moreover, the finest boss is liable to deal unfairly with a subordinate when having a bad day or feeling inordinate pressure to get results. In short, some organization leaders saw that the quality of management can be improved if a manager's prerogatives are limited and a subordinate's rights are expanded. Managers need the discipline; management power needs the counterbalance.

Third, rights-minded top executives saw civil liberties as a kind of organizational tonic. An abusive discharge or demotion has a chain effect. The tragedy of the persecuted employee objector, they saw, is the silence that falls all around afterward, like the gloom of night overtaking a forest. "If the boss won't like it, keep it to yourself," the brooding organization whispers to the would-be dissident. "A closed mouth catches no flies." "You can only improve on saying nothing by saying nothing often." "Don't rock the boat." And so when the next would-be critic perceives a breach of ethics or the law, he or she discreetly looks the other way or swallows the whistle. The worst tragedy is not what happens to the whistleblower, devastating as that may be—the loss in income, the rupture of a career, the emotional turmoil. It is what happens to would-be whistleblowers, the collective decision of other employees to remain silent. It is the buttoned-up, buttoned-down, uptight, self-inhibited, guilty atmosphere of a factory or office policed by the belief that to get along one must go along.

Fourth, these organization leaders saw in employee rights expansion a magnificent opportunity to strengthen society and, through that strengthening, improve organizations. Organizations and society operate in a yin-yang relationship. Society is not over here, the corporation or agency over there. Society *is* the organization, and the organization *is* society. If I learn to be dishonest in my organization, chances are I will become dishonest in my community. If you are irresponsible in your community, chances are you will be irresponsible in your employer organization. Farsighted organization leaders sensed that every time a corporation pollutes society, it pollutes itself. Every time it disillusions an employee by winking at dishonesty, or sickens an employee because scabrous treatment must be observed silently without protest, or corrupts an employee by compelling him or her to accept intrusions, invasions of privacy, or complicity in deception, it poisons the well from which it must drink in the future.

These leaders saw, in other words, that there is more to the much-discussed notions of corporate social responsibility than financial contributions to the arts, technical help for minority businesses, donations to education, and similar grants, important and indispensable as they are. Perhaps the most valuable contribution of all that an organization can make to the public interest is to train employees in such traditional American values as individualism, respect for others' rights, and the dignity of the individual.

At a large midwestern bank, I talked with a young man who had criticized some slipshod and possibly dishonest practices in the department where he had served as an accountant. He was earnest, intelligent, and loyal; he had made no "waves" about the wrongdoing but had gone dutifully up the line to the assistant manager. For his pains and conscientiousness he was fired by an angry boss. He appealed to a section of the personnel department that had been set up to investigate such cases. The investigator—the kind of troubleshooter often referred to as an ombudsperson—listened to him and then his boss, set up an informal hearing, saved his job for him, and arranged for his transfer to another section. There he has since prospered. On the other hand, the abusive manager, apparently unable to change his ways, left the organization.

This young man has had a heartening experience with the practice, values, and realities of free speech that he will not forget as long as he lives. The experience will serve him invaluably as a citizen and voter. His employer organization has served America in the highest possible way.

> In our country, we have those three unspeakably precious things: freedom of speech, freedom of conscience, and the prudence never to practice either.
>
> MARK TWAIN

APPENDIX:
A SAMPLING OF
JUDICIAL OPINION

═══ The excerpts from appellate court decisions that follow show how some judges view employee rights and civil liberties. These excerpts are not intended to represent the strength and following of different judicial attitudes, only different approaches taken by judges during the past decade. In view of the fact that in 1969 there was only a glimmer of diversity in this area—principally the U.S. Supreme Court's *Pickering* decision and the California Supreme Court's *Petermann* decision—the variety of opinion that exists today is remarkable.

Bear in mind that the opinions reported here are interpretations of the law, not of the facts (which are left to trial courts to decide). Indeed, to get at the legal issues more quickly judges may take for granted, for purposes of the opinion rendered, a plaintiff's or defendant's allegations of fact, concentrating on what the law should be *if* the allegations can be supported when the case is returned to a trial court for argument.

For the sake of simplicity, footnotes are omitted from the excerpts.

Martin v. Platt
386 N.E. 2d 1026
Court of Appeals of Indiana, Third District, 1979

This court's opinion, which some observers might unceremoniously call the "middle ages" view, reflects the venerable notion that, as a judge once put it, an employee can be be fired "for cause, for no cause, or for cause morally wrong." Although during the past decade this view has been subjected to many inroads and attacks, it is still strong in many state courts, especially in corporate cases. The bulk of the Indiana court's opinion follows.

Gerald Martin and Keith Niemann (employees) brought this action against their former employer, the Magnavox Company (Magnavox) claiming retaliatory discharge. Joined as individual defendants were Alfred di Scipio and Robert Platt (officers) who were the vice president and president of Magnavox. . . .

The record reveals the following background. The employees were executives with Magnavox. Di Scipio was their immediate superior, and Platt was di Scipio's superior. Both employees were employees at will. In 1974 they reported to Platt information that di Scipio was soliciting and receiving "kickback" payments from Magnavox suppliers. After Magnavox investigated the charges, no action was taken against the officers. However, the employees were discharged.

The employees maintain that the officers intentionally and maliciously caused Magnavox to discharge them in retaliation for truthfully reporting the kickbacks and to suppress the information they had obtained.

I. Interference with Business Relationship

The employees contend they have a claim against the officers individually on the ground that they tortiously interfered in the employment relation between the employees and Magnavox.

Indiana has long recognized that an action will lie for an unjustifiable interference with the contractual and prospectively advantageous business relationship one enjoys with another. *Daly v. Nau* (1975), Ind.App, 339 N.E.2d 71; *Kiyose v. Trustees of Indiana University* (1975), Ind.App., 333 N.E.2d 886; *Fort Wayne Cleaners & Dyers Assoc., Inc. v Price* (1956), 127 Ind.App. 13, 137 N.E.2d 738.

[1,2] However, such an action involves the intervention of a third party. *Geary v. United States Steel Corp.* (1974), 456 Pa. 171, 319 A.2d 174. It will not lie against a party to the contract. *Daly, supra; Kiyose, supra;* Prosser, *Torts,* § 129 (4th Ed. 1971). In addition, an officer or director of a corporation will not be held independently personally liable for inducing the corporation's breach of its contract, if the officer or director's action is within the scope of his official duties on behalf of the corporation. *Daly, supra; Kiyose, supra. See also H. F. Phillipsborn & Co. v. Suson* (1974), 59 Ill.2d

465, 322 N.E.2d 45; *Widger v. Central School Dist. No. 1* (1964), 20 A.D.2d 296, 247 N.Y.S.2d 364.

[3] In the present case it is undisputed that Platt and di Scipio were the supervisors of Martin and Niemann. It is uncontroverted that the decision to hire and fire executive level employees at Magnavox rested with the employee's immediate superior. The discharges were within the scope of the duties of Platt and di Scipio, and no action will lie against them on the theory of interference with a contractual relationship. The trial court correctly held the officers were entitled to judgment as a matter of law.

II. Retaliatory Discharge

[4] The employees also contend that they had a cognizable legal claim that their employment was terminated in retaliation for their truthful reporting of di Scipio's improper activities. The issue we face is whether an employee at will can maintain an action for retaliatory discharge.

[5] The general rule and great weight of authority is that where the duration of the employment cannot be determined from the terms of the contract, the contract is at will and either party may terminate it with or without cause at any time in the absence of contractual limitations. *Pearson v. Youngstown Sheet & Tube Co.* (7th Cir. 1964), 332 F.2d 439; *Speeder Cycle Co. v. Teeter* (1897), 18 Ind.App. 474, 48 N.E. 595.

An exception exists, of course, where an applicable statute prohibits discharge for a specified reason. *See, e. g., Phelps Dodge Corp v. N.L.R.B.* (1941), 313 U.S. 177, 61 S.Ct. 845, 85 L.Ed. 1271, 133 A.L.R. 1217.

In *Frampton v. Central Ind. Gas Co.* (1973), 260 Ind. 249, 297 N.E.2d 425 our Supreme Court found that such a discharge would be precluded where the reason was to punish the employee and dissuade other employees from claiming Workmen's Compensation benefits. The court termed such a discharge a "device" within the meaning of IC 22-3-2-15 prohibiting employers from avoiding their obligations under the Workmen's Compensation Act.

A few cases have extended the prohibition to situations where the employee was discharged for complying with a statutory duty. *See Nees v. Hocks* (1975), 272 Or. 210, 536 P.2d 512 (performing jury service); *Petermann v. Int'l. Bro. of Teamsters* (1959), 174 Cal.App.2d 184, 344 P.2d 25 (refusing to commit perjury).

Two cases have considered the issue on broad public policy grounds. In *Geary v. United States Steel Corp.* (1974), 456 Pa. 171, 319 A.2d 174 the Pennsylvania Supreme Court in a divided opinion refused to permit an action for retaliatory discharge by a former at-will employee who asserted he had been discharged for giving warnings concerning a company product he considered dangerous. Justice Roberts, dissenting, urged recognition of the social and economic desirability of enabling unorganized employees to rely upon a reasonable expectation of continued employment.

The same year in *Monge v. Beebe Rubber Co.* (1974), 114 N.H. 130, 316 A2d 549, the New Hampshire Supreme Court, with Justice Grimes dissenting, affirmed the right to such an action upon the ground of general public policy where a female employee alleged the reason for her discharge was her refusal to date her foreman.

Both decisions discuss the historical evolution of the concept of employment at will. We need not do so here. Nor do we dispute the lack of utility in an employer discharging a faithful capable employee without reason.

The parties do not suggest, however, that it is our proper present function to outlaw employment contracts at will. The employees urge only that we declare unlawful a discharge under such a contract where the reason for the discharge is contrary to general public policy. Normally, of course, the determination of what constitutes public policy, or which of competing public policies should be given precedence, is a function of the legislature.

Even if we were to exercise our power in this regard, what would be the measure of actual damages? If the employment could be truly terminated at any time for no reason at all, how would one carry the burden of proving more than nominal damages? It appears to us that the practical remedy would come, then, from recovering punitive damages. Such damages are allowable for reasons of public policy. We would thus create an action based upon an undeclared public policy where the measure of damages was governed only by the same source. We decline the opportunity to do so. Such broad determinations should be left for the legislature.

Geary v. U.S. Steel Corporation
319 A. 2d 174
Supreme Court of Pennsylvania, 1974

George B. Geary's story appeared earlier in this book (chapter 4), including a brief description of the decision against him by Pennsylvania's highest court. Since 1974 the reasoning of Justice Samuel J. Roberts' dissent has gained favor in an ever-widening circle of state judges. Because of its persuasion, the dissent is reproduced almost in full below. For a short while only, the 4–3 decision against Geary represented, because of its closeness, the high-water mark in the state courts for employee civil liberties in corporations.

I cannot accept the view implicit in the majority's decision that today's jurisprudence is so lacking in awareness and vitality that our judicial process is incapable of affording relief to a responsible employee for an arbitrary and retaliatory discharge from employment. I dissent.

For fourteen years appellant George B. Geary served the United States Steel Corporation as a salesman. Abruptly, on July 13, 1967, he was summarily discharged without cause or notice. The majority now holds "that where the complaint itself discloses a plausible and legitimate reason for terminating an at-will employment relationship and no clear mandate of public policy is violated thereby, an employee at will has no right of action against his employer for wrongful discharge." I am unable to agree that this case presents only "a plausible and legitimate reason for terminating" Geary's employment or that "no clear mandate of public policy" has been violated.

In the particular circumstances of this case, appellant's discharge demonstrates the arbitrary dismissal power exercisable by an employer. The managers of this publicly-held corporation determined that George B. Geary should be dismissed because he called to the attention of his superiors that the steel pipe manufactured by his employer and which Geary was required to sell was a defective and dangerous product. His suggestion that the unsafe steel pipe be withdrawn from the market to protect both the public from danger and his employer from liability was in complete harmony with his employer's best interest. Nevertheless, Geary was discharged.

As a salesman, Geary was required to know intimately the products he was selling. He represented United States Steel and it was expected that he would be alert to protect his employer's reputation. Likewise, it was natural that he would seek to shield himself and his employer from the consequences of a dangerous product. When he correctly recognized that the defective steel pipe had strong potential for causing injury and damage, he immediately notified his superiors. His reward for loyalty was dismissal. Of course, had Geary not informed his superiors of the defective product, he may well have been discharged for his failure to do so.

Geary's assessment of the danger of the steel pipe was correct, since after his notification, the corporation removed the steel pipe from the market. On these pleadings, it is manifestly clear that the employer realized Geary was right and that its interest lay in withdrawing from the market the dangerous product. Despite Geary's candor in seeking within the corporate family to advance the corporation's best interest, his employer fired him.

There is no doubt that strong public policies of this Commonwealth have been offended by Geary's discharge. First, the product asserted by appellant to be defective was, after appellant notified his supervisors, withdrawn from the market. The manufacturer and distribution of defective and potentially dangerous products does not serve either the public's or the employer's interest. Our courts have granted relief to those injured by defective merchandise. E. g., Kassab v. Central Soya, 432 Pa. 217, 246 A.2d 848 (1968); Webb v. Zern, 422 Pa. 424, 220 A.2d 853 (1966). See Restatement (Second) of Torts § 402A (1965). The majority, however, fails to perceive that the prevention of injury is a fundamental and highly desirable objective of our society.

Second, appellant as an employee was "subject to a duty to use reasonable efforts to give his [employer] information which is relevant to affairs entrusted to him, and which, as the [employee] has notice, the [employer] would desire to have and which can be communicated without violating a superior duty to a third person." Restatement (Second) of Agency § 381 (1958). Had Geary refrained from notifying his superiors of the defective product, he could have been discharged for violating this duty to come forward with information. No responsible policy is served which permits an employee to be discharged solely for obeying his legal duty to communicate information to his superiors. Indeed, the policy underlying this duty to communicate is frustrated by denying Geary the opportunity to present his case to the court.

The majority admits, as it must, that precedents barring a cause of action for wrongful discharge are "scant" and that "economic conditions have changed radically" since the date of the only Pennsylvania case on point. Henry v. Pittsburgh & L. E. R. R., 139 Pa. 289, 21 A. 157 (1891). Unlike the majority, I believe the time has surely come to afford unorganized employees an opportunity to prove in court a claim for arbitrary and retaliatory discharge.

The majority concedes the employment relationship is a proper subject for judicial action. Still, it refuses to afford Geary the opportunity to establish his claim of wrongful discharge. The majority justifies its refusal to act by assuming that to recognize a cause of action on the facts alleged will unleash "an increased case load and . . . thorny problems of proof," and by further assuming that these problems will plague our judicial system. The majority's thinking is nothing more than an unarticulated fear of the mythological Pandora's box. Not only are both assumptions unwarranted, but the majority fails to perceive the realities of twentieth century industrial organization. The reality is that recognizing a cause of action for wrongful discharge in these circumstances will help to check a serious menace in our society, the arbitrary dismissal power of employers.

The genius of the common law is that the case-by-case analysis permits opening and closing of the doors to the courtroom.

> [I]n view of the fact that, from the day Magna Charta was signed to the present moment, amendments to the structure of the law have been made with increasing frequency, it is impossible to suppose that they will not continue, and the law be forced to adapt itself to new conditions of society, and particularly, to the new relations between employers and employes, as they arise.

Holden v. Hardy, 169 U.S. 366, 387, 18 S. Ct. 383, 386, 42 L.Ed. 780 (1898). In my judgment, the assertion that appellant should be denied relief because his case represents the opening wedge of a theory which might produce further litigation is an inappropriate judicial consideration. Niederman v. Brodsky, 436 Pa. 401, 412-413, 261 A2d 84, 89 (1970).

It would, however, be misleading to imply that docket considerations alone account for the majority's reticence. "Of greater concern [to the majority] is the possible impact of such suits on the legitimate interest of employers in hiring and retaining the best personnel available." The instant case itself illustrates the fallacy of this argument. If the existence of the tort of wrongful discharge in these circumstances (assuming, as we must, the truth of all facts alleged) will keep employees like George Geary on corporate payrolls, both the employer's and the public's interest will have been served. Affording relief for arbitrary and retaliatory discharge in no way impinges upon the employer's right to discharge for cause. That difficult line-drawing may be involved is of no great moment, since courts are daily confronted with the task of separating wheat from chaff.

As Professor Lawrence E. Blades has noted, "[t]he industrial revolution made an anachronism of the absolute right of discharge by destroying the classical ideal of complete freedom of contract upon which it is based." Blades, Employment at Will vs. Individual Freedom: On Limiting the Abusive Exercise of Employer Power, 67 Colum.L.Rev. 1404, 1418 (1967). Further, although a single nineteenth-century Pennsylvania case stated that an employer can dismiss an employee with or without cause, it does not necessarily follow that this right is absolute and unrestrained. "[T]he word 'right' is one of the most deceptive of pitfalls; it is so easy to slip from a quality meaning in the premise to an unqualified one in the conclusion. Most rights are qualified." American Bank & Trust Co. v. Federal Reserve Bank, 256 U.S. 350, 358, 41 S.Ct. 499, 500, 65 L.Ed. 983 (1921) (Holmes, J.).

It is public policy which here qualifies the "right." See id. at 359, 41 S.Ct. at 501. When a seemingly-absolute right or the conditions of an existing relationship are contrary to public policy then a court is obligated to qualify that right in light of current reality. See Burne v. Franklin Life Insurance Co., 451 Pa. 218, 301 A.2d 799 (1973). Here, the employment relationship, as the majority and Geary's employer view it, clashes with the public's interest in keeping dangerous products from being sold and used.

The Supreme Court of Indiana has recently provided a discharged employee an opportunity to prove a claim for wrongful and relatiatory discharge. Frampton v. Central Indiana Gas Co., 297 N.E.2d 425 (Ind. 1973). There, the plaintiff was dismissed after she filed a claim for workmen's compensation. The Indiana court observed that "[i]f employers are permitted to penalize employees for filing workmen's compensation claims, a most important public policy will be undermined" 297 N.E.2d at 427. A California court similarly recognized a cause of action for wrongful discharge where the employee had been dismissed after he refused to commit perjury. Petermann v. Teamsters Union, 174 Cal.App.2d 184, 344 P.2d 25 (1959).

The principle underlying these decisions should apply to the present case. Contrary to the majority's assertion, society's interest in protecting itself from dangerous products manifestly presents a mandate to the court to recognize a cause of action for wrongful discharge. That a loyal and responsible employee should be summarily and without cause or notice discharged for complying with his duty to communicate relevant information to his superiors provides further justification for affording appellant an opportunity to present his claim. That appellant was discharged without cause for doing that which, had he failed to do, he would have been subject to dismissal with cause amply demonstrates the illogic of the majority's refusal to recognize in these circumstances a cause of action for wrongful discharge.

Our society has long been apprehensive of the arbitrary dismissal power of employers, and has sought through various solutions to remedy the problem. To countervail employers' dismissal power, unions were created. Congress has sought to safeguard certain classes of employees from wrongful and capricious discharges. And our Legislature has decided that certain state employees must be guarded from the abuses of arbitrary discharge.

Yet, under the majority's view, unorganized employees remain unprotected. Here, Geary's discharge is directly contrary to the societal interest in preventing injury due to defectively-manufactured products. See Restatement (Second) of Torts § 402A (1965). Moreover, Geary was dismissed for simply fulfilling his duty to notify his superiors of a potentially dangerous situation. See Restatement (Second) of Agency § 381 (1958). The majority, however, refuses to recognize a cause of action in these particular circumstances. In my view, this Court should take this first step and protect Geary and unorganized employees from arbitrary and retaliatory discharges.

"The judiciary has not been reluctant to expand the meaning of constitutional provisions in order to protect the individual from governmental oppression. It is something of a paradox that the courts have so far displayed no similar bent for invention and improvisation when it comes to protecting individuals, particularly in their highly vulnerable status as employees, from the private establishments upon which they are becoming increasingly dependent. Instead, there has been a blind acceptance of the employer's absolute right of discharge. This outmoded doctrine has been supported by technical principles of contract law." Blades, Employment at Will vs. Individual Freedom: On Limiting the Abusive Exercise of Employer Power, 67 Colum.L.Rev. 1404, 1435 (1967).

Courts are duty-bound to fashion remedies for the changing circumstances of economic and social reality. And it is far too late in the day for this Court to indulge itself by fictionalizing that the doctrine of freedom of contract justifies insulation of an employer's arbitrary and abusive exercise of his power of discharge.

The majority concedes, as it must, that tort law is uniquely suited for judicial action. Further, it cannot be denied that prevention of injuries is a substantial, clear, and compelling objective of our society. See Restatement (Second) of Torts § 402A (1965); cf. Restatement (Second) of Agency § 381 (1958).

This Court should, in my view, fulfill its societal role and its responsibility to the public interest by recognizing a cause of action for wrongful discharge where the dismissal offends public policy. George B. Geary has presented just such a case.

Holodnak v. Avco Corporation

514 F. 2d 285
U.S. District Court, Connecticut, 1975

Seeking restitution for loss of his job in Avco's Avco–Lycoming Division, Michael Holodnak first went to arbitration. When, as noted in Chapter 3, he lost in that hearing, Holodnak appealed to the U.S. District Court. As the following portions of the lengthy decision indicate, the court decided that Holodnak's Constitutional rights had been infringed. The opinion is illuminating not only for its reasoning but also for its references to Federal court decisions in cases concerning employees of government and other public organizations. This was the first decision rendered by a Federal or state court in favor of a corporate whistleblower. Portions of the opinion follow.

At the time of the plaintiff's discharge, the Avco plant in Stratford was owned by the government, as was virtually all the machinery and the land upon which it was located. Military personnel were present at all times to guarantee quality control of the plant's output. Eighty percent of the production of the plant was in the form of military hardware: nose cones for missiles, helicopter engines, and constant speed drives for fighter planes. The plant in Stratford as well as one in South Carolina is part of the Avco-Lycoming Division of the Avco Corporation, a widely diversified conglomerate . . .

Here we are concerned with substantial governmental involvement at Avco's Stratford plant. The fact that Avco-Lycoming Division also operated a second plant in South Carolina engaged in other production and is part of a far-flung conglomerate does not alter the conclusion that there is governmental action. The right here involves the basic right of freedom of speech and press and the firing of Holodnak for expressing his views is "offensive." See *Wahba, supra,* 492 F.2d at 102. For present purposes, the court concludes that there was sufficient governmental action for the First Amendment to apply.

In light of this governmental presence, the plaintiff's discharge for writing an article must be analyzed to determine if First Amendment rights have been infringed. The First Amendment does not guarantee an absolute right of free speech. Concerning discharges of public employees, the Supreme Court has held that the interest of the employee in free speech must be balanced against the employer's interest in job efficiency. *Pickering* v. *Board of Education,* 391 U.S. 563, 568 (1968). See also *Linn* v. *Plant Guards, Local 114,* 383 U.S. 53 (1963).

Both the company and the union claim that precedents have already resolved this balance adversely to Holodnak. The company places particular emphasis on the Supreme Court's decision in *Arnett* v. *Kennedy,* 42 U.S.L.W. 4513 (April 16, 1974). While in *Arnett* the court upheld the discharge of a civil service employee pursuant to a statute authorizing discharges of civil servants for "such cause as will promote the efficiency of the service," 5 U.S.C. § 7501 (1970), it made clear that it was only deciding that the statute was not overbroad on its face. Noting that the statute did not reach "constitutionally protected speech," the plurality opinion by Mr. Justice Rehnquist placed particular emphasis on the fact that the discharged employee had not been discharged for protected speech, but for making recklessly false and defamatory statements that another civil servant, whom he had named, had taken a bribe.

The union relies on cases upholding discharges of teachers who made statements which were potentially disruptive of classroom activities. See, e.g., *Birdwell* v. *Hazelwood School District*, 352 F. Supp. 613. (E.D.MO. 1972), *aff'd*, 491 F.2d 490 (8th Cir. 1974).

The situation here is markedly different from both *Arnett* and *Birdwell*. Unlike *Arnett* Holodnak never accused anyone of illegal activity and has not identified those individuals who, he believed, had not acted in the best interests of the workers. Indeed throughout the grievance and arbitration proceedings Holodnak has evidenced great reluctance to disclose the identities of those he had in mind in writing the article. In no way can Holodnak's comments, constitutionally speaking, be said to be of and concerning any particular individual. *New York Times Co.* v. *Sullivan*, 376 U.S. 254, 288-92 (1964).

Unlike *Birdwell*, relied on by the union, we do not have here potentially disruptive speech in the refined atmosphere of a classroom but rather speech in the rough-and-tumble of labor relations. The record in this indicates that Holodnak's article was no more harsh in its descriptions of management than the union's own leaflets. See generally *Linn* v. *Plant Guards, Local 114, supra*, 383 U.S. at 58. From this record, the court concludes that use of vituperatives alone, such as at issue here, could not have interfered with production at Avco.

Since the cases cited by defendants are not in point, the court must balance the competing interests as suggested in *Pickering*. Read fairly, Holodnak's article is an analysis of why unions lose their militancy. It is largely composed of Holodnak's opinions concerning labor-management relations at Avco and as such is a matter of employee interest clearly protected. Furthermore, many of the statements in the article that could be read as statements of facts are more reasonably read as rhetorical hyperbole, and as such are constitutionally protected. *Greenbelt Cooperative Publishing Assn.* v. *Bresier*, 398 U.S. 6, 11-14 (1970); *cf. Watts* v. *United States*, 394 U.S. 705 (1969). Finally, as noted above, none of the statements concerned any particular person. Thus it must be concluded that Holodnak's article was constitutionally protected regardless of the truth or falsity of the few statements of facts in it. See generally *Gertz* v. *Robert Welch, Inc., supra; New York Times Co.* v. *Sullivan, supra.*

Against Holodnak's interest in having his say, Avco's interest in maintaining efficiency in production is insufficient. As noted above, vituperative articles such as Holodnak's were quite common at Avco and evidently they have not interfered with production. Avco strongly argues that Holodnak's article favored wildcat strikes, which were a problem at Stratford. But the article in fact questions the effectiveness of such strikes and does not advocate them. While Holodnak's belief, expressed at the arbitration hearing, that workers had a constitutional right to engage in a wildcat strike was mistaken, see *Boys Markets, Inc.* v. *Retail Clerks, Local 770,* 398 U.S. 235 (1970), his article falls far short of being "incitement to imminent lawless action," *Brandenburg* v. *Ohio,* 395 U.S. 444, 449 (1969).

The balance, therefore, clearly tips in favor of Holodnak's right to free speech. It is noteworthy that even in private enterprise where the guarantees of the First Amendment do not apply, federal statutes have given employees the right to speak their minds on labor relations. Section 7 of the National Labor Relations Act, 29 U.S.C. § 157, gives employees the "right to self-organize, to form, join, or assist labor organizations, to bargain collectively through representatives of their own choosing, and to engage in other concerted activities for the purpose of collective bargaining or other mutual aid or protection. . . ." Interference with these rights by an employer is an unfair labor practice. 29 U.S.C. § 158 (a) (1). Only recently in *NLRB* v. *Magnavox Co., supra,* 42 U.S.L.W. 4300, the Supreme Court upheld a finding of an unfair labor practice where a company rule forbade the distribution of pro- and anti-union literature within the plant, even though the collective bargaining agreement authorized the rule. See also *Republic Aviation Corp.* v. *NLRB,* 324 U.S. 793 (1945). Of course, the question of whether Holodnak's discharge is an unfair labor practice is not for a district court to decide. See notes 9 & 10, *supra.* But *Magnavox* by analogy supports the conclusion that the First Amendment can allow no greater restrictions by a public employer on the right of employees to write articles which are circulated outside the plant and which in no way interfere with production.

Moreover, Congress has shown its interest in ensuring the right of employees to speak out on matters of union representation in § 101 (a) (2) of the Labor-Management Reporting and Disclosure Act, 29 U.S.C. § 411 (a) (2), which provides: "Every member of any labor organization shall have the right to meet and assemble freely with other members; and to express any views, arguments or opinions. . . ."

While this statute is principally concerned with preserving the right of the worker to speak out on union matters without being punished by the union, it clearly evidences a concern by Congress that the worker should be free to speak his mind on the important question of the quality of representation he is receiving. This is precisely what Holodnak sought to do. *Cf. Cole* v. *Hall,* 462 F.2d 277 (2d Cir. 1972), *aff'd,* 412 U.S. 1 (1973).

In light of the foregoing, the court must conclude that Avco's dismissal of Holodnak infringed on his First Amendment rights and that Holodnak was not discharged for "just cause" as required by Article v, § 1.a. of the collective bargaining agreement.

In conclusion, we would do well to remember that the Supreme Court said 34 years ago in *Thornhill* v. *Alabama,* 310 U.S. 88, 103 (1940):

> Free discussion concerning the conditions in industry and the causes of labor disputes appears to us indispensable to the effective and intelligent use of the processes of popular government to shape the destiny of modern industrial society.

Fortune v. National Cash Register Company
346 N.E. 1251
Supreme Judicial Court of Massachusetts, 1977

In this case a 61-year-old salesman who had worked for NCR for 25 years was fired when he was on the brink of successfully completing a sale. He sued NCR on the grounds that the motive for the discharge was to keep him from collecting bonuses he would ordinarily have collected, an act of bad faith that constituted a breach of contract. Since in common law there would be no breach of contract for bad faith in such a case, the decision of Massachussetts' highest court qualifying that doctrine is significant. A portion of the opinion follows.

[1] The central issue on appeal is whether this "bad faith" termination constituted a breach of the employment at will contract. Traditionally, an employment contract which is "at will" may be terminated by either side without reason. See *Fenton v. Federal St. Bldg. Trust*, 310 Mass. 609, 612, 39 N.E.2d 414 (1942); *Mechanics Foundry & Mach. Co. v. Lynch*, 236 Mass. 504, 505, 128 N.E. 877 (1920); *Gebhard v. Royce Aluminum Corp.*, 296 F.2d 17, 18-19 (1st Cir. 1961); 9 S. Williston, Contracts § 1017 (3d ed. 1967); Restatement (Second) of Agency § 442 (1958). Although the employment at will rule has been almost uniformly criticised, see Blades, Employment at Will vs. Individual Freedom: On Limiting the Abusive Exercise of Employer Power, 67 Colum.L.Rev. 1404 (1967); Blumrosen, Workers' Rights Against Employers and Unions: Justice Francis—A Judge for Our Season, 24 Rutgers L.Rev. 480 (1979), it has been widely followed.

The contract at issue is a classic terminable at will employment contract. It is clear that the contract itself reserved to the parties an explicit power to terminate the contract without cause on written notice. It is also clear that under the express terms of the contract Fortune has received all the bonus commissions to which he is entitled. Thus, NCR claims that it did not breach the contract, and that it has no further liability to Fortune. According to a literal reading of the contract, NCR is correct.

[2] However, Fortune argues that, in spite of the literal wording of the contract, he is entitled to a jury determination on NCR's motives in terminating his services under the contract and in finally discharging him. We agree. We hold that NCR's written contract contains an implied covenant of good faith and fair dealing, and a termination not made in good faith constitutes a breach of the contract.

We do not question the general principles that an employer is entitled to be motivated by and to serve its own legitimate business interests; that an employer must have wide latitude in deciding whom it will employ in the face of the uncertainties of the business world; and that an employer needs flexibility in the face of changing circumstances. We recognize the employer's need for a large amount of control over its work force. However, we believe that where, as here, commissions are to be paid for work performed by the employee, the employer's decision to terminate its at will employee should be made in good faith. NCR's right to make decisions in its own interest is not, in our view, unduly hampered by a requirement of adherence to this standard.

[3] On occasion some courts have avoided the rigidity of the "at will" rule by fashioning a remedy in tort. We believe, however, that in this case there is remedy on the express contract. In so holding we are merely recognizing the general requirement in this Commonwealth that parties to contracts and commercial transactions must act in good faith toward one another. Good faith and fair dealing between parties are pervasive requirements in our law; it can be said fairly, that parties to contracts or commercial transactions are bound by this standard.

Harless v. *First National Bank in Fairmont*
246 S.E. 2d 270
Supreme Court of Appeals of West Virginia, 1978

The full story of the plaintiff in this precedent-setting case appears in Chapter 3. Justice Thomas J. Miller's opinion is interesting not only for its reasoning but also for the cases cited from other courts. His decision is cited frequently by attorneys and judges in American courts. This was the first case decided by a state court in favor of a corporate whistleblower.

[2] The chief defense asserted was that the plaintiff's employment was for no fixed term and therefore terminable at the will of either party, with or without cause. This undoubtedly is an established rule. *Wright v. Standard Ultramarine and Color Co.*, 141 W. Va. 368, 382, 90 S.E.2d 459, 468 (1955); *Adair v. United States*, 208 U.S. 161, 28 S.Ct. 277, 52 L.Ed. 436 (1908); see Annot., 62 A.L.R.3d 271 (1975).

However, the general rule does not dispose of the issue in this case. There is a growing trend that recognizes that an employer may subject himself to liability if he fires an employee who is employed at will if the employee can show that the firing was motivated by an intention to contravene some substantial public policy.

Two recent decisions of the Oregon Supreme Court serve to illustrate some of the principles involved. In *Nees v. Hocks*, 272 Or. 210, 536 P.2d 512 (1975), plaintiff claimed she was fired for performing jury duty. The court, after citing several statutory and constitutional provisions relating to jurors, concluded there was a substantial public policy favoring jury duty and that the plaintiff had a cause of action against her employer.

In *Campbell v. Ford Industries*, 274 Or. 243, 546 P.2d 141 (1976), the plaintiff sought to rely on the public policy theory when he was fired after exercising his statutory right as a corporate shareholder to examine his employer's books and records. The court refused to sustain his cause of action, holding that the statutory right to examine a corporation's books is not founded on any substantial public policy, but is designed as a protection of the private and proprietary interests of stockholders.

Pennsylvania has suggested it may recognize the doctrine of retaliatory discharge in *Geary v. United States Steel Corporation*, 456 Pa. 171, 319 A.2d 174 (1974). In speaking of the cases supporting the doctrine, it states:

> It is not necessary to reject the rationale of these decisions in order to defend the results we reach here. In each case where a cause of action was found, the mandates of public policy were clear and compelling; that cannot be said of the instant case. [319 A.2d at 180, n.16]

Geary involved an employee who contended that a pipe designed and manufactured by the defendant employer was unsafe and should not be marketed. When his immediate supervisors took no action, he took his complaint to their superiors. The complaint alleged that although the company ultimately withdrew the product, his firing was in retaliation for his complaints about the safety of the product.

Indiana and Michigan have utilized the doctrine to permit an employee to maintain an action where a claim is made that the firing occurred in retaliation for filing a workmen's compensation claim against the employer. In *Sventko v. Kroger Co.*, 69 Mich.App. 644, 245 N.W.2d 151 (1976), and *Frampton v. Central Indiana Gas Co.*, 260 Ind. 249, 297 N.E.2d 425 (1973), the courts reviewed their state workmen's compensation statutes and concluded their legislatures had expressed a strong public policy that workmen's compensation claims were not to be frustrated.

In *Jackson v. Minidoka*, 98 Idaho 330, 563 P.2d 54 (1977), the Idaho Supreme Court stated the doctrine in the following fashion, although it declined to apply it under the particular facts of that case:

> As a general exception to the rule allowing either the employer or the employee to terminate the employment relationship without cause, an employee may claim damages for wrongful discharge when the motivation for the firing contravenes public policy. [563 P.2d at 57]

The Arizona Appeals Court also appears to recognize the doctrine, although it was found not applicable upon the facts presented to it in *Larsen v. Motor Supply Co.*, 117 Ariz. 507, 573 P.2d 907 (1977). There, two employees were discharged when they refused to take lie detector tests mandated by the company for all its employees.

The Washington Supreme Court has discussed the doctrine at some length, but determined it was not necessary to decide whether it would adopt the doctrine in *Roberts v. Atlantic Richfield Company*, 88 Wash.2d 887, 568 P.2d 764 (1977).

Two states have created a broader concept. In *Monge v. Beebe Rubber Co.*, 114 N.H. 130, 316 A.2d 549 (1974), the court stated:

> We hold that a termination by the employer of a contract of employment at will which is motivated by bad faith or malice or based on retaliation is not in the

best interest of the economic system or the public good and constitutes a breach of the employment contract. [114 N.H. at 133, 316 A.2d at 551]

In that case, a female employee claimed she was fired because she refused to go out with her foreman. There was evidence that he had reassigned her to more menial jobs and also ridiculed her, causing the court to conclude that the jury was correct in finding "that the dismissal was maliciously motivated." The court considered the cause of action to arise out of the employment contract.

Massachusetts, following the *Monge* case, permits a breach of contract action to lie where there is a "bad faith" termination of an employment contract at will. *Fortune v. National Cash Register Co.*, 364 N.E.2d 1251 (Mass. 1977). In *Fortune*, a salesman was fired after twenty-four years with the company after he claimed he was entitled to certain sales commissions. He asserted the firing was in "bad faith" because the company wanted to avoid paying the balance of the commissions due him. The court enunciated its rule as follows:

> We believe that the holding in the *Monge* case merely extends to employment contracts the rule that "in *every* contract there is an applied covenant that neither party shall do anything which will have the effect of destroying or injuring the right of the other party to receive the fruits of the contract, which means that in *every* contract there exists an implied covenant of good faith and fair dealing." [364 N.E.2d at 1257]

California dealt with the doctrine in *Petermann v. International Brotherhood of Teamsters,* 174 Cal.App.2d 184, 344 P.2d 25 (1959), where a union employee was discharged when he refused to testify falsely before a legislative committee. The court held that the strong public policy against perjury required that an employer be liable civilly to an employee discharged under such circumstances. In *Glenn v. Clearman's Golden Cock Inn,* 192 Cal.App.2d 793, 13 Cal.Rptr. 769 (1961), several employees were discharged because they had applied for union membership. The court concluded that the state's statute giving employees an unfettered right to organize manifested a strong public policy that should give rise to a cause of action against an employer who discharged employees for joining a union.

The California Supreme Court approved and utilized the principle of *Petermann* and *Glenn* in *Schweiger v. Superior Court of Alameda County,* 3 Cal.3d 507, 90 Cal.Rptr. 729, 476 P.2d 97 (1970), where it authorized the defense of retaliatory eviction in a landlord's actions for ejectment, stating:

> Both *Glenn* and *Petermann* persuasively instruct us that one may not exercise normally unrestricted power if his reasons for its exercise contravene public policy. Clearly, sections 1941 and 1942 express the policy of this state that landlords in the interest of public health and safety have the duty to maintain leased premises in habitable condition and that tenants have the right, after notice to the landlord, to repair dilapidations and deduct the cost of the repairs from the rent. The policy expressed in these sections cannot be effectuated if landlords

may evict tenants who invoke the provisions of the statute. Courts would be withholding with one hand what the Legislature has granted with the other if they order evictions instituted in retaliation against the exercise of statutory rights. [476 P.2d at 102]

There is substantial support from commentators for reformation of the rule of nonliability for employers on discharge of at will employees without regard to the circumstances surrounding the discharge.

The question of whether we recognize an exception to the traditional rule is a matter of first impression in this jurisdiction. Some suggestion of the applicability of equitable principles can be found in *Chicago Towel Co. v. Reynolds*, 108 W.Va. 615, 152 S.E. 200 (1930). There, the court found inequitable the employer's firing of an at will employee "without notice and without excuse or attempted justification for its action." The employee had signed a covenant not to engage in the same business and the employer sought an injunction to prevent his employment with another linen company. This Court dissolved the lower court's injunction based on the employer's inequitable discharge of the employee.

[3] We conceive that the rule giving the employer the absolute right to discharge an at will employee must be tempered by the further principle that where the employer's motivation for the discharge contravenes some substantial public policy principle, then the employer may be liable to the employee for damages occasioned by the discharge.

[4] Here, the plaintiff's complaint refers to intentional violations of W.Va.Code, 46A-1-101, *et seq.*, made by the defendants, which he endeavored to have stopped. This statutory provision is commonly known as the West Virginia Consumer Credit and Protection Act, W.Va.Code, 46A-1-101. We need not discuss the Act in detail in order to conclude that it represents a comprehensive attempt on the part of the Legislature to extend protection to the consumers and persons who obtain credit in this State and who obviously constitute the vast majority of our adult citizens.

Not only did the Legislature regulate various consumer and credit practices, but it went further and established the right to civil action for damages on behalf of persons who have been subjected to practices that violate certain provisions of the Act. In addition, criminal violations are sanctioned for certain wilful violations. W.Va. Code, 46A-5-101, *et seq.*

Moreover, under Article 7 of the Act, the Attorney General is given broad powers to supervise, investigate and prosecute violations in order to see that compliance with the Act is maintained. Notwithstanding the broad grant of powers to the Attorney General, the Act still preserves the "remedies available to consumers under this chapter or under other principles of law and equity." W.Va.Code, 46A-7-113.

We have no hesitation in stating that the Legislature intended to establish a clear and unequivocal public policy that consumers of credit covered by the Act were to be given protection. Such manifest public policy should not be frustrated by a holding that an employee of a lending institution covered by the Act, who seeks to ensure that compliance is being made with the Act, can be discharged without being furnished a cause of action for such discharge.

Tameny v. Atlantic Richfield Company
164 Cal. Rptr. 839, 610 P. 2d 1330
Supreme Court of California, 1980

This significant case concerns a veteran employee who alleged he was fired for refusing to participate in an illegal scheme to fix retail gasoline prices. "The days when a servant was practically the slave of his master have long since passed," states Justice Tobriner. Most of the court's opinion is reproduced here.

According to the complaint, plaintiff was hired by Arco as a relief clerk in 1960, received regular advancements, merit increases and commendatory evaluations in his initial years with the company, and, in 1966, was promoted to the position of retail sales representative, the position he held when discharged by Arco in 1975. His duties as a retail sales representative included among other matters the management of relations between Arco and the various independent service station dealers (franchisees) in his assigned territory of Bakersfield.

The complaint alleges that beginning in the early 1970s, Arco, Arco's district manager McDermott, and others engaged in a combination "for the purpose of reducing, controlling, stabilizing, fixing, and pegging the retail gasoline prices of Arco service station franchisees." According to the complaint, defendants' conduct in this regard violated express provisions of the Sherman Antitrust Act (15 U.S.C. § 1 et seq.), the Cartwright Act (Bus & Prof. Code, § 16720 et seq.), and a specific consent decree which which had been entered in a federal antitrust prosecution against Arco.

The complaint further asserts that during the early 1970s, defendants increasingly pressured plaintiff to "threaten [and] cajole . . . the so-called 'independent' service station dealers in [his] territory to cut their gasoline prices to a point at or below a designated level specified by Arco." When plaintiff refused to yield to his employer's pressure to engage in such tactics, his supervisor told him that his discharge was imminent, and soon thereafter plaintiff was fired, effective March 25, 1975. Although at the time of the discharge Arco indicated in its personnel records that plaintiff was being fired for "incompetence" and for "unsatisfactory performance," the complaint alleges that "the sole reason" for plaintiff's discharge was his refusal to commit the "grossly illegal and unlawful acts which defendants tried to force him to perform."

On the basis of the foregoing allegations, plaintiff sought relief on five separate theories. The complaint alleged, in particular, three tort causes of action (wrongful

discharge, breach of the implied covenant of good faith and for dealing, and interference with contractual relations), an action for breach of contract, and an action
for treble damages under the Cartwright Act. Defendants demurred to the complaint, and the trial court sustained the demurrer as to all counts except for the
count alleging a breach of contract. Thereafter, plaintiff voluntarily dismissed the
contract count and the trial court then dismissed the entire action and entered
judgement in favor of Arco. Plaintiff appeals from the adverse judgment.

2. *An employee discharged for refusing to engage in illegal conduct at his employer's request may
bring a tort action for wrongful discharge.*

Under the traditional common law rule, codified in Labor Code section 2922, an
employment contract of indefinite duration is in general terminable at "the will" of
either party. Over the past several decades, however, judicial authorities in California and throughout the United States have established the rule that under both
common law and the statute an employer does not enjoy an absolute or totally
unfettered right to discharge even an at-will employee. In a series of cases arising
out of a variety of factual settings in which a discharge clearly violated an express
statutory objective or undermined a firmly established principle of public policy,
courts have recognized that an employer's traditional broad authority to discharge
an at-will employee "may be limited by statute . . . or by considerations of public
policy." (*Petermann* v. *International Brotherhood of Teamsters* (1959) 174 Cal.App.2d 184,
188 [344 P.2d 25] (discharge for refusal to commit perjury); see, e.g., *Glenn* v. *Clearman's Golden Cock Inn, Inc.* (1961) 192 Cal.App.2d 793, 796-797 [13 Cal.Rptr. 769]
(discharge because of union membership and activity); *Wetherton* v. *Growers Farm
Labor Assn.* (1969) 275 Cal.App.2d 168, 174-175 [79 Cal.Rptr. 543] (same); *Montalvo*
v. *Zamora* (1970) 7 Cal.App.3d 69 [86 Cal.Rptr. 401] (discharge for designation of
nonunion bargaining representative); *Nees* v. *Hocks* (1975) 272 Ore. 210 [536 P.2d
512] (discharge for serving on jury); *Frampton* v. *Central Indiana Gas Company* (1973)
260 Ind. 249 [297 N.E.2d 425] (discharge for filing worker's compensation claim);
Harless v. *First Nat. Bank in Fairmont* (1978)—W. Va.—[246 S.E.2d 270] (discharge for
reporting violations of consumer protection laws).)

Petermann v. *International Brotherhood of Teamsters, supra,* one of the seminal California
decisions in this area, imposes a significant condition upon the employer's broad
power of dismissal by nullifying the right to discharge because an employee refuses
to perform an unlawful act. In *Petermann,* the plaintiff, who had been employed as a
business agent by defendant union, brought a "wrongful discharge" action against
the union alleging that he had been dismissed from his position because he had
refused to follow his employer's instructions to testify falsely under oath before a
legislative committee, and instead had given truthful testimony. Emphasizing that
the employer's instructions amounted to a directive to commit perjury, a criminal
offense, plaintiff maintained that the employer acted illegally in discharging him for
refusing to follow such an order.

The *Petermann* court recognized that in the absence of contractual limitations an
employer enjoys broad discretion to discharge an employee, but concluded that as a

matter of "public policy and sound morality" the employer's conduct, as alleged in the complaint, could not be condoned. The court explained:

> The commission of perjury is unlawful. (Pen. Code, § 118). . . . It would be obnoxious to the interests of the state and contrary to public policy and sound morality to allow an employer to discharge any employee, whether the employment be for a designated or unspecified duration, on the ground that the employee declined to commit perjury, an act specifically enjoined by statute. . . . The public policy of this state as reflected in the Penal Code sections referred to above would be seriously impaired if it were to be held that one could be discharged by reason of his refusal to commit perjury. To hold that one's continued employment could be made contingent upon his commission of a felonious act at the instance of his employer would be to encourage criminal conduct upon the part of both the employee and employer and serve to contaminate the honest administration of public affairs. . . . (174 Cal.App.2d at pp. 188-189.)

Thus, *Petermann* held that even in the absence of an explicit statutory provision prohibiting the discharge of a worker on such grounds, fundamental principles of public policy and adherence to the objectives underlying the state's penal statutes require the recognition of a rule barring an employer from discharging an employeee who has simply complied with his legal duty and has refused to commit an illegal act.

As the statement of facts set out above demonstrates, the present case closely parallels *Petermann* in a number of essential respects. Here, as in *Petermann,* the complaint alleges that the defendant employer instructed its employee to engage in conduct constituting a criminal offense. Plaintiff, like the employee in *Petermann,* refused to violate the law and suffered discharge as a consequence of that refusal.

Arco concedes, as it must in light of *Petermann,* that the allegations of the complaint, if true, establish that defendants acted unlawfully in discharging plaintiff for refusing to participate in criminal activity. Arco maintains, however, that plaintiff's remedy for such misconduct sounds only in contract and not in tort. Accordingly, Arco asserts that the trial court properly sustained its demurrer to plaintiff's tort causes of action, and correctly precluded plaintiff from recovering either compensatory tort damages or punitive damages.

In support of its contention that an action for wrongful discharge sounds only in contract and not in tort, Arco argues that because of the contractual nature of the employer-employee relationship, an injury which an employer inflicts upon its employee by the improper termination of such a relationship gives rise only to a breach of contract action. California decisions, however, have long recognized that a wrongful act committed in the course of a contractual relationship may afford both tort and contractual relief, and in such circumstances the existence of the contractual relationship will not bar the injured party from pursuing redress in tort.

Sloane v. *Southern Cal. Ry. Co.* (1896) 111 Cal. 668 [44 P. 320] illustrates the early application of these principles. In *Sloane*, a passenger who had purchased a railroad ticket to San Diego and had been wrongfully ejected from the train before her destination sued the defendant railroad for damages in tort. In response, the railroad contended that the passenger's "only right of action is for breach of the defendant's contract to carry her to San Diego, and that the extent of her recovery therefor is the price paid for the second ticket, and a reasonable compensation for the loss of time sustained by her. . . ." (111 Cal. at p. 676).

The *Sloane* court rejected the defendant's contention, declaring that

> [t]he plaintiff's right to action . . . is not . . . limited to the breach of [the] contract
> to carry her to San Diego, but includes full redress for the wrongs sustained by
> her by reason of the defendant's violation of the obligations which it assumed in
> entering into such a contract . . . [S]he could either bring an action simply for the
> breach of the contract, or she could sue . . . in tort for [defendant's] violation of
> the duty . . . which it assumed upon entering into such a contract. (111 Cal. at pp.
> 676-677.)

Numerous decisions in the 80 years since *Sloane* confirm that "it [is] well established in this state that if the cause of action arises from a breach of a promise set forth in the contract, the action is ex contractu, *but if it arises from a breach of duty growing out of the contract it is ex delicto.*' " (Italics added.) (*Eads* v. *Marks* (1952) 39 Cal.2d 807, 811 [249 P.2d 257] (quoting *Peterson* v. *Sherman* (1945) 68 Cal.App.2d 706, 711 [157 P.2d 863]); see, e.g., *Jones* v. *Kelly* (1929) 208 Cal. 251, 254 [280 P. 942]; *Heyer* v. *Flaig* (1969) 70 Cal.2d 223, 227 [74 Cal.Rptr. 225, 449 P.2d 161]; *Distefano* v. *Hall* (1963) 218 Cal.App.2d 657, 678 [32 Cal.Rptr. 770].) In conformity with this principle, recent decisions have held that a month-by-month tenant who is wrongfully evicted for exercising the statutory "repair and deduct" remedy may maintain a tort action for compensatory and punitive damages against his landlord. (See, e.g. *Aweeka* v. *Bonds* (1971) 20 Cal.App.3d 278, 281 [97 Cal.Rptr. 650].)

In light of the foregoing authorities, we conclude that an employee's action for wrongful discharge is ex delicto and subjects an employer to tort liability. As the *Petermann* case indicates, an employer's obligation to refrain from discharging an employee who refuses to commit a criminal act does not depend upon any express or implied " 'promise[s] set forth in the [employment] contract' " (*Eads* v. *Marks, supra,* 39 Cal.2d at p. 811), but rather reflects a duty imposed by law upon all employers in order to implement the fundamental public policies embodied in the state's penal statutes. As such, a wrongful discharge suit exhibits the classic elements of a tort cause of action. As Professor Prosser has explained:

> [Whereas] [c]ontract actions are created to protect the interest in having prom-
> ises performed," "[t]ort actions are created to protect the interest in freedom
> from various kinds of harm. The duties of conduct which give rise to them are
> imposed by law, and are based primarily upon social policy, and not necessarily

upon the will or intention of the parties. . . . (Prosser, Law of Torts (4th ed. 1971) p. 613.)

Past California wrongful discharge cases confirm the availability of a tort cause of action in circumstances similar to those of the instant case. In *Kouff* v. *Bethlehem-Alameda Shipyard* (1949) 90 Cal.App.2d 322 [202 P.2d 1059], for example, the court held that an employee who had been improperly discharged from his job for acting as an election poll official could maintain a tort cause of action against his employer for compensatory and punitive damages. Similarly, in *Glenn* v. *Clearman's Golden Cock Inn, Inc., supra,* 192 Cal.App.2d 793, *Wetherton* v. *Growers Farm Labor Assn., supra,* 275 Cal.App.2d 168, 174-175 and *Montalvo* v. *Zamora, supra.* 7 Cal.App.3d 69, the courts sanctioned the right of employees, who had been discharged for joining unions or otherwise exercising their statutory right to choose a bargaining representative, to maintain tort causes of action against their employers for wrongful discharge

Although Arco attempts to distinguish these past wrongful discharge cases from the instant action on the ground that the discharges in the former cases were specifically barred by statute, the suggested distinction does not withstand analysis. In *Glenn, Wetherton* and *Montalvo,* as in *Petermann* and the instant case, no statute expressly prohibited an employer from discharging an employee on the stated ground; instead, the courts simply recognized that the general statute affording employees the right to join a union or choose a bargaining representative articulated a fundamental public policy which the employer's discharge clearly contravened. As the court observed in *Glenn:* "It would be a hollow protection indeed that would allow employees to organize and would then permit employers to discharge them for that very reason, unless such protection would afford to the employees the right to recover for this wrongful act." (192 Cal.App.2d at p. 798.)

Moreover, California courts have not been alone in recognizing the propriety of a tort remedy when an employer's discharge of an employee contravenes the dictates of public policy. In *Nees* v. *Hocks* (1975) 272 Ore. 210 [536 P.2d 512], for example, the Oregon Supreme Court upheld an employee's recovery of compensatory damages in tort for emotional distress suffered when her employer discharged her for serving on a jury. Similarly, in *Harless* v. *First Nat. Bank in Fairmont* (1978)—W.Va.—[246 S.E.2d 270], the Supreme Court of West Virginia upheld a wrongful discharge action by a bank employee who was terminated for attempting to persuade his employer to comply with consumer protection laws, reasoning that "where the employer's motivation for [a] discharge contravenes some substantial public policy principle, then the employer may be liable to the employee for damages occasioned by the discharge," and concluding that the employee's cause of action "is one in tort and it therefore follows that rules relating to tort damages would be applicable." (*Id.,* at p. 275, fn. 5.)

Indeed, the *Nees* and *Harless* decisions are merely illustrative of a rapidly growing number of cases throughout the country that in recent years have recognized a common law tort action for wrongful discharge in cases in which the termination contravenes public policy. (See, e.g., *Frampton* v. *Central Indiana Gas Co., supra,* 260 Ind. 249, [297 N.E.2d 425, 63 A.L.R.3d 973]; *Kelsay* v. *Motorola, Inc.* (1979) 74 Ill.2d 172 [384 N.E.2d 353, 358, 370]; *Jackson* v. *Minidoka Irrigation Dist.* (1977) 98 Idaho 330 [563 P.2d 54, 57–58]; *Sventko* v. *Kroger Co.* (1976) 69 Mich.App. 644 [245 N.W.2d 151]; *Reuther* v. *Fowler & Williams* (1978) 255 Pa. Super. 28 [386 A.2d 119]; see also *Pierce* v. *Ortho Pharmaceutical Corp.* (1979) 166 N.J. Super. 335 [399 A.2d 1023, 1025–1026].)

These recent decisions demonstrate a continuing judicial recognition of the fact, enunciated by this court more than 35 years ago, that "[t]he days when a servant was practically the slave of his master have long since passed." (*Greene* v. *Hawaiian Dredging Co.* (1945) 26 Cal. 2d 245, 251 [157 P.2d 367].) In the last half century the rights of employees have not only been proclaimed by a mass of legislation touching upon almost every aspect of the employer-employee relationship, but the courts have likewise evolved certain additional protections at common law. The courts have been sensitive to the need to protect the individual employee from discriminatory exclusion from the opportunity of employment whether it be by the all-powerful union or employer. (See *James* v. *Marinship Corp.* (1944) 25 Cal.2d 721 [155 P.2d 329, 160 A.L.R. 900]; *Gay Law Students Assn.* v. *Pacific Tel. & Tel. Co.* (1979) 24 Cal.3d 458 [156 Cal.Rptr. 14, 595 P.2d 592].) This development at common law shows that the employer is not so absolute a sovereign of the job that there are not limits to his prerogative. One such limit at least is the present case. The employer cannot condition employment upon requirement participation in unlawful conduct by the employee.

We hold that an employer's authority over its employee does not include the right to demand that the employee commit a criminal act to further its interests, and an employer may not coerce compliance with such unlawful directions by discharging an employee who refuses to follow such an order. An employer engaging in such conduct violates a basic duty imposed by law upon all employers, and thus an employee who has suffered damages as a result of such discharge may maintain a tort action for wrongful discharge against the employer.

Touissaint v. *Blue Cross & Blue Shield*
408 Mich. 579
Michigan Supreme Court, 1980

In this important decision, presented jointly with the judges' decision in the case of *Ebling* v. *Masco Corporation,* Michigan's highest court adds to the judicial literature one more restriction on management's right to discharge. If management makes a commitment, either through a publication such as a personnel manual or by an oral agreement, to dismiss an employee only for certain causes, or only for "just cause," it must stick to the commitment, the

Michigan Supreme Court rules. The traditional common law doctrine does not give management an out. A portion of the court's opinion follows.

Touissaint and Ebling contend that their employer's agreement not to discharge "as long as I did my job [Touissaint]" or "[I was] doing the job [Ebling]" was an agreement not to discharge except for good cause. The issues submitted to both juries, without objection in this regard, were whether there was an agreement to terminate employment only for good cause and whether the employee had been discharged for good cause. In light of the jury verdicts we proceed on the basis that the contracts provided that the employee would not be discharged except for good cause.

We see no reason why an employment contract which does not have a definite term—the term is "indefinite"—cannot legally provide job security. When a prospective employee inquiries about job security and the employer agrees that the employee shall be employed as long as he does the job, a fair construction is that the employer has agreed to give up his right to discharge at will without assigning cause and may discharge only for cause (good or just cause). The result is that the employee, if discharged without good or just cause, may maintain an action for wrongful discharge.

Suppose the contracts here were written, not oral, and had provided in so many words that the employment was to continue for the life of the employee who could not be discharged except for cause (including as a cause, if you will, his attaining the company's mandatory retirement age). To construe such an agreement as terminable at the will of the employer would be tantamount to saying as did the Court of Appeals in *Touissaint*, that a contract of indefinite duration *"cannot* be made other than terminable at will by a provision that states that an employee will not be discharged except for cause" (emphasis supplied) and that only in exceptional circumstances, where there are "distinguishing features or provisions or a consideration in addition to the services to be rendered," would an employee be permitted to bargain for a legally enforceable agreement providing job security.

Where the employment is for a definite term—a year, five years, 10 years—it is implied, if not expressed, that the employee can be discharged only for good cause, and collective bargaining agreements often provide that discharge shall only be for good or just cause. There is, thus, no public policy against providing job security or prohibiting an employer from agreeing not to discharge except for good or just cause. That being the case, we can see no reason why such a provision in a contract having no definite term of employment with a single employee should necessarily be unenforceable and regarded, in effect, as against public policy and beyond the power of the employer to contract.

Touissaint and Ebling were hired for responsible positions. They negotiated specifically regarding job security with the persons who interviewed and hired them. If Blue Cross or Masco had desired, they could have established a company policy of requiring prospective employees to acknowledge that they served at the will or the pleasure of the company, and, thus, have avoided the misunderstandings that generated this litigation. . . .

Touissaint's testimony was sufficient to create a question of fact for the jury whether there was a mutual understanding that it was company policy not to discharge an employee "as long as [he] did [his] job," and that this policy, expressed in documents (which said "for just cause only"), assertedly handed to Touissant when he was hired, would apply to him as to other Blue Cross employees.

We do not, however, rest our conclusion that the jury could properly find that the Blue Cross policy manual created conversation with the executive who interviewed and hired him.

While an employer need not establish personnel policies or practices, where an employer chooses to establish such policies and practices and makes them known to its employees, the employment relationship is presumably enhanced. The employer secures an orderly, cooperative and loyal work force, and the employee the peace of mind associated with job security and the conviction that he will be treated fairly. No pre-employment negotiations need take place and the parties' minds need not meet on the subject, nor does it matter that the employee knows nothing of the particulars of the employer's policies and practices or that the employer may change them unilaterally. It is enough that the employer chooses, presumably in its own interest, to create an environment in which the employee believes that, whatever the personnel policies and practices, they are established and official at any given time, purport to be fair, and are applied consistently and uniformly to each employee. The employer has then created a situation "instinct with an obligation."

Blue Cross offered no evidence that the manual and guidelines are not what they purport to be—statements of company policy on the subjects there addressed, including discipline and termination.

The jury could properly conclude that the statements of policy on those subjects were applicable to Toussaint although the manual did not explicitly refer to him. The manual, by its terms, purports to apply to all employees who have completed a probationary period. The inference that the policies and procedures applied to Toussaint is supported by his testimony that he was handed the manual in the course of a conversation in which he inquired about job security.

Although Toussaint's employment was for an indefinite term, the jury could find that the relationship was not terminable at the will of Blue Cross. Blue Cross had established a company policy to discharge for just cause only, pursuant to certain procedures, had made that policy known to Toussaint, and thereby had committed itself to discharge him only for just cause in compliance with the procedures. There were, thus, on this separate basis alone, special circumstances sufficient to overcome the presumptive construction that the contract was terminable at will.

We hold that employer statements of policy, such as the Blue Cross Supervisory Manual and Guidelines, can give rise to contractual rights in employees without evidence that the parties mutually agreed that the policy statements would create contractual rights in the employee, and, hence, although the statement of policy is signed by neither party, can be unilaterally amended by the employer without notice to the employee, and contains no reference to a specific employee, his job description or compensation, and although no reference was made to the policy statement in preemployment interviews and the employee does not learn of its existence until after his hiring. . . .

In *Cain v Allen Electric & Equipment Co*, the employer adopted a "supervisory and office personnel policy" declaring:

> The keynote of our policy as herein related is an endeavor to achieve fairness with due consideration for the feelings of the employees to whom this is directed, and will be of particular assistance to new or temporary employees.

> When it becomes necessary to terminate the services of an office employee on a permanent basis, such individual will be paid separation pay [in?] lieu of notice as stated in table given to each employee.

An executive having 5 to 10 years employment was entitled to two months separation pay.

Less than four months after the policy announcement, Cain tendered his resignation, effective in two months. He was immediately discharged, without notice, and sought two months' separation pay. The employer appealed a judgment awarding such pay arguing that its declarations of personnel policy "were not of a promissory or contractual nature and did not constitute an offer capable of acceptance . . . but were a mere gratuitous statement of policy or intention."

This Court asked: "Is it the fact that dismissal compensation is purely a gift? That there is no consideration to the company from the adoption and operation of such a plan?", canvassed the literature and case law on the subject, and concluded:

> We cannot agree that all we have here is a mere gratuity, to be given, or to be withheld, as whim or caprice might move the employer. An offer was made, not merely a hope or intention expressed. The words on their face looked to an agreement, and assent. The cooperation desired was to be mutual . . . *The essence of the announcement was precisely that the company would conduct itself in a certain way with the stated objective of achieving fairness, and we would be reluctant to hold under such circumstances that an employee might not reasonably rely on the expression made and conduct himself accordingly.* . . .

The Blue Cross Manual, too, promised that the company would conduct itself in a certain way with the stated objective of achieving fairness. "The cooperation desired was to be mutual"—both employer and employee were to adhere to stated procedures, and no doubt those policies contributed to a "spirit of cooperation and friendliness." Since Blue Cross published and distributed a 260-page manual establishing elaborate procedures promising "[t]o provide for the administration of fair, consistent, and reasonable corrective discipline" and "to treat employees leaving

Blue Cross in a fair and consistent manner and to terminate employees for just causes only," its employees could justifiably rely on those expressions and conduct themselves accordingly.

Recognition that contractual obligations can be implicit in employer policies and practices is not confined to cases where compensation is in issue. Corbin's observation that the law of employment is undergoing rapid change was soon substantiated in *Perry v Sindermann,* concerning a claim of a right to continued employment absent sufficient cause for discharge. The United States Supreme Court observed:

> A written contract with an explicit "tenure provision clearly is evidence of a formal understanding that supports a teacher's claim of entitlement to continued employment unless sufficient 'cause' is shown. Yet absence of such an explicit contractual provision may not always foreclose the possibility that a teacher has a 'property' interest in re-employment. For example, the law of contracts in most, if not all, jurisdictions long has employed a process by which agreements, though not formalized in writing, may be 'implied.' Explicit contractual provisions may be supplemented by other agreements implied from 'the promisor's words and conduct in the light of the surrounding circumstances. And, [t]he meaning of [the promisor's] words and acts is found by relating them to the usage of the past.'
>
> A teacher, like the respondent, who has held his position for a number of years, might be able to show from the circumstances of this service—and from other relevant facts—that he has a legitimate claim of entitlement to job tenure. Just as this Court has found there to be a 'common law of a particular industry or of a particular plant' that may supplement a collective-bargaining agreement, so there may be an unwritten 'common law' in a particular university that certain employees shall have the equivalent of tenure. This is particularly likely in a college or university, like Odessa Junior College, that has no explicit tenure system even for senior members of its faculty, but that nonetheless may have created such a system in practice.
>
> In this case, the respondent has alleged the existence of rules and understandings, promulgated and fostered by state officials, that may justify his legitimate claim of entitlement to continued employment absent 'sufficient cause.'

This court adopted this analysis in another context.

The right to continued employment absent cause for termination may, thus, because of stated employer policies and established procedures, be enforceable in contrast just as are rights so deprived to bonuses, pensions and other forms of compensation as previously held by Michigan courts.

One amicus curiae argues that large organizations regularly distribute memoranda, bulletins and manuals reflecting established conditions and periodic changes in policy. These documents are drafted "for clarity and accuracy and to properly advise those subject to the policy memo of its contents." If such memoranda are held by this Court to form part of the employment contract, large employers will be severely hampered by the resultant inability to issue policy statements.

An employer who establishes no personnel policies instills no reasonable expectations of performance. Employers can make known to their employees that personnel policies are subject to unilateral changes by the employer. Employees would then have no legitimate expectations that any particular policy will continue to remain in force. Employees could, however, legitimately expect that policies in force at anven time will be uniformly applied to all. If there is in effect a policy to dismiss for cause only, the employer may not depart from that policy at whim simply because he was under no obligation to institute the policy in the first place. Having announced the policy, presumably with a view to obtaining the benefit of improved employee attitudes and behavior and improved quality of the work force, the employer may not treat its promise as illusory.

Perks v. Firestone Tire & Rubber Company
611 F. 2d 1363
U.S. Court of Appeals, Third Circuit, 1979

This is unusual because it deals with an aspect of employee privacy. Although, as the opinion indicates, the employee really was guilty of wrongdoing, that was not known at the time of management's controversial action, hence the legal question was still a live one. Note, too, that while a Federal court rendered the decision, the outcome hinged on a state "anti-lie-detector" law. Most of the opinion is reproduced.

Plaintiff was an employee of Firestone for 30 years. He served as a production coordinator for the four years preceding his discharge at Firestone's plant in Pottstown, Pennsylvania. In that capacity, Perks had numerous contacts with a supplier of Firestone, Tri-Stone Technical Sales Corporation and its representative, G. Joseph Pilotti.

Sometime in 1976, the auditors of Firestone commenced an investigation concerning allegations that certain employees had accepted gratuities from representatives of suppliers. During the investigation, the auditors conducted two interviews of Pilotti. The initial interview occurred on December 28, 1976. Pilotti admitted that he procured prostitutes for employees of Firestone, but did not mention plaintiff.

The second interview occurred on January 4, 1977. Pilotti related that Perks was one of the employees who utilized the services of a prostitute provided by him. On or about November 10, 1977, over 10 months following the discharge of plaintiff, and approximately three months after suit was filed, Pilotti provided further details for the auditors, stating that plaintiff was advised of the availability of prostitutes at a Chem Show in New York, in December, 1975, and later that evening, Perks accepted the offer. At the time of the second interview, these details were not available to Firestone.

The Company, armed with the results of two interviews with Pilotti, confronted Perks with the allegations. He denied the charges. As a result, plaintiff's supervisor, Carl J. Kleinert, requested that Perks submit to a polygraph examination to verify the denial. According to evidence adduced by Firestone, the polygraph test was requested to "give [Perks] an opportunity to persuade us that his version of what happened at the Chem Show was accurate. . . . [T]he polygraph test was a final chance for Mr. Perks to persuade us otherwise. . . ." Plaintiff refused the gambit and, within one week, he was discharged.

Following discovery, Firestone moved for summary judgment averring that: (1) Perks was an employee at will and subject to discharge at the pleasure of the Company; and (2) plaintiff was terminated for accepting gratuities furnished by a supplier of Firestone in violation of corporate policy. The district court declined to determine whether a discharge for failure to submit to a polygraph examination is violative of Pennsylvania law. Rather, the court held that, as a matter of law, Perks was discharged for trangressing the Company policy concerning gratuities.

We reverse and hold that: (1) the discharge of an employee at will because of a refusal to submit to a polygraph examination required by an employer gives rise to a cause of action for tortious discharge under Pennsylvania law; and (2) the existence of a genuine issue of material fact concerning the reason for plaintiff's discharge precludes the entry of summary judgment.

Pennsylvania law, which is controlling, traditionally followed the common law doctrine that either party may terminate an employment relationship for any reason when the employment is at will. See, Henry v. Pittsburgh & Lake Erie Railroad Co., 139 Pa. 289, 21 A. 157 (1891). The harsh principle came under increasing attack, and various courts began to recognize that the economic relationship between the parties required some modification of the unfettered right to discharge.

The Supreme Court of Pennsylvania reexamined the question in *Geary v. United States Steel Corp.*, 456 Pa. 171, 319 A.2d 174 (1974). In *Geary*, a salesman and an employee at will alleged that he was discharged for notifying the company of serious defects in several products marketed by the company. In affirming the dismissal of the complaint, the court indicated that in some circumstances an employee would have a cause of action for wrongful discharge. The court stated:

It may be granted that there are areas of an employee's life in which his employer has no legitimate interest. An intrusion into one of these areas by virtue of the employer's power of discharge might plausibly give rise to a cause of action, particularly where some recognized facet of public policy is threatened.

. . . We hold only that where the complaint itself discloses a plausible and legitimate reason for terminating an at-will employment relationship and no clear mandate of public policy is violated thereby, an employee at will has no right of action against his employer for wrongful discharge.

456 Pa. at 184-185, 319 A.2d at 180.

Relying on this broad language, the Pennsylvania Superior Court recently held that an employee, who is discharged for responding to a notice of jury service, has a cause of action against the employer because the discharge violates a clear mandate of public policy. *Reuther v. Fowler & Williams, Inc.*, 255 Pa.Super. 28, 386 A.2d 119, 121 (1978).

The General Assembly of Pennsylvania enacted a relevant statutory provision proscribing the use of polygraph examinations by employers. The Act provides:

A person is guilty of a misdemeanor of the second degree if he requires as a condition for employment or continuation of employment that an employee or other individual shall take a polygraph test or any form of a mechanical or electrical lie detector test.

18 Pa.C.S.A. § 7321(a). The purpose of this statute was ably summarized in an analysis of a similar statute by the Supreme Court of New Jersey:

There is no judicial control when an employer subjects his employee to a lie detector test and there is no licensing or other objective method of assuring expertise and safeguard in the administration of the test and the interpretation of its results. Nor is there any assurance of true voluntariness for the economic compulsions are generally such that the employee has no realistic choice. Organized labor groups have often expressed intense hostility to employer requirements that employees submit to polygraph test which they view as improper invasions of their deeply felt rights to personal privacy and to remain free from involuntary self-incrimination.

State v. Community Distributors, Inc., 64 N.J. 479, 317 A.2d 697, 699 (1974).

[1]   We are satisfied that Pennsylvania's anti-polygraph statute embodies a "recognized facet of public policy" of the type proscribed by the Pennsylvania courts in *Geary* and *Reuther*. Thus, if Perk's discharge resulted from a refusal to submit to a polygraph examination, a cause of action exists under Pennsylvania law for tortious discharge.

[2]   In granting summary judgment, the district court concluded that there is "no record evidence which would support a factual inference that plaintiff was fired for refusing to take a polygraph test." We disagree. The affidavits submitted by Firestone characterized the offer to submit to a polygraph test as a "final chance" to plaintiff. Contrary to the district court's assertion, plaintiff stated in his deposition that the refusal to submit to a polygraph examination may have caused the discharge. More importantly, at the time the auditors confronted plaintiff with Pilotti's allegations, they possessed no other evidence. The corroborating details supplied by

Pilotti, which consisted of plaintiff's alleged remarks on the evening in question, were procured subsequent to Perk's discharge. From this evidence, it can be inferred that Firestone gave undue consideration to plaintiff's refusal to take a polygraph test, and used that refusal as the basis for the discharge.

[3,4]   Firestone contends that the discharge was based on plaintiff's acceptance of gratuities from a representative of a supplier in violation of corporate policy. It correctly points out that, even when an important public policy is involved, "an employer may discharge an employee if he has a separate, plausible, and legitimate reason for doing so." *Reuther* v. *Fowler & Williams, Inc., supra,* 386 A2d at 122. However, as the *Reuther* court emphasized, when the fact-finder can infer one conclusion which violates public policy and one which is plausible and legitimate, invasion of the jury's province is improper. *Id.* While the district court believed that the conflicting evidence weighed heavily in Firestone's favor, "a motion for summary judgment should not be granted on the ground that if a verdict were rendered for the adverse party the court should set it aside against the weight of the evidence." *Rosenthal v. Rizzo,* 555 F2d 390, 394 (3d Cir. 1977); 6 J. Moore, Federal Practice ¶ 56.-04[2], at 2067 (2d ed. 1976).

Accordingly, we conclude that the district court erred in finding an absence of a genuine issue of material fact regarding the reason for plaintiff's discharge. The judgment of the district will be reversed and the case remanded for further proceedings.

INDEX

377